Black Inc.
Agenda

WHITEWASH

Wh

WHITEWASH
On Keith Windschuttle's
Fabrication of Aboriginal History

EDITED BY ROBERT MANNE

Published by Black Inc. Agenda
An imprint of Schwartz Publishing
Level 5, 289 Flinders Lane
Melbourne Victoria 3000 Australia
email: enquiries@blackincbooks.com
web: http://www.blackincbooks.com

Front cover image: Admiralty Library Portfolio I/6: 'Captain Cook's Interview
with Natives in Adventure Bay - Van Diemen's Land. January 29, 1777'.

Index by Michael Ramsden

National Library of Australia Cataloguing-in-Publication entry:

Whitewash : on Keith Windshuttle's fabrication of Aboriginal history.

> Bibliography.
> ISBN 0 9750769 0 6.

> 1. Aborigines, Australian - History. 2. Aborigines,
> Australian - Treatment. 3. Historiography - Australia. I.
> Manne, Robert (Robert Michael), 1947- . (Series : Agenda
> (Melbourne, Vic.)).

994.0049915

Contents

Introduction

Robert Manne

In 1968, the anthropologist W. E. H. Stanner delivered what turned out to be perhaps the most consequential lecture ever broadcast on the ABC. Stanner called his lecture 'The Great Australian Silence'. The point he was making has often been misunderstood.[1] Stanner did not mean that scholars and others had failed to show an interest in traditional Aboriginal society. As he understood better than most, anthropology was probably the most distinguished and developed of the social science disciplines in Australia. What Stanner meant was that both scholars and citizens had, thus far, failed to integrate the story of the Aboriginal dispossession and its aftermath into their understanding of the course of Australian history, reducing the whole tragic and complex story to what one historian had called 'a melancholy footnote' and another a mere 'codicil'.

According to Stanner, this silence was no accident.

> Inattention on such a scale cannot possibly be explained by absent-mindedness. It is a structural matter, a view from a window which has been carefully placed to exclude a whole quadrant of the landscape. What may well have begun as a simple forgetting of other possible views turned under habit and over time into something like a cult of forgetfulness practised on a national scale. We have been able for so long to disremember the aborigines that we are now hard put to keep them in mind even when we most want to do so.

Stanner, who possessed sensitive cultural antennae, was aware that at the time he wrote this lecture the cult of forgetfulness was coming to an end.

> I hardly think that what I have called 'the great Australian silence' will survive the research that is now in course. Our university and research institutes are full of young people who are working actively to end it. The Australian Institute of Aboriginal Studies and the Social Science Research Council of Australia have both promoted studies which will bring the historical and contemporary dimensions together and will assuredly persuade scholars to renovate their categories of understanding.[2]

The silence of which Stanner spoke was, in fact, broken by the three-volume study sponsored by the Social Science Research Council and authored by Charles Rowley – *The Destruction of Aboriginal Society, Outcasts in White Society* and *The Remote Aborigines*, published in 1970.[3] Rowley's trilogy represents one of the great scholarly and moral achievements of Australia's intellectual history. With its publication and absorption into the nation's bloodstream, Australia became a significantly different country.

Henry Reynolds was one of the young historians inspired by Stanner's lecture. In part because of Stanner he was persuaded to give his life to an exploration of the meaning of the dispossession, from many different angles.[4] One of the books Reynolds wrote, *The Other Side of the Frontier*, was another important landmark, generally still regarded as a classic in its field.[5] Yet in this work of discovery Reynolds was not alone. From the late 1960s, hundreds of books and articles on the dispossession by dozens of scholars were published. Through their collective work the great Australian silence was shattered.

As it happens, and perhaps not accidentally, the flowering of post-settlement Aboriginal history coincided with the end of the era of assimilation, which Stanner identified as an impossible and inhumane policy which instructed the Aborigines to remake their identity, or, as he put it, 'to un-be'.[6] After the end of assimilation, politics and history were intertwined in many, complex ways. A deepened historical consciousness and a sharpened moral conscience concerning the dispossession played a vital part in the granting of land rights, in the creation of national representative Aboriginal political structures, in the acceptance of native title, in the attempts to write a treaty between indigenous and non-indigenous Australians and, when this failed, in the struggle for reconciliation.

Sometimes the new historians of the dispossession played an even more direct legal or political role. Reynolds' histories were important in the thinking of the High Court judges who in 1992 at Mabo discovered native title in the common law.[7] Without the pioneering historical research of Peter Read, the inquiry commissioned by the Keating government into Aboriginal child removal might never have been held.[8] In the quarter-century, then, between the last year of the McMahon government and the fall of Keating, while historians deepened understanding of the dispossession, governments and courts discovered, within the limits of the legally and politically possible, both practical and symbolic ways to overturn aspects of what Justices Gaudron and Deane had called Australia's 'national legacy of unutterable shame'.[9] Of course there was considerable resistance from economic interest groups and political conservatives to the post-assimilation trajectory of Aboriginal policy and law, and even one or two feeble attempts to discredit the new historians.[10] In general, however, during this quarter-century, the resistance to the emergence of a new Australian consciousness on the question of the dispossession failed.

The Howard government was elected in March 1996. Before the election Howard told the nation that he intended to govern for 'all of us', a phrase which the Aboriginal leader Noel Pearson instantly understood as a coded message about the government's intention to distance itself from 'minorities', like Aborigines, and to govern on behalf of 'the mainstream'. Howard also told us that he hoped to make Australians feel 'comfortable and relaxed' about their past, whose most unsettling dimension was, of course, the destruction of Aboriginal society. From the American neo-conservative movement Howard had inherited the thought that left-wing elites bullied ordinary people into submission on questions concerning class, gender and race, by a process known as 'political correctness'. He soon let it be known that he intended to release Australians from its thrall.

Following the Howard election a series of cultural battles took place on key questions of Aboriginal law and policy. The Howard government soon faced a second High Court native title judgement (Wik) which found that, in certain very limited circumstances, native title might survive on land over which pastoral leases had once been granted. The government used this judgment as the occasion to amend substantially the Keating government's *Native Title Act* and, almost as significantly, to exclude Aboriginal political leaders almost altogether from the process of negotiation.[11]

The Howard government inherited from the period of Keating the report of the Human Rights and Equal Opportunity Commission into Aboriginal child removal policies and practices, *Bringing them home*. Although the report initially received an overwhelmingly sympathetic response from the media and the public, the Howard government's eventual reaction was, in part, hostile and, in part, cool. It treated *Bringing them home*'s genocide conclusion as risible. On semantic grounds it denied the existence of any 'stolen generations'. It refused the recommendation for financial compensation to the separated children. It refused to offer to the members of the stolen generations in particular or to the Aboriginal people in general a formal government apology.[12] In a parliamentary motion negotiated with the new Aboriginal Senator Aden Ridgeway, John Howard made it clear that while he was prime minister his government would go no further than to express its 'regrets' concerning what had been done to Aborigines in what was conceded to be the most 'blemished' chapter of Australia's history.[13]

On the eve of the centenary of federation, throughout the year 2000, hundreds of thousands of citizens walked across the bridges of Australia's capital cities, as a symbol of their desire for reconciliation and the opening of a new era in our national life. Following the most important of these walks, across the Sydney Harbour Bridge, the Prime Minister, as anticipated, spurned the suggested declaration handed to him by the Council for Aboriginal Reconciliation. John Howard was unwilling to accept any form of words that suggested a government apology or that referred to policies of Aboriginal 'self-determination', a formula which might have been acceptable to every Australian prime minister since Gough Whitlam, but was not acceptable to him.

The Howard government now abandoned the decade-long dream of some grand act of reconciliation with talk of something it called 'practical reconciliation', that is to say improvements in Aboriginal education, employment and health. Yet even its interest in practical reconciliation was thin. The government replaced the outgoing Minister for Aboriginal and Torres Strait Island Affairs, Senator Herron, with a part-time minister, Philip Ruddock, the bulk of whose time and energy was necessarily devoted to the complex and controversial areas of immigration and refugee affairs. In 2001, public interest in Aboriginal reconciliation or native title or questions of injustice bequeathed by history quickly died away. It was replaced by (necessary) discussions about the breakdown of life in the remote Aboriginal communities and the (undeniable) failings of the current leadership of the representative Aboriginal body, ATSIC.

More deeply, during the Howard years, a counter-revolution in sensibility concerning the dispossession of the Aborigines – no less real than the revolution which had begun in the late 1960s and early 1970s, in the days of Stanner and Rowley – was swiftly gathering momentum. The counter-revolution first crystallised around the question of Aboriginal child removal. A campaign against *Bringing them home* was conducted by the conservative magazine *Quadrant* and supported by a number of right-wing commentators in the daily press – the editor of *Quadrant*, Paddy McGuinness, Frank Devine, Piers Akerman, Michael Duffy, Andrew Bolt, Christopher Pearson and Ron Brunton. The campaign characterised Aboriginal witnesses as notoriously unreliable. It claimed that before World War II the 'half-caste' children had been removed to 'rescue' them from ostracism by the tribe and after the war from parental neglect and abuse. It accused the authors of *Bringing them home*, and those who defended the report, of sentimentality, moral vanity, political correctness and hatred for Australia. It treated the question of genocide raised by *Bringing them home* as beyond discussion and beneath contempt. In the course of this campaign, attitudes towards the question of historic injustices suffered by the Aboriginal people, at least as measured by the tone of public discourse, began noticeably to harden.[14]

As this campaign was reaching its conclusion, towards the end of

2000, a 35,000-word essay, of a kind which had not been published in Australia for a generation or more, appeared in three issues of *Quadrant*. The theme of the essay was the supposed left-wing myth concerning British settler massacres of Aborigines.[15] Its author was the formerly obscure, retired Sydney academic Keith Windschuttle, once an ultra-radical leftist who had moved, during the 1990s, rather rapidly to the right, at the time when his positivistic attack on deconstruction-ism and postmodernism, *The Killing of History*, had been championed by *The New Criterion*, the starchy neo-conservative New York cultural magazine. By the late 1990s, Windschuttle's journey from Pol Pot enthusiast to apologist for the British Empire was complete.[16]

Windschuttle had never previously written at any length about Aborigines or the Australian frontier. In his *Quadrant* essay his starting point, for reasons that were never satisfactorily explained, was four massacres mentioned by the journalist Phillip Knightley in his new portrait of Australia. In three of these cases Windschuttle attempted to show, either by drawing on others' work or by a far from convincing chain of evidentiary reasoning, that no massacres had taken place. He also attempted to show that the tentative estimates of 20,000 Aboriginal killings on the frontier between the late 1780s and the late 1920s which had been independently arrived at by Henry Reynolds and Richard Broome, and which had been regarded as a reasonable guess by the most conservative of all contemporary Australian historians, Geoffrey Blainey, was a vast exaggeration and, indeed, a 'fabrication'. Wind-schuttle, who had at that time done no systematic historical research on settler–indigenous relations (or on anything else), claimed to know for certain that the number of Aborigines killed at the frontier had been very small. How did he know this? Windschuttle argued that because of the British settlers' Christian faith and because of their civil-isation's fidelity to the idea of the rule of law, large numbers of killings could be excluded in advance as a cultural impossibility. He expressed astonishment at the discovery that Henry Reynolds' estimate of 20,000 killings, which he had previously accepted on trust, was not even based on a tabulated list of every occasion on which Aborigines had been killed. For Windschuttle, it appeared clear that a death which was unre-ported and thus undocumented was a death which had not occurred.

(By the use of a methodology equivalent to Windschuttle's it would be possible to prove that virtually no sexual abuse of children occurred in Western societies before the 1970s.) Windschuttle apparently could not imagine the kind of rough frontier society where settlers killed Aborigines who threatened their livestock or their lives; where such deaths went officially unidentified; and where government officials tacitly agreed, in regard to settler violence, to turn a blind eye. He also appeared to know next to nothing of the fifty-year history of killings carried out by the Queensland Native Police.[17]

Although many of the arguments in Windschuttle's *Quadrant* essay were unpersuasive and unsupported either by independent research or even familiarity with the relevant secondary historical literature, it was remarkable how seriously they began to be taken. Windschuttle was invited to debate Henry Reynolds on ABC television and at the National Press Club.[18] Because of the seriousness with which his challenge was taken, he was invited to participate in a conference of historians at the National Museum in Canberra, which eventually produced an impressive book.[19] Many criticisms of Windschuttle's essay were mounted. In response he either failed to answer his critics adequately, or at all, or pretended that the only criticism he encountered was, in essence, mere *ad hominem*.[20] Unlike the historians he attacked, Windschuttle claimed implausibly, but with an apparently straight face, to have no political agenda of his own. He was simply interested, he claimed, in establishing the truth by discovering and presenting the unembellished 'facts'.[21] Among Australia's conservative intelligentsia, and beyond, support for Windschuttle grew. Clearly he was singing a song many people wanted to hear.

For historians it is customary to begin investigations with hunches but to defer the arrival at definitive conclusions until research is complete. With Windschuttle the order appears to have been reversed. Having convinced himself in a few months in 2000 that no significant killings of Aboriginals had occurred on the Australian frontier, and having staked his reputation on the conclusion already reached, Windschuttle now embarked upon the necessary archival research, promising that he would produce three revisionist volumes of, in total, 500,000 words. For his first volume he chose Van Diemen's Land or

Tasmania where, for the past 170 years, since the conduct of a British parliamentary inquiry, civilised opinion had accepted that a terrible human tragedy had taken place.

The first volume of Windschuttle's *The Fabrication of Aboriginal History* was published towards the end of 2002, after perhaps eighteen months of research and writing. Clearly he was proceeding with furious energy. He did not grasp that writing history invariably takes imagination, absorption in the sources, and also time. Windschuttle argued here that the indigenous Tasmanians were a 'primitive', 'maladapted' and 'dysfunctional' people who had survived for 35,000 years or so, more or less by luck. He argued that the 'full-blood' Aborigines had died out within seventy years of the arrival of the British, in part because of their susceptibility to European diseases and in part because, as 'agents of their own demise', the men had traded away their women to the whites.[22] Windschuttle argued that the Tasmanian Aborigines had no sense of 'property' and hence no idea of 'trespass' or even strong bonds of attachment to their lands. It followed, then, that the fierce attacks they mounted on British settlers, especially in the 1820s, were not patriotic, nor in defence of territory, nor reasonably understood as acts of war, but mere expressions of their criminal proclivities, the lust for plunder of consumer goods and the unprovoked desire of savages for murder and revenge.[23] As Windschuttle pointed out, the Tasmanian Aborigines did not know the meaning of the Christian virtue of 'compassion'.[24]

Windschuttle regarded almost all previous writers on Aboriginal–settler conflict in Tasmania, from the 1830s to the present day, as belonging to what he called the 'orthodox school'.[25] What bound this extremely heterogeneous group of writers together was, apparently, their agreement that in Tasmania a terrible tragedy had occurred and that in that tragedy it was the Aborigines, the ancestral inhabitants of the disputed lands, who were the party which had been more seriously wronged. In these clashes Windschuttle could see no British wrongdoing. If there was a tragedy here, he argued, it rested only in the self-destructive futility of Aboriginal behaviour, in Aboriginal callousness towards their women and in the absence of an Aboriginal leadership wise enough to grasp the benefits of the 'civilisation' offered by the British arrival and to submit.[26]

Most importantly of all, Windschuttle argued that it was certain that in Tasmania, despite the reduction of the Aboriginal population to a few hundreds by the early 1830s, there had been more killings of British settlers by Aborigines than of Aborigines by settlers.[27] He was determined, by what he claimed to be a scrupulous investigation of sources and footnotes, to demonstrate that all recent members of the 'orthodox school', but especially three historians – Henry Reynolds, Lloyd Robson and Lyndall Ryan – had not merely made mistakes in their discussions of settler motives and Aboriginal killings but had deliberately fabricated evidence concerning the behaviour of the British during the settler–Aboriginal clash.[28]

When the self-published but lavishly produced first volume of *Fabrication* appeared, it was accompanied by a quotation from the editor of *The New Criterion*, Roger Kimball, not previously known to be an expert on either Australia or Aborigines, who hailed it as 'a scholarly masterpiece ... destined to become an historical classic, changing forever the way we all look at the opening chapter of Australian history'. Besides the words of the man who launched *Fabrication* in Sydney, Professor Claudio Veliz, Kimball's praise seemed positively lukewarm. In characteristically baroque style, Veliz described the Windschuttle book as 'meticulously well-researched', 'courageous', 'illuminating', 'immensely readable' and 'masterful'. The author not only brought 'devastating stylistic understatement to his subject'; he also refrained (as no doubt Henry Reynolds and Lyndall Ryan would be amused to learn) 'from translating his findings into inelegant personal attack'. Veliz thought *Fabrication* 'without doubt one of the most important books of our time'. He was reported to have likened the settlement of Australia, at the launch, to a 'nuns' picnic'. When his launch speech was printed in *Quadrant* these instantly notorious words had, for some reason, disappeared.[29]

Quadrant chose a former editor, Peter Coleman, as the appropriate reviewer for *Fabrication*. Coleman's unfamiliarity with frontier history was so comprehensive that he still apparently believed that, apart from Myall Creek (1838) and Coniston (1928), every other massacre of Aborigines was mere unsubstantiated rumour or, in lawyer's jargon, 'alleged'.[30] He duly praised the book's painstaking and devastating scholarship, although he regretted the entire absence from *Fabrication* of a sense of tragedy. Coleman was apparently not aware that the period of left-wing cultural hegemony in Australia had passed. He believed it unlikely that Windschuttle would be noticed by the mainstream media.[31] As it happens, he could not have been more wrong.

One of the media's most important powers is its agenda-setting capacity. On the publication of the first volume of *Fabrication*, the editors of *The Australian* decided to promote, within their pages, a wide-ranging Windschuttle debate. Even Windschuttle was surprised and gratified by what he called, at the launch, 'the rather good press' that his book had received by that time.[32]

On publication, *The Australian* published an opinion piece by Windschuttle and a sympathetic portrait of its author by a senior journalist, Bernard Lane. Lane also reported in its news pages Claudio Veliz's 'nun's picnic' speech; a talk delivered by Windschuttle to the Sydney Institute, whose director Gerard Henderson had already described Windschuttle as someone who had made 'a valuable contribution to Australian history'; and an enthusiastic review of *Fabrication* in *The New Criterion* by Geoffrey Blainey, which argued that *Fabrication* was 'one of the most important and devastating [books] written on Australian history in recent decades'.[33]

In response to the initial promotion of Windschuttle, three academics, Stephen Muecke, Marcia Langton and Heather Goodall, wrote a letter to the editor of *The Australian* complaining about the paper's boosting of a right-wing polemicist such as Windschuttle.[34] Muecke and his fellow authors had accurately discerned the cultural meaning of the promotion but badly misread the political mood. They were soon rebuked by two fellow historians, Bob Reece and Tim Rowse, no friends of Windschuttle, and by *The Australian* itself, for their illiberal censoriousness.[35]

It was certainly not the case that in their sponsorship of the 'sorely needed' Windschuttle debate *The Australian* published only articles favourable to *Fabrication*. In the coming weeks it would publish a review by Henry Reynolds, a self-defence by Lyndall Ryan and *contra* Windschuttle pieces by Bain Attwood and Dirk Moses as well as *pro* Windschuttle commentaries by Roger Sandall, Peter Ryan ('One welcomes – indeed one stands up to cheer – Keith Windschuttle's fresh examination of Australia's black–white frontier'), Geoffrey Blainey, Janet Albrechtsen and Windschuttle himself.[36] Yet it was also obvious to anyone following the coverage of the controversy in *The Australian* where the sympathies of the paper lay. *The Australian* twice editorialised favourably on Windschuttle.[37] It pursued Windschuttle's targets with real tenacity, contacting, for example, the Vice-Chancellor of Lyndall Ryan's university and her publisher, Allen & Unwin, in order to enquire of them what they intended to do.[38] It dismissed the claim that Windschuttle, the defender of old-fashioned scholarly standards, had copied out or lightly paraphrased a number of passages from the American anthropologist, Robert Edgerton, as 'a diversionary tactic'.[39] And it recycled a 7000 word personal attack on the academic who had noticed the borrowings (a certain Robert Manne), which was written by the wife of the editor-in-chief of *The Australian*, Chris Mitchell, and which had been published in *The Courier-Mail* eighteen months before.[40] Chiefly because of the promotion by *The Australian*, the publication of the first volume of *Fabrication* became a major cultural event.

By their nature historical debates of the kind raised by the appearance of the first volume of Windschuttle's trilogy cannot be resolved in the pages of newspapers. Their resolution requires space. This book is aimed at readers who are interested in the early history of Australia and in a thorough, expert discussion of Windschuttle's case. In my opinion the sum total of the chapters which follow reveal that, although it is written at a higher level of maturity and surface plausibility, the first volume of Keith Windschuttle's *Fabrication* contributes to Australian history what Helen Demidenko's *The Hand that Signed the Paper* contributed to Australian fiction – counterfeit coin. Readers will, of course, make up their own minds.

What was so dispiriting about the Demidenko affair was the lapse of critical judgment in so large a part of Australia's literary intelligentsia.[41] What is even more alarming in the reception of *The Fabrication of Aboriginal History* is the way so many prominent Australian conservatives have been so easily misled by so ignorant, so polemical and so pitiless a book. The generation after Stanner broke the great Australian silence concerning the dispossession. It might be the task of the next generation, if the enthusiasm for Windschuttle is any guide, to prevent the arrival in its place of a great Australian indifference.

NOTES

1. Most recently by Keith Windschuttle, *The Fabrication of Aboriginal History: Volume One, Van Diemen's Land 1803–1947*, Sydney, Macleay Press, 2002, pp. 406–11. For a valuable discussion, S. G. Foster, 'Contra Windschuttle', *Quadrant*, March 2003.

2. W. E. H. Stanner, *After the Dreaming: The Boyer Lectures 1968*, 'The Great Australian Silence', Australian Broadcasting Commission, 1969, pp. 25, 27.

3. C. D. Rowley, *The Destruction of Aboriginal Society, Outcasts in White Society, The Remote Aborigines*, Canberra, Australian National University Press, 1970.

4. Henry Reynolds, *Why Weren't We Told? A Personal Search for the Truth of Our History*, Ringwood, Penguin, 1999, pp. 91–2.

5. Henry Reynolds, *The Other Side of the Frontier: Aboriginal Resistance to the European Invasion of Australia*, rev. ed., Ringwood, Penguin, 1990.

6. Stanner, *After the Dreaming*, p. 57.

7. Bain Attwood (ed.), 'Introduction', *In the Age of Mabo: History, Aborigines and Australia*, St Leonards, NSW, Allen & Unwin, 1996. Reynolds, *Why Weren't We Told?*, ch. XIII.

8. Peter Read's writing on the stolen generations has been collected in Peter Read, *A Rape of the Soul So Profound: The Return of the Stolen Generations*, St Leonards, NSW, Allen & Unwin, 1999.

9. Attwood (ed.), *In the Age of Mabo*, p. xxxii.

10. For example, Geoffrey Partington, *The Australian History of Henry Reynolds*, AMEC, 1994.

11. These items are discussed in Robert Manne, *The Barren Years: John Howard and Australian Political Culture*, Melbourne, Text Publishing, 2000.

12. The attitude of the government was made clear in its April 2000 submission to the Legal and Constitutional Committee of the Senate.

13. Manne, *The Barren Years*, pp. 66–69.

14. These issues are discussed in Robert Manne, *In Denial: The Stolen Generations and the Right* (Quarterly Essay 1), Melbourne, Schwartz Publishing, 2001.

15. Keith Windschuttle, 'The myths of frontier massacres in Australian history', Parts I–III, *Quadrant*, October, November, December 2000. The text can be found at http://www.sydneyline.com.

16. Jane Cadzow, 'Who's right now, then?', *Good Weekend*, 17/5/03; Keith Windschuttle, 'Rewriting the History of the British Empire', *The New Criterion*, May 2000, at http://www.sydneyline.com/Launch%20speech.htm.

17. These matters are discussed in Manne, *In Denial*, pp. 93–101.

18. http://www.abc.net.au/lateline (16/4/01) and http://www.sydneyline.com/National%20Press%20Club%20debate.htm (19/4/01).

19. Bain Attwood & S. G. Foster, *Frontier Conflict: The Australian Experience*, National Museum of Australia, Canberra, 2003.

20. He responded, for example, to the powerful critique of Raymond Evans and Bill Thorpe, 'The massacre of history', *The Age*, 7/7/01 by pointing to one or two

factual errors. Keith Windschuttle, 'When history falls victim to politics', *The Age*, 14/7/01.

21. Windschuttle, *Fabrication*, pp. 400–04 and Keith Windschuttle, 'Why I'm a Bad Historian', *The Australian*, 12/2/03.

22. Windschuttle, *Fabrication*, ch. 10.

23. *Ibid*, ch. 4.

24. *Ibid*, p. 406.

25. *Ibid*, pp. 11–15 and *passim*.

26. *Ibid*, ch. 10.

27. *Ibid*, ch. 10.

28. *Ibid*, *passim*.

29. Claudio Veliz, 'History as Alibi', *Quadrant*, March 2003. The original report was 'British arrival a "benign picnic"', *The Australian*, 10/12/02.

30. Peter Coleman, 'Accidentally on Purpose', *The Australian*, 28/7/01.

31. Peter Coleman, 'The Windschuttle Thesis', *Quadrant*, December 2002.

32. http://www.sydneyline.com/Launch%20speech.htm (9/12/01).

33. *The Australian*, 6/12/02; 10/12/02; 12/2/03; 5/4/03. Henderson's views are found in *The Age* and *The Sydney Morning Herald*, 24/12/02.

34. *The Australian*, letters, 11/12/02.

35. *The Australian*, letters, 16/12/02; editorial, 28/12/02.

36. *The Australian*, 14/12/02 (Reynolds); 17/12/02 (L. Ryan); 23/12/02 (Sandall); 6/1/03 (Attwood); 10/1/03 (P. Ryan); 13/1/03 (Moses); 12/2/03 (Windschuttle); 14/4/03 (Blainey); 7/5/03 (Albrechtsen).

37. *The Australian*, editorials, 14/12/02; 28/12/02.

38. *The Australian*, 11/1/03. Lane told me he telephoned the Vice-Chancellor at the University of Newcastle.

39. *The Australian*, editorial, 28/12/02.

40. Deborah Cassrels, 'History of Manne', *Courier-Mail*, 2/6/01 was reprinted with minor changes as 'Evolution of Manne', *The Australian*, 28/12/02. Happily the evidence concerning Windschuttle's use of Edgerton can be found at http://www.sydneyline.com/Manne%20reply%20table.htm.

41. These issues are discussed in Robert Manne, *The Culture of Forgetting: Helen Demidenko and the Holocaust*, Melbourne, Text Publishing, 1996.

OVERVIEW

Fantasy Island

James Boyce

Keith Windschuttle needs to spend much more time in Tasmania. Then, perhaps, he would rely less on tourism web pages for weather information and refrain from describing the climate of windy Flinders Island as 'much like that of a southern Mediterranean port'.[1] An extended sojourn might also have helped give his book something it so obviously lacks: a solid foundation in the experience of life on this island, past and present. As it stands, *The Fabrication of Aboriginal History: Volume One, Van Diemen's Land 1803–1847* primarily reflects a pre-determined national political agenda that is summarised in some detail in the introductory chapter.

Windschuttle can impose his contemporary conclusions on Van Diemen's Land history only by limiting his selection of sources, thereby silencing not just ordinary Van Diemonians but – with almost unheard-of presumption – even the privileged classes. *Fabrication* relies on government documents that, in relation to Aborigines, hardly began to appear until 1827. Yet the Aboriginal issue was so central to life on the island from 1803 to 1833, so interrelated with the realities of frontier life that occurred largely beyond the official gaze, that this over-reliance on one kind of source inevitably leads to a series of gross oversights and mistakes.

The number of elementary errors in *Fabrication* will soon exclude it from serious historical debate. The political and cultural impact of the book, however, is more complex, given the appeal of its claim to be upholding truth in the face of politically motivated intellectuals who are setting us all up for an unwarranted guilt trip. It is perhaps fortunate, therefore, that Windschuttle has picked Tasmania as the place to begin his national campaign, for knowledge of the extensive black–white violence here is certainly not a product of post-1960s academia, as Windschuttle would have the rest of the nation believe. *Fabrication*'s arguments are contradicted not only by contemporary academics but by literally scores of writers, of all political shades, from 1820 onwards. Local cultural resistance is thus well prepared: 170 years of scholarship, 200 years of well-accessed and widely read records, will leave this particular attempt to deny our story looking very shallow indeed.

It is true that the Tasmanian tradition did weaken substantially from about 1880 to 1970, as those with direct experience of the ferocity of the conquest died and a great silence descended on all matters Van Diemonian. Social Darwinism also emerged to corrupt the white perspective. Even in this period, however, when the strength of Aboriginal resistance, Aboriginal adaptation and – ultimately – Aboriginal survival was sidelined, the reality of the violence was never forgotten.

To present this tradition as a unified 'Tasmanian orthodoxy' is another matter entirely, though, as is *Fabrication*'s related claim that the orthodoxy has 'overt political objectives'.[2] The nineteenth-century writers are the most overtly political of the Tasmanian historians, but they are not the sort of left-leaning academics Windschuttle has in his sights. For this reason, they are largely ignored in *Fabrication*. Even the Rev. John West's *History of Tasmania*, published in 1852, escapes serious consideration, although it has been the foundation stone of Tasmanian historical scholarship for 150 years – perhaps the idea of West, a distinguished and remarkable man, being so deceived about the horrible reality of the 'Black War' was simply too preposterous a case to argue.[3]

Still, Windschuttle is correct in lumping all these diverse writers together on one central matter: their agreement that, from 1824 to 1832 in particular, the Aborigines conducted 'a violent, protracted, but ultimately tragic war in defence of their homeland against European invaders'.[4] Windschuttle's alternative to this claim is the only real question for debate, as it is the only matter on which *Fabrication* is, in substance, saying anything new.

Two key conclusions are presented. The first, and less significant, is that it is possible to make a definitive statement that few Aborigines were killed by the British. Windschuttle claims 118 'plausible' Aboriginal deaths occurred at the hands of whites, and argues that:

> whatever adjustments are eventually made to these figures, another thing is also clear. The number of Aborigines killed by colonists was far fewer than the colonists who died at Aboriginal hands ... the over-all conclusion appears inescapable: during the so-called 'Black War', more than twice as many whites were killed as blacks.[5]

Since the 1820s, a number of writers have suggested that massacres have been exaggerated and that, especially in the later stages of the war, Aborigines had the best of the fighting. For example, J. E. Calder, one of the four nineteenth-century writers *Fabrication* claims is responsible for the development of the 'orthodox' view, claimed that, 'Numerous fictitious fights are recorded as having taken place in the early times of the colony, and which, though still repeated by the marvellous and hor-rible, were found to be utterly false on investigation.' Calder believed that Aborigines 'had by far the best of the fight'.[6]

However, no one before Windschuttle had been prepared to nomi-nate such a definitive body count or draw a correspondingly firm con-clusion about the low level of Aboriginal casualties. Windschuttle's present attempt to do so will be shown as transparently flawed.

The second and more critical new conclusion presented in *Fabrication* is that the frontier violence did not represent any defence of territory by Aborigines – indeed, they had no notion of a communal interest, be it land or otherwise, to defend. Aborigines are described as 'a people who not only had no political objectives but no sense of a col-lective interest of any kind'. Thus, for Windschuttle there was no Aboriginal–British conflict in a collective sense, merely a series of indi-vidual outrages, motivated by nothing more than 'crime or revenge'. Aboriginal attacks are explained as raids primarily to obtain European goods, while 'the reason [...] why Aboriginal thieves had little com-punction about killing anyone they found in their way' was because 'their own culture had no sanctions against the murder of anyone out-side their immediate clan ... They were killed simply because they could be.' According to Windschuttle, Aborigines committed 'nothing more than what would be recognized as crimes in any human culture [except apparently the Tasmanian Aboriginal?]: robbery, assault and murder'.[7]

With regard to its central argument, *Fabrication* should be seen not simply as a critique of post-1960s academia, or even of 170 years of previous study in this field. In fact, it is a denial of what those who met, lived and fought with Aborigines wrote. *Fabrication*'s findings are consistently contradicted by the primary source record itself.

This point is much more serious than Windschuttle's silencing of Rev. John West and most other nineteenth-century authors, or his ignorance of almost all recent research, including any academic thesis written since 1977. *Fabrication*'s fatal flaw, the source of its many factual mistakes, is the exclusion of almost all primary source material from the period in question, 1803 to 1847.

Fabrication's Sources

Any history of Van Diemen's Land must rely on two types of primary source: the published and the unpublished documents written at the time. Van Diemen's Land historians are fortunate to have an extensive collection of biographies, travel journals, settler guides and exploration accounts written and published in the 1803–1847 period by people who had spent time on the island. There are over 30 such books relevant to *Fabrication*'s themes, but only three have been directly cited: Henry Melville's *History of Van Diemen's Land from the year 1824 to 1835 inclusive*, James Backhouse's *Narrative of a Visit to the Australian Colonies* (twice) and, on one occasion, Charles Jeffreys' *Van Diemen's Land*. In its bibliography, *Fabrication* does list two other titles: the 1807 French edition of François Péron's record of the Baudin expedition and Edward Curr's 1824 account of the island. However, these latter sources are only quoted when cited by others, their main themes are never dealt with, and the evidence in them that could easily have corrected some of Windschuttle's more basic errors is overlooked – suggesting, at best, a cursory read.

A most startling omission is that of the records left by French explorers. If, as claimed, Windschuttle really has read in French the rare first edition of Péron's account of the Baudin expedition, why are all the quotes from it taken from Ling Roth's work published in 1899?[8] Further, how can he possibly have made the elementary error that places Péron's visit as occurring 'from 1807 to 1816' – actually the dates of the publication?[9]

In addition, Windschuttle does not even pretend to have looked at Labillardière's account of the d'Entrecasteaux expedition. Other records left by the French that have been translated and published in more recent times, including Baudin's comprehensive journal, have also been ignored. The accounts left by the British explorers have fared no better.

The significance of these omissions cannot be overstated. The neglected texts are our only written sources concerning Aboriginal society before British settlement. Anyone making bold statements about pre-contact Tasmanian Aboriginal life – and, as will be seen, Windschuttle makes the boldest that have been made in at least a century – without having read the only documentary sources available must surely relinquish their credibility at the outset.

For the ambitious task Windschuttle sets himself, at least some of the other neglected publications of the post-settlement period are also essential reading. The thoughtful observations of Van Diemonians like David Burn and James Ross are not optional extras for any serious student of the period.[10] These men did not shy away from presenting the full horror of war. Burn, for example, recalled seeing:

> The remains of a stock keeper, slain upon the writer's estate, [who] presented an appalling picture of their fury. The eyes were torn out of their sockets, and waddies [sticks not unlike office-rulers] thrust into the apertures. The skull was dreadfully smashed, and the mouth filled with cow dung. It was conjectured the waddies were placed to resemble the horns of oxen, and that their revenge was emblematical of the occupation of their victim – a cattle-herd.

But Burn also understood the underlying causes of violence:

> the atrocities which were perpetrated against these unoffending creatures may well palliate the indiscriminate, although heart-rending

slaughter they entailed. Both governor and governed were placed in a dilemma; they scarcely knew how to act to preserve their own lives, and yet protect those of their sable foes. It is true, there were those who had no scruple on that head; but the reflecting portion of the community knew well that they were 'invaders', who had despoiled the original possessors of their hunting-fields and that therefore what some folks denominated murder, was virtually 'slaying the enemies of their country', according to their mode of battle, and that, however the grantee might endeavour or reconcile his acquisition as a gift of the British crown, still it was a legalised plunder, which the flattering unction, that he was converting an inadequately appropriated wilderness into a resort for civilised man, could not entirely smooth away.[11]

The extent of the pre-1847 output makes nonsense of Windschuttle's claims that 'Melville, Robinson, Calder and Bonwick ... were the four most influential nineteenth-century voices in framing opinion about the fate of the Tasmanian Aborigines' and that they were first responsible for the Tasmanian orthodox 'deception'.[12] Only Melville's 1835 *History of Van Diemen's Land* and a very small selection of Robinson's writings (most of which were private papers not yet publicly available) would even have been read by the many writers who described frontier violence in the period up to 1847. The other two nominated by Windschuttle wrote later. Robinson and Melville were indeed influential figures, but they were but two in a diverse and wide-ranging discussion.

Windschuttle goes on to dismiss the conclusions reached by even his select Van Diemonian duo. He counters the extensive evidence presented by Robinson as to the nature and causes of the violence with psychological speculation. Apparently Robinson is attempting to salve 'his own conscience' for not handing over 'Aborigines who were guilty of the murder of his fellow settlers'.[13] Equally weak is the argument that Melville's feud with Lieutenant-Governor Arthur explains his conclusions that Aborigines were 'legitimate owners of the soil', the settlers were 'invaders' probably subject to Aboriginal law, Aboriginal defence represented 'guerilla war', and a captured Aborigine should be seen as a 'prisoner of war ... defending his country against cruel intruders'.[14]

However different Melville's assessment of Arthur on other matters, like most of the Van Diemonian writers in the 'Tasmanian orthodoxy' he was broadly sympathetic to the Governor's policy dilemma in relation to the Aborigines – arguing, for instance, that the Black Line was undertaken 'with the best intentions' and 'that something was necessary, either to intimidate the blacks or the capture of them, there cannot be a question'.[15]

Yet these published accounts of Van Diemen's Land are not Windschuttle's most serious omission. In terms of primary source material, there is another hole of such magnitude that it alone should discredit *Fabrication*'s central arguments. Windschuttle has almost completely ignored the extensive collection of diaries and letters available from the relevant period, even most of those that were published later, although these provide the only test of his central claim that little unrecorded killing of Aborigines occurred on the Tasmanian frontier.

Windschuttle at least acknowledges in *Fabrication* the obvious point that to rely – as he largely does – on the documented accounts of Aboriginal deaths as a reliable indicator of the actual numbers of Aborigines killed by whites would seem to mislead, because almost all the killing was likely not to be recorded, as it was usually illegal. As many have pointed out, most of the killings of Aborigines throughout Australia, both by local authorities and by settlers and their workers, convict and hired, did not make their way into the documented records. Windschuttle, however, claims that the extent of the surviving record means that this is 'definitely untrue of Van Diemen's Land'.[16]

The test for such claims must surely be the unofficial documents, those not intended for public consumption. It is this source alone which contains what people privately admitted about conflict with Aborigines when there was not the danger of official reprimand. And it is this source that Windschuttle almost completely ignores. Whether by deliberate neglect, laziness or oversight, it scarcely matters: the material in these documents leaves *Fabrication*'s central argument in tatters.

The only unpublished diary or letter Windschuttle even claims to have looked at from the relevant period is George Hobler's. His claim to have consulted these diaries, however, is either untrue or Windschuttle has deliberately ignored their contents, as the material they contain directly contradicts *Fabrication*'s arguments. Readers are surely entitled to ask what Windschuttle made of Hobler's claim that on 15 December 1827, after one of his splitters was speared by Aborigines, 'I have armed four men who I hope will get sight of their night fires and slaughter them as they be around it.' How does *Fabrication*'s claim that the settlers were held back from killing Aborigines by the Evangelical Christian revival hold up against Hobler's statement that on 11 May 1830, he 'shot a very beautiful bird of the thrush kind, but my pellets were meant for kangaroos or Black Fellows, so that my bird was unfit to be preserved'? The diaries make it abundantly clear that for Hobler at least, this war was serious business indeed, noting on 6 October 1830 that:

> these horrid savages have committed many cruel murders of late and if not severely chastised will destroy the exposed settlements and materially check the progress of the colony – One fellow taken a short time ago who could speak English said that the different tribes had leagued together sinking their own disputes and determined to exterminate the whites if possible.

Perhaps the Hobler family motto could have served as a reality check to the man who has now become the most infamous of Hobler's contemporary readership: 'Not what I seem but what I am.'[17]

If Windschuttle had read some of the other Van Diemonian diarists and letter writers, he would have found his central arguments similarly challenged. For instance, Christian pacifism seems also to have been lacking in Michael Steele, as he revealed in a letter to his brother Joseph on 21 February 1827: when the Aborigines were seen, 'I instantly armed all my men some on horseback and some on foot' and set off in pursuit. The next day, 'we fell in with them on the top of a mountain and poured a strong fire into them and killed their leader and one more ... had the country been even and clear we should have killed or taken the whole of them.' They also killed 50 of the Aborigines' heroic dogs: 'it would have astonished you to have witnessed the dogs when the attack was first made how they bravely defended their masters.'[18]

One of the most respectable of the early east coast settlers, Adam Amos, also knew and dealt with frontier realities. On 13–14 December 1823, not long after his arrival, when the Aborigines attempted to continue their customary burning regime, Amos immediately acted to defend his home, crops and family. On 13 December, he sent his 'oldest son to shoot them again but missed by minutes'. On 14 December, 'the natives who have of late been in the woods near my hutt [*sic*] have this day set the grass on fire near my farm … sent my oldest son who was joined by two of Mr Meredith's men who fired at them and wounded one of the mob … [who] fled over the hill they pursued them for some time and returned after dark with a quantity of spears.' It was an ongoing and difficult struggle. On 18 January 1824:

> I had a hunt after the natives on Friday they appeared above my plain. The boys and me set after them, when we came up to their fires they were gone across the river. We followed them for two hours and found them on a marsh about two miles from my farm on the east side. About 30 men. We fired they run away and left their dogs and spears which we destroy and brought some of them home and two dogs.

Amos did not relish this conflict, and there is no reason to doubt his closing lament, 'I hope they will trouble us no more.' However, there is equally no reason to doubt that the violent conflict continued. For example, on 23 May 1824, he was again 'after natives' and on 12 July 1824 he recorded, 'My son James returned from hunting the blacks without ever seeing them.'[19]

It seems almost incomprehensible that Windschuttle could claim that he has been able to 'to record every killing of an Aborigine between 1803 and 1834 for which there is a plausible record of some kind' without looking at such crucial and readily accessible primary source material.[20] Some of his omissions have even been published in widely read works that are basic textbook material for study of the period. For example, the diaries of the surveyor J. H. Wedge contain this entry for 11 June 1829: 'Surveying on the South Esk … Mr McLeod's shepherd fell in with the natives about three miles from hence, and after a skirmish he shot one of the women.'[21]

Other sources, if he knew them, Windschuttle would probably dismiss. Hamilton Wallace wrote to his father in 1825 to report that, 'on the second day under the Ben Lomond Tier we fell in with about 250 Aborigines.' These were pursued on horseback, with the Aborigines eventually spearing a stock-keeper. But it would presumably be another left-wing trick to imply even the possibility of Aboriginal casualties in this case, since none is admitted to.[22]

Given how little information there is concerning life at and beyond the frontier, it is equally extraordinary that Windschuttle ignores the published evidence of those who cannot possibly have had any vested interest in, or prejudicial exposure to, the 'Tasmanian orthodoxy'. For example, Rosalie Hare was on board the *Caroline* which visited the fledgling Van Diemen's Land Company headquarters at Circular Head between January and March 1828. Her account records that:

> Natives are terrible robbers and do all the mischief they can to the set-tlers ... Burning the huts of the shepherds and stealing their dogs are also the works of these incendiaries ... But we are not to suppose the Europeans in their turn take no revenge. We have to lament that our own countrymen consider the massacre of these people an honour. While we remained at Circular Head there were several accounts of considerable numbers of natives having been shot by them [the com-pany's men], they wishing to extirpate them entirely if possible. The master of the Company's Cutter, *Fanny*, assisted by four shepherds and his crew, surprised a party and killed 12. The rest escaped but after-wards followed them. They reached the vessel just in time to save their lives.[23]

Although Windschuttle devotes an entire chapter to dismissing the likelihood of more than a few killings in the north-west of the island, he ignores this source, as he does almost all other 'non-official' voices, in *Fabrication*.

Reviewing the footnotes confirms that instead of such core pub-lished and unpublished primary source material, *Fabrication* relies almost entirely on a select number of published secondary sources. The exceptions are easily listed and just as easily explained. Knopwood's diary, Robinson's journal, the Historical Records of Australia and the early *Hobart Town Gazette*s all have indexes and, with the exception of Robinson's journals, seem mainly to have been read only where they make specific mention of Aborigines.[24] Newspapers, except for known significant dates, have also mostly been ignored. As will be seen later, this selective reading leaves Windschuttle profoundly ignorant of some of the basic realities of Van Diemonian frontier life, meaning that his work consistently lacks the correct context.

What remains of *Fabrication*'s primary sources is Windschuttle's purported *coup de grace*: the Colonial Secretary Office papers relating to Aborigines from 1827 to 1833. This is the most familiar, widely accessed and well-known part of the primary record. Indeed, some of this material was first extensively used by yet another informed contemporary commentator of whom Windschuttle seems ignorant, James Bischoff, in his *Sketch of the History of Van Diemen's Land*, published in 1832. J. E. Calder's first words in his 1875 book, *Some Account of the Wars, Extirpation, Habits etc of the Native Tribes of Tasmania,* are to thank the 'gentlemen' in the 'Office of the Colonial Secretary' for allowing him to consult the 'immense correspondence on the subject of the Aborigines of Tasmania'.[25] For Lyndall Ryan, 'The 17 volumes of records in the Tasmanian State Archives ... were my inspiration.'[26] There was no 30-year rule in place; most of these papers were put together precisely so they could be easily accessed and the government's position communicated. And they have indeed proved an enduring Arthurian legacy. The papers are a worthy place for Windschuttle's research to begin; given his ambitious claims, they are a grossly inadequate place for it to end.

The over-reliance on the government's records grossly distorts Windschuttle's understanding of the realities of frontier life for two reasons. First, despite *Fabrication*'s claim that 'except for a handful of gaps, there are good records of the activities of almost the entire colonial population from 1803 to the 1840s,'[27] it was not until 1824 that Governor Arthur instituted a comprehensive system of public record-keeping. The preceding two decades of government records have enormous gaps. So few records of Governor Collins' time (1804–10) survive that in 1925 his burial cask was re-opened in a search for long-lost documents.[28] In 1820, Commissioner Bigge heard many excuses about this topic. Governor Davey (1813–17) claimed that he had sent most of the many documents missing from his term of office to the Earl of Harrowby.[29] One senior civil servant gave the excuse to the commissioner that 'very considerable difficulties arise from the insufficiency of stationery.'[30] Another claimed that 'about a year ago a case containing all my papers was stolen.'[31]

Government record-keeping improves somewhat with the arrival of Sorell in 1817, except in relation to documents pertaining to Aborigines. Sorell virtually never mentions Aborigines in his dispatches to London and ignores them altogether in his lengthy hand-over report to Arthur in 1824. Even the meticulous Arthur largely followed the same practice of keeping London out of the Aboriginal issue until 1827. Quite simply, like any good administrator, neither Sorell nor Arthur actively sought information in those areas they would rather not know about, let alone apprised a meddling London of the uncomfortable facts. Only when the level of killing became such a prominent public issue from 1827 onwards, with such a dramatic impact on profit, colonisation and the operation of the penal system, did Arthur change tack.

Relying for the most part on the official government record for information on the Aborigines before 1827 is therefore grossly inadequate. *Fabrication*'s claim that 'Few colonial encounters anywhere in the world are as well documented as those of Van Diemen's Land' is only true for the years 1827 to 1832.[32]

And once the violence got out of hand, almost the opposite problem faces the historian. Arthur was very aware of the political implications of the violent dispossession and possible extinction of the Aborigines. The wide reporting of the violence had caused concern to grow among the politically powerful missionary societies in Britain, who were well connected to the House of Commons and other seats of power. Arthur – once again like any other competent administrator – now set out to cover his own and the government's back by sharing the responsibility for actions and policies and documenting every move. The government's very real policy dilemmas, and its genuinely difficult choices, are thus well recorded at this time. Committees were set up whenever possible, and settler input sought, to ensure that 'blame' was widely shared. None of this is to imply that Arthur lacked a genuine humanitarian concern. It is simply to point out that this governor was the finest administrator of the Van Diemonian era, that running a large penal colony doubling as a rapidly growing settlement on another people's land was no easy matter, and that it was not by chance that he was one of the two governors of Van Diemen's Land before 1850 to leave the posting with his career prospects enhanced and his official reputation intact. Such hidden considerations do not mean the 17 volumes of official records are not a very important source. Windschuttle, however, is too easily duped when he confuses quantity for completeness. The fact that Arthur covered himself so well does not mean that he revealed – or even knew – every aspect of the conflict.

By relying to such a degree on the government record of the time, Windschuttle remains ignorant of the period until 1827 and inherits a distorted and unbalanced perspective on the height of the war years. This is true not only of the direct conflict with the Aborigines but also of the realities of European life outside the main settlements. The narrow selection of sources results in a profound ignorance of the basics of Van Diemonian economy, society and politics, which in turn leads to a series of elementary errors.

Fabrication's Estimates of Aboriginal Deaths

Windschuttle does acknowledge that he might have missed a killing or two in arriving at his figure of 118 'plausible' Aboriginal deaths at the hands of whites, but seems so unaware of the extent of his omissions that he believes his overall conclusions will remain definitive. 'British colonists', he says, 'killed very few Aborigines in Van Diemen's Land … whatever adjustments are eventually made to these figures … the overall conclusion appears inescapable: during the so-called "Black War", more than twice as many whites were killed as blacks.'[33]

In responding to criticism of his neglect of critical primary source material – material he undoubtedly needs to make his claims credible – Windschuttle may well reply that he has largely and openly relied on N. J. B. Plomley's research undertaken for his book *The Aboriginal/Settler Clash in Van Diemen's Land*.[34] However, this is profoundly unsatisfactory, as Plomley sought to estimate white casualties, not black. He documented only those incidents that were officially recorded or made it into the press, these being reasonably reliable indicators of how many Europeans were killed by Aborigines. The Aboriginal death rate, however, is an entirely different matter, for – as

Plomley himself pointed out in the introduction to his book – 'The written record as a whole suffers from one particular defect: it is only concerned with attacks by the Aborigines on the settlers.'[35] Plomley was well aware that privately recorded details of attacks on Aborigines very rarely went into the detail of a body count, whether from fear, shame, 'respect' or 'decency'. Such sources were therefore of limited use for Plomley's purposes, but they are obviously essential to any credible attempt to make even a rough estimate of Aboriginal casualties.

It was not his political sensitivities, as Windschuttle implies, that held Plomley back from drawing *Fabrication*'s conclusions about the very low Aboriginal death rate.[36] Plomley was not a person to keep quiet out of either respect or fear; indeed, he showed himself as willing as Windschuttle to have his say no matter whom in the Aboriginal community or white society he offended. The difference between the two men is not courage or politics; it is simply that Plomley recognised that his research did not – and could not – indicate how many Aborigines died at the hands of whites in Van Diemen's Land.

The limited application of Plomley's research should have been immediately obvious to Windschuttle, given that Plomley does not make use of the evidence of Aboriginal fatalities contained in George Augustus Robinson's 1829–1834 journals, of which Plomley was the editor. Windschuttle doesn't seem to have asked the obvious question: if Plomley had left out even the many details of Aboriginal war dead in *Friendly Mission*, could not many other sources, equally pertinent to his own but not Plomley's research, have similarly been omitted? Regardless, the fact is they have been ignored, and Windschuttle's 'Table 10', his 'attempt to record every killing of an Aborigine between 1803 and 1834 for which there is a plausible record of some kind',[37] is essentially *Friendly Mission* incidents tacked on to those detailed in *The Aboriginal/Settler Clash*.

Windschuttle's twin reliance on *The Aboriginal/Settler Clash* and *Friendly Mission* means that even well-known incidents which are referred to in the text of *Fabrication* don't make it into the much-publicised Table 10.[38] Thus, the infamous admissions of one of the better-known Van Diemonians, John Batman, about the activities of his roving party in September 1829 is left out of the tally, despite a sanitised version of this incident, in which Windschuttle concedes two Aboriginal deaths, being presented elsewhere in his text.[39] Here is the actual account by the 'founder of Melbourne' of one bloody engagement of the Tasmanian war:

> In pursuit of the Aborigines who have been committing so many outrages in this district ... I fell in with their tracks and followed them with the assistance of the Sydney native blacks until we came to a number of huts ... we proceeded in the same direction until we saw some smoke at a distance. I immediately ordered the men to lay [*sic*] down; we could hear the natives conversing distinctly, we then crept into thick scrub and remained there until after sunset ... and made towards them with the greatest caution. At about 11 o'clock pm we arrived within 21 paces of them. The men were drawn up on the right by my orders intending to rush upon them before they could arise from the ground, hoping that I should not be under the necessity of firing at them, but unfortunately as the last man was coming up, he struck his musket against that of another party, which immediately alarmed the dogs (in number about 40) they came directly at us. The natives arose from the ground, and were in the act of running away into the thick scrub, when I ordered the men to fire upon them, which was done, and a rush by the party immediately followed, we only captured that night one woman and a male child about two years old ... next morning we found one man very badly wounded in the ankle and knee, shortly after we found another. 10 buckshot had entered his body, he was alive but very bad, there were a great number of traces of blood in various directions and learnt from those we took that 10 men were wounded in the body which they gave us to understand were dead or would die, and two women in the same state had crawled away, besides a number that was shot in the legs ... We shot 21 dogs and obtained a great number of spears, waddies, blankets, rugs, knives, a tomahawk, a shingle wrench etc etc. On Friday morning we left the place for my farm with the two men, woman and child, but found it impossible that the two former could walk, and after trying them by every means in my power, for some time, found I could not get them on I was obliged to shoot them.[40]

The captured woman was later sent on to Campbell Town jail and separated from her son, Rolepana, who was kept by Batman. Batman's own estimate was that the band they had fired on numbered 60 to 70 men, women and children, and that about 15 had been killed or would die from the wounds. This incident was reported to Arthur, who noted the shooting of the injured Aborigines. Later, Arthur wrote of Batman's sympathy for the Aborigines, but that he also 'had much slaughter to account for'.[41]

The analysis that underpins *Fabrication*'s central claim that 'British colonists killed very few Aborigines in Van Diemen's Land' is just as flawed as the attempt to ascertain an Aboriginal body count. Windschuttle does not dispute Plomley's figures of 187 whites killed and 211 whites wounded in the main period of fighting from 1824 to 1831, although these are probably underestimates as there were always unaccounted-for convicts and a significant number of vagrants on the edges of official white society. Living in the bush in Van Diemonian times, their deaths could easily be missed. Even on the 1830 population numbers (and there was a rapid annual increase at this time), Windschuttle accepts that these figures represent a casualty rate of about 2% of the white population, considerably higher than in any other conflict except World War I.[42] Excluding Hobart and Launceston and the more densely populated and basically secure areas of settlement surrounding these towns, this represents a casualty rate on the frontier area of somewhere between 5% and 10%.[43]

Readers can decide for themselves just how likely it is that 187 whites died in those seven years alone while only 118 Aborigines were killed over thirty years. It is by any measure an extraordinary claim to make that ethical, legal, and technical factors limited white retaliation to such a degree. Windschuttle's lack of understanding of the realities of Van Diemen's Land means that his arguments to support this ambitious case are full of elementary mistakes.

First, his claim regarding the significant impact of the Evangelical revival in the Church of England on colonial policy and behaviour is an exaggeration.[44] Certainly, the Evangelical influence in London was growing stronger at this time and did have some influence on colonial policy (a point much more fully and effectively made by Henry

Reynolds in *Fate of a Free People*). Certainly, those figures Windschuttle mentions, Arthur, Robinson and O'Connor, did have a Christian faith which influenced their perspective. Nevertheless, the impact of Evangelical Christianity in Van Diemen's Land was limited. Unlike in Sydney, no ministers of the church took a public stand on Aboriginal issues, although Norman and Bedford supported Robinson's work. Compared with the actions of the likes of the Church Missionary Society in London, the local church was largely irrelevant. Its response reflected the realities of the war.[45]

Before the 1820s, in contrast to New South Wales, it is hard to find a prominent Evangelical in Van Diemen's Land. The broad-minded approach to religious and moral matters shown by the likes of the first chaplain, Knopwood, and all of the early governors up to and including Sorell, is familiar to all students of Van Diemen's Land. Even in 1824, Arthur saw the majority of the settlers as of little help in 'the moral improvement and discipline of the convicts ... their habits almost universally encourage dissipated tendencies'. At the frontier it was 'worse': 'The whole population of the interior are totally destitute of religious instruction and the Sabbath is a day of the most excessive dissipation.'[46]

Even relatively sympathetic and sensitive men were prepared to kill once their own property and lives were directly threatened. George Lloyd, who had much peaceful interaction with Aborigines in the pre-war era, admitted (in yet another of *Fabrication*'s neglected texts) to 'the telling delivery of 7 double-barrelled guns, heavily charged with good duck shot' that left such a 'wholesome impression upon the notoriously cruel Big River Tribe that most of them, more or less severely wounded, immediately retired'. Lloyd acknowledged the usual ethical compromises of war: 'to turn the other cheek is a grace but rarely to be met with ... not in erring mortals like myself.'[47] While one of Windschuttle's Christian exemplars, Roderick O'Connor, told the Aborigines Committee in 1830 that Douglas Ibbens had killed half the 'eastern mob' by 'creeping upon them and firing amongst them', not in order to have such behaviour publicly condemned, but as evidence for his argument that 'some of the worst characters would be the best to send after them.'[48]

Thus, to equate the Evangelical influence in London, or even in sections of the Hobart and settler establishment, with a significant restraint on frontier behaviour at the height of a bloody conflict is to exaggerate its impact grossly. As for legal prohibitions against killing and government orders forbidding violence, Windschuttle's analysis falls down in assuming a level of official control outside the major centres that simply did not exist. In his extensive discussion of this issue, Windschuttle presumes some kind of automatic correlation between government intent, expressed as an order or proclamation, and on-the-ground frontier reality: 'The Lieutenant-Governors of Van Diemen's Land … had little reason to be over-concerned about how well their pronouncements were received locally. When they proclaimed a government order they expected it to be obeyed.'[49] In fact, all the early governors struggled to maintain order even in the vicinity of the major centres and were well aware of the limits of their power. Davey could hardly venture safely out of Hobart Town because of the power of the bushrangers. Even Sorell and Arthur documented their considerable struggles to impose economic and social control beyond the main towns, a challenge that was integral to developing an effective penal system.

Until the mid-1820s, the military force available to the governors was both inadequate and hard to discipline. Few options existed for punishing convicts other than corporal punishment before Macquarie Harbour was built in 1821, and even as late as 1820 the island did not have a secure jail. Punishing emancipated convicts and free settlers was even more difficult until a higher court was established in 1824. Before then, all serious cases, including murder, had to be trialled in Sydney, and the expense and time involved meant that much crime escaped a formal hearing. It was not until the Supreme Court was established in 1824 and the colony was administratively separated from New South Wales in 1825 that the governor's hand was significantly strengthened. Moreover, there was also a serious labour shortage until this time and extracting any sort of efficient work output, as Maxwell-Stuart has shown, was not an uncomplicated matter.[50] This was particularly true of the shepherds' and stockmen's domain of the 'crown' lands; in return for enduring the hardships of frontier life, these men were given a very large degree of autonomy provided that the essential work was done.

Until the late 1820s, then, the British governors of the island were well aware of the world of difference between formal power and real power. As Arthur told Earl Bathurst, explaining the delay in introducing new measures to control the convicts:

> In resigning the command into my hands, Colonel Sorell expressed the opinion that the period had now arrived when measures of coercion and restraint might in greater safety be enforced towards the convicts; my predecessor however, had not himself ventured to take any step, and the only one I have presumed upon has convinced me that more rigid discipline cannot be introduced without opposition, and therefore with the present military force I cannot feel justified in attempting it.[51]

Arthur later recalled that on his arrival:

> the Colony was destitute of any buildings except a small Penitentiary in which the convicts could be safely lodged, and the prisoners were consequently alone kept passive by a system of extreme indulgence, which I am sure the comprehensive mind of Colonel Sorell would never have suffered to exist had he not been cramped in all his measures and unable to follow the dictates of his own judgment ...[52]

As late as 1827, Arthur reported that he hoped through 'encreased [*sic*] means of coercive labour and new penal settlements' to ensure that assignment 'may be made the consequence of good conduct', and

> there would then be no difficulty in reducing transportation to that salutary punishment which it is in Your Lordship's desire to see in operation, but which, to attempt without these means, I am confident, would deeply affect the prosperity, if not the safety of the colony.[53]

And if Sorell and Arthur struggled to control the behaviour of the convicts, this was as nothing compared to their efforts to curb the independent power wielded by the wealthy settlers. As a frustrated Arthur told Under Secretary Horton in September 1825, 'it is utterly impossible to do one's duty and give satisfaction to the settlers and merchants ... [they] instantly declare their determination to call a public meeting and report home.'[54]

On the Van Diemonian frontier, such independence was even more pronounced. Wealthy cattle barons like Edward Lord and William Field had far more real authority on these lands, until the mid-1820s at least, than did the British governor. Lord had politically influential contacts in London and Sydney, and, with his wife, made enormous profits from cattle and trade. In 1822, he told London he was owed £70,000 by the settlers of the colony.[55] This was many times the total annual government revenue (which didn't reach half this figure until 1827) and left the governor and other senior officers, all on salaries of less than £500 per annum, looking like paupers. There is no doubt that the influence of such men was enormous, and that the governor's real, rather than formal, capacity to prosecute a stockman for murdering an Aborigine was very limited indeed without a boss's acquiescence.

Government influence over the 'gentleman' land grantees of the late 1820s was greater, but even here real control was limited. Such men largely controlled the administration of justice in their localities, and there was little prospect of a land-owner pushing for the prosecution for murder or violence of a worker defending his master's stock or property from an Aborigine. The chances of the government being able to do so independently were even less. No wonder it never happened.

Windschuttle quotes Melville, Ryan and Morgan who, among others, point this out, stating that, 'Despite their confident tone and their mutual confirmation', their claims that no European was ever charged for killing an Aborigine 'are untrue ... the very first case before the Supreme Court of Van Diemen's Land in May 1824 was ... a convict charged with the manslaughter of an Aborigine.'[56] What is the available evidence on the matter? In May 1824, William Tibbs was indeed sentenced to three years transportation for manslaughter. The dead man is described as a 'black man' by the name of 'John Jackson'. At this time Aborigines were generally not described in these terms, but as 'natives'. The source document, the *Hobart Town Gazette*, is consistent on this, even when referring to 'civilised' Aborigines. Most likely, then, the man killed was what he was purported to be, a black man, many of whom spent time in what was already a cosmopolitan port. Hobart was an important supply depot for the whalers of the southern ocean, and black crew were common on these ships. Most likely, too, the charge was indeed manslaughter, the result of a pub brawl or some other alcohol-related violence. Convicts and sailors at this time still shared the rough hospitality of the towns' 'licensed victuallers'. Given the limited evidence, there is admittedly a small chance that John Jackson was a 'civilised' Aborigine living in the settled districts, one of the many Aboriginal children raised by whites. If so, the killing was still likely to have been manslaughter and the result of a brawl, not frontier conquest.[57] As for Windschuttle's claim that other legal prosecutions of whites for violence to Aborigines may come to light as the newspaper records are perused – it is possible but extremely unlikely. Such a trial would almost certainly have attracted publicity and is likely to have been documented in more than one source. Finally, Windschuttle's conclusion that the authorities were genuinely motivated to prosecute such cases may indeed be true, in the early 1820s at least. But if so, the point needing explanation is surely the factors that prevented them from doing so.

The gap between the law and its implementation was everywhere apparent in the real Van Diemen's Land. For example, government orders until the late 1820s banning convicts keeping dogs for hunting, maintaining stock on the thirds system and keeping Aboriginal children had to be regularly repeated because they were just as regularly ignored. Legal conditions relating to land grants were also usually disregarded. The occupation of more remote 'crown' land by many whites often violated government regulations. Rules about stock were widely ignored. As the land commissioners reported in 1827:

> It is evident from these facts that it is only the truly conscientious man who is determined to adhere to the laws and regulations of the colony, that suffers in his prospects, he sees the 'old hands' around him rioting and reveling in their luxuries and enjoyments … the consequence is that throughout the colony we have found the people who have bid defiance to the Government restrictions, independent, and in affluence, whereas the bona fide settler, is too often, we are grieved to say, labouring under distress and difficulties.

In short, to the commissioners many a settler 'may properly be termed a complete outlaw'.[58]

To put it mildly, the Van Diemonian frontier was a wild and unruly place where, as Levy has put it, 'The King's writ ran weakly.'[59] In this turbulent and difficult environment, even when the governor heard about the killing of an Aborigine, enforcing the law was virtually impossible. While the wide-ranging reforms Arthur instituted from 1825 to 1830 and the changing nature of settlement did have a dramatic impact on the level of social and political power exercised by the government, places like the Central Plateau, the Bass Strait islands and much of the north-west remained largely beyond official control. And, as Arthur told Bathurst, it remained true everywhere that 'where master and servant have an interest in deceiving, it is almost next to impossible to detect their scheme.'[60] Windschuttle's belief that the governors' regular orders not to kill Aborigines were carried out because of the near-absolute legal power possessed by the official autocrat is thus, at best, extraordinarily naive.

It also leaves unanswered the question of why, on *Fabrication*'s own terms, the orders warning against committing acts of violence against Aborigines were even necessary. Why was one issued in January 1810 when, according to Windschuttle, no Aborigines had been killed by whites for two years? The order of June 1813 is even more perplexing, since by then apparently not a single killing had occurred in five years. And for Windschuttle the March 1819 Government Order (quoted below) must be nothing more than uninformed slander, given his belief that only one 'plausible' killing of an Aborigine had occurred since August 1816:

> It is undeniable that in many former instances, cruelties have been perpetrated repugnant to humanity and disgraceful to the British character ... The impression remaining from earlier injuries are kept up by the occasional outrages of miscreants whose scene of crime is so remote as to render detection difficult; and who sometimes wantonly fire at and kill the men, and at others pursue the women for the purpose of compelling them to abandon their children ...[61]

Fabrication's point about the many difficulties faced by whites in killing Aborigines is much stronger. However, none of these arguments, about gun inaccuracy, the influence of dogs, Tasmanian topography and so on is new. Most have been made best in recent times by Henry Reynolds in his *Fate of a Free People*, although they are restraints many Van Diemonian writers also acknowledged. To these should be added the related point that until 1820 or so the balance of power beyond the major settlements and their environs rested with the Aborigines. It was this combination of factors that led to a comparatively low level of British killings of Aborigines in the first phases of white settlement and enabled a significant degree of cultural meeting and exchange. Characteristically, though, Windschuttle pushes this argument much too far in suggesting that only seven Aborigines were killed from March 1808 to November 1826.

In proceeding to deny so many Aboriginal deaths at the height of the war from 1827 to 1831, Windschuttle takes the blundering-British thesis to ridiculous extremes. He can do this only by assuming that the foot soldiers of the 40th Regiment were the principal white force; he seems unaware that these troops were in fact peripheral to the main struggle. As early as 1826, the British placed their reliance on experienced Van Diemonian bushmen who knew many of the Aboriginal migratory routes and preferred camping sites reasonably well after a generation of peace; and on masses of convict cannon fodder seeking indulgences and freedom. Arthur had discovered in the 1825–6 struggle with the bushrangers that the key to an affordable and effective military force was arming the convicts. Of all the various strategies employed to achieve a degree of political, social and economic control over the frontier, this was Arthur's masterstroke. As he told Bathurst in 1827:

> I was driven during the heat of bush-ranging to strengthen the establishment by the appointment of a field police, formed from the very best conducted prisoners, and stimulated to exertion by the hope of a mitigation of their sentence, which is promised after uniform good conduct for three years ... it was objected to by some on account of the danger which they apprehended from putting arms into the hands of prisoners ... The objection however proved totally groundless, and ... I venture to hope that the appointment of this band altogether supersedes the necessity of any militia or yeomanry or any other *local* military force, and supersedes it most advantageously.[62]

Scholars of the period have moved a long way from seeing the conflict as a series of one-sided massacres. As Reynolds has concluded, 'there is a tendency among writers sympathetic to the Aborigines to exaggerate the number so killed in order to emphasise the brutality of the colonial encounter ... this ... greatly inflates the capacity of the European and underestimates the ability of the Aborigines.'[63]

Again, however, Windschuttle goes far beyond reason or evidence in dismissing virtually all large-scale killing of Aborigines. Undoubtedly some massacres have been exaggerated, but it is equally likely that others remain unknown to us. Similarly, although large-scale killings are not likely to have been a feature of the later stages of the war – the period Windschuttle focuses on – they were much more likely to have occurred in the earlier phases when whites could still predict trade and migration routes, likely camping and gathering places, and when babies, children, pregnant women and the elderly and sick were still part of community life. The phases of war varied considerably across the island. Massacres were still possible in the newly settled north-west in the late 1820s, long after the potential for these had disappeared from the midlands.

In assessing massacre tolls, *Fabrication* attempts to draw definitive conclusions about what is, to a large extent, unknown. For example, we simply do not know how many Aborigines died at Risdon Cove in May 1804. Three deaths were confirmed, but how many more occurred will forever remain a mystery. Even the whites present did not know, as most of the injured (and possibly dying) were removed. The impact of firing muskets and a cannon into a large mob of people must have been chaos – as the leaving behind of a small boy suggests. The evidence compiled by the Aborigines Committee which Windschuttle largely draws on, as any researcher must, reviewed the events nearly 27 years after they occurred. All of those giving accounts were not actually present except Edward White, the one direct witness, who claimed that 'a great many of the Aborigines [were] slaughtered and wounded'.[64]

A little Van Diemonian context and knowledge exposes Windschuttle's detailed attempt to dismiss White's evidence as simply silly. He claims that 'White's awareness of events was not good' because the huts of two of the settlers he mentions were on the same side of the creek, not opposite sides as White recalled, and reproduces Bowen's

September 1803 sketch of the settlement to 'prove' this.[65] The sketch was made in the same month as the settlement was founded. Governor King had instructed Bowen to erect 'tent huts' on landing.[66] These could be put up very quickly and were not intended as permanent structures but as a substitute for imported canvas which had proved less than satisfactory in Australian conditions.[67] Bowen's sketch is simply the site of initial camping places. It is very likely that by May the following year one of the settlers had chosen to relocate across the creek.

Windschuttle's dismissal of White's testimony about the former surgeon Jacob Mountgarret sending Aboriginal bones to Sydney is similarly unsound. Of course convicts like White could have 'direct knowledge' of what the 'elite' were doing at this time – there were only 49 people there. Moreover, Mountgarret subsequently showed an interest in the scientific study of Aborigines, as did a number of his superiors in Sydney. His dissection of one of the Aboriginal dead was probably for science, and he would have been very reluctant to 'waste' his 'ownership' of the first bones of a 'new' people. Mountgarret even disobeyed Collins' order for the Aboriginal infant, christened Robert Hobart May by Knopwood, to be returned, and took him to Sydney and then on to his new posting at Port Dalrymple.[68]

Windschuttle's claim that 'the settlement did not have any quantity of lime at its disposal', so that the bones could not be 'packed in lime' as White claimed, is simply wrong.[69] Limestone had not yet been discovered, but convicts were already permanently stationed at Ralph's Bay burning oyster shells – probably Aboriginal midden deposits – thus ensuring a regular supply of lime to both Risdon Cove and Sullivan's Cove.

Finally, Windschuttle claims that 'Mountgarret had no ostensible reason to downplay the conflict. He was not part of the military. He had been replaced as colonial surgeon ...'[70] This radically misses the point. Since the arrival of Collins, Mountgarret had effectively become unemployed, quite unwillingly, and he had a very good reason to maintain positive relations with those in Sydney who could, and did, secure him another official position. Overall, the reliability of Edward White's evidence to the Aborigines Committee about the Risdon massacre therefore looks reasonably good.

Nevertheless, significant uncertainty surrounds the events at Risdon Cove and no definitive conclusion is possible. For this reason, *Fabrication*'s statement that 'three Aborigines were shot dead'[71] has no more historical credibility and is as politically driven as the statements of those who claim 100 deaths and a bloodbath. The balanced conclusions, based directly on the limited evidence available, are provided by the historians Windschuttle so derides. Ryan says that 'at least three Aborigines were killed.'[72] Reynolds doesn't risk a figure at all, using it as an example of how difficult it is to estimate numbers of Aboriginal deaths.[73]

Acknowledging the role of introduced diseases in Aboriginal population decline is also not new. It is common to virtually all nineteenth and twentieth-century works. Deaths from disease *might* have been widespread, even *the* major cause of the population decline, but Windschuttle's claim that 'the evidence for disease … as the major cause of depopulation is compelling'[74] is nonsense. All of the evidence *Fabrication* cites is from after 1829, except for one conversation documented by Bonwick,[75] and by this time much of the population decrease had already occurred, traditional Aboriginal lifestyles had been extremely disrupted except on the west coast, and there was close, ongoing and concentrated contact with large numbers of whites.

Moreover, there are also substantial problems with the disease thesis that Windschuttle does not acknowledge. *Fabrication* points out that smallpox soon largely wiped out the Aboriginal people living in the vicinity of Sydney, and that many deaths from disease occurred rapidly at Port Phillip.[76] The problem for this argument, however, is that Van Diemen's Land had no equivalent visible epidemics, despite the extensive cultural contact characteristic of the pre-1820 period.[77] Aborigines were never observed dying in large numbers. Indeed, smallpox, as well as many other diseases, was unknown on the island.

Overall, the extended sailing time from England, whereby diseases were 'burnt out' on arrival, the small population, the low level of movement of people and an effective smallpox vaccination program, combined with plenty of clean water and an excellent protein-rich diet, made Van Diemen's Land probably the healthiest outpost of the British empire, at least until around 1818. There were definitely very few white deaths from disease. The limited sources available suggest this could have been true of Aborigines too.

Surgeon Mountgarret told Commissioner Bigge in 1820 that at Port Dalrymple there was little disease and his main work was complications from old war wounds received by ex-soldiers and sailors on active service.[78] While in Hobart Town, Surgeon Luttrell told the Commissioner, 'Measles, hooping cough, smallpox … None of them are known here, nor is scarlet fever.' In response to a follow-up question concerning the diseases of the Aborigines, Luttrell replied, 'I don't know any other than the cutaneous [skin] eruption I have just mentioned. We have had some in the hospital, that have been brought in the last stage of dysentery.'[79]

In late 1819, Luttrell also ran a sort of temporary hospital specifically for Aborigines in Hobart, in response to a number being ill. None seems to have died, however, and Sorell told the surgeon he wanted it closed: 'The Lieutenant Governor finding Mr Luttrell's report that the native peoples are in good health, excepting the cutaneous disorder to which they are more or less liable, will desire that they may be conveyed into the country, so that the hire of the place occupied by them may cease on Saturday next.'[80]

Moreover, as none of the sources concerning Aborigines between 1804 and 1820 has been cited by Windschuttle, he is presumably unaware that the available evidence suggests Aboriginal population numbers held up fairly well during this period and observers saw few signs of diseases or epidemics. For example, Kelly's circumnavigation of the island in an open five-oared boat in the summer of 1815–16 involved a number of meetings with large groups of Aboriginal people, including women and children.[81] He reported nothing to suggest widespread illness.

Robinson's observations on the west coast also suggest that prior to intensive concentration with European people, the incidence of disease might have been quite low. The West Coast people, even in 1833, had a full demographic, including the elderly and infants – those most prone to death by disease. However, once confined and concentrated with whites at Macquarie Harbour, their death rate was tragically high.

The limited evidence available leans towards the likelihood that disease played only a limited role up to 1820, while between 1820 and 1830 the balance between violent deaths at the hands of whites and disease is not clear. Only from 1832 is the leading role of disease in the Aboriginal death rate conclusive. Perhaps the juxtaposition of the two issues is misleading anyway. The drastic changes in lifestyle demanded by the dramatically expanded conflict, including the constant movement, the loss of fires, the need to winter inland and sometimes in subalpine areas, the difficulty of hunting and obtaining fresh meat, and the subsequent substitution of flour and sugar for meat and seafood are likely to have made the Aborigines more vulnerable to white disease from the mid-1820s.

The final serious flaw in Windschuttle's analysis of the Aboriginal death rate is his use of the category of 'implausible' for those deaths where there is insufficient evidence to ascertain the truth of the matter. Any fair and balanced assessment must list these incidents as 'uncertain', 'unknown' or 'possible but no supporting evidence'. For example, why is the death described in the *Hobart Town Gazette* on 20 March 1819 so implausible, since even for Windschuttle revenge is one cause of Aboriginal violence? The white man David Kemp's killing by the Aborigines at Grindstone Bay is recorded by the *HTG* on 28 November 1818. On 20 March 1819, the paper then claimed that, 'It is well known that some time before Kemp was killed, a native man was shot in the woods by some of the stockmen to the eastward.' Why is this 'implausible', given we have no other information?[82] That an Aboriginal death occurred cannot be said to be unlikely; on the limited evidence available, it is possible but unknown.

It is also not at all clear what level of proof is needed for a death to be 'highly plausible'. For example, concerning the deaths described in the *Colonial Times* on 3 September 1830, there is a statement from both a white and an Aborigine directly involved, each of whom confirms the deaths. The latter evidence Windschuttle considers of such value that he quotes it elsewhere as evidence to 'clinch his argument … the kind that advocates of the patriotic war thesis have never been able to produce to support their own case; testimony from a tribal Aborigine explaining his actions'.[83] Given the value and rarity (although not uniqueness) of such corroborated evidence, and given that those involved agreed on the substance of what occurred, why is it that when compiling Table 10, Windschuttle believed such significant doubts remained that the deaths only warranted a 'plausible' ranking?[84] To rank the deaths resulting from this incident as even 'highly plausible' is conservative. Evidence in this difficult research field just doesn't get better than this, except perhaps in those few examples where Aborigines were killed in close proximity to the principal British settlements.

The fact that Aborigines died at the Risdon settlement in May 1804 had never been questioned in 199 years – even by those responsible for the killings. In *Fabrication*'s extensive discussion of the incident, Windschuttle raises no evidence to cast any doubt that some Aborigines died. Yet in his infamous tally these deaths are described as no more than 'plausible'.

Whatever the unknown basis of Windschuttle's plausibility assessments, their fundamental flaws are transparently evident in his bizarre conclusions. *Fabrication* claims there exist only two accounts of 'highly plausible' killings of Aborigines – involving a total of four deaths – and none at all until October 1830. Four 'highly plausible' Aboriginal deaths, only about 2% of the equivalent white figure, is self-evidently a ridiculous claim and shows how flawed is any analysis that equates the level of uncertainty with plausibility. The likelihood of truth can only be claimed where there is evidence to support it. The fact that the documentary record of Aboriginal deaths is incomplete does not mean that we *know* 'few Aborigines were killed'.

Windschuttle's Aboriginal death rate figure has no credibility, even as a starting point for further research. The case for – at the very least – acknowledging significant uncertainty concerning the number of Aboriginal deaths is compelling. It is true that both Reynolds and Ryan make suggestions about the number of Aboriginal war dead. Reynolds believes that Ryan's figure of 700 is 'probably too high' and suggests a range of 250 to 400.[85] Calder also believed it to be less than 500.[86] But these figures only purport to be general estimates based on a broad perusal of the evidence available, not definitive claims. In the end, there is only one certainty on this matter, and that is, as Reynolds put it, 'We will never know with any certainty.'[87] Definitive body counts and firm statements about the low level of violence Aborigines experienced are not evidence-based. *Fabrication*'s low Aboriginal death rate figure at the hands of whites, headlined in much of the book's promotion, reflects the author's political agenda, not serious historical research.

Windschuttle's mistakes in his analysis of the Aboriginal death rate result from his failure to consider most of the extensive published and unpublished Van Diemonian primary source material for himself. This should deny him any academic, cultural or political credibility, even on his own terms. As he points out, 'There is a world of difference between historians who go to the past to *investigate* the evidence about this subject and those who go to *vindicate* a stand they have already taken.'[88]

The Causes of Violence

Windschuttle's failure to investigate Van Diemonian sources is just as evident in other embarrassing factual mistakes that similarly discredit *Fabrication*'s second principal conclusion: not only did few Aborigines die at the hands of the British, but Aboriginal violence against whites did not represent the defence of any communal interest.

Windschuttle makes a considerable effort to show in *Fabrication* that Aborigines had 'no sense of a collective interest of any kind'.[89] He sets out to show that around 200 European deaths, the widespread and documented destruction of white property and the evacuation of large areas of the island was not due to an Aboriginal defence of their resources, land, culture or any other communal interest, but rather a series of individual outrages by Aborigines occasionally seeking revenge, but usually after white food and household goods.[90] In the quest for plunder, Europeans were killed 'simply because they could be'.[91]

To establish his case, Windschuttle attempts to discredit the two main causes contemporaries and subsequent scholars have generally given for the explosion in violence from the mid-1820s: as he puts it, 'the destruction of native game ... and the alienation of Aborigines from their traditional lands'.[92] However, his ignorance of the realities of Van Diemonian life means that his arguments on both issues are based on claims that can easily be shown to be wrong, not just in interpretation but in fact.

1. *The Competition for Game*

In endeavouring to prove that competition for game could not have been one of the triggers for violence, Windschuttle claims that 'in the early days of the colony the white settlers themselves supplemented their supplies by hunting native game, mainly kangaroo. However, this only lasted until January 1811 when more reliable supplies of traditional British food became available.'[93] Moreover, he argues that the end to white hunting, combined with Aboriginal population decline, meant that kangaroo and game numbers must have increased in the subsequent years as 'A decline in the number of hunters, other things being equal, will always cause an increase in the number of the hunted.'[94]

Besides the comparatively small fact that Windschuttle is two years out on the final government purchase of kangaroo meat, the problem is that hunting by whites in the years after 1813, especially from 1818, dramatically increased, not decreased, as any number of overlooked Van Diemonian sources reveals. Hunting was such a defining feature of Van Diemonian life that by the late 1820s the forester kangaroo and emu, except in the unsettled north-east and parts of the Central Plateau, had largely been exterminated in a killing frenzy that parallels the near-extinction of the bison on the American prairie a generation later.

Windschuttle seems to be unaware that forester kangaroos and emus only lived on the frequently burnt, largely open, native grass plains, the main Aboriginal-developed and Aboriginal-managed hunting grounds, and that in these areas the introduction of the dog, previously unknown on the island, had an enormous impact on fauna numbers.

Hunting kangaroo with dogs was the main occupation of a large part of the population. Government orders (presumably again Windschuttle's only source) were issued repeatedly to stop convict stockmen and shepherds hunting, but the practice instead escalated with the development of the export skins market after 1818. To give some idea of the extent of the plunder, we might note that two ships only are recorded as entering George Town in 1819–20: the *Governor Macquarie*, with 1400 sealskins and 520 kangaroo skins on board, and the *Little Mary*, with 3300 sealskins and 4700 roo-skins.[95] In 1819, over 3600 kangaroo skins left the port of Hobart for Sydney alone.[96]

James Gordon told Commissioner Bigge about the principal occupation of Van Diemonian stockmen and shepherds: they 'derive subsistence from killing kangaroos, and they derive a profit from the sale of the skins'. Indeed, the temptation to hunt kangaroo, Gordon confirmed, caused them to 'desert flocks' regularly.[97]

A reading of almost any account of life in Van Diemen's Land will confirm the centrality of hunting. Even Windschuttle's restricted sources should have been enough to reveal his mistake. For example, on 17 December 1831, Robinson lamented, on being confronted by another group of vagabond hunters, that, 'This is another proof of the folly of masters to allow their servants to keep dogs, who only employ themselves in hunting when they ought to look after their master's business.'[98] A fuller reading of the *Hobart Town Gazette* beyond its indexed references to Aborigines might have helped too. The paper's Christmas Day message in 1819 was, 'It would be found very beneficial if the owners of stock were to limit or to get rid entirely of the dogs, which are now generally kept at the interior stockyards, and which induce the men to employ almost all of their time in hunting, losing sight of the flocks for days together.'

Jeffreys' *Van Diemen's Land* should also have been sufficient for Windschuttle to correct his error about the end of large-scale hunting. Jeffreys believed the numbers of kangaroos killed:

> diminish the idea of sport, as the dogs themselves destroy great quantities, flock succeeds flock in such abundance, that 26 kangaroos have been killed in one morning, and persons have been said to have filled two bullock carts before 9 o'clock with these animals and emus ... it is to be hoped that this lavish system of butchery will be laid aside ... indiscriminate destruction should be prohibited; if some measure of this kind is not adopted, a total extinction of these valuable animals in this island will be the consequence.[99]

Windschuttle's narrow reading of sources thus causes a principal occupation of the white population, and its consequent impact on Aborigines, to disappear. Real men like old Thomas Toombs, the

Calcutta convict who had lived in Van Diemen's Land since 1804, have no place on *Fabrication*'s fantasy island. As Toombs said in a statement dated 3 May 1835, 'I have no property whatsoever, except some kangaroo dogs. I now reside – with Mr Anstey's permission – in Michael Howe's Marsh, and I gain a living by hunting kangaroo and selling the skins – I am the person who discovered that lake between Malony's Sugar Loaf and the Eastern Coast, which now bears my name.'[100] Toombs had been a kangaroo hunter by 1835 for three decades. 'Tooms Lake' is one of the comparatively few significant vernacular Van Diemonian place names to survive to the present. It is a continuing reminder that there was more to Van Diemonian life than what government regulations proclaimed.[101]

Of course, a decline in the numbers of forester kangaroos and emus does not mean that wallabies, possums, wombats and other Aboriginal meat sources were equally affected. There is some evidence to suggest that Aboriginal population decline in this period may even have caused an increase in the numbers of those animals not extensively hunted by Europeans (mainly those animals not vulnerable to the dog). It is also true that the Aborigines travelling with Robinson generally had no trouble securing game, so long as they stayed in the more open country where the dogs could hunt effectively. Windschuttle's jump from this evidence to the conclusion that plenty of food was available for Aborigines is a misleading one, however. The Aborigines with Robinson could secure plenty of game precisely because of the freedom from attack afforded by Robinson's protection. It is a great mistake to believe that other Aborigines had such opportunities. Indeed, the possibility of safe hunting and food-gathering was a main attraction of membership of Robinson's party, and the prospect of this becoming permanent once work was completed was the most important inducement Robinson offered. For example, on 23 November 1830, he told the Aborigines with him that 'if they had attended to my orders ... all our troubles would be at an end, and we and the Lairmairrener (Big River) natives might go and hunt among the settlers.'[102] The small groups of Aboriginal people Robinson met with near the settled districts usually agreed to accompany him on the understanding that they would have the right to hunt peacefully their ancestral lands. For example, on 29 August 1831, at a meeting with seven Aborigines, Robinson said he 'made known to them the wish of the Government; that if they would not spear white men they might remain and hunt, and they seemed glad and lifted up their hands'.[103]

Besides the native grass plains, the other principal location of Aboriginal food was the coast. *Fabrication* claims that 'the settlers occupied only a very small proportion of the coastline and estuaries from which several tribes gained food such as shellfish, crayfish … swans, ducks and eggs', and cites Jorgen Jorgenson's belief that tribal visits were 'left uninterrupted' even during the height of the Black War.[104]

In fact, the plunder on the Van Diemen's Land coast and offshore islands had increased progressively since 1798, and by 1830 core foods like seals, swans, ducks and their eggs had been decimated, mainly for skins and feathers. Boats came from far abroad to access these resources, and the story of the permanent and semi-permanent 'sealers' (who killed much more than seals) is relatively well known. Such roving raiding parties journeyed well past Bass Strait – the Baudin expedition, for instance, passed a group heading to the east coast in 1803. Less well known is that seasonal raids had also become an established part of 'ordinary' Van Diemonian life well before 1820. The *Hobart Town Gazette* in 1818 described a typical bounty from such a foray. A party of five men had gone to Oyster Bay and procured 300 lbs of swan feathers, 60 swan-skins, 100 kangaroo skins, 34 live swans and 151 sealskins. They had with them four kangaroo dogs, three muskets, some ammunition and sealing knives.[105]

The result of such cumulative plunder was that Louisa Meredith, who arrived at Great Swanport in 1839, lamented that 'the swans were nearly all gone and we rarely see more than a few wild ducks or teal in a season, although formerly every lagoon teemed with them, and with legions of bald coots, but the latter are now so rare, that I have not yet seen one.'[106] Seals too had long gone from the Tasmanian mainland and largely from the offshore islands.

It was not only the depletion in the amount of coastal game, but the severe interruption to traditional coastal access that caused such disruption and harm to Aborigines. Aborigines were forced to abandon many of their most important sites, especially the easily accessible bays and estuaries of the east coast. As noted above, Windschuttle's only source for claims of largely uninterrupted coastal access through the height of the war years is a remark by Jorgen Jorgenson.[107] A fuller reading of the cited document would have corrected his mistake: 'As a great number of armed parties were sent in quest of the hostile Aboriginal tribes they became so harassed that they avoided all their former haunts.' Or again, 'the poor blacks had taken alarm, they were in utter consternation, they had nearly been encompassed and reduced to a state of starvation; they could not see that the Colonists were unable to remain constantly in the field, and carry on an expensive war without ample finances.'[108]

Or, in closing, as Windschuttle makes the claim that the 'Tasmanian orthodoxy' never quote 'tribal' Aborigines, this attempt at direct language translation by Jorgenson may also interest him: 'When I returned to my country I went hunting but did not kill one head of game. The white men make their dogs wander, and kill the game, and they only want the skins.'[109]

2. The Competition for Land

Windschuttle makes a similarly basic mistake in dismissing competition for land as another trigger for Aboriginal violence. He points out, correctly, that up to and including 1823, only 527,241 acres had been granted, 3.1% of the island, the great majority of it in 1823. His mistake is to claim this well-known statistic as proof that the 'account of the growth of the pastoral economy up to 1824 is grossly exaggerated', and that Lyndall Ryan is wrong to claim that whites had by this time occupied 15% of the island, including the main hunting grounds of the Oyster Bay and North Midlands tribes.[110]

Windschuttle's error is to equate land ownership with land occupation. He seems not to understand that on this island formal land title usually followed many years of other forms of increasingly intense white occupation and resource exploitation. The full-time kangaroo hunters were only the first such wave. By 1820, stockmen and shepherds, and a range of hard-to-occupationally-define vagabonds, had joined the hunters, sometimes in the service of those with formal tickets of occupation, sometimes without any formal sanction. It is a matter of easily demonstrable fact, not interpretation, that by this time the British lived throughout the native grass pasture lands of the island.

There is no shortage of evidence nor any doubt about this. Much of the land was legally leased. The surveyor G. W. Evans described tickets of occupation to Commissioner Bigge in 1820 as an 'annual license'. They were 'numerous ... very large tracts comprehending from 3 to 10 miles in extent selected at the will and for the convenience of the parties'. There were, he said, 'no limits' to the lands allowed to be occupied.[111]

James Gordon pointed out to Bigge how many of the small settlers also occupied – rather than owned – 'crown' land in the interior. There are '"not many" sheep and cattle in the district', he told the Commissioner; instead they graze them, 'in the interior of the country and at a distance of 40 and 50 miles from the settlement ... (with) a ticket of occupation describing in very general terms the tract of land that he is to occupy'.[112]

The extensive nature of the 102 'licenses for grazing occupations' which were 'renewed and granted for 12 months from September 29 1819' are listed in the official returns of 1820. These licences obliged the holder to erect a stockyard 'convenient to contain the whole of his cattle or sheep'. Stock huts adjacent to this were erected for the stockmen and shepherds. Some of the licences issued that year included one to 'Stines and Troy' on the 'East Coast' from 'Prossers Plains to Oyster Bay'.[113] Yet Windschuttle claims that, 'The first settler to discover land suitable for pastures at Oyster Bay was George Meredith in April 1821 and the first white man known to inhabit the district was William Talbot later that year.' Meredith was in fact advised of the availability of excellent ungranted pasture land at Oyster Bay by the government within a few days of his arrival in the colony. Meredith says he first met with Sorell, who suggested the east coast, and then the Surveyor, Evans, 'and was favoured ... with a written report of the country contiguous to Oyster Bay for my better information'.[114] At a time when the main form of transport was by sea, Oyster Bay was not as remote as many inland regions. Sorell had sent an official exploration party to the east coast in the summer of 1819–20 in part to try and find an easier overland route to this well-known and widely accessed area. To believe that Meredith discovered such pastures, and that Talbot was the first to inhabit them, is to be blind to a whole generation of Van Diemonian land use. Yet on the basis of such ignorance Windschuttle denigrates the late Lloyd Robson who, in discussing a possible east coast massacre of Aborigines in 1815 in *The History of Tasmania*, assumed the presence there of white men and sheep. *Fabrication* concludes that since there 'was adequate information about land settlement available when Robson prepared his book', such claims reflected 'poorly on his scholarship, or ... poorly on his integrity'.[115]

Windschuttle's complete ignorance of the existence of tickets of occupation even causes him to include Scott's 1821 sketch of Stocker's stock hut on the Macquarie River in *Fabrication* as an example of a 'land grant'; he is unaware that this property, too, was leasehold, documented in the 1820 returns, but not yet existing in the official land grants on which he places exclusive emphasis.[116]

Furthermore, these tickets of occupation were only an attempt by Sorell to exert some control over an already extensive informal land occupation.[117] And many land users never bothered to obtain a ticket. Although Windschuttle concedes the possibility of some 'unrecorded illegal squatting by graziers beyond the officially sanctioned settlements',[118] he describes what was largely a later mainland phenomenon. Certainly, wealthy cattle and sheep barons sent their men and stock largely where they pleased, but in Van Diemen's Land it was mainly poor whites, without capital or legitimate claim to land grants or leases, who moved onto the 'crown' land, often grazing the stock owned by others on a system known as 'the thirds' while also hunting game or participating in somewhat less legal activities, particularly stock theft. As Burn recalled, before Arthur's time, 'crown lands' were 'overrun with men free by servitude or ticket of leave'.[119] For example, James Ross found he had established neighbours on the Shannon River although he was the first official grantee: 'The sheep which this man tended, belonged to three or four different proprietors, one of whom had put them under his charge, and without further license or ceremony he had set himself down with them in this secluded spot.' 'Dennis' and his sheep may exist in no government documents, and thus have no chance of appearing in the pages of *Fabrication*, but to Aborigines and whites alike they were real nevertheless.[120]

Cubit has documented the large gap between official and unofficial occupation of the north-west, fully revealed when the Van Diemen's Land Company sought to take up its grant on what was officially 'empty' and remote land. When Curr, the company's agent, crosses the Meander River in April 1826, he finds instead herds of cattle and sheep well settled in, and even carts had passed through.[121]

The speed of expansion in land occupation at this time can also be seen in the rapid growth of livestock numbers. In 1817, there were 104,236 sheep and 11,116 cattle in Van Diemen's Land, excluding those owned by the civil and military officers and the government. In 1818, there were 127,883 sheep and 15,356 cattle; by November 1819, 172,128 sheep and 23,124 cattle. Cattle numbers had thus more than doubled and sheep nearly doubled in two years, although few land grants were made during this time. By contrast, only 8330 acres were in cultivation in 1819.[122] By that year Van Diemen's Land had more than twice the number of sheep of New South Wales.[123]

Windschuttle is thus quite wrong to conclude that 'settlement in the early 1820s was characterised by the same kind of small mixed farming as the previous two decades', and that Ryan's 'account of the growth of the pastoral economy up to 1824 is grossly exaggerated'.[124] On the contrary, Ryan's analysis is, if anything, too conservative. Van Diemen's Land was a pastoral economy well before 1824, and the tiny land grants cited in *Fabrication* are no indicator of the extent or nature of land use. Moreover, the increasingly intensive occupation would clearly have had major implications for the other primary users of the plains, the Aborigines.

This elementary error is not Windschuttle's only mistake in his analysis of the competition for land. *Fabrication* virtually ignores the implications of the million acres formally granted from 1824 to 1831, although this coincided directly with the outbreak of serious and sustained hostilities.[125] By the conclusion of this process, almost all the native grasslands of the island – the main Aboriginal hunting fields, except for the north-east and Central Highlands – were in private ownership. As Arthur reported to London as early as August 1825:

... the accounts which have been published in England respecting Van Diemen's Land have been highly exaggerated. A tract of country extending from Hobart to Launceston, 120 miles, may be considered one extensive vale and, within this space, the land is generally very fine ... but all the country to the westward is very mountainous, the climate severe ... The great misfortune seems to have been portioning out the valley in such extensive grants.[126]

Five years later Arthur again reminded London of the realities of Tasmanian topography: 'no country that I am acquainted with has so large an extent, in proportion to its areas, of wild, unproductive, impervious, rugged mountains and dense forest.'[127] Control of the limited grassland plains, the home of both the native and introduced herbivores, was thus the key to profit and power for the large land-owners, and the key to survival itself for most Aborigines.

Windschuttle also fails to understand how these formal grants transformed the nature of land use in the mid-1820s. *Fabrication* makes much of the point that there was still very little fencing in the 1820s, and argues from this that Aborigines were not significantly affected by white land occupation. Indeed, this point forms the bulk of his argument against the competition for land triggering war.[128] It is true that fences were indeed rare until well into the 1830s. However, the implications of this are the reverse of what *Fabrication* suggests. Before the mid-1820s, hardier varieties of sheep were almost exclusively kept for domestic meat consumption, and some form of black–white co-existence was possible. After this, the much more valuable and vulnerable merinos were increasingly kept for the export wool trade. The investments required to import breeding stock (often directly from Spain and Germany) and improve the flocks were considerable. What Windschuttle misses is that the lack of fencing now exacerbates the conflict between this form of land use and continued Aboriginal occupation. The need to separate the flock, graze the land more intensively and maintain a much greater level of supervision and control was in direct conflict with Aboriginal hunting and land-management techniques, which used both dogs and fire. Moreover, the new settlers built substantial homes and planted crops and gardens that were not easily replaced when burnt. Aborigines were thus moved on to protect the unfenced flocks and associated investments, and, as all the best land was similarly taken up, force was increasingly required to achieve this. It is not surprising that the forms of co-existence that had been possible when white land use was associated with hunting, wild cattle and largely unsupervised sheep, and with the temporary abodes of stockmen and shepherds, now rapidly broke down, especially given the associated explosion in white population numbers. The unwillingness or incapacity to make the significant capital investment required to build fences thus added to, not mitigated, the potential for violent conflict.

The widely known facts – which Windschuttle chooses not to cite – are that from 1823 to 1831, the period that coincides with intense fighting, 1,899,332 acres were granted, over 95% of the total area of land granted in Van Diemen's Land.[129] The size of each grant also dramatically increased: small land grants of less than 100 acres virtually cease and land is now granted in proportion to capital held. A new type of 'gentleman' immigrant, seeking profit and social status, increasingly dominates land ownership. The overall white population increases from 3114 in 1817 to 7400 in 1821 to 26,640 in 1831. Sheep numbers also explode, increasing five-fold in the seven years to 1830.[130] As a result, Van Diemen's Land overtakes New South Wales in wool exports in the late 1820s, and very large profits indeed are made in the period from 1828 to 1835. On the back of this wealth, the 200 largest land-owners form a self-proclaimed 'gentry' establishment, wielding considerable political, social and economic power.

The conflict with the Aborigines was widely seen to be a threat to this wealth and prosperity, justifying the direct expenditure of £30,000 on the Black Line – about half the government's annual budget – and the arming of over 1000 convicts to back up 550 regular troops and numerous citizen volunteers in a sweep across much of the state that was meant to settle the issue once and for all. The senior government official G. T. W. B. Boyes, another of *Fabrication*'s neglected diarists, explained the campaign on 31 October 1830 in these terms:

> Our papers were filled weekly with the atrocities of the Blacks and it
> has become apparent that unless means were devised for making them

prisoners … in some well adapted part of this country, or, otherwise exterminating the race, that the country must be abandoned … The Lt Governor has taken the field with almost all the military – the Ticket of Leave men, Constables and as many assigned servants as could be spared, have been marshaled, equipped for the field, and distributed like soldiers along the line, or formed into parties scouring the bush. Many of the young men, Clerks in public offices, have put the knap-sack upon their backs, rations in their pouches and guns upon their shoulders and have marched in charge of ten or twelve men, each to the destined scene of action.[131]

If this dramatically escalated conflict with the Aborigines cannot be explained solely by the far-reaching changes in the form and intensity of British land occupation during the 1820s, they surely provide its essential context. Acknowledging the relevance of the explosion in sheep, people and profit cannot be dismissed as a 'quasi-Marxist explanation'.[132] The importance of these changes has been accepted by almost all writers, of all political persuasions, since the late 1820s, and this is certainly not a 'post-1960s' interpretation originating with Ryan, Reynolds or any other contemporary academic. Windschuttle attempts to counter the importance of these factors in explaining the dramatic increase in Aboriginal resistance after 1824 by noting the low level of formal land grants to 1823 and the lack of fencing after this. But these factors support, rather than challenge, the 'orthodox' view once they are seen in the context of the changing economic and social realities of Van Diemen's Land.

Windschuttle's final point on this question of land is also flawed: 'The strongest argument that the colonists' possession of their land was not the reason behind the Aborigines' violence was that they took so long to respond to the British presence.'[133] In fact, Aborigines soon met with each of the three groups of British settling at Risdon Cove, Sullivan's Cove and Port Dalrymple over the period 1803–4.

The details of the first meeting at Risdon, which pre-dates Bowen's arrival, have been lost, although Bowen confirmed to King on 26 September 1803 that others had 'seen' Aborigines.[134] Whether there was some show of force by the British to frighten off any Aboriginal reception party cannot now be known. Certainly, the NSW Corps was not by then known for its discipline or restraint, and such a small party would have felt quite vulnerable. Details from a February 1804 encounter suggest that by then the Aborigines were feeling far from neutral about the British arrival. The surveyor Meehan's notebook records that somewhere to the north of the settlement on the Derwent, they were,

> infested with a considerable body of natives who endeavoured to sur-round us – had taken one of my marking sticks – am obliged to fire on them ... The natives are in a considerable body – assembled again and endeavoured to steal behind a hill – on which, fired another gun and they dispersed for the night. Tuesday morning. – the natives again assembled in a large body on a hill over us – all around with spears and in a very menacing attitude. They followed us a short distance and then stopped. They appear to be very dexterous at throwing stones. Them who surrounded us yesterday in such multitudes had no arms but a few waddys, but several of them picked up stones ...[135]

The Derwent was a tribal boundary, and negotiations went much better at Sullivan's Cove, where the experienced and astute David Collins was in charge. There were a number of peaceful early exchanges. The first contact on 9 March 1804 is recorded by Knopwood: 'natives all around ... Cap Mertha and Mr Brown had an interview with them on the shore near the Ocean.'[136]

At Port Dalrymple, Paterson, after arriving on 5 November, chose a hill site that he saw as 'well situated for the protection of the settlement'. He recorded that:

> On the 12th a body of natives consisting of about 80 in number, made their approach within about 100 yards from the camp; from what we could judge they were headed by a chief, as everything given to them was given up to this person ... from this friendly interview I was in hopes we would have been well acquainted with them ere this, but unfortunately a large party (supposed to be the same) attacked the guard of marines, consisting of one sergeant and 2 privates ... the Guard was under the unpleasant act of defending themselves, and

fired upon them, killed one and wounded another; this unfortunate circumstance I am fearful will be the cause of much mischief hereafter, and will prevent our excursions inland, except when well armed.[137]

Despite the violence, negotiations continued, and Paterson had a friendly meeting with 40 Aborigines, involving the exchange of more goods, on 9 December 1804.[138]

3. Fabrication's *Own Claims*
The argument presented in *Fabrication* for alternative causes of violence between the Aborigines and British is contradictory and cannot explain the increase in violence from the mid-1820s. It is claimed that:

> Overall, then, the spread of white settlement in the 1820s was certainly a major cause of the increase in black violence; but not for the reasons the orthodox school proposes. Far from generating black resentment, the expansion of settlement instead gave the Aborigines more opportunity and more temptation to engage in robbery and murder, two customs they had come to relish … It was a tragedy the Aborigines adopted such senseless violence.[139]

According to Windshuttle, so many British died because Aboriginal 'culture had no sanctions against the murder of anyone outside their immediate clan'. Europeans were 'killed simply because they could be'.[140]

Again, it is the distinctiveness of the Van Diemonian story that causes Windschuttle's politically driven themes to unravel. On this island, much less conflict occurred in the first generation after white settlement than occurred almost anywhere else. After considerable resistance in the 1805–8 period, when white hunters first went beyond the secured environs of the settlements seeking new supplies of kangaroo, a generally peaceful access to land developed from the widespread exchange of goods.[141] In particular, tea, tobacco, sugar, flour and dogs were sought by the Aborigines. While most such meetings went unrecorded, the many texts and documents neglected by *Fabrication* contain sufficient evidence to show how extensive was this early cultural contact, trade and largely peaceful co-existence.

For example, in James Kelly's account of his circumnavigation of the island in the summer of 1815–16, he records that on 12–13 January they saw a 'large mob' of natives on the north-east coast. The latter saw 'Briggs, whom they knew particularly well'. Briggs had taken the trip 'hoping he might fall in with some of his black relations near Cape Portland'. One of the Aborigines, Lamanbunganah – 'Briggs called him Laman' – was his 'father in law'. Briggs was 'fluent' in the language. The Europeans traded seal carcasses for kangaroo skins, and by 22 January had procured 122 sealskins and 246 kangaroo skins, with a value of £180 in Hobart. This meeting and associated trade concluded with 'dancing' involving around '300 natives'.[142]

Henry Barrett, of George Town, reported to Bigge in April 1820 that Aborigines have been 'encouraged here to mix with the Europeans … I have had 9 or 10 in my house together. They will be very contented for a time and then they will throw their cloaths [sic] away and run into the bush.'[143]

James Ross had largely peaceful interactions with the Aborigines at the Shannon in the early 1820s,[144] as did Lloyd at Pitt Water and beyond.[145] Even in Hobart, a number of peaceful visits took place, especially between 1815 and 1818, as recorded by Knopwood and others. Archibald Campbell's Aboriginal partner who lived with Campbell on South Arm acted as the intermediary. This now unnamed woman died in January 1820 at Coles Bay, guiding a party of exploration overland to the east coast.[146] However, as late as November 1824, another 66 Aborigines visited Hobart.[147] Launceston had similar encounters in the pre-war era.[148]

Many Aborigines thus had extensive contact with the British, and tobacco, sugar, flour and tea were widely used by them well before 1824. So the question that must be faced by any serious historian of Van Diemen's Land is, why was there so little 'robbery' and 'murder' for the first 20 years of settlement, and so much after this?

Windschuttle's answer to this question, that there was 'more opportunity and more temptation' because there were more whites, does not hold up. If anything, the opportunity to steal and kill in the early days, when the stock-keepers were more isolated, there was no regular military presence in the interior, and stock huts had not yet been turned into defensive fortresses, would seem the greater.[149] Some of the stockmen in the pre-war days were even unarmed. Edward White, for example, lived near the Great Western Tiers for three years without ever carrying a gun.[150]

The inherent contradiction in *Fabrication*'s argument is obvious. Why did a people with 'no sanctions against the murder of anyone outside their immediate clan' kill so few of the isolated shepherds, kangaroo hunters and stock-keepers spread across the main Aboriginal hunting grounds of the island before 1824? As Sorell pointed out in 1819, 'It is ... most certain that if the natives were intent upon destruction ... the mischief done by them to the owners of cattle or sheep, which are now dispersed for grazing over so great a part of the interior country, would be increased a hundred fold.'[151] Readers may well wonder how there could be such peaceful contact and exchange of goods and technologies, well documented from the time of the French explorers on, with a people who, according to Windschuttle, had no cultural restraints on killing, and killed whites simply because 'they could'.

In a last attempt to show that Aboriginal violence was chiefly motivated by an enjoyment of plunder, Windschuttle presents as clinching evidence, 'testimony from a tribal Aborigine explaining his actions', that is, the account in the *Colonial Times* of the interrogation of an Aborigine captured after another violent exchange on the frontier:

> all that could be got from him was that the white man had destroyed several of his companions, and that he had most reason to complain; that when the tribe attacked the hut it was in order to obtain food, and such articles as the whites had introduced amongst them, and which now instead of being luxuries as formerly, had become necessities, which they could not any other way procure.[152]

When placed in Van Diemonian context, this quote highlights the point that many Aborigines had long obtained certain British goods from stock-keepers and others without violence, but these arrangements had now broken down. The only way now to procure what had become essential goods – and perhaps any food at all – was by force. It is only by largely ignoring the pre-1824 period and the extensive cultural contact that characterised it that Windschuttle can present such evidence as providing support for his argument.

To support his case that Aborigines did not have 'a collective interest of any kind', let alone a defence of it, Windschuttle also claims that
they 'never in twenty-five years made any political approaches to the
British ... and never attempted any kind of meeting, bargaining or
negotiation with them'.[153] The first meetings and the extensive cultural
contact and trade already described directly contradict this claim.

For most readers of Robinson's journals, this would also seem a
very odd conclusion, given that the diaries are basically a long and
detailed record of such meeting, bargaining and negotiation.
Robinson was understood by all parties to be representing the governor. For example, on 27 December 1831, just days before the crucial
negotiations with the Big River people that essentially ended the
Tasmanian War, Robinson noted that, 'in conference with my natives
[I] explain[ed] to them the purport of the Governor's letter, when
they all evinced a strong desire to communicate with the people.'[154]
Robinson's mission was described as an 'embassy', and on occasion the
Aborigines requested and were granted direct audiences with Arthur,
such as in Launceston on 5 October 1831.[155] A range of other evidence
is well presented in *Fate of a Free People* and need not be repeated here.
Certainly, thoughtful Van Diemonians were in as little doubt as Reynolds today that a deal had been done, given that only on the west
coast had any force been used to bring about the 'surrender' of their
formidable foe. 'From the time of Mr Robinson's extraordinary capture, or rather persuasion of the natives to follow him,' Louisa
Meredith records,

> a complete change took place in the island; the remote stock stations
> were again resorted to, and guns were no longer carried between the
> handles of the plough. The means of persuasion employed by Mr
> Robinson to induce the natives to submit to his guidance has ever been
> a mystery to me. He went into the bush ... and used such argument
> with them as sufficed at length to achieve his object.[156]

Despite the information contained in *Friendly Mission*, no one can be
completely sure what these arguments were. That they existed, and that
negotiations therefore occurred, was, and is, beyond any reasonable
doubt.

Windschuttle simply has no explanation for the outbreak of extensive fighting from the mid-1820s. He sees no external changes, no matter how dramatic, as significantly impacting on Aborigines. The cause of the violence is seen to lie in the inherent nature of Aboriginal society, even if its murderous propensities apparently lay dormant for 20 years. *Fabrication* thus explains neither the outbreak of war, nor the peace that preceded it. The distinctive and complex Van Diemonian story refuses to fit into Windschuttle's prefabricated box.[157]

Fabrication's View of Tasmanian Aboriginal Society

As *Fabrication* moves towards its close, there is a hint that even Windschuttle may be aware of the weakness of his arguments. At any rate, he changes tack markedly and makes comments about Aboriginal society which imply that all the preceding material in the book is ultimately besides the point, for however many of them the British killed, or whatever the reason for their fight, the Aborigines were doomed. The decline of the Tasmanian Aborigines, *Fabrication* argues, was rooted not in their encounter with the British but in the very nature of Tasmanian Aboriginal society. Indeed, the unfolding tragedy was their own fault for not changing their destructive ways when they had the chance:

> The real tragedy of the Aborigines was not British colonization *per se* but that their society was, on the one hand, so internally dysfunctional and, on the other hand, so incompatible with the looming presence of the rest of the world. Until the nineteenth century, their isolation had left them without comparisons with other cultures that might have helped them reform their ways. But nor did they produce any wise men of their own who might have foreseen the long-term consequences of their own behaviour and devised ways to curb it. They had survived for millennia, it is true, but it seems clear that this owed more to good fortune than good management. The 'slow strangulation of the mind' was true not only of their technical abilities but also of their social relationships. Hence it was not surprising that when the British arrived, this small precarious society quickly collapsed under the dual

weight of the susceptibility of its members to disease and the abuse
and neglect of its women.[158]

The political implications of such a bizarre assessment are crudely
obvious: responsibility for the past tragedy rests with Aborigines themselves, and therefore any claims for compensation on the basis of past
wrongs have no justification. However, these statements are so lacking
in reason, so unsubstantiated by any evidence, that the book at this
point, if it has not already done so, degenerates into slander.

Windschuttle's strongest interest, it seems, is in domestic relations:
'The aspect of their society that left them most vulnerable in the face of
the European arrival was the treatment of their women.' Aborigines
were 'active agents in their own demise because their men hired out
and sold off their women without seriously contemplating the results.
Only men who held their women cheaply would allow such a thing to
happen.' To back up such slurs, *Fabrication* claims there is 'abundant
evidence of the violent nature of relations between the sexes'.[159]

What 'abundant evidence'? Windschuttle quotes Robert Edgerton, a
contemporary American writer, to support his claims. Edgerton – who
knows even less of Tasmania than Windschuttle does – believes that
Tasmanian Aborigines were a 'profoundly maladapted population' who
'failed to devise social and cultural mechanisms to control their
destructive tendencies'.[160] Such theorising, however, is not evidence.
What information does Windschuttle provide from people who actually met with and observed Tasmanian Aborigines?

Given the 'abundance' of evidence, it seems rather strange that the
only direct observation *Fabrication* provides of the violent nature of
male–female relations is from November 1830, when a group of
Aborigines were detained on Swan Island, supplemented by a few other
Robinson journal entries during this last period of tribal disintegration. By then, these people had been exposed to a long period of systematic brutalisation on the front-line of the war, including a long
period of forced separation. Just as in Aboriginal communities today,
dispossession and severe cultural disruption almost always bring a
range of tragic social impacts. These, however, do not provide any evidence at all about traditional Aboriginal customs or practices.

Windschuttle states that, 'The first European observers called the men "indolent" and "extremely selfish" and said they treated their women like "slaves" and "drudges".'[161] But what is his actual source for these claims? It is Ling Roth's 1899 book, written at the height of Social Darwinist orthodoxy. To his credit, Ling Roth actually presented a varied range of contemporary opinion, but Windschuttle's quotes are selected from only two of Roth's sources: the French naturalist Péron and someone who did not even arrive until 1829, J. E. Calder, who is thus hardly a 'first observer' of Aborigines. Péron observed scars on the women and believed this to be evidence of domestic violence.[162] However, Péron did not witness such violence, nor was he provided with any information on the matter. Other observers of such scarring understood it as a cultural practice. Cook, for example, pointed out that the Aborigines were 'masters of some contrivance in the manner of cutting their arms and bodies in lines of different lengths and directions'.[163] He further pointed out that men and women's bodies were 'marked with scars in the same manner'.[164] Peron's speculation as to the cause of the women's scars therefore probably says more about his experience of French society than of Aboriginal.

Certainly, Péron was a less sympathetic observer of Aborigines than other 'first observers' such as his countrymen accompanying d'Entrecasteaux or the other members of his expedition, including the commandant himself, Baudin. The observations of these explorers, all ignored by Windschuttle, do not support *Fabrication*'s claims. In fact, even Péron's views differ significantly. The naturalist had a friendly meeting at Port Cygnet with the Aborigines, including three men, two women and four children, 'providing the most striking example we had ever had of attention and reasoning among savage people'. The Aborigines shared a meal of abalone around the fire with the French, who in turn sang to them, much to the joy and amusement of the Aborigines. 'Everything seems to combine to form in us feelings of the most tender interest,' Péron recalled. 'Their family life', he concluded, 'had moved us deeply.'[165]

Péron would also have profoundly disagreed with *Fabrication*'s claim that, 'Traditional Aboriginal society placed no constraints on the women's sexual behaviour with men.'[166] Péron was repeatedly rebuffed and kept at a safe distance when he tried to make any physical contact at all with Aboriginal women. Baudin believed that none of the amorous French crew had any sexual relations with the Bruny Island people, and it was not for want of trying.[167] The same people's very different behaviour a generation later with the whalers at Adventure Bay on Bruny, the behaviour that Windschuttle cites as evidence for his claim, is self-evidently a product of the extensive disruption of traditional life that had occurred by then. Only someone who is totally blind to the impact of changing power relations, of declining choices, of the profound impact of cultural disintegration and recurring violence and abuse, let alone the simple imperatives of survival, could cite the unfolding tragedy at Bruny Island in this period as evidence for the sexual mores and domestic relations of pre-invasion Aboriginal society.

Those seeking a more balanced and sympathetic view than that provided by *Fabrication* need simply do what Windschuttle has not done and read the only documentary sources on the matter, the French, and to a lesser extent the British, explorers.[168] Not content, however, with such uninformed slander, and just in case we are missing the point that these were not a people with any concern or capacity to defend themselves, their children, their families, their land, their culture or way of life, Windschuttle now throws in some unsubstantiated asides about the primitiveness of the Aborigines: 'their faeces deposited close to the fires where they slept ... They went about completely naked, even in the snow-covered highlands ... they could not make a fire, a skill that even Neanderthal Man had mastered.'[169] The first bizarre statement is not supported by direct observation. The two pieces of 'evidence' provided for it are an account by Backhouse of what he believed were Aborigines' former customs that, anyway, makes no mention of faeces or toilet practices; and a settler's observations of an abandoned east coast camping site made during the height of the war in February 1830.

The next two statements, while still unfortunately part of popular folklore, are directly contradicted by those who actually met the Aborigines. Windschuttle would have been well advised to remember his own criticism of historians who 'have not checked the original sources' and who repeat old claims 'without corroboration'.[170] When the Aborigines were reported to be 'naked', European observers usually meant that they did not cover their genitals – the European cultural meaning of nakedness – not that they wore no clothes. This began with Cook: 'The females wore a kangaroo skin tied over their shoulders and round their waist ... it did not cover those parts which most nations conceal.'[171] In warm weather, when nothing was needed, the men in particular frequently went naked. However, Baudin noted that as soon as the weather turned bad, even in summer, all the natives wore kangaroo skins.[172] Jeffreys also noted the climatic variations, and that during winter the natives dressed in kangaroo skins and 'the women are always partially clad in a robe of the same kind.'[173] There are no accounts of what Aborigines wore in the 'snow-clad highlands', mostly because, until forced to do so by the imperatives of war, they usually chose not to be there in the winter. The notion that they would not use warm skins in such circumstances, a clothing of such effectiveness that it often replaced European fabric for all races on the frontier, is too silly to merit any serious response.[174]

As for the repetition of Plomley's 1962 claim that Aborigines couldn't make fire, Windschuttle would again have been better served by reading the primary sources for himself. The Aborigines, like the British in this era before matches, carried fire with them. As Thornley noted, 'They have discovered ... that two pieces of lighted stick, or charcoal, crossed and in contact will keep alight ... [T]he settlers have borrowed this trick from the natives.'[175] Most people in Van Diemen's Land, though, believed that the Aborigines already knew how to make fire. The only significant evidence that they didn't is that an Aborigine once told Robinson this was the case. However, as Shayne Breen's review of this issue has pointed out, there are many examples of Aborigines withholding cultural information from Robinson by giving him a misleading answer, and taken alone this evidence counts for little.[176]

As Windschuttle's arguments unravel in the face of such Van Diemonian difference, he resorts to the semantics of a modern spin doctor. For him, Arthur's use of the word 'warfare' is 'a figure of speech, a surrogate term for mere violence'. It can't be war because Aborigines didn't attack troops directly but rather stockmen, who, although armed, 'had to put down their guns while they worked' and were usually 'assaulted or killed while they were unarmed'.[177] Convict workers, like the convict field police, don't fight and don't get killed in what *Fabrication* calls 'real warfare'.[178] Perhaps their dead bodies were just nineteenth-century 'collateral damage', although Windschuttle's definition of legitimate 'war' belongs to a far earlier era than this.

To hold the crumbling edifice of its argument together, *Fabrication* keeps a tight grip on any Van Diemonian voice that manages to sneak its way through the censor's barricade. Again and again the reader is left looking for some reference to a published or unpublished primary source beyond the tiny selection noted earlier. Given that even the middle-class and upper-class letter, journal and book writers are ignored, the complete dismissal of Aboriginal voices comes as no surprise. Very little direct evidence of the Aboriginal perspective has made it into the documentary record, but this doesn't stop Windschuttle dismissing the small selection he has made from this.[179] There cannot have been any notion of patriotism because no statements were 'made by a tribal Aborigine during the Black War that expressed a patriotic or nationalistic sentiment'.[180] It doesn't count when these are recorded in Robinson's journal because 'this is Robinson speaking, not an Aborigine'.[181] Another comment is dismissed because the Aborigine is not 'tribal'.[182] To pass this man's dictation test for authentic evidence, we apparently need a white person recording the tribal words of an Aborigine who must have had neither extended contact with Europeans nor a knowledge of English. And all this at the height of a bloody conflict. The fact that almost all surviving Aborigines in Tasmania outside the west coast spoke some English by 1830, and probably no literate whites were fluent in Aboriginal languages, is either unknown to him or irrelevant. In Tasmanian speak, this sure is a tough call. It would have done White Australia policy-makers proud.

Conclusion

Aborigines thus join white Van Diemonians in being excluded from a hearing in *The Fabrication of Aboriginal History*. An over-reliance on five years of government record-keeping indeed silences almost everyone.

Windschuttle has read almost nothing of what has been written about life in Tasmania over the past 200 years. He is familiar with very few of the island's many historians. He knows almost none of our letter writers, diarists and other people who recorded their views and experiences of life here. All recent research is ignored: no academic thesis written in the past 25 years has been looked at. He knows little, it is embarrassingly evident, of the Tasmanian land. Whatever else this book is, it is not a Tasmanian story.

Fabrication represents a view of the past disconnected from the lives of the real people who lived in Van Diemen's Land. At best, it is a description of what those with power wanted but because of the economic and political facts could never achieve. It is the fantasy island created by imperial correspondents, not the messy and bloody reality of our beautiful Van Diemonian earth.

Devoid of context, *Fabrication* develops in its place an obsession with the character and morality of a few prominent individuals, such as Robinson and Arthur. But at the same time Windschuttle must avoid hearing the personal, the local voices that can get us beyond the limitations of the official view. Private writings don't count and passed-on experience misleads. There is apparently too much uncertainty and ambiguity in the human domain. But in a careful selection of some official reports – here, we are told, we can at last find truth.

The deep mystery, our overwhelming ignorance in relation to Tasmanian Aborigines, is smothered by this obsessive and arrogant pretence to certainty. *Fabrication* dismisses the unknown, treating with contempt the empty tomb that confronts every history rooted in Van Diemen's Land earth. Some awe, wonder and pain in the face of what happened here is a rational response to an extraordinary tragedy that we can now only glimpse, not a left-wing conspiracy to deceive.

Many will understandably want to ignore Windschuttle's book, dismissing it as either very bad academic history or a poisonous political tract, both of which are true. But in the end, the Tasmanian community will need to find a language and framework – as other groups have been forced to do – to deal with the material in the text that is not concerned with academic debate but constitutes a slander on the custodians and creators of our land. This is not just up to Aborigines or activists: some respect for those almost-timeless generations who lived and developed this island before us is surely beyond race or politics; it simply flows from a love of the place.

I don't think Tasmanians can say our history is not for others to tell. But we can demand some respect. Firstly, for the accounts provided by our ancestors and the sources they left behind. And secondly, and most importantly, respect for the people who lived here for at least 35,000 years and for their descendants today.

Windschuttle's attempt to lump such a diversity of writers together as the 'Tasmanian orthodoxy' does produce what is for me the one comfort of the book. *Fabrication* should at least open our eyes to the extent that we have had something very special here. From at least 1830, the reality of frontier violence and of the Aboriginal defence of their homeland has at least been acknowledged and discussed. I know how limited such discussion has been, and how rigidly and with what tragic outcomes the past has been disconnected from the present. But now, with the alternative paradigm before us, our passed-on story seems to have a newfound intrinsic worth.

Windschuttle is perhaps right in one thing. Historians may have assumed a 'framework'[183] for our research that has left many in the community behind. *Fabrication* provides the opportunity to articulate this and the extensive sources on which it rests. It is to be hoped that greater awareness of the nature and richness of this unique tradition, which chronicled the horrors of invasion, dispossession and war, will now bring opportunities for an equally distinctive but radically new Van Diemonian story that is built on far firmer earth than the easy absolution offered by *The Fabrication of Aboriginal History*.

NOTES

1. Keith Windschuttle, *The Fabrication of Aboriginal History: Volume One, Van Diemen's Land 1803—1847*, Sydney, Macleay Press, 2002, p. 230.
2. *Ibid*, p. 28.
3. Windschuttle does not even include West in *Fabrication*'s list of the four most influential nineteenth-century writers: Melville, Robinson, Calder and Bonwick. The Black War is covered in considerable detail by West, and in broad terms his views set the parameters for debate well into the 1970s. He remains an important source today. Either Windschuttle is ignorant of West's arguments and influence or

the leading anti-transportationist, forerunner of Federation and eventual long-time editor of *The Sydney Morning Herald* is just too impressive a figure to try to fit into *Fabrication*'s prefabricated box.

4. Windschuttle, *Fabrication*, p. 4.
5. *Ibid*, p. 364.
6. J. E. Calder, *Some Account of the Wars, Extirpation, Habits etc of the Native Tribes of Tasmania*, Hobart, Fullers Bookshop, 1972, pp. 7–8, 25.
7. Windschuttle, *Fabrication*, pp. 99, 101, 128.
8. *Ibid*, p. 379.
9. *Ibid*, p. 105. This is not a 'typo', as the error is repeated on p. 379. *Fabrication* is also a decade out with the D'Entrecasteaux Expedition, placing this voyage as occurring in 1800.
10. D. Burn, *A Picture of Van Diemen's Land*, Hobart, Cat and Fiddle Press, 1973; J. Ross, *The Settler in Van Diemen's Land*, Melbourne, Marsh Walsh Publishing, 1975.
11. Burn, *Ibid*, pp. 12, 23.
12. Windschuttle, *Fabrication*, p. 37.
13. *Ibid*, p. 221
14. Windschuttle, *Fabrication*, p. 35; H. Melville, *The History of Van Diemen's Land from the Year 1824 to 1835 inclusive*, Sydney, Hortivity Publications, 1965, pp. 30, 33, 37, 56, 80–1.
15 Melville, *ibid*, p. 90.
16. *Ibid*, pp. 4–5.
17. G. Hobler, *The Diaries of Pioneer George Hobler, October 6 1800–December 13 1882*, C. & H. Reproductions, 1992, pp. 40, 176, 187.
18. G. Dow and H. Dow, *Landfall in Van Diemen's Land: The Steels Quest for Greener Pastures*, Footscray, Footprint, 1990, p 45.
19. Diary of Adam Amos, *Tasmanian State Archives*, NS323/1.
20. Windschuttle, *Fabrication*, p. 364.
21. J. H. Wedge, J. Crawford et al., *The Diaries of John Helder Wedge, 1824–1835*, Royal Society of Tasmania, 1962, pp. 56–7.
22. Hamilton Wallace to his father, James Wallace, 10/9/1825, in J. Richards, *Fifteen Tasmanian Letters, 1824–52*, unpublished manuscript, no page numbers.
23. R. Hare and I. Lee, *The voyage of the Caroline from England to Van Diemen's Land and Batavia in 1827–28*, London, New York, Longmans, 1927, pp. 40–1.
24. The evidence for this finding is that all the material in these texts that could have corrected basic errors and provided broader Van Diemonian context has been ignored. There are even hints that Robinson's journals have not been read completely. For example, as will be seen, Windschuttle has not picked up how widespread white hunting was even after 1811, although many references to this practice appear in the journals. Windschuttle also believes that the artist John Glover only saw Aborigines at Robinson's Hobart home (p. 219), although the journals record that the Aborigines with Robinson visited Glover at his country property.
25. Calder, *Some Accounts of the Wars*, p. 3.
26. L. Ryan, *The Aboriginal Tasmanians*, St Lucia, University of Queensland Press, 1981, p. 2.
27. Windschuttle, *Fabrication*, p. 5.
28. J. Currey, *David Collins: A Colonial Life*, Melbourne, Melbourne University Press, 2000, p. 2.

29. Sorell to Bigge, *Historical Records of Australia*, Series 3, vol. 3, Library Committee of the Commonwealth of Australia, 8/5/1820, p. 651.

30. Evidence of T. Bell, Acting Engineer and Inspector of Public Works, *HRA*, 3/3, 26–29/2/1820, p. 236.

31. Evidence of Surgeon Mountgarret, 26/4/1820, *HRA*, 3/3, p. 421.

32. Windschuttle, *Fabrication*, p. 5.

33. *Ibid*, p. 364.

34. *Ibid*, p. 363.

35. N. J. B. Plomley, C. Goodall et al., *The Aboriginal/Settler Clash in Van Diemen's Land, 1803–1831*, Launceston, Queen Victoria Museum & Art Gallery, 1992, p. 97.

36. Windschuttle, *Fabrication*, p. 362.

37. *Ibid*, p. 363.

38. For example, what Windschuttle (incorrectly) believes to be a legal conviction for killing an Aborigine in 1824 is ignored.

39. Windschuttle, *Fabrication*, pp. 156–7.

40. Batman to Anstey, 7/9/1829, CSO1/320/7578 *TSA*, cited in A. H. Campbell, *John Batman and the Aborigines*, Melbourne, Kibble Books, 1987, pp. 31–2.

41. Campbell, *ibid*, p. 32. Windschuttle, *Fabrication*, pp. 156–7, reduces the tally to 'several' wounded on the basis that 'Tasmanian natives could not count to ten'.

42. Windschuttle, *Fabrication*, p. 84.

43. In 1830, just over half the population lived in the towns of Hobart and Launceston, and the proportion was much higher still when the nearby, relatively highly concentrated agricultural districts were included.

44. *Ibid*, pp. 297–301.

45. J. Boyce, *God's Own Country? The Anglican Church and Tasmanian Aborigines*, Hobart, Anglicare Tasmania, 2001, ch. 2.

46. Arthur to Bathurst, 15/8/1824, *HRA*, 3/4, pp. 161–3.

47. G. T. Lloyd, *Thirty Three Years in Tasmania and Victoria*, London, Houlston and Wright, 1862, pp. 110, 117.

48. *Van Diemen's Land: copies of all correspondence between Lieutenant Governor Arthur and His Majesty's Secretary of State for the Colonies on the subject of the Military Operations lately carried on against the Aboriginal inhabitants of Van Diemen's Land (including minutes of evidence taken before the Committee for the affairs of the Aborigines 1830*, Hobart, Tasmanian Historical Research Association, 1971, pp. 54–5.

49. Windschuttle, *Fabrication*, p. 190.

50. H. Maxwell-Stewart, 'The Bushrangers and the convict system of Van Diemen's Land, 1803–1846', PhD thesis, University of Edinburgh, 1990, esp. pp. 119–28, 230–1.

51. Arthur to Bathurst, 15/8/1824, *HRA*, 3/4, pp. 161–3.

52. Arthur to Bathurst, 23/3/1827, *HRA*, 3/5, p. 621.

53. *Ibid*, p. 624.

54. Arthur to Horton, 14/9/1825, *HRA*, 3/4, pp. 366–371.

55. *HRA*, 3/4, pp. 475–6.

56. Windschuttle, *Fabrication*, p. 191.

57. The available primary source material is given at www.law.mq.edu.au/sctas. I am grateful to Stefan Petrow for information on this case, although responsibility for the analysis and conclusions is solely mine.

58. A. McKay (ed.), *Journals of the Land Commissioners for Van Diemen's Land*,

1826–28, Hobart, University of Tasmania in conjunction with the Tasmanian Historical Research Association, 1962, p. 54.

59. M. C. I. Levy, *Governor George Arthur: A Colonial Benevolent Despot*, Melbourne, Georgian House, 1953, p. 271.
60. Arthur to Bathurst, 7/1/1827, *HRA*, 3/5, p. 480.
61. *Hobart Town Gazette*, 13/3/1819.
62. Arthur to Bathurst, 24/3/1827, *HRA*, 3/6, pp. 691–706.
63. H. Reynolds, *Fate of a Free People*, Ringwood, Penguin, 1995, p. 77.
64. *Ibid*, p. 77.
65. Windschuttle, *Fabrication*, pp. 22–23.
66. M. Glover, *History of the Site of Bowen's Settlement Risdon Cove*, Hobart, National Parks and Wildlife Service, 1978, p. 6.
67. J. Boyce, 'Journeying Home: A New Look at the British Invasion of Van Diemen's Land 1803–1823', *Island*, vol. 66, 1996, pp. 49–51.
68. The fact that Robert May was taken to Port Dalrymple is revealed by the fact that he is listed in the 1805–6 smallpox vaccination list for that settlement. I am grateful to Kaye Price for bringing this to my attention.
69. Windschuttle, *Fabrication*, p. 24.
70. *Ibid*, p. 17.
71. *Ibid*, p. 26.
72. Ryan, *The Aboriginal Tasmanians*, p. 75.
73. Reynolds, *Fate of a Free People*, pp. 76–77.
74. Windschuttle, *Fabrication*, p. 375.
75. *Ibid*, pp. 372–6.
76. *Ibid*, p. 372. Windschuttle wrongly dates the smallpox epidemic among the Aboriginal population near Sydney. It occurred in 1789, not 1788.
77. See Boyce, 'Journeying Home…'
78. *HRA*, 3/3, p. 418.
79. *Ibid*, p. 501.
80. Sorell to Luttrell, 7/12/1819, *HRA*, 3/2, pp. 741–2.
81. J. E. Calder (ed.), *The Circumnavigation of Van Diemen's Land in 1815 by James Kelly and in 1824 by James Hobbs*, Hobart, Sullivan's Cove, 1984, pp. 21–34.
82. Windschuttle, *Fabrication*, p. 388. The likelihood that Windschuttle has not even superficially investigated such killings is shown by the fact that the claimed Aboriginal death is listed for the year of the *HTG* report, 1819, when Kemp was killed the year before, and if it was a revenge killing, the Aborigine must have died some time before that.
83. Windschuttle, *Fabrication*, p. 129.
84. *Ibid*, p. 394.
85. Reynolds, *Fate of a Free People*, pp. 76, 81.
86. Calder, *Some Accounts of the Wars*, p. 25.
87. Reynolds, *Fate of a Free People*, p. 81.
88. Windschuttle, *Fabrication*, p. 402.
89. *Ibid*, p. 101.
90. *Ibid*, ch. 4, esp. pp.129–130.
91. *Ibid*, p. 128.
92. *Ibid*, p. 77.
93. *Ibid*, pp. 88–9. Windschuttle unfairly sources this to Fels, who was only considering the period to 1811.

94. *Ibid*, p. 89.

95. *HRA*, 3/3, p. 723.

96. *Ibid*, p. 532.

97. *HRA*, 3/3, p. 250.

98. N. J. B. Plomley (ed.), *Friendly Mission: The Tasmanian Journals and Papers of George Augustus Robinson 1829–1834*, Hobart, Tasmanian Historical Research Association, 1966, pp. 557–8. Robinson's journals contain numerous other examples of him meeting white hunters, often convict stockmen. See for example 8/11/1830 & 17/11/1830, pp. 507, 521.

99. C. Jeffreys, *Van Diemen's Land: geographical and descriptive delineations of the island of Van Diemen's Land*, London, J. M. Richardson, 1820, pp. 100–101.

100. E. Fitzsymonds and C. Sullivans, *Mortmain: a collection of choice petitions, memorials, and letters of protest and request from the convict colony of Van Diemen's Land*, Hobart, Sullivan's Cove, 1977, p. 50.

101. Because of the implications for social order, a series of orders banned convict stockmen from having dogs – see the proclamation of Sorell on 30/6/1821, given in full in Edward Curr, *An Account of the Colony of Van Diemen's Land*, Hobart, Platypus Publications, 1967, pp. 152–61, repeating in full his order of 4/11/1820. Such orders were nearly universally ignored until the 1830s. They thus provide another example of the gap between government intent and frontier reality.

102. Plomley, *Friendly Mission*, p. 528.

103. *Ibid*, p. 415.

104. Windschuttle, *Fabrication*, p. 89.

105. *HTG*, 28/11/1818.

106. Meredith, *My Home in Tasmania*, p. 245.

107. Windschuttle, *Fabrication*, p. 89. Windschuttle acknowledges here Jorgenson's use of the term 'Black War' which must have occurred before 1841 (when Jorgenson died), although on p. 196 Windschuttle claims that 'the earliest usage I have observed' was West in 1852. This claim is even more odd given that Melville's 1835 *History of Van Diemen's Land*, discussed in *Fabrication*, makes use of the term (e.g. p. 90), and it was widely used from the time of the 1830 Black Line onwards. Windschuttle's claim therefore provides further evidence of both his narrow selection of sources and his selective reading of these.

108. N. J. B. Plomley, *Jorgen Jorgenson and the aborigines of Van Diemen's Land: being a reconstruction of his 'lost' book on their customs and habits, and on his role in the Roving Parties and the Black Line*, Hobart, Blubber Head Press, 1991, pp. 183, 109.

109. *Ibid*, p. 63.

110. Windschuttle, *Fabrication*, pp. 77–8.

111. *HRA*, 3/3, p. 320.

112. *Ibid*, p. 250.

113. *Ibid*, pp. 575–7.

114. Meredith to Sorell, 10/11/1821, *HRA*, 3/3, p. 441.

115. Windschuttle, *Fabrication*, pp. 145–6. Robson's discussion of the possible east coast killings is in fact only one sentence in the context of a paragraph which has as its lead sentence, 'it is very difficult to assess the relationship between the Europeans and the invaded Aborigines because a great deal of data, hearsay and opinion was collected only in the late 1820s and early 1830s …' (L. Robson, *A History of Tasmania, Vol. 1*, Melbourne, Oxford University Press, p. 50) Robson's argument in

this section of his book is that comparatively little conflict occurred in these early years although the information is very incomplete. Thus he is not trying to promote 'Hobbs's massacre story' (Windschuttle, *Fabrication*, p. 146). Robson's only – but important – mistake is to attribute to Hobbs a direct observation on a matter Hobbs had only heard of. Contrary to what *Fabrication* argues in its three-page rebuttal (pp. 143–146) of this one sentence, whether the killings occurred or not is – yet again – unknown. Hobbs had held a land holding at Little Swanport since 1824 and had obviously heard accounts of some early incident. These may not have been accurate, or have been only partially accurate, but we are now in no position to know. Hobbs would have known the 'unofficial' history of land settlement in the region better than most, and certainly better than present-day historians. Further, despite Windschuttle's claim that the soldiers could not have been there, in 1815 the military regularly left Hobart in pursuit of the bushrangers. The bushranging threat, through Michael Howe, was then at its peak. The bushrangers and many other whites accessed Oyster Bay, and there is no reason why the soldiers in pursuit might not have gone there. Indeed, one of Howe's gang, Jones, was eventually killed in the area. It is quite possible sheep were occasionally grazed there. It is possible there was a reprisal killing. We simply do not know. The surviving records from 1815 are far too incomplete to permit a definitive finding: there are no newspapers, very few diaries or letters, and big gaps in the government documents. We do know, however, that the claims made by Windschuttle in his attempt to refute it definitively are wrong.

116. Windschuttle, *Fabrication*, p. 154; *HRA*, 3/3, pp. 575–7.
117. Windschuttle is either ignorant of Tasmanian geography or presenting contradictory material on this issue. As part of an attempt to refute Robson, Windschuttle notes Knopwood's claim that 930 sheep were killed at '"Scantland Plains"' (Scanlans Plains), near the settlement of Oatlands' in 1815. Not only does he seem unaware that there was no settlement nor even a district named 'Oatlands' as yet, but, more importantly, he claims in the very next paragraph, 'In 1815 farming and pastoralism were still clustered around the two principal settlements …' (*Fabrication*, p. 145).
118. Windschuttle, *Fabrication*, p. 146.
119. Burn, *A Picture*, p. 10.
120. J. Ross, *The Settler in Van Diemen's Land*, Melbourne, Marsh Walsh Publishing, 1975, p. 33.
121. S. Cubit, 'Squatters and Opportunists: Occupation of Lands to the Westward to 1830', *THRA Papers and Proceedings*, 34, 1, 1987, pp. 9–10.
122. Return of Agriculture and livestock, *HRA*, 3/3, p. 584.
123. R. Paddle, *The Last Tasmanian Tiger: The History and Extinction of the Thylacine*, Cambridge, Cambridge University Press, 2000, pp. 102-3.
124. Windschuttle, *Fabrication*, pp. 77–8.
125. *Ibid*, pp. 77–82.
126. Arthur to Bathurst, 10/8/1825, *HRA*, 3/4, p. 315.
127. Arthur to Murray, 20/11/1830, in J. Bischoff, *Sketch of the history of Van Diemen's Land: illustrated by a map of the island, and an account of the Van Diemen's Land Company*, London, J. Richardson, 1832, p. 59.
128. Windschuttle, *Fabrication*, pp. 77–82.
129. S. Morgan, *Land Settlement in Early Tasmania: Creating an Antipodean England*, Cambridge, Cambridge University Press, 1992, p. 22.

130. Ryan, *Aboriginal Tasmanians*, p. 83.

131. P. E. Chapman, *The Diaries and Letters of G. T. W. B. Boyes, Volume 1, 1820–1832*, Melbourne, Oxford University Press, 1985, pp. 378–80.

132. Windschuttle, *Fabrication*, p. 79.

133. *Ibid*, p. 111.

134. Glover, *History of the site*, pp. 10–11.

135. H. Ling Roth, *The Aborigines of Tasmania*, p. 2.

136. R. Knopwood and M. Nicholls, *The diary of the Reverend Robert Knopwood, 1803–1838: first chaplain of Van Diemen's Land*, Hobart, Tasmanian Historical Research Association, 1977, p. 46.

137. Paterson to King, 26/11/1804, *HRA*, 3/1, pp. 605–7.

138. Paterson to King, 27/12/1804, *HRA*, 3/1, p. 621.

139. Windschuttle, *Fabrication*, pp.129–30.

140. *Ibid*, p. 128.

141. M. Fels, 'Culture Contact in the Country of Buckinghamshire, Van Diemen's Land 1803–1811', *THRA Papers and Proceedings*, 29, 2, 1982; J. Boyce, 'Surviving in a New Land: The European Invasion of Van Diemen's Land 1803–1823', BA Hons thesis, University of Tasmania, 1994.

142. Calder (ed.), *Circumnavigation*, pp. 21–34.

143. *HRA*, 3/3, p. 381.

144. J. Ross, *The Settler in Van Diemen's Land*, Melbourne, Martin Walsh Publishing, 1975.

145. Lloyd, *Thirty Three Years*.

146. M. Tipping, *Convicts Unbound: The Story of the Calcutta Convicts and their Settlement in Australia*, Melbourne, Viking O'Neil, 1988, pp. 260–1.

147. T. Parramore William and D. C. Shelton, *The Parramore letters: letters from William Thomas Parramore, sometime Private Secretary to Lieutenant Governor Arthur of Van Diemen's Land, to Thirza Cropper, his fiancée in Europe and England, the majority from 1823–1825*, Epping, NSW, D. and C. Shelton, 1993, p. 60.

148. See for example Roth, *Aborigines*, p. 135.

149. Robinson described the new style of stock huts on 8 November 1830: 'This stock hut is like most stock huts, a formidable construction. It is made by piling large solid logs horizontally upon each other, halved together at the ends, with port holes to fire out of. The roof is barked and covered with turf so as not to ignite.' Plomley, *Friendly Mission*, p. 508.

150. *Van Diemen's Land: copies of all correspondence*, p. 53.

151. *Hobart Town Gazette*, 13/3/1819.

152. Windschuttle, *Fabrication*, p. 129.

153. *Ibid*, p. 101.

154. Plomley, *Friendly Mission*, p. 566.

155. *Ibid*, p. 483. On 12/9/1831, Robinson received a letter from Arthur agreeing to the Aborigines' request for a meeting – see pp. 476–7. Direct discussions with Arthur were also part of the agreement reached with the Big River people in the New Year of 1832, and this condition was fulfilled.

156. Meredith, *My Home in Tasmania*, p. 153.

157. Windschuttle also argues that a couple of individuals, Musquito and the Aborigine known to whites as Black Tom or Tom Birch, were primarily responsible for the comparatively small-scale violence of 1824–26. (Windschuttle, *Fabrication*, pp. 65–77) But even if this were true, it would only highlight further the lack of reason

provided for the escalation in fighting from 1827 to 1832, when Musquito was dead and Tom was no longer active in the Aboriginal resistance.

158. Windschuttle, *Fabrication*, p. 386.

159. *Ibid*, pp. 379–80, 386.

160. *Ibid*, p. 382.

161. *Ibid*, p. 379.

162. N. J. B. Plomley, *The Baudin Expedition and the Tasmanian Aborigines 1802*, Hobart, Blubber Head Press, 1983, p. 32

163. A. W. Reed (ed.), *Captain Cook in Australia: Extracts for the Journal of Captain James Cook, giving a full account in his own words of his adventures and discoveries in Australia*, Wellington, A. H. and A. W. Reed, 1969, p. 180.

164. *Ibid*, p. 173.

165. Plomley, *The Baudin Expedition*, pp. 19–23.

166. Windschuttle, *Fabrication*, p. 384.

167. Plomley, *The Baudin Expedition*, pp. 33, 41.

168. Windschuttle is so short of evidence for his claims in this area that even later commentators who had no direct personal knowledge of the matter are misrepresented. Windschuttle claims on p. 383 that, 'The travelling Quaker James Backhouse described one case on the west coast where local Aborigines traded a fourteen-year-old girl to the pilot at Macquarie harbour in exchange for a dog.' What Backhouse actually recorded (J. Backhouse, *A Narrative of a Visit to the Australian Colonies*, London Hamilton Adams, 1843, p. 58) is that one Aborigine 'exchanged a girl of about 14 years of age, for a dog, with the people at the Pilot station; but the girl not liking her situation was taken back, and the dog returned'. This is evidence of a much more complex cultural situation, even in post-settlement times, than that presented in *Fabrication*.

169. Windschuttle, *Fabrication*, p. 377.

170. *Ibid*, pp. 254, 43

171. Reed, *Captain Cook in Australia*, p. 173

172. Plomley, *The Baudin Expedition*, pp. 40–1.

173. Jeffreys, *Van Diemen's Land*, pp. 125–6.

174. Bigge noted that 'a great many of the convicts in Van Diemen's Land wore jackets and trowsers [sic] of the kangaroo skin, and sometimes caps of the same material,' as cited in R. W. Giblin, *The Early History of Tasmania: Vol. 2, 1804–1828*, Melbourne, Melbourne University Press, 1939, p. 235. Such clothing was thus not confined to stock-keepers and bushrangers, on whom it was nearly universal. Even soldiers often wore such garb when in the bush (see for example Burn, *A Picture*, p. 67) as until the mid-1820s European clothing was ineffective, indeed dangerous, in Tasmanian conditions.

175. W. Thornley and J. Mills, *The adventures of an emigrant in Van Diemen's Land*, London, Hale [etc], 1973, p. 113.

176. S. Breen, 'Tasmanian Aborigines – Making Fire', *THRA Papers and Proceedings*, 39, 1, 1992.

177. Windschuttle, *Fabrication*, p. 99.

178. *Ibid*, pp. 97–99.

179. For example, none of the Aboriginal views for the period after 1832 is considered by Windschuttle. Yet these inevitably contain most of what we know of the Aboriginal perspective on the fighting, the causes of the conflict and the basis of the negotiations to end it. A comparatively large body of evidence from the period

of the Flinders Island exile concerns this matter and the strength of the Aboriginal attachment to their native land.

180. Windschuttle, *Fabrication*, p. 99.

181. *Ibid*, p. 100.

182. *Ibid*, p. 101. Windschuttle's rigid distinction between tribal Aborigines and others is a false one. Tom Birch had a continuing tribal identity and was bilingual. Nor are the statements recorded by Melville in 'American Negro vernacular' as *Fabrication* claims. We know that Tom spoke English well, but we do not know he could, or chose to, speak 'like an Englishman'. A form of Aboriginal English had emerged by this time and was commonly used by both races in communication. As Robinson recorded in his diary on Sunday, 18 October 1835 at Wybalenna, 'I conversed with Mr. Clark (the catechist) after the service and suggested his discontinuing the use of gibberish so common on the settlement ... it was not the natives' language.' N. J. B. Plomley, *Weep in Silence*, Hobart, Blubber Head Press, 1987 p. 304.

183. *Ibid*, p. 28.

IN GENERAL

The Character of the Nation

Martin Krygier & Robert van Krieken

If, as Cyril Connolly and George Orwell both alleged, within every fat man there is a thin man struggling to get out, we might ask if this also applies to works such as Keith Windschuttle's *The Fabrication of Aboriginal History*. This portly if handsome volume on the history of relations between Europeans and Aborigines in Tasmania is apparently to be followed by two more dealing with the rest of Australia. The result is to add up to some 500,000 words. But what is this tubby tome about?

The author's own answer is unequivocal: History, the job of which is to establish Facts. This is why much of the book is occupied with sieving and separating facts, no-longer-facts, not-quite-facts, never-were-facts, about the nature of frontier violence in Australian history. Much of its size derives from the painstaking detail of its examination of a range of accounts of frontier violence in colonial Tasmania.

Windschuttle regards 'orthodox' historians of these matters much as a somewhat obsessed ferret might regard rabbits: as nothing but prey. He hunts for incompetence, sloppiness, ideologically driven false-hood and fantasy, and he reckons he finds them everywhere. He seems convinced that the British just weren't the massacring sort, so wherever there is an account of a massacre, the hunt is on to show either that it never occurred, that there weren't very many Aborigines killed, or that it was all a mistake. In almost all cases these are the conclusions *Fabrication* shepherds us towards.

However, you don't just need to get the facts right, which the 'orthodox' apparently never do; you also need the right attitude, which they never have. That attitude is one of 'detachment'. Windschuttle has it, his 'orthodox' quarries lack it. What mars their work, apart from living in a 'black armband' fantasy land, is that they have 'overt political objectives' and fail to 'adopt the traditional stance of the academic historian and profess at least a modicum of detachment from their subject'.[1] Here they are true to the spirit of the 1960s that spawned them, a spirit that 'turned the traditional role of the historian, to stand outside contemporary society in order to seek the truth about the past, on its head'.[2] The errant results, Windschuttle informs us, follow necessarily from their (misguided and insidious) political motivation.

There is a problem here. These methodological strictures actually serve as an embarrassment for Windschuttle: the more they convince us, the more they weaken *Fabrication* itself, because whatever the outcome of the disputes between him and his targets, it soon becomes obvious that this book is not a politically disengaged pursuit of facts at all. As his own introduction observes, correctly, 'the debate over Aboriginal history goes far beyond its ostensible subject: it is about the character of the nation and, ultimately, the calibre of the civilization Britain brought to these shores in 1788.'[3] These are matters on which members of any nation are generally not detached, and rightly so.

Most of us *care* deeply about both the character of the nation to which we belong and the calibre of the civilisation we embody. It is because we care that discussions of Aboriginal history under settler-colonialism have evoked the attention, not to mention the passions, sometimes hatreds, often pain, which they have in this country. The historical understanding of issues like frontier violence is never going to be detached, because history lies at the heart of identity. What one of us wrote about recent debates about child removal can be generalised: an observer of the way these debates are conducted and the heat they arouse,

> is forced to conclude that at issue is not really, or at any rate not merely, the past *wie es eigentlich gewesen,* but the present. Or, more precisely, that the imagined past is being treated as a crucial part of the present, and it is *that* present-past that is the focus and explanation for the

passions these past events still manage to inspire. This suggests that as important as the subjects of the debate, and the texts that are their vehicles, are the subtexts that fuel them.[4]

When we consider the history and character of our nation, we do not immunise ourselves against either emotions or politics, we are thoroughly *engaged,* as is, of course, Windschuttle. Thus he opens his book with a denunciation of the former governor-general Sir William Deane, assorted journalists and judges, and indeed anyone over the last 200 years who has worried that the character of the nation and its civilisation might be sullied in any way, and this is clearly his own version of such an engagement. If Windschuttle were less shy about the role of the subtext that fuels his narrative, he would not have to suggest, implausibly and unconvincingly, that he is Ranke to his opponents' Marx.[5] Rather, he could recognise that there are better and worse ways of engaging in debate about the 'character of the nation', and that proud boasts of detachment are neither necessary nor sufficient to distinguish those who participate well from those who do not. Historians participate in these debates without being disqualified by their vocation from doing so, and without making them any lesser historians.

Much more can be said about the fat book. For example, Windschuttle is keen to be a revisionist historian, to turn the accepted approach to his topic upside down, and this can be a thoroughly honourable occupation. However, he pursues this aim with such a heavy hand that it threatens to turn into, or at least invite, self-parody.[6] It would not be entirely misguided to treat the accusations it levels at others as an excellent guide to understanding the inner logic of *Fabrication* itself, it comes so close to being comically self-referential. But the fat book is the subject of most of the other chapters in this collection. Our focus is different: the other, slimmer volume contained within, which embodies a particular style of thinking about the meaning, bearing and significance of our shared history for understanding and appreciating 'the character of the nation' and the 'calibre of British civilization'. For just as many of us are driven most by what we acknowledge least, it is this subtext that provides the motivation, rationale, the indefatigable energy and the spine of the larger work.

Black v. White Myths

Fabrication presents debates over our past as a highly scripted Manichaean drama. In such drama, and so in such historiography, there are always two major mythical characters, negative images of each other, locked in battle. The drama is heightened by certain rules of the genre: each character is portrayed in starkly contrasting tones: black–white, no shades of grey. They must be mutually exclusive: no combination, no partly this partly that, will do. They must exhaust the field: no other possibilities, nothing else, nothing more, and they must be opposites: what is white can be inferred inversely from black, and vice versa. In *Fabrication* itself, the protagonists are, on the one hand, what we might call the 'black myth' generated by 'orthodox' historians, on the other Windschuttle's 'white myth', although of course he calls it truth. Only one of them can be allowed to remain standing: gunfight at Suicide Bay.

Not only is the black myth itself a homogenised, identikit mélange, but so is its collective author, the hydra-headed mythologist of 'orthodoxy', whose many mouths apparently all speak with one voice. It includes historians who do make strong claims about massacres and violence, others who do not but still see the tragedy involved in white settlement; journalists and media figures, some of whom, like John Pilger, seem to believe that in talking about our past, worse is better and worst is best; others who simply want to try to understand and then come to terms with that past; political figures; parties to current legal and political disputes. These are all mixed up to give the impression that, in the last analysis, as Marxists used to say, they all believe the same, that our past was an unqualified Hell populated by white demons and black angels. Having everyone agree with everyone else is convenient for an attacker in a hurry, since any criticism of one 'orthodox' historian will also do for all of them. Those who pursue a complex argument about the possibility of a genocidal 'moment' in the twentieth-century policies of child removal involving no killings are thrown in the mix with those who use the word to describe killings in the nineteenth, and with others who do not use the word at all. All of them end up among the 'orthodox' and all are then taken to be purveyors of the black myth.

The result, attributable to the malign influence of leftist historical orthodoxy, is that the story of the nation is shrouded in guilt, deriving from calumny, in turn supporting a perverse desire to hand over most of the continent to a handful of Aboriginal people clearly unable to do anything with it under the name of 'native title'[7]. Whites, according to this myth, were bent on nothing other than exploitation, dispossession and extermination; blacks were skilful guerilla warriors defending their land, usually heroically; systematic and large-scale carnage of the latter by the former was the order of the day. Most odious and despicable of all, we appear to have been led to think of our history as on a par with Nazism. Although Windschuttle does not appear able to find a historian who actually said as much, the orthodox are nevertheless culpable for the views of those journalists who do. We must not underestimate how cunning the orthodox school is, for, writes Windschuttle, 'While the historians themselves might not have overtly used the Nazi comparison, they have created a picture of widespread mass killings on the frontiers of the pastoral industry that not only went unpunished but had covert government support. They created the intellectual framework and gave it the imprimatur of academic respectability.'[8] One might note in passing that the Nazis did more than give covert support to frontier massacres, but this bagatelle passes Windschuttle by.

Once the black myth is delineated, the contrary position generates itself on automatic pilot. Such a counter-myth constitutes *Fabrication*'s deep structure, its underlying grammar, burrowing into Windschuttle's prose, the epithets he chooses, the targets of his anger, the structure of his arguments, the mirror-image symmetry between what he denounces and what he insists upon. He explains that it is true that white settlement provoked black violence, but not for any of the retaliatory 'political' (still less military) reasons suggested in the black myth, and certainly not out of resentment. European settlement simply 'gave the Aborigines more opportunity and more temptation to engage in robbery and murder, two customs they had come to relish'.[9] Where particular Aborigines indulged in violence, not only were their actions 'not noble: they never rose beyond robbery, assault and murder'.[10] Those alleged to be 'warrior patriots' were 'simply outlaws ... bushrangers who happened to be black'.[11] They gave 'no evidence of anything that deserved the name of political skills at all', and as for military organisation, which might have 'elevated Aboriginal violence into something more than criminal behaviour ... [it] is conspicuous by its absence'.[12]

In response to these venal representatives of a sick civilisation just teetering for 30,000 years before collapsing in 40, far from seeking to exterminate them, whites were desperate to civilise the blacks. Notwithstanding the 'agonising dilemma that the continuation of Aboriginal violence created for the settlers' (others' 'agonising dilemmas' are not recorded), killings of blacks were not systematic, were merely 'sporadic'. Since not everyone agreed even then with this picture of generalised benevolence occasionally thwarted by its benighted beneficiaries, the ones who don't agree are denigrated throughout the book. That is true of the historians who are its immediate targets, but it is also true of *anyone* who purported to 'protect' blacks (with the implicit suggestion that they might need some protection). Thus missionaries, thus George Augustus Robinson, thus anyone over the past couple of centuries, who experiences a 'whispering in [their] hearts'.

There are other ways of doing this. If there are indeed mythological elements to the currently dominant approach to Aboriginal history, it is possible to show that such a myth is historical caricature without lurching towards an equally flat, monochrome counter-caricature. As many historians, among them Henry Reynolds, have shown, the story is altogether more complex, both factually and morally, than either caricature allows. A worthy job for a historian might be to probe and reveal some of those complexities, but it is precisely *Fabrication*'s political concerns which prevent it from doing so.

A favourite writer among those who pursue the approach to history represented by *Fabrication* is Paul Hasluck, who remains today the leading intellectual of the anti-self-determination, assimilationist position, with its current proponents a mere pale shadow of his much more sophisticated understanding. *Fabrication* approvingly quotes this passage from Hasluck's *Black Australians*, a history of Aboriginal policy published in 1942:

> There have been two colossal fictions in popular accounts of the treatment of natives in Australia. One suggests that settlers habitually went

about shooting down blacks; the other, framed as a counterblast, is that every settler treated natives with constant kindness. There is no evidence to support either statement in Western Australia.[13]

Fair enough: it would be hard to find anyone who would explicitly argue with this point. But, perversely, most of *Fabrication* effectively does: we get Pilgerism *à rebours*, in the form of Windschuttle's own counterblast. The only *un*kindness he is willing to acknowledge is that of *misguided* kindness (the protectionists), but everyone else who sought the civilisation of Australian Aborigines appears unable to do much wrong.

Yet even Hasluck, who might be accused of constructing another fiction that every *assimilationist* 'treated natives with constant kindness', was much more prepared to acknowledge complexity. He observed, for example, that the reluctance of 'civilised' white Australians to incorporate Aborigines into their communities was as much a barrier to assimilation as anything to do with the policies pursued by governments or church agencies, or the characteristic capacities and inclinations of Aboriginal people themselves.[14] On the question of frontier violence, what he called the 'direct action' pursued by settlers, Hasluck was able to argue in favour of the *character* of the men who engaged in such violence without finding it necessary to deny its morally problematic features:

> That policy of direct action on the frontier did not come from any peculiar viciousness in individuals, it arose out of the nature of contact. Men who if they had been in England on those days or in an armchair in the present day would probably have abhorred the shooting down of natives, were brought by fear, rivalry and exasperation to kill men or to condone the killing by others. It was recognised as a means of establishing order and peace.[15]

His point was that one should see frontier violence as a product of a particular situation or structural context rather than of character flaws, without denying the reality and damaging effects of that violence. Hasluck's plea was not to attribute all frontier violence to Aboriginal criminal tendencies, but to ask ourselves 'why it was that men of decent habit and usually of controlled passions were moved to a tolerance of violence and even to its commission';[16] in other words, to investigate what it was about the frontier situation that led apparently civilised people to behave in barbaric ways.

Some commentators[17] have said that *Fabrication* lacks a sense of the tragedy of Aboriginal history. This is an observation at the same time perceptive, incomplete and not completely accurate. It is *perceptive* because this is a disturbingly heartless book, even about the deaths and miseries (attributed to 'the dual weight of the susceptibility of its members to disease and the abuse and neglect of its women'[18]) that are acknowledged. It is *incomplete* because it sees this inattention to the tragedy of the end of a civilisation and its human carriers in the space of a few decades as an independent, accidental blemish, rather than an integral component of the white myth embodied by *Fabrication*. But it is also *not completely accurate*, because there are some points in *Fabrication* where tragedy is acknowledged: for example, Windschuttle thinks it was a tragedy that 'the Aborigines adopted such senseless violence' during the Black War in Van Diemen's Land, of which they were themselves the primary victims.[19] Later we are also informed that the 'real' tragedy was 'not British colonisation *per se*, but that their society was, on the one hand, so internally dysfunctional and, on the other hand, so incompatible with the looming presence of the rest of the world'.[20]

What is wrong with this? If you call someone a Nazi, unfairly, it is indeed right for them to deny it and show that they are not. But what of those such as Stanner, Elkin or Rowley, who talked not of Nazism, but of a colonial history, inevitably fraught with tragedy though not only that, better than some worse than others, peopled with good people and bad, good motives and bad, events of which we can be proud and others of which we should be ashamed, yet a history which, with both its achievements and its calamities is *ours*, and which, for all its real factual and moral complexity, had comprehensively catastrophic consequences for the original inhabitants of this country, not all of them unintended?

And what of a view less concerned with individuals and their motives than with situations and their imperatives? The settler-colonial situation has had tragedy written into it for a very long time. It is hard for settler-colonists to behave well whatever their intentions, because of power-imbalance, contradictory interests, cultural distance, conde-scension built into the missionary impulse and the 'civilising mission', cluelessness, carelessness and many other things. One can very easily do harm without meaning to, even when meaning to do good, not because like Windschuttle's missionaries and historians, one is hopelessly cap-tivated by a romantic ideology of noble savagery, but because the situation is good for some and bad for others, and good for some because bad for others, all at the same time. *Fabrication*'s approach to history is not concerned about even this small level of complexity, because its myths and counter-myths are all equally simple. It is defeated by real complexity and ambiguity, unable to grasp the distance between what a debunking detection may have revealed and what really needs to be shown to make out the counter-myth.

One way this conceptual inability is manifested in this particular book is the talismanic role, sometimes bad sometimes good, it gives particular words. The bad are massacre, genocide and Aboriginal self-determination; the good are (some versions of) Christianity, civilisa-tion and the rule of law. Let us briefly consider them.

Genocide, Civilisation, the Rule of Law

If deliberate massacres characterised our history, the character of the nation bears deep scars and we have reason to think more deeply about the calibre of our civilisation. If it turns out that what happened in par-ticular circumstances cannot fairly be called either a 'massacre' or 'geno-cide', that is good news. The Europeans who came to Australia certainly did see themselves as aiming to civilise the blacks whose condition they 'pitied' – to begin with, at any rate.[21] This meant, suggests Windschuttle, that notwithstanding the settlers' 'agonising dilemma', they were only provoked to kill blacks occasionally, and therefore, his narrative sug-gests, such killings were of little significance. Certainly not worth wear-ing a black armband for. How could it have been otherwise, since the whites were Christians *and* carriers of the Enlightenment *and* of the rule of law. 'It was this rule of law', writes Windschuttle, 'that made every British colony in its own eyes, *and in truth*, a domain of civilization.'[22]

Massacres and Genocide

If massacres cannot be unequivocally shown to have occurred, according to rather strenuous conditions of proof, then the verdict in *Fabrication* is not the Scottish 'not proven' but 'non-existent'. If no extermination or extirpation, then the only harm done was that effected by those 'humanitarians' – missionaries and others – who purported to be saving Aborigines from non-existent threats of extermination, and by initiating 'separatism' did them in with their fraudulent ministrations. Yet even the settlers whose voices we hear in *Fabrication* itself had a more complex understanding of where the blame for the violence lay.[23]

In any event, does our understanding of the character of European civilisation really begin and end with massacres, with whether we 'exterminate all the brutes', and should we set settler-colonial dispossession aside as an issue unless it is organised around killing? However many deliberate murders occurred, and various historians have already cast doubt on the ubiquity of massacres while still insisting that killings were widespread,[24] they do not exhaust the pain of the encounter, and they are not the only things that can be done to colonised peoples about which later generations of settler-colonists might feel uneasy. Many of those who have written about settler–Aboriginal relations have been concerned with aspects of these encounters besides massacres, and those aspects too must be registered in any appraisal of the character of the nation. What of all the slights, humiliations, hurdles, obstacles involved in the colonial encounter? Moreover, even if there had been no massacres at all in Australian history, the violence of colonial dispossession itself does not count for nothing.

In his masterly book *The Decent Society*, Avishai Margalit points out that apart from the degree to which the institutions of a society are 'bridled' so as not to inflict physical suffering without restraint, societies differ in the degree to which they are what he calls 'decent', using that word to mean 'non-humiliating'. The essence of humiliation is rejection, and two general ways in which people are likely to be humiliatingly rejected by social institutions generally, and by colonial invaders typically, is, first, when they are not treated as human by them, and second, when they are denied control over their vital interests.

Where such rejection occurs, the humiliation exists no matter how noble the motives of the colonist might be.

We do not have to go to extermination camps, then, to find systematic and humiliating disrespect. That can happen whenever we are 'human-blind', and that, as Margalit points out, does not mean failing literally to see people, bumping into them as if they were invisible, or thinking of them literally as machines or dogs. It means seeing them 'under a physical description without the capacity to see them under a psychological one'. It commonly involves *overlooking* them, that is 'not paying attention to them: looking without seeing … [it] does not strictly mean seeing them as things, but rather not seeing them fully or precisely.' Many colonial regimes, Margalit points out, were:

> often more restrained in their physical cruelty than the regimes they replaced. Nevertheless, the colonial regimes were usually more humiliating, and more rejecting of their subjects as human beings, than the local tyrants, who considered their subjects their fellow nationals or fellow tribe members and thus equal to them as human beings.[25]

Apart from massacre and humiliation, what of the small matter of dispossession? It is conceivable, we concede, that that could be done without killing a flea, even with the utmost politeness, but it is hard to conceive it being done without injury to those dispossessed. Apart from its practical implications, there is a point that Raimond Gaita has made about the significance of dispossession, in his suggestion that:

> For many of the settlers, the Aborigines were not the kind of limit to our will, to our interests and desires, that we mark when we speak of respecting someone's rights, or treating them as ends rather than as means, or of according them unconditional respect, and so on.[26]

Henry Reynolds, who in less philosophical fashion has made this the point of his life, makes a poignant observation in this connection:

> The injustice was gross regardless of whether the Aboriginal circumstances were compared with those of the settlers or those of indigenous people in other Anglo-Saxon colonies of settlement … whose native title was recognised …

The contrast between the respect accorded Aboriginal property rights and those of everyone else in early colonial Australia was even greater [than the latter] ... Convicts – and marines as well – were hanged for theft while Sydney was still only a few months old. Hangmen and flagellators continued to enforce the sanctity of private property for the first two generations of settlement. A community with such priorities could not find a more decisive way to illustrate its fundamental disrespect for another society than to ignore its property rights. Even an enemy beaten in battle might receive more consideration.[27]

Whenever *Fabrication* touches on dispossession, by contrast, it fudges the boundary between reporting and endorsing, with some actors' perception being subject to no critical scrutiny at all, but presented as 'fact':

... when British eyes of the eighteenth century looked on the natives of Australia, they saw nomads who hunted but who had no agricultural base, and who therefore did not possess the country they inhabited. In contrast, the British colonists took up the land and 'improved' it – a term persistently employed by the first settlers. By 'improving' the land, the colonists thereby regarded themselves acquiring right of possession. They were not dispossessing the natives. Instead, colonisation offered the indigenous people the gift of civilization, bringing them all the techniques for living developed by the Old World.[28]

Again the binary logic: either one is dispossessing the native, or one is bringing the gift of civilisation. One of the more central points, however, of understanding the impact of European civilisation on the rest of the world is grasping the ways in which 'civilisation' is, as the German sociologist Norbert Elias suggests, precisely the 'watchword' of colonisation:[29] it is through 'bringing the gifts of civilisation' and effecting the changes in the behaviour and dispositions of the colonised necessarily accompanying those 'gifts' that colonisers execute and above all legitimate their dispossession of indigenous populations.

Fabrication appears to find it difficult to subject the cognitive and moral universe of the settler-colonist to very much analytical scrutiny at all. More precisely, the assertions and the motives of any colonist who suggests that white violence was a problem are always mercilessly cross-examined and usually pilloried. By contrast, when settlers give justifications, whether theological or legal, for dispossession of Aborigines, we are simply invited to understand their *Weltanschauung*. A good example of this is the use made of Anthony Pagden's work on the distinction between Spanish and British discourses of colonisation.[30] *Fabrication* makes much of Pagden's contrast between the Spanish concern with the conquest of peoples and the British focus on the governance of things, particularly land, constructing the British approach as not 'really' constituting colonial dispossession of the indigenous inhabitants of the Australian continent. Instead of the Spanish inclination to conquer indigenous peoples in order to extract their gold and silver, John Locke, his imagination no doubt fired by his work as secretary for the proprietors of the colony in Carolina,[31] was among those who developed an alternative type of explanation for why British settler-colonists were entitled to the use of lands inhabited by indigenous peoples, one which American settler-colonists found extremely congenial, as did Australian settlers. In this construction, land which had not been cultivated through human labour did not 'really' belong to the people that used and lived on it, indeed it was the solemn natural duty of cultivators like the British and the French to put such 'virgin' land to use for the benefit of all humanity.

In *Fabrication* this account of some of the features of British colonial discourse is presented as an effective *defence* of 'the calibre of British civilisation' against critical analysis of its dynamics and impact. Since 'the British *regarded* their settlements as peaceful exercises, mutually beneficial to both colonist and native,' and since 'the early British *objectives* towards the indigenous people were primarily to trade useful products and to demonstrate by example the benefits of the civil and polite customs of Europe,'[32] for Windschuttle this becomes how things actually were and it immunises British settlement of Australia against criticisms of the legitimacy of colonial dispossession. Apart from a range of comments one could make on the logic of this position, it is also a mischievous misreading of Pagden.

His book, *Lords of All the World*, emphasises the *shared* historical roots of both Spanish colonial ideas and practices on the one hand, and

British and French on the other, in Ancient Roman imperialism, so that they both remained different translations of an essentially similar 'will to empire'. If the British and French ended up emphasising commerce and trade rather than conquest and exploitation, this was not because of the calibre of their civilisation, as Walter Raleigh's conquistadorial ambitions show, but more because the Spanish had got to most of the gold and silver first:

> It was only when it became obvious that there was no new Mexico or Peru to be conquered, that both Cartier's 'Suguenay'; and Raleigh's 'Large, Rich and Beautiful Empire of Guiana' were fictions, that the British and the French turned, half-reluctantly, to regard their colonies as sources not of mineral or human, but of agricultural and commercial wealth.[33]

The British emphasised domination over things (land) not as an *alternative* to dominion over people, but as a *means* to such dominion. Property and the argument concerning the cultivation and improvement of land was, to the mind of the English administrator, both at home and in the colonies, precisely *how* one governed a people. In the colonial situation, how one effectively conquered them without having to call it that, thus gaining a particular rhetorical advantage of being able to claim that it was only the barbaric Spaniards that did such a cruel thing. Pagden cites Arthur Young reminding his readers in 1772 of the illusory nature of the Lockean discursive 'solution' to the normative legitimacy of colonial dispossession: his distinction between occupation and possession of land was not one which held any meaning for that land's indigenous people themselves, and 'since ... they were unlikely to accept the colonists' claims without protest, any attempt to displace them would become *de facto* a conquest'.[34]

What *Fabrication* presents as a detached description of the inner nature of British colonisation and its actual consistency with humanitarian values, is in Pagden's book an analysis of the rhetorical strategies pursued by the British (and the French) to legitimise colonisation so as to *render* it consistent with those humanitarian values. The various rhetorical strategies concerning the legitimacy of colonial settlement were also, we have to remember, pursued primarily in relation to the competition between the different European powers over their prop-erty rights vis-à-vis each other, not in relation to the persuasion of any indigenous populations, whose ultimate fate was largely to endure, with greater or lesser degrees of resistance, being elbowed out of the way by the Europeans.

Like other contributions to these sorts of debates, much of *Fabrication*'s argumentation also revolves around the appropriateness of applying the concept 'genocide' to the Australian settler-colonial context, and works with a simple dichotomous opposition between genocide and extermination on the one hand, and civilisation and modernisation on the other.[35] However, the problem with talking about genocide is that there are a number of unresolved, and possibly irre-solvable, disagreements about what it means and refers to. The concept is possibly most 'essentially contested' when it comes to the treatment of indigenous populations by European colonists and settlers, with the divergence of views organised around a distinction between physical and cultural destruction.

There are certainly strong and persuasive arguments in favour of saying that if it is not a case of deliberate *physical* extermination, like the Armenian genocide, the Holocaust, Cambodia, Rwanda and so on, then we should not be using the word genocide. Michael Ignatieff proposes, for example, that rather than operating as a 'validation of every kind of victimhood', the concept of genocide should be reserved for 'genuine' horrors and barbarisms.[36] The United Nations Genocide Convention was written at a time when just about every member state of the United Nations would have presumed that assimilation of indigenous populations was generally unproblematic and that it was desirable that 'primitive' cultures be modernised, making it very difficult to argue that the UNGC was intended to include the concept of non-physical, 'cultural' genocide. The remaining problems with 'forced assimilation' were meant to be dealt with in another arena, that of the protection of minority populations.[37] Any legal action based on the UNGC also generally fails on the convention's requirement of a demonstrable *intention* to destroy a cultural group, making it virtually impossible to pin down any state or administration that is not silly enough actually to declare this intention. This is why the person who first drew our attention to the fact that Aboriginal people often regard the destruction of their social and familial life as 'genocidal', Hal Wootten,[38] also regards the 'finding' of genocide in the *Bringing them home* report a 'quite unnecessary legal ruling' which has generated 'pointless controversy'.[39]

However, this does not exhaust the discussion. It is also worth recalling that the word was coined by the Polish jurist Raphaël Lemkin *before* Auschwitz, and a core concern for Lemkin was not simply 'obvious' examples of killing but the whole colonising regime of the Axis powers in the occupied countries, a very particular kind of legal order based on a variety of 'techniques of occupation'. For Lemkin, such techniques of occupation constituted 'a gigantic scheme to change, in favour of Germany, the balance of biological forces between it and the captive nations for many years to come', aiming 'to destroy or cripple the subjugated peoples in their development' so that Germany would be placed in a position of 'numerical, physical and economic superiority' regardless of the military outcome of armed conflict.[40]

'Genocide' was thus 'effected through a synchronised attack on different aspects of life of the captive peoples', in the realms of politics, society, culture, economics, biology, physical existence (starvation and killing), religion and morality.[41] The concept was intended to capture:

> a coordinated plan of different actions aiming at the destruction of essential foundations of the life of national groups, with the aim of annihilating the groups themselves. The objectives of such a plan would be disintegration of the political and social institutions, of culture, language, national feelings, religion, and the economic existence of national groups, and the destruction of the personal security, liberty, health, dignity, and even the lives of the individuals belonging to such groups. Genocide is directed against the national group as an entity, and the actions involved are directed against individuals, not in their individual capacity, but as members of the national group.[42]

Outright killing was one, but not the only, part of a multi-faceted political rationality and a multi-dimensional set of legal and administrative forms and practices, and Lemkin was keen to point out the heterogeneity of ways in which the destruction of human groups could take place.[43]

Although one can argue about what constitutes a 'national group', it remains unsurprising that those peoples subjected to colonialism in all its forms have come to recognise their own experience in these words, and that they experience the well-intentioned modernisation and civil-isation of their ways of life as something other than 'bringing the gifts of civilisation' to them, indeed as an often violent and destructive process. Even if we agree that for the most effective use of the concept of genocide, we should exclude its application to this sort of question, this does not dispose of the issue: it simply generates a need to find some other word and idea.[44]

Rather than assuming that the only kind of violence and destruc-tion which challenges the character of the nation and the calibre of our civilisation is that of massacres and physical genocides, it is important to give some consideration to the various other ways in which it is pos-sible to 'destroy' a human group. For example, we could reflect upon the remark of Alexis de Tocqueville, that great observer and admirer of American civilisation, on the contrast between the approaches of the Spanish and the Americans to the peoples they colonised:

> The Spanish, with the help of unexampled monstrous deeds, covering themselves with an indelible shame, could not succeed in exterminat-ing the Indian race, nor even prevent it from sharing their rights; the Americans of the United States have attained this double result with marvellous facility – tranquilly, legally, philanthropically, without spilling blood, without violating a single one of the great principles of morality in the eyes of the world. One cannot destroy men while being more respectful of the laws of humanity.[45]

It is not just a matter, then, of deciding whether it is true or false that relations between Europeans and Aborigines could be described as genocidal, but also one of choosing between different perspectives on colonisation and state formation. Although there is some support for the position represented by *Fabrication*, that genocide should be nar-rowly conceived, this does not in any way diminish the need to recog-nise what remains problematic about the Lockean approach and what remains violent and destructive about otherwise civilised settler-colonisation in the name of the rule of law. Certainly these are not issues to be decided merely by contemptuous fiat.

Civilisation: British and Christian

Not all the words which fascinate Windschuttle mark out things to be avoided. On the contrary, some – particularly Christianity, civilisation and the rule of law – do sterling service and are lavishly commended. If settlers were Christian, how could they mean to do harm? Similarly with civilisation. If the government did not intend extermination, perhaps even felt a mission to civilise, how could anyone – least of all the putative civilisees – complain? If it was charged to establish the rule of law, how could one talk of lawlessness on the frontier?

Christianity has two roles in Windschuttle's dramaturgy. On the one hand, its official representatives are accused of all sorts of self-aggrandising lies about massacres, and essentially blamed for all the ills of Aborigines that flowed from regimes of 'protection' that bred separatism and were the real source, apart from their self-inflicted wounds, of the misery of the Aboriginal peoples of this country. On the other hand, the fact that settlers were Christians is supposed to render spurious the allegations that they were involved in anything terrible.

There is no doubt that many of the leading colonists were indeed believing Christians, children of the Enlightenment, earnest 'civilisers' and avatars of the rule of law. But is this all that needs to be said? Bringing salvation or improvement or civilisation to those believed to lack it is commonly an intrusive business, most of all if you are really convinced it is as good for them as it has been for you, particularly if they are unconvinced. Sometimes it doesn't even depend on your motives: the very attempt has consequences, many of them irreversible, some tragic, some salutary, some both tragic and salutary at once and for the same reasons.[46]

One of *Fabrication*'s sources for the settlers' beliefs is John Gascoigne's *The Enlightenment and the Origins of European Australia*, but the representation of that book is highly selective. Not only were Christianity and a civilising mission not inconsistent with dispossession and harm,[47] they could often allow the harm done to be ignored, or even done with an honest and clear conscience. These are points that Gascoigne makes several times, all the while recognising the complexity of motivation and effect, not trying to reduce it to *Fabrication*'s binary moral repertoire. He observes the tendency among nineteenth-century social theorists to relegate the Australian Aborigines to 'an increasingly lowly position', a mode of theorising 'invoked to justify dispossession and white supremacy'.[48] Unlike Windschuttle, Gascoigne is prepared to use the word domination, and is able to note that Australia was '*regarded* as a piece of waste land writ large requiring to be brought into productive use' without suggesting that this is how we today should also regard it.

> The traditional inhabitants of these 'waste lands' were seen as rather like the squatters on the commons who were obliged to make way for improvements which were for the greatest good of the greatest number. Some hoped that, like the British squatters, they, too, would benefit from the increased and more regular employment that agricultural improvement brought but, ultimately, tradition had few rights in the headlong rush to transform the land as it gathered momentum, so the belief in improvement began to permeate the society more generally.[49]

This analysis does not condemn Christianity or civilisation as base, still less demonic, but it does acknowledge that they come at a price which its exactors are not generally well situated or disposed to recognise.

Is this to demonise our ancestors, to put them on trial and find them guilty? Not at all. We're not a court, still less a kangaroo court. Some people do bad thinking it good. Others do good, but with terrible consequences. Many sad results were not intended, and few people who did evil thought that was what they did. People rarely do, but what does that tell us? Lots of otherwise decent people do otherwise indecent things, because they believe what everyone believes or do what everyone else does. And what everyone believes is rarely anyone's specific invention. To understand systematic historic injustices, individual motives are rarely decisive. They don't explain patterned and structured behaviours, and that is what later generations typically need to understand. In any event, what individuals thought they were doing is not decisive on how we now should regard what they did.

We are members of a nation, seeking to come to terms with what our inherited culture made available and our forebears did. Of course, interpretation of the past must exhibit tact and humility, depends on thoughtful, sensitive appraisal of the facts, and should avoid simple all-purpose characterisations of complex matters. And morality is not the only relevant register. Tragedy was almost certainly written into our national history as soon as whites decided to come here, and whatever we did. Nevertheless we did come here and we did some things and not others. We must come to terms with what we did.

Rule of Law

One thing we did, according to Windschuttle, is bring the rule of law. There is deep truth in that. There is no way of understanding the convict story in Australia, for example, without appreciating that convicts were not merely prisoners but prisoners with legal rights, who knew that, demanded respect for their rights, and did so from officials who were not at liberty to ignore them. That has been convincingly demonstrated in a number of studies, particularly David Neal's *The Rule of Law in a Penal Colony*.[50] What happened to convicts, however, was only part of the story, and could not, in the nature of the colonial encounter, represent the whole.

It is a complicated matter to assess the extent to which the rule of law exists in any society at any time, though these complications do not appear to delay Windschuttle at all. It is enough for him to cite the colonial governors' commitment to the rule of law to move to the conclusion that Aborigines were regularly safeguarded by it. But how could that be?

The rule of law requires, at a low minimum:[51] systematic restraint and channelling by law of the activities of officials; equally systematic restraint and channelling of the power of powerful citizens; law that is knowable and generally known; and the capacity of citizens, in their interactions with each other and with officials, routinely to appreciate the authority of the law and its relevance to their encounters, and to be prepared to invoke it. The rule of law must not only be proclaimed, or even endorsed by officials, for whether it exists and matters is a social matter. It must *count* in the social world. But in settlers' relations with Aborigines this could not routinely be the case. Charles Rowley identifies the logic of the situation thus:

> The problem of a cultural frontier in the colonial situation is basically the same everywhere. If the frontier is expanding, law and order depend on the government leading the way and taking charge of the processes of trade, settlement, recruitment of labour; and establishing by use of superior force the best approximation to a rule of law possible in these very difficult conditions. This has happened only rarely in colonial history ... In any case, more 'development' is necessary for more revenue. Development involves the taking of land: and in spite of legal theories about certain lands being 'waste and vacant', practically all land is the object of indigenous claims to ownership. There may be violent resistance, and reprisals by the settlers taking the law into their own hands. Efforts by police to keep the peace tend to come later. In practice, the police will go where there is 'trouble'; and the nature of the trouble will be described for them by the settler community. So the first contact of the Aboriginal with the police has been characteristically in the role of an avenging force.[52]

Settlers were often isolated, frightened[53] and, in the nature of things, on the make. This is precisely the sort of situation Hobbes envisaged, and that stems from a truth often enough manifested and noted: *homo homini lupus*, man is a wolf to man. Sometimes it was better, and not infrequently it was worse, helped along as it was by the weakness of restraints on the frontier, the superior power of the settlers, the fact that real interests were at stake, and beliefs that Aborigines were barbarian, not quite human, anyway nothing like us.

And if the settlers had all been of goodwill and devoted to the rule of law, what then? In the first stages of contact, with a few exceptions, law had yet to be devised specifically for Aborigines. The 'law in the books' was generally that which applied to convicts. But contact brought out in the most dramatic and extreme forms the depth of those truisms of sociology of law that stress the distance between 'law in books' and 'law in action', or between official law and what the legal sociologists Eugen Ehrlich and Leon Petrazycki, respectively, call 'living' or 'intuitive' law.[54] Those distances exist in every society, however familiar and obedient to law. But some societies are not at all familiar with it, and among those who are, not all are obedient. In this connection, we would repeat the following observation, born of reflection on eastern Europe, which is even more dramatically applicable here:

> for the rule of law to *count*, rather than simply to be announced or decreed, people must *care* about what the law says – the rules themselves must be taken seriously, and the institutions must come to matter. They must enter into the psychological economy of everyday life – to bear both on calculations of likely official responses *and* on those many circumstances in which one's actions are very unlikely to come to any officials' attention at all. They must mesh with, rather than contradict or be irrelevant to the 'intuitive law' of which Leon Petrazycki wrote, in terms of which people think about and organise their everyday lives. None of this can be simply decreed.[55]

Whatever the formal law was like, settlers would often find themselves in circumstances where they faced opportunities and temptations to flout it, and Aborigines did not and for a long time could not know it, or understand it. If Poles under Russian or Prussian or Austro-Hungarian rule throughout the nineteenth century, or under communism in the twentieth, took the law to be alien and imposed, were reluctant to enlist the legal system and not much used to doing so, then early nineteenth-century Aborigines, assailed with the finest fruits of the common law tradition, were astronomically less well placed. As Hasluck comments:

> These new British subjects did not know British law and they did not believe it was a good law, and even if they had known and believed, their situation and condition meant that the law was not accessible to them and that they were not amenable to it. They knew nothing of the process of sworn complaint, warrant, arrest, committal for trial, challenging the jury, pleading, legal defence, recovery of costs, suit for damages, summons for assault, evidence on oath, and so on. Those living in the bush did not know that it was wrong to resist arrest or

hinder a policeman in the execution of his duty and they also frequently refused to stop when called upon to do so.[56]

The pretension in such circumstances of Aborigines *using* the law
on more than rare occasions is absurd.[57] That is dramatically true of
criminal law, where the process was in the hands of whites, and it was
even more true of civil law. For, as Hasluck reminds us, 'in any civil
relation ... the move for redressing injury or maintaining a right rests
with the wronged person'.[58] It takes a rich imagination to conjure up
crowds of avid Aboriginal litigants in the early years of settlement. Still
less the far more important service that the rule of law is supposed to
provide in informing and supporting the relations of citizens who
never go to court but act on understandings of the law in countless
routine individual acts, accidents and forms of co-operation in daily
life. None of this 'tacit knowledge' was or could quickly be available to
the Aborigines upon which the penal colony had been inflicted. In the
long meantime, at so many levels in so many ways, British law contradicted exactly that 'living', 'intuitive' law that legal sociology has shown
to be fundamental to people's ordinary lives, and to the structures,
roles, culture and expectations that underpin them.

The rule of law, then, presupposes a lot to be effective and a lot to
be good. In early contact with Aboriginal society its presuppositions
did not exist even where the will to adhere to it did. And that often
did not exist either. Most unsettling for ardent adherents to the rule
of law, among them ourselves, is that it is hard to see how a will more
concerned to bring the rule of law could have done much to alter the
tragedy that became the Aboriginal story in our country. Indeed, in the
context of early colonialism, and even more in the light of the relative
impotence of the imposed law for much of the century, talk of the rule
of law could serve to justify, mythologise and may well have blinded the
perpetrators to the horror of relationships of domination and exploitation out of which, systematically and unavoidably, there could be only
one set of winners. Again, this is a systemic problem, not necessarily a
problem of anyone's ill will. But Aborigines might be forgiven for not
noticing the distinction.

Conclusion

In *Fabrication* we read that there is a difference between scholars who do their research in order to 'investigate' a topic and those who seek to 'vindicate' a pre-existing standpoint.

> The former usually begin with an idea of what they hope to find but are always prepared to change their expectations and conclusions in the light of what the evidence itself reveals. The latter, as the sorry example of Aboriginal history in this country reveals, only select evidence that supports their cause and either omit, suppress or falsify the rest.[59]

This distinction is an important one, and commonly ignored in debates about the character of nations. Think of the *Historikerstreit* in Germany,[60] the more recent Polish debate over the wartime massacre of Jews by their neighbours in the village of Jedwabne,[61] not to mention the entrenched positions of so many participants in our own debates. So many words, so much invective, so little change to original positions. Hard though it might be to keep faith with it when the stakes seem high, what *Fabrication* recommends should be a regulative ideal, not only for Rankean historians but for all who are concerned about their nation's past.

But if Windschuttle is claiming to be an 'investigator' and not a 'vindicator', the claim collapses under any serious scrutiny. A rough guide to whether one is reading investigative or vindicatory history is the possibility of *surprise*. Vindicators leave few loose ends. Everything fits, seamlessly. Investigators, by contrast, can be puzzled and taken by surprise, led to new and different conclusions. But nothing appears to puzzle or surprise Windschuttle. Who, reading his *Quadrant* articles,[62] written before he had completed his Tasmanian research, would be startled by how that research was going to turn out in his hands? Who expects to be taken off guard by the conclusions of Volumes 2 and 3? Indeed, who can even *conceive* Windschuttle saying after a few more years in the archives, 'Whoops! Got it all wrong. Hats off to Henry.' Unless, of course, he has yet another across-the-board ideological conversion, in which case all bets are off.

We need go no further than Paul Hasluck, again, to identify precisely one of the core psychological problems for settler-colonists and for the kind of historiography purveyed by *Fabrication*. As well as observing even-handedly that there were 'a number of cases of both white men and black men suffering death or injury at each other's hands in circumstances of gross savagery', Hasluck felt that it was important to look at the 'grim history' of frontier violence in the interest of seeing 'what it reveals of the attitude of the whites', not what it reveals about the dysfunctionality of Aboriginal society. Moreover, he wrote,

> the occurrence of a phase of violence in the early stages of contact
> is important because inevitably it left antagonism between the races,
> while some degree of shame or the need to justify what happened
> brought a tendency to defame the primitive defender of his soil as
> treacherous, black at heart, murderous and open to no instruction
> except by force.[63]

In the face of this sort of historical and moral sensitivity, the impression Windschuttle's book will make most firmly on the minds of its readers may be its industrial-strength obtuseness, but we would suggest that it deserves a more careful analysis. *Fabrication* is worth reading, if only to remind us that the tendency identified by Hasluck more than half a century ago remains an integral part of the culture and civilisation characterising Australian society, and that it continues to play a real and effective role in Australian political and cultural life. Title's terrific, too.

NOTES

1. Keith Windschuttle, *The Fabrication of Aboriginal History: Volume One, Van Diemen's Land 1803–1847*, Sydney, Macleay Press, 2002, p. 28.
2. Windschuttle, *Fabrication*, p. 402.
3. *Ibid*, p. 3.
4. Martin Krygier, 'Neighbours. Poles, Jews and the Aboriginal Question,' *Australian Book Review*, April 2002, p. 41.
5. Noting, incidentally, that Leopold von Ranke's remark about history dealing with 'what actually happened' was not a historiographical injunction, but a modest observation on the confined aspirations of his first book, written when he was in his twenties. His words were '*er will blos zeigen, wie es eigentlich gewesen*', i.e. 'it [the

book] aims only to show what actually happened' (Letter by Fritz Stern to *The New York Review of Books*, 24/2/2000).

6. For examples of either lazy or rapid reading, of the sort Windschuttle finds inexcusable in others, see S. G. Foster, 'Contra Windschuttle', *Quadrant*, vol. 47, no. 3, March 2003, pp. 25–28.

7. As it happens, the attempt to link the historiography of frontier violence to the High Court's *Mabo* decision (*Mabo and Ors v Queensland (No. 2)* (1991–1992) 175 CLR 1) reveals primarily a failure actually to read the judgement, let alone understand it: yes, Reynolds' work had an impact on the rhetorical framing of some, and only some, of Justices' decisions, but it had nothing to with the logic of the *legal* outcome. See Robert van Krieken, 'From *Milirrpum* to *Mabo*: the High Court, *Terra Nullius* and Moral Entrepreneurship', *UNSW Law Journal* 23 (1) 2000, pp. 63–77.

8. Windschuttle, *Fabrication*, p. 2.

9. *Ibid*, p. 129.

10. *Ibid*, p. 130.

11. *Ibid*, p. 70.

12. *Ibid*, p. 102.

13. Paul Hasluck, *Black Australians: A Survey of Native Policy in Western Australia, 1829–1897*, Melbourne, Melbourne University Press, 1942, p. 179.

14. *Ibid*, pp. 167–8.

15. *Ibid*, p. 178.

16. *Ibid*, p. 179.

17. Peter Coleman, 'The Windschuttle Thesis' *Quadrant*, volume 46, issue 12, December 2002, p. 80. See also Ron Brunton, quoted in *The Australian*, 28–29 December 2002, p. 3.

18. Windschuttle, *Fabrication*, p. 386.

19. *Ibid*, p. 130.

20. *Ibid*, p. 386.

21. Hasluck, *Black Australians*.

22. Windschuttle, *Fabrication*, p. 186, emphasis added.

23. William Barnes is quoted referring to 'the barbarity and treachery of the whites', and James Scott felt that it was displacement from the best tracts of land which was a cause of Aboriginal violence (*Fabrication*, pp. 334–5). Not, as *Fabrication* claims (p. 130), mere criminal venality.

24. See Bain Attwood, 'Frontier Warfare', *Australian Financial Review*, 28/2/2003.

25. Avishai Margalit, *The Decent Society*, Cambridge, Mass., Harvard University Press, 1996, p. 148.

26. Raimond Gaita, *A Common Humanity*, Text, 1999, pp. 78, 79.

27. Attwood, *Frontier*, 186–87. See also John McCorquodale, 'The Legal Classification of Race in Australia' (1986) 10, 1 *Aboriginal History* 8.

28. Windschuttle, *Fabrication*, p. 186.

29. Norbert Elias, *The Civilising Process*, Oxford, Blackwell, 2000, p. 431.

30. Anthony Pagden, *Lords of all the World: Ideologies of Empire in Spain, Britain and France c. 1500–c.1800*, New Haven, Yale University Press, 1995.

31. Robert A. Williams, Jr. *The American Indian in Western Legal Thought: The Discourse of Conquest*, New York, Oxford University Press, 1990, p. 248.

32. Windschuttle, *Fabrication*, p. 32, emphasis added.

33. Pagden, *Lords*, p. 68.

34. *Ibid*, p. 84.
35. Windschuttle, *Fabrication*, p. 9.
36. Michael Ignatieff, 'The danger of a world without enemies. Lemkin's world', *The New Republic*, 26/2/2001, p. 27.
37. Pieter N. Drost, *Genocide: United Nations Legislation on International Criminal Law. Vol. 2 of Crimes of State* Leiden, A. W. Sythoff, 1959, p. 11; Patrick Thornberry, *International Law and the Rights of Minorities*, Oxford, Clarendon Press, 1991, p. 122.
38. Royal Commission into Aboriginal Deaths in Custody (1989) *Report of the Inquiry into the Death of Malcolm Charles Smith* by Commissioner J. H. Wootten, Canberra, Australian Government Publishing Service, p. 5.
39. Hal Wootten, 'Ron Brunton and *Bringing Them Home*', *Indigenous Law Bulletin* 4 (12) 1998, p. 6.
40. Raphaël Lemkin, *Axis Rule in Occupied Europe: Laws of Occupation, Analysis of Government, Proposals for Redress*, Washington, Carnegie Endowment for International Peace, 1944, p. 81.
41. *Ibid*, pp. xi–xii.
42. *Ibid*, p. 79.
43. See also Richard Lawrence Miller, *Nazi justiz: Law of the Holocaust*, Westport, Conn., Praeger, 1995.
44. For example, Pierre Clastres, 'On ethnocide', *Art & Text* 28, 1988, pp. 51–58.
45. Alexis de Tocqueville, *Democracy in America*, volume 1, Part 2, ch. 10, transl., ed. and with an introduction by Harvey C. Mansfield and Delba Winthrop, Chicago, University of Chicago Press, 2000, p. 325.
46. Martin Krygier, 'The Grammar of Colonial Legality. Subjects, Objects and the Rule of Law', in Geoffrey Brennan and Francis G. Castles (eds), *Reshaping Australia. 200 Years of Institutional Transformation*, Cambridge, Cambridge University Press, 2002, 220–60; Robert van Krieken, 'The barbarism of civilisation: cultural genocide and the "stolen generations"', *British Journal of Sociology* 50 (2) 1999, pp. 295–313; 'Reshaping civilisation: liberalism between assimilation and cultural genocide', *Amsterdams Sociologisch Tijdschrift*, 29 (2) 2002, pp. 1–38.
47. Alice L. Conklin, *A Mission to Civilise: The Republican Idea of Empire in France and West Africa, 1895–1930*, Stanford, Stanford University Press, 1997.
48. John Gascoigne, *The Enlightenment and the Origins of European Australia*, Cambridge, Cambridge University Press, 2002, p. 13.
49. *Ibid*, pp. 70–71.
50. David Neal, *The Rule of Law in a Penal Colony*, Cambridge, Cambridge University Press, 1992. See also Alan Atkinson, *The Europeans in Australia. A History, Volume One: the Beginning*, Melbourne, Oxford University Press, 1997; John Braithwaite, 'Crime in a Convict Republic', *The Modern Law Review*, 64, 2001, pp. 11–50; John Hirst, *Convict Society and its Enemies*, Sydney, Allen & Unwin, 1983; Martin Krygier, 'Grammar'.
51. For more on what the rule of law requires, see Martin Krygier, 'The Rule of Law', *International Encyclopedia of the Social and Behavioral Sciences*, editors-in-chief Neil J. Smelser and Paul B. Bates, Oxford, Elsevier Science, 2001, vol. 20, pp. 13403–408; and Martin Krygier, 'Transitional Questions about the Rule of Law: Why, What, and How?' *East Central Europe/L'Europe du Centre-Est*, 28 (pt 1) 2001, pp. 1–34.
52. C. D. Rowley, *The Destruction of Aboriginal Society*, Canberra, ANU Press, 1970, pp. 123–24.

53. The significance of fear in the frontier setting is emphasised by, among others, Henry Reynolds in *Frontier,* Sydney, Allen & Unwin, 1996, pp. 9–31, 44–50.

54. Eugen Ehrlich, *Fundamental Principles of the Sociology of Law,* trans. Walter L. Moll, Transaction Books, New Brunswick, 2002, [1913]; Leon Petrazycki, *Law and Morality,* trans. Hugh W. Babb, Johnson Reprint 1968 [1955], A. Podgórecki, 'Unrecognised father of the sociology of law: Leon Petrazycki', *Law & Society Review* 15 1980, pp. 183–202; Reza Banakar, 'Sociological Jurisprudence' in Reza Banakar & Max Travers (eds), *An Introduction to Law and Social Theory,* Oxford, Hart, 2002, pp. 33–49.

55. Martin Krygier, 'Institutional Optimism, Cultural Pessimism, and the Rule of Law', in Martin Krygier and Adam Czarnota (eds), *The Rule of Law after Communism,* Dartmouth, Ashgate, 1999, pp. 89–90.

56. Hasluck, *Black Australians,* p. 123.

57. *Ibid,* p. 143.

58. *Ibid,* pp. 147–48.

59. Windschuttle, *Fabrication,* pp. 402–3.

60. For overviews, see M. S. Peacock, 'The desire to understand and the politics of Wissenschaft: an analysis of the *Historikerstreit*', *History of the Human Sciences,* 14 (4) 2001, pp. 87–110; W. Wippermann & A. Umland, 'Whose fault? From the *Historikerstreit* to the Goldhagen controversy' *European History Quarterly* 29 (4) 1999, pp. 603–607; S. Gallagher, 'The *Historikerstreit* and the critique of national-ism', *History of European Ideas,* 16 (4–6) 1993, pp. 921–926; M. Travers, 'History Writing and the Politics of Historiography – The German *Historikerstreit*', *Australian Journal of Politics & History* 37 (2), 1991, pp. 246–261.

61. Jan T. Gross, *Neighbors: the destruction of the Jewish community in Jedwabne, Poland,* Princeton, Princeton University Press, 2001.

62. Keith Windschuttle, 'The myths of frontier massacres in Australian history, Part I: The invention of massacre stories', *Quadrant* 44 (10) 2000, pp. 8–21; 'The myths of frontier massacres in Australian history, Part II: The fabrication of the Aboriginal death toll', *Quadrant* 44 (11) 2000, pp. 17–24; 'The myths of frontier massacres in Australian history, Part III: Massacre stories and the policy of sepa-ratism', *Quadrant* 44 (12) 2000, pp. 6–20. The texts can be found at http://www.sydneyline.com.

63. Hasluck, *Black Australians,* p. 179.

Terra Nullius Reborn

Henry Reynolds

There is no doubt about Keith Windschuttle's ambition. He seeks to bring the concept of *terra nullius* back to life. That is a central feature of *The Fabrication of Aboriginal History*. He tells us that the notions of the exclusive possession of territory and the defence of it either by law or force 'were not part of the Aborigines' mental universe'. In short the Tasmanians 'did not own the land'. The concept of property was 'not part of their culture'.[1]

Much follows from this assertion. The incoming Europeans were not taking land belonging to someone else. They introduced tenure to a place where none had previously existed. Aboriginal attacks on the settlers had nothing to do with resisting encroachments on their land because they had no sense of trespass. In the absence of such motivation they must have been spurred to violence by baser, more personal motives – by the desire for vengeance and for plunder. Therefore the Tasmanians were not at war with the settlers. They were criminals – burglars and cutthroats, not warriors or patriots.

Much then turns on this question. Remove this building block and much of the argument in *The Fabrication of Aboriginal History* collapses. It is not possible, as some reviewers have wished, to cast doubt on Windschuttle's vision of *terra nullius* while leaving the rest untouched. The soundness of argument and evidence in this area are all-important.

He begins at a high level of generalisation. Unless it can be proved to the contrary, it must be assumed that hunters and gatherers have no sense of land ownership. It's an heroic claim which flies in the face of 200 years of jurisprudence and at least 150 years of ethnography. Windschuttle provides no evidence, no references to ground this heroic proposition. We are expected to receive it as an axiom that is beyond argument. But it is not a good start. And things get worse.

The most powerful proposition we are presented with is that the Aborigines did not have a word for property. This argument has caught the public's eye and has been repeated numerous times in reviews. Clearly it has been seen to be a clincher – an argument of great discursive power. But we should begin with Windschuttle's own words:

> The Aborigines did not even have a word for it. None of the four vocabularies of Tasmanian Aboriginal language compiled in the nineteenth century, nor any of the lists of their phrases, sentences or songs, contained the word 'land'. Nor did they have words for 'own', 'possess' or 'property' or any of their derivatives.[2]

The source for these claims is a series of appendices in the 1899 book, *The Aborigines of Tasmania*, by H. Ling Roth.[3] Given the great significance of the linguistic evidence it is remarkable that Windschuttle has apparently read nothing on Tasmanian Aboriginal linguistics published in the twentieth century. But leaving that aside, two points should be made. We have no idea at all of what percentage of total Aboriginal vocabularies were ever recorded – particularly by the informants whose work is reprinted in Roth. A modern authority has written:

> Only limited and generally quite unreliable notes and materials, mostly word lists and some sentence materials, had been collected in the Tasmanian languages, from which only a superficial picture of them can be obtained. Those few short texts that are available are of dubious value, as they were compiled by Europeans with, it seems, little real knowledge of the languages.[4]

Other scholars support this proposition.[5] So while we know how many words *were* listed by European witnesses we have no idea of how many *weren't*.

N. J. B. Plomley, the doyen of Tasmanian Aboriginal scholarship, observed that 'we are quite ignorant of the range of Aboriginal thought because so few topics were explored in conversation with them'.[6] All Windschuttle can legitimately say is that words for land don't appear in the vocabularies printed in Roth. That is a much-diminished claim. The word lists themselves create further difficulties. Apart from George Augustus Robinson, whose extensive vocabularies weren't available to Roth, 'no one did more than record in a desultory way the aboriginal words for common words and activities'.[7] If the European enquirers didn't ask the Aborigines about land, ownership and trespass, they didn't hear the relevant words or write them down for posterity. It is as simple – and as obvious – as that. The only significant collection of words consulted by Windschuttle was the one compiled by Joseph Milligan on Flinders Island in the 1840s. Plomley observed that Milligan's vocabulary contained no tribal names at all, which is not all that surprising given that his informants had already been living in exile on Flinders Island for ten years.[8] He may have made no enquiries about tribal organisation as it had once been. However Milligan's lists included the names of 31 men and 24 women. Each is accompanied by a reference to their homeland – e.g. a native of Ben Lomond, a native of Circular Head District, a native of George's River, a native of Port Davey.[9] For all we know, this may have been the way that Milligan's informants characterised themselves – identifying with a clearly defined, specific homeland.

Roth himself did not draw the conclusion that Windschuttle extracts from the vocabularies. In his chapter on 'Nomadic Life' he adduces, without comment, numerous nineteenth-century authorities who observed that the Tasmanians confined themselves to their own well-defined territory.[10] It seems particularly perverse to say that linguistic evidence proves that the Aborigines had no sense of property. The problem is that so few settlers showed any interest in Aboriginal thought or languages. To use that fact in order to establish that Tasmania was a *terra nullius* demonstrates a determination to make totally fragmentary records reveal what the author desires them to reveal.

But the most serious problem with the Windschuttle position is that he didn't consult the most important contemporary work on Tasmanian languages – N. J. B. Plomley's 1976 book, *A Word List of the*

Tasmanian Aboriginal Languages. The result of 26 years' research in Australia and Europe, it represents a benchmark in relevant scholarship – an authority which cannot lightly be dismissed. So how does Plomley's work help us to pursue the question of land ownership? At first sight it would appear to support the Windschuttle position. There are no entries for 'land', 'property' or 'possess'. But everything is not as it seems.

When Aborigines talk about land, they most commonly refer to 'country'. Hence we hear of 'caring for country', 'returning to country', 'claiming country', 'living on country'. It was not unreasonable, then, for Plomley to categorise all words relating to land under the rubric of country. And it's there that all the words will be found – a page and a half of them – 23 relating to country, three meaning 'my country', six meaning 'where is your country?' Some of the entries are variations of a single word. But each one was collected separately. And they come from all over Tasmania – from the Western, Northern, North Eastern and South Eastern tribal groups. The record is even more geographically specific, with relevant words recorded at Port Sorell, Bruny Island, Cape Grim, West Point, Mount Cameron, Cape Portland, Ben Lomond, Oyster Bay. The majority were collected by George Augustus Robinson, who was the only person among the settlers who had even a slight grasp of the Tasmanian languages. But other words were contributed by Charles Robinson, Jorgen Jorgenson and Alexander McGeary. In his commentary on the words relating to country, Plomley wrote:

> Although the phrases 'my own country' and 'where is your country?' clearly refer to a tribal territory, it does not follow that all the words translated as 'country' do so. Many of them almost certainly have the meaning of tribal territory, but at least one may have the meaning of countryside.[11]

The fact that Robinson's papers have so many references to Aboriginal tribal divisions and sense of property makes nonsense of Windschuttle's claim that 'nowhere, in Robinson's extensive diaries … is there any suggestion of land as property'. On the basis of those diaries Plomley drew up both a table and a map of Aboriginal tribes and their territories. He observed that, 'along the coast at any rate the natives lived within a defined territory, which was regarded by other groups as belonging to it'.[12]

If Windschuttle had looked more carefully at his word lists, he would have found numerous references to 'country'. Joseph Milligan's vocabulary incorporated the translation of a legend on the origin of fire. It contained two pertinent references – one to 'a hill in my own country', the other to 'my countrymen', a phrase which is mentioned twice.[13] In another song published by T. H. Braim, there is a line that runs:

> When I returned to my country I went hunting but did not catch any game.[14]

The vocabulary provided by Alexander McGeary included two words relating to country – one related to 'the country all around' but the other clearly referred to country as territory.[15]

Where does this leave Windschuttle's claim that the Aborigines had no words relating to territory or ownership or possession? Clearly it cannot be sustained. But was he simply unaware of Plomley's linguistic work? Was it just a case of not doing his homework? It does seem extraordinary that he was willing to rest such a critical argument on what was known at the end of the nineteenth century. Is it possible that he actually consulted the *Word List* but did not like what he saw? He listed nine other Plomley works in his bibliography. If one were to adopt Windschuttle's own view of things and employ his inimitable language, we would have to assume that this was one piece of information that he was 'careful to keep from' his readers.[16]

If the use of linguistic evidence leaves much to be desired, the treatment of the historical record is equally flawed. This is particularly so when Windschuttle comes to discuss the views about Aboriginal land ownership current among the colonists in the nineteenth century. In one sense his response is – and has to be – pre-determined. If you start from the *a priori* assumption that the hunter-gatherers have no sense of property, that they don't own the land and have nothing in their language to suggest otherwise, then contemporaries who thought differently must have been mistaken. In that situation one would know in advance that they were imposing their Eurocentric views on the indigenous people. An alternative strategy is to deny that there is any evidence at all relating to the question. Windschuttle therefore insists, as he logically must, that there is no contemporary evidence that the Tasmanians had a sense of territory or property. The solution to the problem is simply to leave out evidence to the contrary. And yet there is an unbroken tradition in European writing from the 1820s to the present which has recognised Aboriginal land ownership. Many of the witnesses are people whom Windschuttle himself quotes approvingly when other issues are concerned.

The Land Commissioner Roderick O'Connor, who travelled extensively throughout the settled districts during the Black War, argued that the various tribes composed 'as it were so many different nations, each having its Chief and each possessing particular lots of hunting ground'. They were as 'tenacious of their hunting grounds as settlers are of their farms'.[17] The Quaker missionaries James Backhouse and George Washington Walker, who twice visited the Aboriginal settlement on Flinders Island, had similar views about Aboriginal territorial arrangements. Walker concluded that each tribe confined itself to a specific, known district,[18] while Backhouse observed that:

> Though the mode of holding property differed among the aborigines
> of Van Diemen's Land from that used among English people, yet they
> had their property: each tribe was limited to its own hunting ground;
> and into such hunting grounds the island was divided.[19]

Governor George Arthur informed the Colonial Office that 'each tribe claims some portion of territory which they consider peculiarly their own'.[20] As we have already seen, G. A. Robinson's journals and reports are mines of information about tribal groups, the names applied to their country and their territorial boundaries. He was confident that he could use his notes to compile a map of Tasmania on Aboriginal principles because:

> he could truly say that the island was divided and subdivided by the
> natives into districts, and contained many nations. Their divisions he
> intended at some future time to point out, as he intended to execute a
> map of the island on aboriginal principles, with the aborigines' names
> for mountains, rivers and districts.[21]

Robinson informed members of the Executive Council that Aboriginal society was 'divided into various tribes under chiefs occupying particular districts'.[22]

The colonial historian John West summed up what was widely understood about Aboriginal territoriality in the middle of the nineteenth century. 'It is true', he wrote:

> they had no permanent villages, and accordingly no individual property in land; but the boundaries of each horde were known and trespass was a declaration of war.[23]

There were, then, many contemporary observers who believed that the Tasmanians had a strong sense of territory and lived within recognised, well-understood boundaries. It is, of course, possible to dismiss their assessment of the situation and argue, as Windschuttle does, that they were projecting European ideas onto the property-less Aborigines. There is no evidence that this was the case. It can only be supposition, and it rests entirely on the virtually unsupported assumption that hunter-gatherers, by definition, lacked any sense of ownership. On the other hand Windschuttle alludes to no contemporary witness who could support his position. There were a few people who did argue the case, but they lacked any particular knowledge of traditional society.

The question of land is also critical to an assessment of Windschuttle's interpretation of the Black War. Assuming that the Tasmanians didn't own the land, had no sense of property and traditionally knew nothing of trespass, the conflict itself could not have been about land. That being so, the Aborigines were not patriots, not even warriors. They were criminals engaged in murder, assault and theft. They were largely responsible for the violence and they brought their own fate on themselves. This may appear extreme, but it is a fair rendition of the Windschuttle thesis. Most of the actions of the Aborigines, he argues, 'were nothing more than what would be recognised as crimes in any human culture, robbery, assault and murder'.[24] Contemporary European witnesses who believed the Tasmanians were motivated by anything more elevated than the desire for plunder and revenge are either ignored in *The Fabrication of Aboriginal History* or dismissed with an insouciance that is breathtaking.

Many experienced settlers made the connection between the rapid spread of settlement through the Midlands in the 1820s and the outbreak of conflict. Land Commissioner Roderick O'Connor observed that the Aboriginal tribes were displeased when they found 'houses built or persons hunting' on their land and 'this causes them to attack remote stock huts'.[25] Richard Dry, who had been in the colony since 1807, attributed the emergence of a 'determined spirit of hostility' to the 'Rapid increase of Settlers who now occupy the Best portions of the Land, extensive plains and fine tracts …'[26] Another settler attributed Aboriginal hostility to the fact that 'all the best tracts of land in the Island where they used originally to find abundance of game' had been taken from them 'by settlers, arriving year after year from England'.[27] Governor Arthur commented in 1828 in a dispatch to the Colonial Office that the Aborigines:

> already complain that the white people have taken possession of their country, encroached upon their hunting grounds, and destroyed their natural food …[28]

Running through these observations – and many similar ones – is the awareness that the Aborigines resented and reacted to the presence of uninvited Europeans on their land. But Windschuttle knows better. The Tasmanians, he is convinced, had no sense of possession and trespass. Yet even if one assumed that traditional society had little sense of trespass, this in itself would not preclude the likelihood that such a sense would develop rapidly after settlement, with utterly alien people occupying territory without observing any of the known protocols. Windschuttle's conviction leads him off into several long investigations of the extent of fencing and actual availability of game in the 1820s, investigations which have antiquarian interest but are of little relevance to the central issue – the Tasmanian complaint that the settlers had taken possession of their country, abundant kangaroos and limited fencing notwithstanding.

But the views of assorted settlers, officials and governors were one thing. What of those handful of Europeans who actually spent time with and talked to the Aborigines? What evidence do they provide?

G. A. Robinson is obviously the most important witness. He first came into contact with the Tasmanians on Bruny Island when he was appointed as a storekeeper with instructions to provide the resident Aborigines with rations. He had his first 'interview with the natives' at the end of March 1829. By the end of May he noted in his journal that he could make himself 'tolerably well understood in their vernacular tongue'.[29] For their part the Aborigines had a smattering of English. This was the first time in the history of the settlement that anyone had been engaged in close and continuous communication with the Tasmanians. A few days later Robinson gave a sermon of sorts in the local dialect. Robinson began to record observations about the way the Aborigines saw the world and understood their situation. On 23 November he recorded in his journal a much-quoted passage:

> It is well known that it is very usual for a number of aborigines, when assembled by their fireside under the open canopy of heaven to recount the sufferings of their ancestors, to dilate upon their present afflictions and to consult upon the best means of being released from their cruel and bloodthirsty foes. They have a tradition amongst them that white men have usurped their territory, have driven them into the forests, have killed their game and thus robbed them of their chief subsistence, have ravished their wives and daughters, have murdered and butchered their fellow countrymen; and are wont whilst brooding over these complicated ills in the dense part of the forest, to goad each other to acts of bloodshed and revenge for the injuries done to their ancestors and the persecutions offered to themselves through their white enemies.[30]

This was not published until 1966, long after Robinson's death. There is no evidence to suggest that, at this early period of his career as protector, it was written with a future audience in mind.

How does it advance the matter at hand? Robinson was not reporting directly the words of a particular person but rather considering a tradition that he had become aware of. He was the first person to be in a position to report on that tradition and to reflect upon it. There is no reason to suppose that he was making it up and it confirms what many well-informed settlers and officials had said independently.

How does Windschuttle respond to what for him is such damaging testimony? He observes that 'this is Robinson speaking not an

Aborigine', which is true but scarcely a compelling refutation, and then remarks that the extract was recorded 'before his expedition started out'[31] (that is, his West Coast expedition). The relevance of this self-evident fact is difficult to determine.

The existence of such a tradition was confirmed by the senior Bruny Island man, Wooraddy, ten years later on Flinders Island. In a speech, recorded by the catechist Robert Clark, he declared:

> My brothers, in our own country a long time ago we were a great many men, a great number. The white men have killed us all; they shot a great many. We are now only a few people here and we ought to be fond of one another.[32]

Windschuttle turns a blind eye in the direction of any evidence which indicates that the Aborigines believed – and were motivated by the fact – that the Europeans had usurped their territory. He argues that although in Robinson's diaries the Aborigines 'give plenty of explanations for their actions based on individual wrongs', such as being assaulted by whites or having their women stolen, there are 'none about defending their country'.[33]

In fact there are many in the Robinson papers. While reporting to the government in January 1832 about his first meeting with the remnants of the Big River and Oyster Bay tribes, he wrote:

> The chiefs assigned as a reason for their outrages upon the white inhabitants that they and their forefathers had been cruelly abused, that their country had been taken from them, their wives and daughters had been violated and taken away, and that they had experienced a multitude of wrongs from a variety of sources.[34]

There seems no reason to doubt that Tongelongter and Montpeliater attributed their attacks on Europeans to the fact that their country had been taken away. That Robinson doesn't actually quote the words they used seems a minor quibble. Robinson was also in close contact with Mannalargenna, another senior Aboriginal leader, for a long period of time and concluded that he was 'fully sensible of the injustices done to himself and people in the usurpation of his country by the white intruders'.[35] Robinson's testimony here is particularly significant because more than anyone in the colony he had a motive to deny Aboriginal land ownership, being the agent who effected their removal to Flinders Island. As he confessed in his journal, 'I have been the borrowed instrument in removing them from the main territory.'[36] He hoped that the Aborigines would transfer their sense of ownership to their settlement on Flinders Island. 'Patriotism is a distinguishing trait in the aboriginal character', he wrote in May 1833, 'yet for all the love they bear their country the aboriginal settlement will soon become their adopted country.'[37]

Gilbert Robertson had considerable contact with several Aborigines and in particular the leading man of the Stoney Creek tribe, Umarrah. This began when Robertson's Roving Party captured five members of the tribe, including two 'Warrior Chiefs'. With the help of an Aboriginal member of his party, Black Tom, Robertson was able 'to hold communication' with the chiefs, who told him that they had been in the area attending a gathering of Oyster Bay, Swan Port and Stoney Creek tribes 'to repel an invasion which the Port Dalrymple tribe made on the hunting grounds of the Swan Port tribe'. In the event all the tribes in question had come to an accommodation – 'some sort of treaty by which the Swan Port tribe have given all the others permission to hunt on their grounds'. Robertson was informed that parties were currently on their way to fight the Big River tribe for the purpose of 'compelling them to give up their hunting ground for the common good' and make common cause with them in 'carrying on their warfare against the white inhabitants'.[38]

Robertson's prisoners were taken before the Colony's Executive Council so that its members could ascertain for themselves if possible 'the cause of their grievances and aggressions against the White Inhabitants'. There was 'considerable communication with the five natives'. The minutes of the council recorded that the Aborigines knew sufficient of the English language 'to hold communication', and that they were assisted by the interpreting of Black Tom. The party denied that they had speared white people but said that the murders in the north of the colony had been carried out by the Port Dalrymple tribe 'because they had been driven off their Kangaroo Hunting Grounds'.[39]

In the most significant meeting between an Aboriginal party and senior officials of the colonial administration, the cause for conflict was said to be the loss of land. This confirmed what Robertson had been told earlier out in the bush: Aboriginal groups had a tradition that trespass was invasion which should occasion an armed response and that inter-tribal politics and diplomacy could determine the outcome of conflict over land.

That these incidents do not appear in *The Fabrication of Aboriginal History* should occasion no surprise. They would complicate things and make it much harder to declare that in existing accounts of internecine conflicts between Aboriginal bands there is not even 'one example of trespass provoking violence', and that the Tasmanians showed no evidence of anything that deserves the name of political skill.[40]

Windschuttle is also keen to scotch any suggestion that the Tasmanians had any patriotic feelings. The fact that no one ever recorded a patriotic speech verbatim leads him to the truly extraordinary proposition that none was ever delivered. 'The reason for historians' inability to produce patriotic statements', he argues, is simple – 'none were made'.[41] As only one or two settlers understood any of the Tasmanian languages, and only a few Aborigines spoke a little broken English, the absence of reporting from the 'front' is scarcely surprising. The number of direct quotations provided by Aboriginal informants on any subject could be counted on one hand. If this were taken to stand in the way of historical interpretation, there could be no history. But it is a standard of proof which Windschuttle applies only to other peoples' interpretations and not to his own.

The settlers who were closest to the Tasmanians – Robinson, Robertson and Darling – each commented on their patriotism. 'The aborigines of Van Diemen's Land are patriots', Robinson noted in his journal, 'staunch lovers of their country.'[42] Robertson came to the conclusion that they had 'ideas of their natural rights which would astonish most of our European statesmen'. He believes that:

> they consider every injury they can inflict upon White Man as an Act of Duty and patriotism and however much they may dread the punishment which our laws inflict on them – they consider the sufferers under those punishments as Martyrs in the cause of their country.[43]

William Darling spent two and a half years as superintendent of Aboriginal settlements in several locations in Bass Strait, during which time he learnt something of the languages and became 'acquainted with their dispositions'. In a letter to Governor Arthur in May 1832, he observed that the Tasmanians had 'considered themselves as engaged in a justifiable war against the invaders of their country'.[44] Nine months later he returned to the subject, writing that:

> it must be obvious to every candid mind, that they are a *brave* and
> *patriotic* people – though reduced to a mere handful, they still for a
> long time maintained their independence and refused to surrender.[45]

None of these observations by Robinson, Robertson or Darling appears in *The Fabrication of Aboriginal History*. They could not be accommodated in a work which with characteristic dogmatism declares that the actions of the Aborigines 'were not noble: they never rose beyond robbery, assault and murder'.[46]

And then there is the question of war. Was the Black War a serious matter of enemies in conflict or a police action aimed at 'saving the Aborigines from the consequences of their own actions'?[47] Windschuttle's answer is both clear and predictable. The British, he declared, had no good reason to regard Aboriginal hostility 'as genuine warfare, nor did they accord the Aborigines the status of warrior'. A military force deployed to quell actions 'that never rose above the level of criminal behaviour was not engaged in warfare'.[48] Here, as so often, he shows his hand all too plainly. The story must be told to deny the Tasmanians the status of warrior, to deny them any motivation above the criminal. A blind eye is turned to any suggestions of skill or courage, or even of suffering that was not self-inflicted.

So what of the British? We know a great deal about their attitudes and policies during the 1820s and 1830s. Any such discussion must begin with Governor Arthur's instructions relating to the Aborigines. These were handed to him in November 1825 by his superior officer (in both a military and bureaucratic sense), General Darling, who called in at Hobart en route from Britain to take up the governorship of New South Wales. They read in part:

the manner in which the Native Inhabitants are to be treated when making hostile incursions for the purpose of plunder, you well understand it to be your duty, when such disturbances cannot be prevented or allayed by less vigorous measures, to oppose force by force and to repel such Aggressions in the same manner, as if they proceeded from subjects of an accredited State.[49]

It was Arthur's *duty* to take military action and to treat the Aborigines as enemies not as criminals. The fundamental difference in policies adopted towards bushrangers and Aborigines during the period in which Arthur was governor makes that obvious.[50]

Arthur carried out his duty. We know that he had these instructions constantly in mind. At critical moments during the Black War he read them to his Executive Council. This was the case in November 1825 when he first raised the prospect of driving the Tasmanians from the settled districts.[51] He did so again in November 1828 when the council took the decision to declare martial law.[52] The truly extraordinary thing is that the instructions are never mentioned in *The Fabrication of Aboriginal History* – not once in 436 pages. And yet Windschuttle has a 12-page section on 'The Legitimization of Colonial Rule' that deals with gubernatorial instructions, policies and proclamations.[53] Such a startling omission will not surprise readers who have read thus far. But the question must be asked: did Windschuttle know of the instructions or not? If not, it undermines his claim to have read the sources in any more than a superficial, selective way. If he did, then he still has a case to answer – and a more serious one – of distortion effected by the suppression of vital evidence.

The development of British policy unfolded logically from the decision to treat the Aborigines as foreign enemies. The declaration of martial law in November 1828 that placed the Aborigines 'on the footing of open enemies of the King, in a state of actual warfare against him' was the inevitable outcome of earlier decisions, given that Aboriginal resistance had persisted.[54] The steps taken in this direction can be quickly outlined. In November 1826 the Governor issued an official notice which read in part:

If it should be apparent that there is a determination on the part of one or more of the native tribes to attack, rob, or murder the white inhabitants generally, any person may arm, and, joining themselves to the military, drive them by force to a safe distance, treating them as open enemies.[55]

The phrase 'open enemies' comes up again and again in official correspondence. Early in 1828, in a dispatch to the Colonial Office, Arthur observed that much should be endured before the blacks were 'treated as open and accredited enemies by the government'.[56]

The British record is full of references to war. Officials from the Governor down had the word constantly on their tongues and at the point of their pens. To cite all the instances and to put them in context would demand more space than is available here. In his correspondence over a five-year period, the Governor referred to 'the lawless and cruel warfare which is now carrying on', 'this mode of warfare', 'the lawless warfare', 'our continued warfare', 'this lamented and protracted warfare', 'the species of warfare which … is of the most distressing nature', 'our unpleasant war with the Aboriginal natives'. Arthur's private secretary, James Burnett, had his own portfolio of phrases referring to 'the warfare with the natives', 'this arduous warfare', 'the present harassing and lengthening warfare'.

Given the sheer weight of evidence regarding British policies and attitudes about how to deal with an 'open enemy', Windschuttle's arguments are perverse. He concedes that Arthur did occasionally use the term warfare but then explains it away by insisting that the usage was merely 'a figure of speech, a surrogate term for mere violence'.[57] Why the resistance to the obvious? Why does he so urgently argue the point? The answer comes in the sentence which runs:

Arthur's use of the term 'warfare' does not concede to the Aborigines any status as warrior counterparts.[58]

But the evidence from the colonists' side cannot be totally ignored. The British, Windschuttle concedes, certainly took military action against the Tasmanians but they (the Aborigines) did:

not wage war themselves. That is, though one side waged war, there was not a state of war between the parties … Hence, even though the

British used military tactics and methods themselves, the lack of recip-
rocation by the Aborigines meant the two were not linked by anything
that deserves the title warfare. In short, the Black War is a misnomer
and the orthodox school of Aboriginal history is mistaken. There was
no frontier war in Van Diemen's Land.[59]

It makes good copy but does little to enhance understanding.
The settlers, the active and retired military officers, the government
officials believed that they were engaged in warfare with the Aborigines
and that the Aborigines in turn were at war with them. Many commentators from George Arthur down knew a war when they saw one,
although they recognised it was a particular 'mode of warfare' or
'species of warfare'. The settler and retired military officer William
Clark thought the Big River tribe was 'at open war with the colony'.[60]
A neighbour reported that every day afforded evidence of determination to destroy 'and their declaration of war with the whites'.[61]
This was the view at the highest level of government. In October 1828
the Executive Council declared that the 'outrages of the aboriginal
Natives' amounted to 'a complete declaration of hostilities against
the settlers generally'.[62] In August 1830 the council concluded that
Aboriginal attacks could be considered 'in no other light than as acts of
warfare against the settlers generally, and that a warfare of the most
dreadful description'.[63] The council determined at the same meeting to
initiate the Black Line, which it believed would 'bring to a decisive issue
a state of warfare which there seems no hope of ending by any other
means'.[64]

The Aborigines themselves had words for war. Milligan recorded
three quite different ones which distinguished between a skirmish and
a battle resulting in serious loss of life.[65] Commenting on these words,
Plomley observed that there was:

> evidence of two styles of intertribal fighting among the Tasmanians,
> the ritual combat between one or two members of each tribe ... and
> the pitched battle involving a number from each tribe.[66]

Given Windschuttle's use of Milligan's vocabulary to prove that land
ownership was not part of the Tasmanians' mental universe, logic

would suggest that warfare was a part of it – that they too knew what a war was when they saw one.

If indeed there was no frontier war in Van Diemen's Land, all we can say is that many contemporaries, including active and retired military officers, were greatly mistaken. But so too are the modern military historians who have written on the subject and who also can recognise a war when they see one.[67]

Which brings us to the question of guerilla warfare, a subject which calls forth Windschuttle's scorn for historians who have imposed onto Aboriginal history 'an anachronistic and incongruous piece of ideology'. Reynolds, he asserts, imagines the Tasmanian Aborigines of the 1820s 'as the indigenous equivalent of Che Guevara or Ho Chi Minh'.[68] Apart from being a flight of fancy this dismissal fails to come to terms with the matter at hand. There are two distinct questions that require answers. Was the conflict in Tasmania considered to be guerilla war at the time? Should it be so described now, given the importance that guerilla warfare attained in the middle of the twentieth century?

The word 'guerilla' entered the English language during the Peninsular War in Spain. It meant literally 'a small war'. It came to mean an irregular war carried on by small bodies of men acting independently and was applied quite commonly to a range of situations and was so employed in Tasmania to refer to both the Aborigines and the European Roving Parties. In February 1830 the *Colonial Times* reported on the activities of '*Guerilla* parties under the command of Gilbert Robertson'.[69] In his *History of Tasmania* John West explained how increasing violence in the 1820s embittered both sides until 'every white man was a *guerrilla,* and every black an assassin'.[70] In his 1835 *The History of Van Diemen's Land* Henry Melville twice referred to *Guerilla* war conducted by the Tasmanians. The Black Line, he explained, was planned to 'put an end to the *Guerilla* war which had been so harassing and murderous in its effect'.[71] In 1847 the Superintendent of the Flinders Island settlement, Henry Jeanneret, outlined a history of the relations between the Tasmanians and the settlers which he had completed after talking at length to the older surviving members of the Wybalenna community. European violence had led the Aborigines to conclude that they were 'irrevocably destined to destruction'. From that period:

they engaged in a kind of guerilla warfare with the European population resorting, not ineffectually, to every resource their daring and cunning could suggest.[72]

The term guerilla war was applied to Aboriginal resistance in both Western Australia and New South Wales in the 1830s.

There is, then, nothing anachronistic about referring to guerilla war in the 1820s, nor is there any incongruity in applying the term to Aboriginal patterns of resistance. In his standard work *Guerrilla: A Historical and Critical Study*, Walter Laqueur pointed out that:

> In actual fact, guerilla warfare is as old as the hills and predates regular warfare. Primitive war was, after all, largely based on surprise, the ambush and similar tactics.[73]

Windschuttle's attempt to judge what happened in the 1820s by what he believes are contemporary benchmarks for guerilla warfare is the endeavour wherein anachronism abounds.

Whether the Black War measures up to modern guerilla war is a far less significant question, and it all depends on how that subject is viewed – there is no generally accepted interpretation of what is, or is not, a guerilla war. Windschuttle's opinion that the Tasmanians couldn't have been guerillas because they didn't attack soldiers and they lacked a political objective is a purely subjective judgement of no particular significance. Leading authorities on the subject think otherwise. Take for instance the views of Major-General John Coates, retired head of the armed forces as well as being one of Australia's leading experts on insurgency and guerilla warfare. In his recent *An Atlas of Australia's Wars*, he observed that there was now a widespread view that frontier conflict was war. 'That it was also warfare of a particular type – guerilla warfare – does not disqualify it.'[74]

Why is Windschuttle so determined to argue that the Aborigines could not have been fighting a guerilla war? It would seem that when he was a young man guerillas had cachet and prestige, attributes which he has assiduously denied to the Tasmanians. Consistent with this is the absence from his work of any of the many commentators who admired the courage and skill of the Aboriginal warriors, who noted the increasing sophistication of their campaigns. Symptomatic of this denial is his attitude to Governor Arthur. The record quite clearly shows in Arthur's reports and dispatches a growing respect for his 'open enemies'. Windschuttle will have none of this and ridicules the view that the Governor 'showed an old soldier's respect for his Aboriginal adversaries'.[75] It will surprise no one that Arthur's lament of 1833 cannot be found in *The Fabrication of Aboriginal History*; that is, his regret at being

> reduced to the necessity of driving a simple but warlike, and, as it now appears, noble-minded race, from their native hunting grounds.[76]

It would be hard to find any statement more subversive of the whole Windschuttle case – the conflict was about land, the Tasmanians were not criminals but noble and warlike. Yet when other historians fail to mention events or observations which Windschuttle thinks important and which, to his way of thinking disrupt their theses, he accuses them of airbrushing such events and observations out of history and pretending they didn't happen.

Closely related to the question of warfare is the issue of the Aboriginal death toll arising from conflict with Europeans. Windschuttle concludes that the total number of 'plausible killings' between 1804 and 1834 was 118 – considerably lower than the 189 Europeans known to have died at the hands of the Tasmanians. This claim made very good copy, but the suggestion that it is remotely possible to find a precise figure for Aboriginal mortality indicates that Windschuttle is more interested in sensation than in sensible historical interpretation. All that he 'plausibly' can do is to argue that he has estimated a figure from the available written records.

His approach can be contrasted with the work of Plomley, whose earlier research provides the basis for Windschuttle's table of Aboriginal deaths. Windschuttle acknowledges his debt to Plomley's *The Aboriginal/Settler Clash in Van Diemen's Land 1803–1831* and observes that among the tables and graphs the author 'declined to make a separate tally of black casualties'.[77] But what Windschuttle fails to do is to make any reference to Plomley's consideration of the subject – based on more than twenty-five years of research. Plomley stressed that the attempt to quantify the results of conflict fails from a paucity of records, particularly for the period between 1811 and 1823. There are almost no early records at all for the settlement of northern Tasmania. All Plomley is able to say of the north is that despite the spread of settlement south into the Midlands,

> the record of Aboriginal affairs in that region has not been studied, if indeed records exist. All we know is that the occupation of the Midlands by the settlers resulted in the decline of the Aboriginal population living there.

The written record is far more extensive in the 1820s. Even in this case, though, it is an act of little more than bravado to assume that it is possible to account for every Aboriginal death directly or indirectly caused by the Europeans during the period of the Black War. Plomley estimated that between 1824 and 1831 the Tasmanian population declined from 1500 to 350. This seems to be a reasonable conclusion: there can be little serious debate about the population in 1831; and although Windschuttle attempts to prove that there were fewer Aborigines on the island than was previously thought, the figure of 1500 seems a reasonable one as well. There was, then, in all likelihood a steep decline in the Tasmanian population during the period of the Black War. What percentage could in any sense be considered to be casualties of war can be debated endlessly. A definite conclusion is beyond us.

Then there is the question of unrecorded killings. Windschuttle is able to leave these out of his calculations. But less acceptable is the fact that he fails to deal adequately with the large amount of testimony throughout the early years of settlement from many settlers about the activities of stockmen, sealers, bushrangers and escaped convicts. The armed and usually mounted stockmen who inhabited the outer fringes of settlement and the sealers living on the Bass Strait islands were almost universally reputed to be the main destroyers of the Aborigines. There seems no compelling reason to doubt that this was the case. In fact it is hard to find anyone who argued this was not so. And it's not as though the matter wasn't constantly discussed in official documents, in letters of the settlers and in newspaper articles. There are literally dozens, if not hundreds, of references to the murderous attacks by the 'borderers' as they were called. There is much more circumstantial evidence about ruthless attacks on the Aborigines than exists to support many of Windschuttle's propositions about frontier conflict. Space forbids more than a brief reference to the extensive literature. Governor Arthur observed in a dispatch to the Colonial Office in 1828 that on arrival in the colony he found that 'the quarrel of the natives with the Europeans' was:

> daily aggravated, by every kind of injury committed against the defenceless Natives, by the stockkeepers and sealers, with whom it was a constant practice to fire upon them whenever they approached ...[78]

The Aborigines Committee also dealt with the question and took testimony from persons of 'long residence in the Colony' who explained that the Tasmanians had been 'sacrificed in many instances to momentary caprice or anger'.[79] Windschuttle's response to the committee's findings about the brutality of convicts and bushrangers is quite characteristic. The report, he noted, found that they were 'probably guilty of a number of atrocities'.[80] To argue that many Aborigines were not killed in unrecorded clashes overlooks a huge body of circumstantial evidence and suggests that large numbers of reputable colonists were suffering from a collective delusion.

There are other serious problems with Windschuttle's calculations of Aboriginal deaths. He lists those Tasmanians killed, by which he presumably means those people who died on the spot or within the view of the Europeans and whose bodies could be counted. But how many more died subsequently of their wounds out of the sight of Europeans? To suppose there weren't any at all beggars belief. Given that Europeans often used shot rather than ball, and that their guns were inaccurate at the best of times, the likelihood of injury rather than immediate death must have been extremely high. Gunshot wounds would have been very hard to treat adequately by traditional means, especially among incessantly moving nomadic bands under enormous pressure for much of the time during the 1820s. It is not unreasonable to assume that as many Tasmanians succumbed to their wounds out of sight of the settlers as died in their view. G. A. Robinson

noted on Flinders Island how many of the inmates carried wounds
from the Black War. There was:

> not an aborigine on the settlement nor an aboriginal that has been at
> the settlement but what bears marks of violence perpetrated upon
> them by the depraved whites. Some have musket balls now lodged in
> them ... Some of the natives have slugs in their bodies and other con-
> tusions, all inflicted by the whites.[81]

Windschuttle shows almost no interest in the impact on Aboriginal
society of the intense pressure applied by the settlers, the soldiers and
the Roving Parties and whatever vigilante groups were roaming about
at the time. The Tasmanians must have assumed that any group of
Europeans was potentially dangerous. The fact that the parties usually
failed to come up with the Aborigines was a testimony to how quickly
and frequently they had to flee. They clearly lived with constant danger and acute anxiety for months and years on end. The military
officer in charge of the detachment at Bothwell observed in March
1830 that the Big River tribe had been able to avoid the military
patrols and that they had:

> suffered but little from our exertions, yet the constant state of alarm
> they must be left in, and the frequent change of positions rendered
> necessary to avoid the parties must be very harassing to themselves
> and their families.[82]

The colonial historians showed an understanding of the hardships
suffered by the beleaguered tribes in the 1820s. John West observed
that:

> in their harassing life, parents and children had been broken up in
> melancholy confusion. ...Infanticide and distress, rapid flight, and all
> the casualties of a protracted conflict, threatened them with speedy
> destruction.[83]

Bonwick pictured the Tasmanians on the eve of their exile:

> They had fought for the soil, and were vanquished. They had lost
> fathers, brothers, sons in war. Their mothers, wives and daughters,

harassed by continued alarms, worn out by perpetual marches, enfeebled by want and disease, had sunk down one by one to die in the forest, leaving but a miserable remnant. Their children had been sacrificed to the cruel exactions of patriotism, and had perished of cold, hunger and fatigue.[84]

The Victorian prose may be unfashionable but both Bonwick and West show the capacity for empathy and compassion so conspicuous by its absence in the pitiless prose of Keith Windschuttle.

In assessing the reason for Aboriginal attacks on the Europeans, Windschuttle determines that the desires for revenge and for plunder were the driving forces. He leaves out the most widely reported reason common to accounts of both Aborigines and settlers alike – rape and abduction of women. G. A. Robinson constantly refers to this in his journal. The complaints made to him were that white men had 'ravished their wives and daughters',[85] had carried the women away into captivity. They had violated them and taken them away from their tribes.[86] In a letter to James Burnett, the Colonial Secretary, Robinson wrote:

> The natives complain in bitter terms of the cruelty to which they and their progenitors have been subjected by the merciless white men … and also complain of their women having been forced away, and they put the question how white men would like Black men to steal white women …[87]

Lieutenant Darling recorded similar complaints following his conversations with the Aborigines recently exiled from mainland Tasmania. In a letter to the Governor, he wrote:

> If Sir, these people appear to us to be savage and bloodthirsty, it can easily be accounted for, without attributing to them any of these qualities. The sealers, stockkeepers and other persons of that description have robbed them of their wives and daughters and otherwise ill-treated them.[88]

European sources contain many similar reports. Governor Arthur determined that it was the constant practice of stock-keepers and sealers 'to deprive them of their women whenever the opportunity offered'.[89]

The Aborigines Committee provides similar evidence. Windschuttle praises this body highly and berates other historians for not treating its reports with sufficient respect.[90] Its reports are central to his thesis about Aboriginal motivation. In pursuing his case that the desire for revenge dominated their behaviour he quotes a long passage from the report of 19 March 1830 which contains the sentence:

> They were sacrificed in many instances to momentary caprice or anger, as if the life of a savage had been unworthy of the slightest consideration, and they sustained the most unjustifiable treatment in defending themselves against outrages which it was not to be expected that any race of men should submit to without resistance, or endure without imbibing a spirit of hatred and revenge.[91]

Having adduced evidence for Aboriginal vengeance Windschuttle brings his quotation to an end. The point of termination is especially significant. The following unquoted passage explains what the committee was actually referring to:

> The Committee allude to these attacks which, it has come to their knowledge, were then frequently made by lawless and desperate characters for the purpose of carrying off Native women and children; attempts which, if resisted, the aggressors did not scruple to accomplish with circumstances of dreadful and unnecessary barbarity.[92]

So there we have it. Windschuttle praises the work of the committee and quotes it at length to establish that the Tasmanians were driven by the desire for revenge. But he leaves out all references to the abduction of women. He does the same a few pages later when he quotes a passage from G. A. Robinson's journal about revenge but chooses one among many which makes no mention of rape and abduction.[93] Not that he avoids the question of sexual relations between white men and Aboriginal women. Far from it. But his interest is in pursuing every possible European reference to Aboriginal men prostituting their women in order to further his campaign of vilification. Not that Windschuttle has any direct evidence from Aboriginal men themselves – that is, the sort of evidence demanded by him of any writer who has viewed the Tasmanians favourably. When questions of land ownership and patriotic sentiment are discussed, Windschuttle demands verbatim statements from the Tasmanians themselves. When he wants to establish that Aboriginal men 'hired out and sold off their women without seriously contemplating the result',[94] any bit of scuttlebutt will do, and direct evidence from Aboriginal men themselves is not required. The topic of sexual relations between white men and black women is a complex one. Windschuttle's crude analysis rests on censoriousness and sensation.

The Fabrication of Aboriginal History is a remarkable book. It is, without doubt, the most biased and cantankerous historical work to appear since the publication of G. W. Rusden's three-volume *History of Australia* in the 1880s. But even Rusden's attacks on his political opponents fail to match Windschuttle's vilification of the Tasmanian Aborigines. And vilification is not too strong a word. The concept of savagery has been reborn.

Sympathy, empathy – even understanding – are missing from Windschuttle's book. He turns a deaf ear to the many reports which exist of bitter Aboriginal complaint about the way they were treated. The most that he can say in response is that there was 'little doubt the Aborigines believed stories of this kind' and used them to justify 'their own attacks on the settlers and their servants'.[95] But he knows better. Almost every contemporary observation expressing respect or admiration for the Tasmanians is 'airbrushed' out of existence. Even in colonial society few writers exhibited such distilled contempt for the Aborigines.

When it comes to assessing evidence, Windschuttle operates a system of filters. When the evidence inclines one way, the finest filters are used to screen out almost everything of relevance. When it leans in the other direction, almost everything passes the checkpoint. The persistent inconsistency in the use of evidence frequently lifts the text into the higher reaches of hypocrisy. Witnesses giving testimony against the Aborigines are treated quite differently from those telling a competing story. The convict whose evidence is useful is an honest man; the one who tells an unwelcome tale is dismissed as a hardened criminal. Things get more confusing when the same witnesses are treated differently according to the colour of their testimony.

At the whim of the author the same person can be a reliable witness or a mendacious scoundrel. Hearsay evidence can be dismissed or accepted according to the demands of the moment. Accounts of Aboriginal behaviour can be either valuable or worthless depending on the circumstances. It's all rather confusing for the attentive reader.

The Fabrication of Aboriginal History is not so much a thesis as an anthology of arguments. And there are hundreds of them. They are all pursued with equal combative vigour whether they are over a minor point in a citation or a major one of interpretation. But there are so many of them that the author loses track. They tumble over one another and contradict each other. Windschuttle tries to bring some order to the yelping disputation by creating a mythical collective called the conventional historians of Tasmania, yoking together writers of different periods, diverse ages, outlooks and attitudes with contrasting and often conflicting interpretations. As a result he can present himself as standing alone struggling heroically under the banner of truth against a disreputable intellectual junta. And what a pack of rascals they are – guilty of fraud, malpractice, fabrication, deception and suppression of information. His most sustained, detailed work is employed to prove everyone else is wrong. He seems to think that the corollary of his attacks on other historians is that he must be right. But many of his own interpretive forays are unsupported by evidence – they are mere assertions which the reader is expected to take on trust because he fills up his text with detail, some of it of antiquarian interest, much of it irrelevant.

How do we explain the animus towards the Tasmanians? Whence comes the passion? Windschuttle himself is no help here. He has told interviewers that he has no political motives and that he is only interested in discovering the truth. It's hard to know whether this is a pose or a reflection of his private thoughts. If this is what he really thinks, we can only look on in amazement at the entire absence of self-reflection – the inability to account for the force and the press of his own passion. But there are intimations here and there which help us to understand some of the deficiencies of *The Fabrication of Aboriginal History*. He has no ear for complexity, no eye for the subtleties of character. He is unable to give life to the people who inhabit the book, even to people as interesting as George Arthur and George Augustus Robinson. We may also be closer to understanding the crudity with which Windschuttle deals with other historians, the reliance on cartoon-like characterisation.

His book is also diminished by its depiction of the Aborigines. Such primitive people lack intellectual or moral depth. They are unable to play a role in a complex story. Windschuttle occasionally uses the word tragedy. But he does not mean this in the sense of loss, of catharsis. The reader who follows him uncritically through the book would have to conclude that such primitives were destined for well-earned oblivion.

Even some of Windschuttle's admiring reviewers have suggested that he has gone too far in his vilification of the Aborigines. And there is much evidence of an egregious lack of judgement. But they miss the point. If the object is to undermine all those staples of contemporary indigenous politics – land rights, self-determination, reparation, even the need for a prime ministerial apology – then the necessary and log-ical path is the one opened up by Windschuttle that leads to the inter-related concepts of savagery and *terra nullius*. If the desire is to forestall the emergence of Aboriginal nationalism, then the way to do it is to rob indigenous communities of anything in their past that might nurture pride and self-confidence.

The bevy of right-wing identities who are now following their pied piper show no concern about the direction or the destination of their journey. They seem to be rejoicing as they go, glad once more that they can feel relaxed and comfortable about their history.

NOTES

1. K. Windschuttle, *The Fabrication of Aboriginal History: Volume One, Van Diemen's Land, 1803–1847*, Sydney, Macleay Press, 2002, p. 111.
2. *Ibid*, p. 110.
3. H. Ling Roth, *The Aborigines of Tasmania*, F. King and Sons, Halifax, 1899.
4. S. A. Wurm, *Languages of Australia and Tasmania*, The Hague, Mouton, 1972, p. 168.
5. See T. Crowley, Tasmanian Aboriginal Language, in M. Walsh & C. Yallop, *Language & Culture in Aboriginal Australia*, Canberra, AIATSIS, 1992, pp. 51–72.
6. N. J. B. Plomley, *A Word List of the Tasmanian Aboriginal Languages*, Hobart, Tasmanian Government, 1976, p. xiv.

7. *Ibid*, p. 4.
8. N. J. B. Plomley, *The Tasmanian Tribes and Cicatrices as Tribal Indicators, etc.*, Launceston, Queen Victoria Museum, 1992, p. 7.
9. Roth, *Aborigines*, appendix B, pp. xlv, xlvi.
10. *Ibid*, pp. 104–5.
11. N. J. B. Plomley, *A Word List*, pp. 191–3.
12. N. J. B. Plomley (ed.), *Friendly Mission: The Tasmanian Journals and Papers of George Augustus Robinson 1829–1834*, Hobart, Tasmanian Historical Research Association, 1966, appendix 5, pp. 968–76.
13. J. Milligan, *Vocabulary of the Dialects of Some of the Aboriginal Tribes of Tasmania*, Hobart, Tas. Govt. Printer, 1890, p. 13.
14. Roth, *Aborigines*, appendix B, p. xlvii.
15. *Ibid*, p. ix.
16. Windschuttle, *Fabrication*, p. 89.
17. Tasmanian State Archives, hereafter TSA, CSO/1/323, p. 66.
18. J. B. Walker, *Early Tasmania*, Hobart, Tas. Govt. Printer, 1914, p. 242.
19. Backhouse to Buxton, 22/10/34 in Select Committee on Native Inhabitants, British Parliamentary Papers, 1836, no. 538, vol. 7, p. 680.
20. Arthur to Goderich, 7/1/1832, CSO/280/33.
21. Walker, *Early Tasmania*, p. 256.
22. A. G. L. Shaw (ed.), *Van Diemen's Land*, THRA, Hobart, 1971, p. 80.
23. J. West, *A History of Tasmania* [1852] ed. A. G. L. Shaw, Sydney, Angus & Robertson, 1971, p. 322.
24. Windschuttle, *Fabrication*, p. 99.
25. Shaw, *Van Diemen's Land*, p. 55.
26. TSA: CSO/1/323, p. 289.
27. T. Scott, Rubicon, TSA: CSO/1/323.
28. Arthur to Goderich, 10/1/1828.
29. Plomley (ed.), *Friendly Mission*, p. 61.
30. *Ibid*, p. 88.
31. Windschuttle, *Fabrication*, p. 100.
32. N. J. B. Plomley (ed.), *Weep in Silence: A History of the Flinders Island Aboriginal Settlement*, Blubber Head Press, Hobart, 1991, p. 733.
33. Windschuttle, *Fabrication*, p. 100.
34. Plomley (ed.), *Friendly Mission*, p. 571.
35. G. A. Arthur Papers, vol. 28, Mitchell Library mss. A2188.
36. G. A. Robinson Papers, vol. 11, Mitchell Library mss. A7032.
37. Plomley, *Weep in Silence*, p. 725.
38. TSA: CSO/1/331, p. 172.
39. TSA: A.O./E.P., p. 383, 19/11/1828.
40. Windschuttle, *Fabrication*, pp. 102, 108.
41. *Ibid*, p. 100.
42. Plomley, *Friendly Mission*, p. 302.
43. TSA: CSO/1/331, p. 175.
44. Plomley, *Weep in Silence*, p. 992.
45. *Ibid*, p. 999 (emphasis original).
46. Windschuttle, *Fabrication*, p. 130.
47. *Ibid*, p. 195.
48. *Ibid*, p. 196.

49. Bathurst to Darling, 14/7/1825, *Historical Records of Australia*, Series 1, vol. XII, p. 21.
50. See H. Reynolds, *Fate of a Free People*, Ringwood, Penguin, 1995, pp. 95–6.
51. TSA: A.O./E.P., p. 230.
52. *Ibid*, p. 370.
53. See pp. 184–96.
54. Alfred Stephen, TSA: GO 33/7, p. 901.
55. Shaw, *Van Diemen's Land*, p. 20.
56. *Ibid*, p. 4.
57. Windschuttle, *Fabrication*, p. 98.
58. *Ibid*.
59. *Ibid*, pp. 197–8.
60. Clark to Burnett, TGO: CSO/1/316/7578.
61. *Colonial Times*, 26/2/1830.
62. Shaw, *Van Diemen's Land*, p. 11.
63. *Ibid*, p. 63.
64. *Ibid*, p. 64.
65. Milligan, *Vocabulary*, pp. 49–51.
66. Plomley, *A Word List*, p. 223.
67. See for instance: J. Connor, *The Australian Frontier Wars, 1788–1838*, Sydney, UNSW Press, 2002; J. Grey, *A Military History of Australia*, Cambridge, Cambridge University Press, 1990; J. Connor, British Frontier War Logistics and the 'Black Line', Van Diemen's Land … 1830, *War in History, vol. 9, no. 2, 2002*, pp. 143–58.
68. Windschuttle, *Fabrication*, pp. 103, 404.
69. *Colonial Times*, 19/2/1830.
70. West, *History of Tasmania*, p. 276.
71. Henry Melville, *The History of Van Diemen's Land*, 1835, p. 91. See also p. 26.
72. TSA: CSO/11/26/455.
73. Walter Laqueur, *Guerrilla: A Historical and Critical Study*, London, Weidenfeld & Nicolson, 1977, p. vii.
74. John Coates, *An Atlas of Australia's Wars*, Melbourne, Oxford University Press, 2001, p. 6. Coates wrote one of the standard works on insurgency. See his *Suppressing insurgency: An analysis of the Malayan Emergency, 1948–1954*, Boulder, Westview, 1992.
75. Windschuttle, *Fabrication*, p. 97.
76. Arthur to Goderich, 6/4/1833, Colonial Office, CO/280/41.
77. Windschuttle, *Fabrication*, p. 362.
78. Shaw, *Van Diemen's Land*, p. 3.
79. *Ibid*, p. 36.
80. Windschuttle, *Fabrication*, p. 118.
81. Plomley, *Weep in Silence*, p. 464.
82. TSA: CSO/1/322, p. 323.
83. West, *History of Tasmania*, p. 309.
84. J. Bonwick, *The Last of the Tasmanians*, London, Sampson Low, Son and Marston, 1870, p. 226.
85. Plomley, *Friendly Mission*, p. 88.
86. *Ibid*, p. 202.
87. Robinson to Burnett, 30/8/1831, Robinson Papers, vol. 21, Mitchell Library mss. A7042.

88. Plomley, *Weep in Silence*, p. 992.
89. Shaw, *Van Diemen's Land*, p. 3.
90. Windschuttle, *Fabrication*, p. 117.
91. Shaw, *Van Diemen's Land*, p. 36.
92. *Ibid.*
93. Windschuttle, *Fabrication*, p. 120.
94. *Ibid*, p. 386.
95. *Ibid*, p. 121.

Re-inventing Social Evolution

Shayne Breen

In *The Fabrication of Aboriginal History*, Keith Windschuttle portrays indigenous Tasmanians as the most primitive society known to man. They are a doomed race treading a path to inevitable extinction. They are robbers, murderers and bushrangers with a natural criminal inclination. Windschuttle claims they were intellectually and organisationally incapable of mounting an effective military challenge to their invaders, that they had no sense of politics and no sense of collective interest. He portrays the men as thugs who sold their defenceless women into prostitution, thereby causing widespread venereal disease and the eventual demise of their people (a classic case of blame the victim). To top it all off, Windschuttle claims Tasmanian Aborigines lacked the defining human virtue of compassion.

The portrayals of Aborigines in Windschuttle's *Fabrication* are drawn from nineteenth-century ethnology. In promulgating them anew, Windschuttle has comprehensively failed to consult the wide range of authoritative scholars who reject the views that he supports. Instead he has relied on the eighteenth-century concept of savagery and the nineteenth-century theory of social evolution. Such images and ideas appeared regularly in colonial newspapers from the time they were first published in Van Diemen's Land, as well as in official documents and in scientific and historical literature.

None of Windscuttle's characterisations is historically or anthropologically verifiable. They reflect opinion, perception and ideology.

Their presence in Windschuttle's work renders absurd his claim that his work is free of ideology. He presents these images as historical truth, and he uses them to support his core arguments. He demands that historians provide forensic proof for their claims, especially in relation to frontier violence, but he offers no forensic proof for the ways in which he characterises Tasmanian Aboriginal society and culture. In fact, as I shall argue here, Windschuttle's images of Tasmanian Aborigines are historical fabrications plundered from the handbook of social evolution and re-invented by Windschuttle.

Social Evolution

The theory of social evolution was constructed following the publication of Darwin's *Origin of the Species* in 1859. Its informal history, however, can be traced to the 2000-year-old concept of the Great Chain of Being, which ordered species on an evolutionary ladder from the most simple organism to the most complex. During the early decades of colonisation, Australian Aborigines were commonly seen as the lowest form of humanity on the Great Chain, and hence as the people most poorly equipped to climb the evolutionary ladder. Darwin's work on evolution in the natural world was appropriated by lesser writers and theorists, in particular Herbert Spencer with his notion of survival of the fittest, and taken as confirmation of the earlier conceptions.[1]

According to the theory of social evolution, peoples passed through three key stages on the path to evolutionary perfection: savagery, barbarism and civilisation. In the Western world-view, this theory assumed the force of natural law. Blacks and hunter-gatherers were savages. Savages had no political organisation, no capacity for ethics or compassion, no sense of land ownership, no artistic refinement, no aesthetic sensibility. Barbarians were those peoples with political and military organisation but without aesthetic or emotional sensibility. The civilised, of course, possessed everything that the others lacked. European society exhibited all the desired characteristics, and the English had the best of them.[2]

Much 'scientific' activity in late nineteenth and early twentieth-century Australia, North America and Europe was conducted in the context of social evolution. The common aim was to prove scientifically that social evolution was not merely a theory but an empirical fact. It was therefore necessary to prove that discrete races existed and that cultural capacities were biologically determined. By the end of the nineteenth century, social evolutionists were asserting that Tasmanian Aborigines were the missing link between apes and man. They were the most primitive people the world had known. The final movement in the theory of social evolution, from the 1880s to the 1930s, is known as 'scientific racism'. Adherents professed to have proved scientifically that some races were inherently or biologically superior to others, and in particular that white races were superior to black. Scientific racism's twentieth-century manifestations included apartheid in South Africa and segregation in the United States and Australia. Its ultimate development was reached in the Nazi extermination camps during World War II.[3]

Certain key words, including 'primitive', 'simple' and 'savage', were used habitually by colonial observers in all British colonies, including Tasmania, to describe tribal cultures. When used in the context of social evolution, these words were not neutral or value-free. They had particular connotations that enabled readers to locate the race under discussion within the social evolutionary framework. The description of a people or their culture as primitive or simple located that people in the evolutionary stage of savagery. Over time, these meanings became embedded in the words. When Windschuttle uses words such as 'primitive' and 'simplistic' to describe Tasmanian Aborigines, he is not using value-free words.[4] These words operate as a code for social evolutionist ideology. If he is not aware of this, he should be, since it has long been clear that much past writing about Tasmanian Aborigines was produced by adherents of social evolution. Yet Windschuttle avoids any discussion of the concept of savagery or of the wider framework of social evolution. In *Fabrication*, social evolution never appears explicitly, but it is everywhere as an assumption.

The Most Primitive Ever

Windschuttle claims that at the beginning of the nineteenth century, Tasmanian Aborigines were 'the most primitive society ever discovered'. In support of this claim, reference is made to the Tasmanian Aborigines' technology, their hunter-gatherer economy, their mobility and their sanitary habits.[5] In making this claim, Windschuttle relies on two writers whose views have undergone substantial challenge and are no longer regarded as authoritative.

According to Windschuttle, the most useful overall view of Tasmanian Aboriginal culture is H. Ling Roth's *The Aborigines of Tasmania*, published in 1899. Windschuttle ignores the verifiable historical fact that Ling Roth's work is steeped in the theory of social evolution. Ling Roth is a primary source for the study of social evolution in Tasmania, not an authoritative source on the nature of Tasmanian society. Windschuttle also ignores Cassandra Pybus's exposition of the extraordinarily simplistic scientific method used by Ling Roth in the 1880s to prove that Fanny Cochrane-Smith was not a full-blood, hence not a real or authentic Aborigine, and hence not entitled to a small land grant. Ling Roth relied on a photograph of Fanny that showed she did not look like Trugannini, and a single strand of hair that he thought was too straight to belong to a full-blood.[6]

Windschuttle's second major source in support of his 'most-primitive-ever' claim is the archaeologist Rhys Jones. Windschuttle invokes an argument, put at the end of the 1960s by Jones, that isolation from mainland Australia caused an inevitable degeneration, or strangulation, of Aboriginal intelligence and culture. Jones argued that as a result of isolation following the flooding of the Bassian Plain some 8000 years ago, Tasmanian Aborigines stopped evolving, were perhaps devolving, so that by the early nineteenth century they possessed the simplest culture in the world. His evidence included the decision to drop fish from their economy some 4000 years ago, an apparently simple tool kit, and a supposed inability to light fire. Isolation, in short, deprived the Tasmanian Aborigines of the opportunity to evolve their culture, and probably caused it to degenerate.[7]

Windschuttle knows that the degeneration claim and the evidence on which it is based are now strongly disputed, at a theoretical level and in relation to Tasmania. He has consulted only a tiny fraction of recent archaeological and anthropological scholarship that challenges the 'most-primitive-ever' claim in a range of technological, economic and cultural contexts. He ignores evidence that a significant cooling of the global climate about 4000 years ago coincided with a major phase of Aboriginal adaptation, not only in Tasmania but also across south-east Australia. Archaeological evidence suggests that some 3000 years ago the Tasmanian population increased and spread into previously unoccupied parts of the island. It seems that 3000 years ago Aborigines at Louisa Bay, in the island's far south, developed seaworthy watercraft that enabled regular seasonal visits across often-treacherous waters to de Witt and Mattsuyker Islands to hunt seals. At the same time, significant artistic developments occurred, and the practice of firing the country to promote pasture growth, maintain pathways and minimise bushfire was introduced over much of the island. These developments, and their concurrence with similar developments in south-east Australia, contradict the strangulation view.[8] But with the same contempt he displays elsewhere for Lyndall Ryan and Henry Reynolds, Windschuttle dismisses these arguments as politically motivated rationalisation.[9]

Although he claims that Tasmanian Aborigines were unable to light a fire, Windschuttle has not even bothered to consult recent work on this topic. As James Boyce has shown elsewhere in this book, the claim that the Aborigines did not have a method for lighting fire is now generally discredited. Windschuttle's source for the claim is Brian Plomley's 1966 publication, *Friendly Mission*. He has not consulted a 1973 paper by German anthropologist Gisela Volger that argues the percussion method was used, nor a 1991 paper by myself that supports and consolidates Volger's arguments, nor a recent paper by Monash University biologist Beth Gott that further consolidates the percussion view, nor solid linguistic evidence for the percussion method currently being advanced by University of Tasmania MA candidate John Taylor.[10]

Windschuttle also seeks to bolster his most-primitive-ever argument with the claim that Tasmanian Aborigines had no sacred sites.[11] This presumably means that in Windschuttle's view they had nothing deserving the name of religion. Rhys Jones argued in 1969 that Tasmanian religion was clearly inferior to that of mainland Australia[12] where, as many anthropologists have shown, an extraordinarily sophisticated religious culture was practised. In which case, it's a pity when he was inventing his *Fabrication* that Windschuttle did not consult Julia Clark's 1987 article which argues that, despite the very limited documentary evidence of Aboriginal religious culture, it is clear from G. A. Robinson's journals that at least four of the seven key metaphysical elements of spirituality that W. E. H. Stanner found on mainland Australia were present in Tasmania. Elements present in Tasmanian myths included the view that the world was full of signs that were transformed into assurances of mystical providence, the view that the material domain was under spiritual authority, and the view that the nature of man and the condition of human life were axiomatic.[13]

Clark also found evidence of several creation myths similar to those found on mainland Australia, and evidence of at least one significant sacred site, at Cox Bight in south-west Tasmania. The story of a large rock at Cox Bight is a common Australian Aboriginal story of transaction and transformation. The large rock is an ancestral being called *Moihernee*, who was hurled down from heaven, died and was transformed into the rock. Clark regards this as a critically important Tasmanian myth because it is the only one of which she is aware that connects living people, ancestral beings and country. These are the types of myths commonly used on mainland Australia to support land claims.[14]

In further support for his most-primitive-ever argument, Windschuttle claims that Tasmanian Aborigines demonstrated no evidence of collective interest.[15] Presumably he means they had no sense of collective interest whatsoever, because if they did, it would have come into play in the conflict with their invaders. Commonsense would suggest that the capacity to survive over 35,000 years would imply some level of collective interest, as would their reciprocal exchange system, but no, Windschuttle's *Fabrication* would have us believe that Aboriginal survival came down to a single factor: 'good fortune'. Presumably he knows this claim is preposterous, but he makes it anyway. Every historian knows that significant events rarely have a single cause, but not Windschuttle. Most thinkers would accept that collective interest is a pre-condition for social survival, so Windschuttle has to claim, which he does, that Tasmanian Aborigines had no ethics and no capacity for compassion.[16] This claim indisputably locates the Aboriginal subjects of Windschuttle's *Fabrication* at the savagery stage of social evolution.

The clearest evidence that Aborigines did have a sense of collective interest can be found in their system of reciprocal exchange, especially of ochre. Ochre was not necessary to material survival, although it clearly was important in ritual and creative life. Groups that controlled access to ochre entered into trade arrangements with others. Groups providing ochre received hunting rights in the country of groups receiving ochre. There is ample evidence of this, and more generally there is ample evidence that the system of reciprocal exchange was as important in Tasmanian social and economic life as it was on mainland Australia.[17]

Robbers and Murderers

In his classical 1852 defence of colonisation, Launceston historian John West elevated Tasmanian Aborigines from the condition of aimless savagery to the second evolutionary stage of barbarism.[18] Windschuttle chronicles a similar shift. Following contact with Europeans, the isolated primitives were transformed into incorrigible barbarians. Windschuttle's shift is evident in his view that Aboriginal attacks against colonists constituted no more than robbery, murder and arson. Further, he asserts that Tasmanian Aborigines were not merely engaging in criminal behaviour but giving vent to a natural criminal inclination and an inherent pleasure in inflicting pain on others.[19]

Two points are important here. The first is that – as Henry Reynolds has shown elsewhere in this book – the British were convinced that there was a guerilla war between the settlers and the Aborigines, and that the Aborigines were fighters acting in defence of their country. They were not mere robbers and murderers. Second, Windschuttle fails to adhere to the standards he seeks to impose on others. He argues, for example, that a direct quotation from an Aborigine is necessary evidence for any claim that they were defending their country,[20] but he provides no direct quotations from any Aborigine, or any linguistic evidence, that they regarded themselves as robbers, murderers and arsonists.

What might be called the 'treacherous criminal' view deployed by Windschuttle is itself a product of the colonial encounter. American historian Winthrop Jordan has argued that freed African Negroes in America were seen to be potentially – if not actually – in a state of insurrection. Black and free equalled insurrection. Barry Morris has argued that force was seen by colonists in New South Wales as a necessary part of black–white contact because Aborigines were perceived to be inherently treacherous. I have put a similar argument for Tasmania. The perception in New South Wales and Tasmania that force was necessary was prompted and legitimated by a conception – based on real and imagined fears – of Aborigines as savages and barbarians inherently inimical to colonisation.[21]

To support his case for inherent criminality, Windschuttle also claims that the Tasmanian Aborigines were incapable of military organisation.[22] Contrary to what Windschuttle claims, there is strong evidence for Aboriginal capacity for military organisation. The intensification of conflict in the late 1820s gives a strong impression of organised attacks, carried out on a seasonal basis. One example is from the central north of the island during the late spring and early summer of 1827. At least 19 separate incidents occurred in this period, including nine between 10 and 24 November. At least eight Europeans were killed, in addition to spearings, other woundings and general harassment. Huts were plundered and burnt, and at least a hundred sheep were killed at Lake River. It is easy to claim that such incidents do not imply considered action, that they occurred coincidentally in the course of seasonal travel. Both claims may be plausible, but it is reasonable to argue that nine incidents in 14 days strongly suggests organised action. More generally, the apparent increase in conflict in the late 1820s, when the Aboriginal population was very low, also suggests organised action.[23]

Aboriginal capacity for military organisation is also evident in the range of tactics used by Aborigines. Official documents and contemporary observers commonly acknowledged and sometimes admired the Tasmanians' tactical skill in conflict. Tactical skill would seem to imply a capacity for military organisation. Tactics used included avoiding military contact in favour of surveillance of colonists, which sometimes culminated in retribution spearings and sometimes killings, both of which derived from traditional warfare practices, as did the use of smoke signals to communicate information. Selective attacks, whether planned or unplanned, lessened the risk of reprisal, as did the skilful exploitation of topographical advantage. Innovations included the theft of British food, which increased mobility and lessened the risk of capture or reprisal. Firearms were taken and sometimes used. Stock was killed, haystacks were burnt and seed was ruined, tactics commonly portrayed by post-colonial historians as economic warfare.[24] These are tactics of the sort adopted by small-scale fighters against heavily armed invaders, tactics commonly referred to as guerilla warfare – a type of warfare that needs to be understood not, as Windschuttle wants, according to some precise definition, but rather according to the specific contexts in which the conflict occurs.

The argument that Aborigines practised economic warfare particularly rankles with Windschuttle. In a long-winded discussion, he embellishes his characterisation of Aborigines as incorrigible criminals with an argument that Aborigines were insatiable plunderers. Plundering is taken by Windschuttle as evidence of criminality, and as evidence of an incapacity for organised military activity.[25] Windschuttle should read some military history. Plunder has always been an integral part of warfare. As Daniel Mannix once said, all wars are trade wars.

Irrespective of the nature of Aboriginal military organisation, it is clear that their actions were militarily effective. This can be discerned from the colonial response, both politically and on the ground. From the mid-1820s, when the pastoral invasion intensified, the military effectiveness of the Aboriginal response can be read in Arthur's Aboriginal policy. Arthur deployed detachments of military to sites of conflict. He introduced martial law, effectively suspending common-law rights for Aborigines and granting to colonists immunity from prosecution. He established roving parties and the Black Line, and with G. A. Robinson he engineered the removal of Aboriginal survivors to Flinders Island.[26]

The military effectiveness of Aboriginal fighters was based on their tactical skill. Aboriginal fighters were reactive to the changing circumstances of colonial occupation, they were advantaged by their knowledge of local topographies and they acted within the limits of their available range of options. They were never going to mount an organised campaign that the British might recognise as warfare waged by civilised states. Windschuttle's argument for a lack of organisational capacity is a furphy.

Chronic Abusers

In addition to being primitive, barbaric and inherently criminal, Tasmanian Aboriginal society was maladaptive, according to Windschuttle. In his view, Aboriginal men were chronic and violent abusers who took advantage of the arrival of Europeans to sell their women into prostitution. This behaviour, Windschuttle asserts, is evidence of a maladaptive society that was culturally vulnerable to the impact of colonisation.[27] Neither of these claims, for chronic male abuse or the selling of women into prostitution, is supported by adequate argument or evidence.

No substantial evidence exists to show that Aboriginal men chronically abused their women. Evidence of harsh treatment and a secondary status for women in tribal society does exist, but this cannot be taken as proof for chronic abuse. Harsh treatment and a secondary status for women are characteristic of many cultures, including Western cultures. The evidence cited by Windschuttle for abuse of women comes almost entirely from the late 1820s, by which time tribal culture and its social protocols were radically altered. It is also clear that by the late 1820s, the concept of savagery had taken root in the colonial imagination, increasing the likelihood that observations made during this period were strongly influenced by a pre-conceived idea of indigenous Tasmanians as treacherous savages.

Nor is there substantial evidence that Aboriginal men sold their women into prostitution. There is no doubt that Aboriginal women had sexual relations with their invaders. But the means by which Aboriginal women came to be involved with European men cannot be reduced to a single factor, let alone to forced prostitution. Several points cast considerable doubt on the prostitution argument. Windschuttle provides no direct quote from any Aborigine, male or female, that supports the claim that women were sold into prostitution. Nor does he provide linguistic evidence for the existence of an Aboriginal concept of prostitution. Windschuttle assumes that Aborigines had such a concept, but since there is no documentary evidence to support him he has no option but to impose the concept upon them.

It is clear that Aboriginal men, especially along the northern and eastern coastlines, used women as commodities in trade with colonisers. But such trade does not equate to prostitution. The women had considerable skill and experience in hunting seals. One could just as easily argue that the women went to work for the sealers. Sexual services might or might not have been included in arrangements made. Sometimes arrangements were culturally sanctioned, sometimes they were not. Sometimes women willingly participated, sometimes they did not.[28]

There is solid evidence that some sealers who benefited from the culturally sanctioned trade involving women failed to honour the arrangements they had made with Aboriginal men. It is also clear that the abduction of Aboriginal women by colonists occurred across the island for much of the period. Indeed, the 1830 Aborigines Committee found that the abduction of women was a major cause of attacks against colonists by Aborigines.[29] Windschuttle's claim that Aboriginal men sold their women into prostitution fails to take adequate account of the substantial and credible documentary evidence of abduction.

The claim that Aboriginal men sold their women into prostitution is important to Windschuttle's frontier conflict argument. It provides an alternative explanation for Aboriginal population decline. If he can demonstrate that prostitution-induced disease was the primary cause of population decline, the focus shifts away from death by violence.

One major cause of population decline, he argues, was that venereal disease rendered Aboriginal women infertile. Prostitution exposed women to venereal diseases, and therefore Aboriginal men were responsible for the fate of their women and general population decline. This argument is not supported by evidence. It is very likely that disease-induced sterility did contribute to a falling birthrate, but the claim that this was a major cause of population decline is a guess. Windschuttle provides no forensic evidence, of the sort that he demands in relation to frontier violence, in support of the claim. His discussion of death from disease relies entirely on Robinson, who began his journals in 1829.

Robinson recorded no stories of the impact of European disease in the early period of occupation. On the basis of Aboriginal deaths at Macquarie Harbour (where Aborigines were briefly imprisoned in 1833) and further deaths on Flinders Island in the 1830s, Windschuttle concludes that 'it was likely' European disease had a 'dramatic effect' on population levels, and that the sealers were 'probably' responsible for introducing such disease. On this basis, Windschuttle argues that the evidence for disease as a major cause of depopulation is 'compelling'.[30]

One variant of Windschuttle's male abuse argument is the claim that Tasmanian Aborigines were unable to feel compassion. According to Windschuttle, compassion is a peculiarly Western characteristic, a claim for which he provides no evidence or citation.[31] The claim that Aborigines had no compassion was commonly made prior to 1850 and by social evolutionists later in the nineteenth century. It is interesting, then, that Peter Coleman and Ron Brunton, both regular *Quadrant* contributors, have detected in Windschuttle's *Fabrication* a lack of compassion for the destructive and painful experience of colonisation endured by indigenous Tasmanians. Alan Atkinson and Tom Griffiths, in relation to Windschuttle's *Quadrant* articles, have noted the same absence.[32]

Perhaps it is futile to expect a social evolutionist to feel compassion for savages, but the point about compassion and who may lack it recalls Winthrop Jordan's discussion of Shakespeare's 'blackness within' and the associated idea that whites have historically treated blacks as if they were external projections of their own capacity for savagery and evil.[33] Interesting, then, that two of Windschuttle's major charges against others – fabrication (by other historians) and lack of compassion (by Aborigines) – have now been levelled against the accuser, and not only by members of the 'orthodox school'.

Fabricated Aborigines

Like many things in Windschuttle's *Fabrication*, present-day Tasmanian Aborigines are fabricated. In the final section of his book, headed 'The Invention of Aboriginality', Windschuttle argues that present-day Tasmanian Aborigines are not authentic Aborigines but rather impostors invented by 1970s radicalism, in particular by Michael

Mansell, in order to access newly available government funds and obtain free land. They have no legitimate claim to reparation for historical injustice because they are descended from whites as well as Aborigines – in fact, they are now virtually whites because they are at least five generations removed from 'real' Aborigines.[34]

Windschuttle's understanding of the concept of authenticity is superficial. He uncritically accepts the notion of authenticity as empirical fact. He offers no discussion of what authenticity might mean in the historical Tasmanian context. He fails to consult, let alone to critically analyse, the considerable body of scholarly writing that challenges the usefulness of the notions of racial and cultural authenticity.[35] He is unaware of Patrick Wolfe's notion of 'repressive authenticity', wherein the claims of 'invented' indigenes in the present are rejected in favour of those whose living actuality more closely resembles 'traditional' culture and society.[36]

In Windschuttle's *Fabrication*, culturally authentic Aborigines are tribal, or 'traditional'. The traditional Aborigine is a timeless, static, prehistoric artefact best embodied in the anthropological stereotype, perched on a rocky outcrop, one leg resting on the other, leaning on his spear, surveying his domain. The consequence of this thinking is that urban Aborigines are de-tribalised and hence not authentic.[37] As Wolfe has shown, the notion that a real Aborigine is a traditional Aborigine has recently been used to deny native title to most indigenous peoples in Australia and North America.[38] It is also commonly used in the cultural tourism industry, where an indigenous cultural experience is seen to be authentic if it replicates some aspect of indigenous culture that existed in the past, especially if the experience offered is located in 'the outback'.[39]

Racial authenticity is similarly embedded in the past, with the key difference that racial authenticity is measured by a combination of blood quantum and the generational distance of a person in the present from a racially authentic ancestor. A racially authentic ancestor is seen as a full-blood. Anything less than full-bloodedness, especially four or five generations distant, means that the present-day individual is not racially authentic. He or she is both racially and culturally too distant from the authentic ancestor to be authentic, or real. As Geoffrey

Blainey puts it in his review of Windschuttle's *Fabrication*, 'most of the thousands who now call themselves indigenous Tasmanians possess only a minority strand of that ancestry'.[40]

The notion of racial authenticity employed by Windschuttle has its roots in nineteenth-century social evolution, where racial authenticity was based on the hypothesis that pure, discrete racial categories (full-bloods) with biologically determined characteristics actually existed. Evolutionary scientists, most notably a group at the University of Melbourne just prior to World War I, tried desperately but failed to prove that racial categories actually existed, that there was such a thing as a pure race. Nevertheless, they persisted with the belief that 'full-bloodedness' conferred authenticity, or purity.[41]

The 'authenticity' of present-day Tasmanian Aborigines has been historically denied on two grounds. First, 'real' Aborigines became extinct when Trugannini died in 1876. Their demise was explained not by British violence but by their evolutionary unfitness, their inherent incapacity to progress to the superior stage of civilisation. They were fated to die out because they lacked the moral and intellectual capacity to progress beyond the stage of barbarism. Second, the 'mixed-blood' descendants of the extinct Tasmanians have had their authenticity repressed through a series of linked categories that have been imposed on them by adherents of social evolutionism. According to late-twentieth-century social evolutionists, including N. J. B. Plomley and Windschuttle, post-1876 Tasmanian Aborigines have moved through the successive stages of half-caste, hybridity and inauthenticity on their way to whiteness.

The first-generation, mixed-blood descendants of Aboriginal women and European sealers were labelled half-castes. Half-castes themselves were doomed to extinction because they could never constitute more than one generation. Half-castes gave way to hybrids, which combined characteristics of races that were supposed to be inherently distinct. The scientists explained away the anomaly of race-mixing by regarding half-castes and hybrids as freaks of nature that violated accepted assumptions of what constituted a natural racial category. Blood mixing was believed to contaminate both white and black races, and was held to cause biological degeneration because mixed-bloods supposedly inherited the worst characteristics of both races.[42] In line with this thinking, evolutionary scientists in the 1920s and 1930s assumed, often despite compelling evidence to the contrary, that Tasmanian hybrids combined the worst characteristics of both races, especially since most were descended from primitive Aborigines and the worst of British convicts.[43]

By the 1970s, few writers, with the notable exception of Plomley, portrayed Tasmanian Aborigines as hybrids. In 1977, Plomley claimed, somewhat obviously, that, 'structurally, physiologically and psychologically hybrids are some mixture of their parents'. He argued that in social terms, hybrids belonged to neither of the races from which they were descended, that they were shunned by both, 'and lacking a racial background they have no history'.[44] In 1987, Plomley repeated the claim that the so-called hybrids were an impoverished people who had lost most of their culture.[45]

The Tasmanian Aboriginal writer Ian Anderson published a detailed discussion of the hybridity issue in 1997, but Windschuttle ignores it.[46] And, from this basis of ignorance, Windschuttle asserts that Aboriginal identity in Tasmania has been lost and Aboriginal culture has become extinct.[47] In addition to Plomley, Windschuttle relies on two other sources, both anecdotal, to support his claim that real Tasmanian Aborigines no longer exist. He quotes an interview with an islander of Aboriginal descent shown in the 1976 film *The Last Tasmanian*, and he quotes Patsy Adam-Smith's 1965 observation that during her time on the islands researching her book *Moonbird People*, the last 'quarter-caste', a man called Walter Beeton, died.[48]

In making his case that real Aborigines no longer exist, Windschuttle ignores a considerable body of evidence that demonstrates the historical continuity of Aboriginal culture in Tasmania. He ignores the detailed historical work of Stephen Murray-Smith. He ignores Irynej Skira's recent doctoral thesis, which demonstrates the centrality of mutton-birding to the maintenance and reproduction of Aboriginal cultural identity. He makes no attempt to consult the range of official documentary sources which strongly suggest that Aboriginal identity was maintained and reproduced down the generations, and that the Aboriginal Islander demand for land rights has an historical basis dating back to at least the early 1850s. Nor does Windschuttle explain why a reserve for Aboriginal half-castes was created with laws that denied common-law rights to Aborigines, nor does he consider the difficulties involved in open identification in a state that had a White Australia policy, nor does he explain why, in the mid-twentieth century, many Tasmanian Aboriginal children were removed from their parents, nor does he consider the memoirs produced by elders Ida West and Molly Mallett, both of whom strongly identify as Aboriginal.[49]

The Islander tradition of political activism illustrates my point. From the 1850s onwards, the Islander community, through letters, petitions and representations to government, actively pursued the return of land. The Islanders believed they should be given control of the mutton-bird rookeries as compensation for the British invasion and theft of their ancestors' lands. Their insistence on the maintenance of a culture based on hunting and community rather than European farming and social individualism brought them into regular conflict with Tasmanian authorities, especially the various missionaries who were sent to 'civilise' them.[50]

The formation in 1897 of an Islander Association to agitate for control of the rookeries resulted in the 1912 *Cape Barren Island Reserve Act*. The Reserve was intended as a place of subjugation to government authority and transformation into peasant farmers. Successive governments offered only limited access to rookeries and unwanted leaseholds on small, infertile agricultural blocks. In subsequent decades, the Islanders regularly challenged the power of local authorities, consistently defied unpopular provisions of the Reserve Act and maintained a lifestyle and an identity clearly linked to their Aboriginal ancestors. When Michael Mansell presented a petition for land rights to Queen Elizabeth in 1976, he was not, as Windschuttle suggests, fabricating Aboriginality, he was adding one more chapter to the long history of Aboriginal Islander activism.[51]

Conclusion

Windschuttle criticises 'orthodox' historians for failing to 'enter the mentality' of Aboriginal people.[52] But he himself comprehensively fails to do just that. He fails to realise that Ryan, Robson and Reynolds have used an approach similar to the one articulated by Rhys Isaac, whereby the actions of non-literate peoples are understood in terms of the cultural values and assumptions which are likely to come into play in incidents described in evidence. Reynolds and Ryan both argue that in their early relations with colonists, the actions of Aborigines in Tasmania were governed by Aboriginal principles of exchange; similarly, in the late 1820s, Aboriginal responses were governed by the perception that their land – and livelihood – was being taken from them. This is a straightforward method in ethno-history: identify key operational principles in the society in question, then apply those principles in efforts to explain reported actions.[53]

Presumably Windschuttle believes that he has entered the mentality of the Aboriginal peoples. Yet his portrayal of Aboriginal culture and society is deeply embedded in the racial strictures of social evolution. Windschuttle has not entered the mentality of Aborigines, rather that of the colonists who dispossessed Tasmanian Aborigines of their land, then invented social evolutionist rationalisations that portrayed Aborigines as subhuman savages. In Windschuttle's *Fabrication*, Aborigines progress from the stage of savagery, as isolated and intellectually regressive primitives, to the intermediate stage of barbarism, where, in the period of dispossession, they are criminals and thugs. Those who survive the coming of the white man ascend to the lower levels of civilisation where they simultaneously become inauthentic Aborigines and assimilated whites.

Windschuttle's preoccupation with verifiable body counts, and with demonstrating what he claims was the inherent barbarism of Tasmanian Aborigines, results in a comprehensive failure to locate his analysis in relevant broader contexts. And, as every historian except Windschuttle knows, no context, no history. In truth, Windschuttle's *Fabrication* is not a work of history, but the simulated proceedings of a neo-conservative kangaroo court in which the self-proclaimed master of the forensically plausible inadvertently demonstrates how not to write history.

NOTES

1. The seminal work on the Great Chain of Being is Arthur Lovejoy, *The Great Chain of Being: A Study in the History of an Idea*, Massachusetts, Harvard University Press, 1957. For discussion of racial ideology in early colonial Australia, see Bernard Smith, *European Vision and the South Pacific*, London, Oxford University Press, 1960; Henry Reynolds, 'Racial thought in early colonial Australia', *Australian Journal of Politics and History*, vol. 20, no. 1, 1974, pp. 45–53; A. T. Yarwood and M. J. Knowling, *Race Relations in Australia: A History*, Sydney, Methuen, 1982, pp. 12–22; Richard Broome, *Aboriginal Australians: black responses to white dominance, 1788–1994*, Sydney, Allen & Unwin, 1994, ch. 2; Andrew Markus, *Australian Race Relations 1788–1993*, Sydney, Allen & Unwin, 1994, ch. 1; Henry Reynolds, *Fate of a Free People*, Ringwood, Penguin, 1995, pp. 70–4.

2. M. C. Hartwig discusses social evolution in 'Aborigines and racism: an historical perspective', esp. pp. 15–18, in F. S. Stevens (ed.), *Racism: the Australian experience*, vol. 2, Sydney, ANZ Book Company, pp. 9–24; and for a discussion of similar views in nineteenth-century USA, see John S. Haller, Jr, 'Race and the concept of progress in nineteenth-century American ethnology', *American Anthropologist*, no. 73, 1971, pp. 710–24.

3. For detailed discussion of scientific racism in Australia, see John Cove, *What the Bones Say: Tasmanian Aborigines, Science and Domination*, Ottawa, Carleton University Press, 1995; Russell McGregor, *Imagined Destinies: Aboriginal Australians and the Doomed Race Theory, 1880–1939*, Melbourne, Melbourne University Press, 1997. For examples of Tasmanian writing located within the framework of social evolution, see for example James Barnard, 'Aborigines of Tasmania', in *Transactions of the Australasian Association for the Advancement of Science*, vol. 2, Hobart, 1890, pp. 597–611; H. Ling Roth, *The Aborigines of Tasmania*, Halifax, F. King & Sons, 1899; and W. L. Crowther, 'The Aboriginal Natives of Van Diemen's Land', *Papers & Proceedings of the Royal Society of Tasmania*, no. 1, 1924, pp. 166–7.

4. Windschuttle, *Fabrication*, p. 377

5. *Ibid*, p. 377

6. *Ibid*, p. 377; Roth, *Aborigines*; Cassandra Pybus, *Community of Thieves*, Melbourne, Heinemann, 1991, ch. 10.

7. *Ibid*, p. 378; Rhys Jones, 'Tasmanian Paradox', in R. V. S. Wright, *Stone Tools as Cultural Markers: Change, Evolution and Complexity*, Ottawa, Carleton University Press, 1977; N. J. B. Plomley, *The Tasmanian Aborigines*, Launceston, Plomley Foundation, 1993.

8. For a survey of these developments, and a discussion of relevant archaeological theory, see Harry Lourandos, *Continent of hunter-gatherers: new perspectives in Australian pre-history*, Cambridge/Melbourne, Cambridge University Press, 1997; and Josephine Flood, *The Riches of Ancient Australia*, St Lucia, University of Queensland Press, 1990, pp. 318–26. Other works include Steve Brown, 'Art and Tasmanian pre-history: evidence for changing cultural traditions in a changing environment', in P. Bahn and A. Rosenfeld (eds), *Rock Art and Prehistory: papers presented to Symposium G of the AURA Congress, Darwin 1988*, Indiana, David Brown, 1991, pp. 96–108; R. L. Vanderwal, 'Pre-history and the archaeology of Louisa Bay', in H. Gee and J. Fenton (eds), *The South West Book: A Tasmanian Wilderness*, Melbourne, Australian Conservation Foundation, 1979, pp. 17–22;

D. R. Horton, 'Tasmanian Adaptation', in *Mankind*, vol. 12, no. 1, 1979, pp. 28–34. Of the five works cited here, only Horton appears in Windschuttle's bibliography.

9. Windschuttle, *Fabrication*, p. 378.

10. N. J. B. Plomley (ed.), *Friendly Mission: The Tasmanian Journals and Papers of George Augustus Robinson, 1829–1834*, Hobart, Tasmanian Historical Research Association, 1966; Gisela Volger, 'Making fire by percussion in Tasmania', *Oceania*, vol. 44, no. 1, 1973, pp. 58–63; Shayne Breen, 'Tasmanian Aborigines: making fire', in *Papers & Proceedings*, Hobart, Tasmanian Historical Research Association, vol. 39, no. 1, 1992, pp. 40–3; Beth Gott, 'Fire-making in Tasmania: Absence of evidence is not evidence of absence', *Current Anthropology*, vol. 43, no. 4, 2002, pp. 650–55; John Taylor, pending, MA thesis, Launceston, University of Tasmania, 2003.

11. Windschuttle, *Fabrication*, p. 110.

12. Jones, 'Tasmanian paradox', p. 201.

13. Julia Clark, 'Devils and horses: religious and creative life in Tasmanian Aboriginal society', in Michael Roe (ed.), *The Flow of Culture; Tasmanian Studies*, Canberra, Australian Academy of the Humanities, 1987, pp. 50–72, esp. p. 58.

14. Clark, 'Devils and horses', pp. 58–9.

15. Windschuttle, *Fabrication*, p. 101.

16. *Ibid*, p. 406.

17. For a discussion of reciprocal exchange in Tasmania, see Rhys Jones, 'Tasmanian Tribes', in N. B. Tindale, *Aboriginal Tribes of Australia*, Canberra, ANU Press, 1974, pp. 343–46; Lyndall Ryan, *The Aboriginal Tasmanians*, second edition, St Leonards, Allen & Unwin, 1996, ch. 1; Claudio Sagona (ed.), *Bruising the Red Earth: Ochre Mining and Ritual in Aboriginal Tasmania*, Melbourne, Melbourne University Press, 1994.

18. John West, *History of Tasmania*, vol. 2, Launceston, Henry Dowling, 1852, pp. 92–6.

19. Windschuttle, *Fabrication*, pp. 95–103 (guerilla warfare), pp. 65–77, 130 (criminals), pp. 109, 127–8 (pleasure in violence).

20. *Ibid*, p. 93.

21. Winthrop D. Jordan, *The White Man's Burden: historical origins of racism in the United States*, London, Oxford University Press, 1974, pp. 221–2; Barry Morris, 'Frontier colonialism as a culture of terror', in Bain Attwood and John Arnold, *Power, Knowledge and Aborigines*, Melbourne, La Trobe University Press, 1992, pp. 72–87.

22. Windschuttle, *Fabrication*, p. 102.

23. N. J. B. Plomley, *The Aboriginal/Settler Clash in Van Diemen's Land, 1803–1831*, Launceston, Queen Victoria Museum & Art Gallery, Tasmania, 1992, pp. 44–51.

24. Plomley, *Tasmanian Aborigines*, p. 30; Ryan, *Aboriginal Tasmanians*, ch. 7; Henry Reynolds, *The Other Side of Frontier*, Melbourne, Penguin, 1982, pp. 103–110.

25. Windschuttle, *Fabrication*, pp. 116–29.

26. A. G. L Shaw (ed.), *Van Diemen's Land: Copies of all Correspondence between Lieutenant Governor Arthur and His Majesty's Secretary of State for the Colonies, on the subject of the Military Operations lately carried on against the Aboriginal inhabitants of Van Diemen's Land*, Hobart, Tasmanian Historical Research Association, 1971.

27. Windschuttle, *Fabrication*, pp. 377–86.

28. Ryan, *Aboriginal Tasmanians*, ch. 3.

29. Aborigines' Committee Report, 1830, in Shaw, *Van Diemen's Land: Correspondence.*

30. Ryan, *Aboriginal Tasmanians*, p. 169; Windschuttle, *Fabrication*, pp. 372–6.

31. Windschuttle, *Fabrication*, p. 406.

32. Ron Brunton, 'Fabrication fury, but the rest is history', *Courier-Mail*, 28/12/2002; Peter Coleman, 'The Windschuttle Thesis', *Quadrant*, December 2002; Alan Atkinson, 'Historians and moral disgust', 2003, pp. 113–19; Alan Atkinson, 'Historians and moral disgust', pp. 113–19, and Tom Griffiths, 'The language of conflict', pp. 135–49, both in B. Attwood and S. G. Foster (eds), *Frontier Conflict*, Canberra, National Museum of Australia, 2003.

33. Jordan, *White Man's Burden*, ch. 1.

34. Windschuttle, *Fabrication*, pp. 431–6.

35. Bill Ashcroft, Gareth Griffiths and Helen Tiffin (eds), *The Post-Colonial Studies Reader*, London/New York, Routledge, 1995; Homi K. Bhabha, *The Location of Culture*, London, Routledge, 1994; Keith Hollinshead, 'The dis-identification of Aboriginal life and traditions', in R. Butler and T. Hinch (eds), *Tourism and Indigenous Peoples*, London, International Thomson Business Press, 1996, ch. 13.

36. Patrick Wolfe, 'The limits of Native Title', in *Meanjin*, vol. 59, no. 3, 2000, pp. 129–144, esp. pp. 134–5.

37. Bain Attwood, *In the Age of Mabo*, Sydney, Allen & Unwin, 1996, 'Introduction', which discusses anthropological representations of Aborigines as timeless.

38. Wolfe, 'The limits of Native Title', pp. 130–2.

39. Heather Zeppel, 'Selling the Dreamtime: Aboriginal culture in Australian tourism', in D. Rowe & G. Lawrence (eds), *Tourism, Leisure and Sport: Critical Perspectives*, Sydney, Hodder Education, 1998, pp. 7–10; Hollinshead, 'The dis-identification of Aboriginal life and traditions', 1996, ch. 13.

40. Windschuttle, *Fabrication*, pp. 431–6; Geoffrey Blainey, 'Native fiction', in *The New Criterion*, no. 21, 2003.

41. Cove, *What the Bones Say*, pp. 62–70.

42. McGregor, *Imagined Destinies*, pp. 124–41.

43. Cove, *What the Bones Say*, pp. 60–5.

44. Plomley, *Tasmanian Aborigines*, p. 66;

45. N. J. B. Plomley (ed.), *Weep in Silence: A History of the Flinders Island Aboriginal Settlement*, Blubber Head Press, Hobart, 1991, p. 1.

46. Ian Anderson, 'I, the "hybrid" Aborigine: film and representation', *Australian Aboriginal Studies*, no. 1, 1997, pp. 4–14.

47. Windschuttle, *Fabrication*, p. 433.

48. *Ibid*, p. 433.

49. Stephen Murray-Smith, 'Beyond the Pale: The Islander community of Bass Strait in the nineteenth century', *Papers & Proceedings*, Hobart, Tasmanian Historical Research Association, vol. 20, no. 4, 1973, pp. 167–200; Irynej Skira, 'Tasmanian Aborigines and Mutton-birding: an Historical Examination', PhD dissertation, Launceston, University of Tasmania, 1993; Lyndall Ryan, 'Outcasts in White Tasmania', *Mankind*, vol. 8, no. 4, 1972, pp. 249–54; National Inquiry into the Separation of Aboriginal and Torres Strait Islander Children from their Families (Australia), *Bringing them home: report of the national inquiry into the separation of Aboriginal and Torres Strait Islander Children from their Families*, Sydney, Human Rights and Equal Opportunity Commission 1997, pp. 91–100; Ida West, *Pride Against Prejudice*, Canberra, Australian Institute of Aboriginal Studies, 1988; Molly

Mallet, *My past – their future: stories from Cape Barren Island*, Hobart, Blubber Head Press, 2001.

50. Ryan, 'Outcasts'; Ryan, *Aboriginal Tasmanians*, chs 15 & 16.
51. Cape Barren Island Reserve Act for Aboriginal half-castes, 1912; several reports were compiled during the 1920s and early 1930s, for example J. S. Needham, 'Cape Barren Island', *Australian Board of Missions Review*, no. 17, 1931, pp. 171–2; for a list of further reports, see Ryan, *Aboriginal Tasmanians*, chs 15 & 16 & pp. 335–6; Ryan, 'Outcasts in White Tasmania', 1972.
52. Windschuttle, *Fabrication*, p. 406.
53. Rhys Isaac, *The Transformation of Virginia, 1740–90*, Chapel Hill, University of North Carolina Press, 1982, pp. 323–29. Bain Attwood also used this approach in *The Making of the Aborigines*, Sydney, Allen & Unwin, 1989, ch. 6.

History and the Nation

Marilyn Lake

> What we need is to forget, and history is the opposite of forgetting.
> – Gaston Clemendot, Address to third Annual Congress of National
> Teachers' Union, France, 1923[1]

I grew up near Oyster Cove, in the D'Entrecasteaux Channel district, where the Aborigines, who had survived the violence of the frontier and subsequent exile to Flinders Island, had been re-settled in 1847, eventually to perish. I grew up completely unaware of this local history and the larger context of colonial dispossession on which white settlement – and our network of family farms – rested.

My great-great-grandfather's people had taken up land at Sandford, on South Arm, south-east of Hobart, in the early 1830s, but the settlement of new land continued up to the present. My grandfather had moved to the Channel district in the 1930s and my father cleared his own land after World War II. In the summer months, we sometimes walked to Oyster Cove to swim at Black Station, an inlet I always assumed was so named because of the charcoal colour of the mudflats, a sharp contrast to the white sands of the beach at Conningham, further along the road. Black Station has since been returned to Aboriginal Tasmanians and I have since realised the significance of the local place name.

I was a keen student of history, but learnt nothing about our colonial past, at school or university, despite the publication of several distinguished and popular histories, in and about Tasmania, including Henry Melville's *The History of Van Diemen's Land*, re-published in 1965, John West's *History of Tasmania*, re-published in 1972 and James Bonwick's *The Last of the Tasmanians*, published in 1870. Tasmanians wanted to forget their violent beginnings, whether located in colonial dispossession or convict transportation. The tourist destination of Port Arthur, with its burned-out convict ruins, merely served to emphasise that the past was dead and gone. The special status of the Tasmanian Hydro-Electric Commission, on the other hand, which powered Electrolytic Zinc and the Cadbury's factory, emphasised our modernity and progress. At the newly opened Taroona High School, where one of my teachers was Henry Reynolds (he taught English), I learnt only American history, using a textbook belonging to my brother, who had earlier studied the same subject at Hobart High School. Clearly history was best kept at a distance.

Nationalist Self-Innocenting

> It was a tragedy the Aborigines adopted such senseless violence. Their principal victims were themselves.
> – Keith Windschuttle, *The Fabrication of Aboriginal History*[2]

Australian history, as taught at university in the late 1960s and into the 1970s, was silent about frontier violence; it was, rather, the story of the development of national identity. Through the writings of Bob Gollan, whose essay 'Nationalism, the Labour Movement and the Commonwealth, 1880–1900' was published in Gordon Greenwood's *Social and Political History of Australia*, Russel Ward in *The Australian Legend*, A. A. Phillips in *The Australian Tradition*, Geoffrey Serle's *The Golden Age* and Manning Clark's *Select Documents* and *Short History of Australia*, we charted the development of national identity through a study of economic development, literary culture and democratic politics. The general interpretation was influenced by what Vance Palmer called *The Legend of the Nineties*, the idea that 'a scattered people, with its origins in all corners of the British Islands and in Europe, had a sudden vision of themselves as a nation, with a character of their own and a historic role to play, and this vision set fruitful creative forces in motion'.[3] The distinctiveness of the Australian culture and tradition and the novelty of its egalitarian political experiments inspired identification and shaped our sense of ourselves as Australian.

The more conservative *New History of Australia*, edited by F. K. Crowley, in reaction against the 'legend of the nineties', located Australia's founding moment in 1787 with its 'conception' as a convict colony. The natives appear on page 6. In an argument Windschuttle would repeat 30 years later, A. G. L. Shaw wrote that because the natives were nomads, they saw no difference between 'plundering and hunting' and did not 'resist the seizure of their [*sic*] land'.[4] Much of the book focused on land settlement, pastoralism and free selection, followed by accounts of the gold rushes, urbanisation, federation, the World Wars and so on. It was a story of white men's achievements: no Aborigines mentioned by name and few women. As I have commented elsewhere, women feature in the index between wombats and wool, with the entries for the latter more numerous. In his preface, F. K. Crowley explained that the book was structured 'to highlight the significant events and turning points in Australia's development, and to emphasise the continuity which exists between contemporary Australia and its recent and distant past'.[5] Whether radical nationalist or conservative, Australian history structured the past as a nationalist narrative to serve the present. There was nothing unusual in this. From its inception, modern history has helped construct the modern nation.[6]

For some time now, historians have pointed to the ways in which the writing of history has been complicit with, and shaped by, the demands of nation-building. 'Modern historical scholarship has its origins in the legitimatisation of the nation-state,' as Adam McKeown has recently noted, 'and historians have been slow to reach beyond those roots.'[7] History has taken as its natural subject the very formation it has helped to construct, but as Jerry H. Bentley noted at the most recent International Congress of Historical Sciences in Oslo, addressing the theme of 'Perspectives on Global History', 'the near-exclusive focus on the experiences of national communities and other ostensibly coherent and distinct groups has blinkered historians' vision and blinded them to processes that transcend single societies.'[8] Processes such as colonialism. These newer historians are arguing for the importance of trans-national frameworks of analysis for understanding historical process, but it has been history's complicity with nation-building – in our case with Australian and Aboriginal nation-building – which has made the interpretation of the past such a fraught and politically invested endeavour.

During the last twenty or so years there has been extensive national discussion about the meaning of Australian history in a debate which assumes an identification between the present and the past, conceptualised as the national heritage.[9] Is this heritage a source of national pride, or of national shame, as the new Aboriginal history, published from the 1980s, began to suggest? So influential was the new historiography on Aboriginal dispossession and frontier conflict that Keith Windschuttle has cast himself as a dissident battling a new 'orthodoxy'. More to the point, he sees himself as defending the honour and reputation of the Australian nation.

Windschuttle opens his book with a quotation from the former Governor-General Sir William Deane, who observed in a speech on the occasion of the centenary of federation that:

> The oppression and injustice to which indigenous Australians were subjected in our land and under our Federation were not merely the acts of individuals who are long since dead and for whose acts living Australians might deny responsibility. They are properly to be seen as acts of the nation itself of which all living Australians are members. As such, that past oppression and injustice remain part of the very fabric of our country. They reach from the past to blight the present and to demand redress and reconciliation in the future.[10]

Past oppressions are 'acts of the nation itself'. Windschuttle's book seeks to answer Deane's charge by rescuing the reputation of the founders of the nation. Rejecting representations of the colonists as brutal, callous murderers acting with genocidal intent, he offers alternative understandings of Lieutenant-Governor Arthur and his associates as conscientious men, shaped by Evangelical humanitarianism, and anxious about the dreadful prospect of escalating frontier violence leading to the extermination of the Aboriginal race.

Windschuttle seeks to redeem the settlers, first, by discrediting the historical scholarship of the 'orthodox school' as careless, inaccurate and unreliable – at worst, a fabrication – and second, by discrediting the Tasmanian Aborigines, describing them as 'the most primitive human society ever discovered'[11] and later, as criminals, thieves and murderers, addicted to white men's 'luxuries'. Aborigines were victims of their own 'senseless violence'. The settlers were innocents: they could not have stolen Aboriginal land because 'the Tasmanian Aborigines did not own the land.'[12]

Windschuttle goes to great pains to prove that Aborigines had no concept of land ownership and thus did not consider the British as trespassers or invaders. Yet, again and again, Windschuttle himself quotes witnesses observing that Aboriginal people bewailed their loss of country and held whites in general responsible for taking their country and its resources from them. 'They have a tradition among them', said George Augustus Robinson, 'that the white men have usurped their country.'[13] Or, as Lieutenant-Governor Arthur wrote to Viscount Goderich in 1828, 'They already complain that the white people have taken possession of their country, encroached upon their hunting grounds …'[14]

It would seem that Windschuttle, unlike Lieutenant-Governor Arthur and many colonists, cannot bring himself to recognise that the British settlement was founded on the violent dispossession of another people. In his narrative, it is the natives who are the plunderers, thieves and intruders, not the settlers. Because they travelled across other clans' country, 'they were intruders just as much as anyone from Europe'.[15] It is also the Aborigines who commit excessive violence: 'It is clear from the contemporary reports about Aboriginal killings of many white settlers that their murders were incidental accompaniments to robbery. The whites were unarmed and posed no deterrent to the Aborigines' main objective. They were killed simply because they could be.'[16] Nationalist narratives are self-innocenting narratives.

In her insightful study of the psycho-dynamics of nationalism in *States of Fantasy*, Jacqueline Rose invokes Christopher Bollas's concept of 'violent innocence' to refer to the nationalist syndrome of denial and defence, through 'projection' of what you least like about yourself on to an other.[17] Her analysis is useful for making sense of the excessive nature of Windschuttle's argument. 'The actions of the Aborigines were not noble,' he asserts, 'they never rose beyond robbery, assault and murder.'[18]

Rose refers readers to Linda Colley's work *Britons: Forging the Nation* in which Colley argues that 'regular *and violent* contact with peoples' defined the emergent nation-state (emphasis original) and its psycho-dynamics. Colley shows the ways in which the English staked out their superiority in their preoccupation 'with virtue in its civilised and potentially civilising mode: civility as detached benevolence, or endeavour, free enterprise, liberty as the sign of moral worth (hence Colley argues the preoccupation … with the freeing of slaves).'[19] And hence, too, Windschuttle's emphasis on the abolition of slavery as a sign of the virtue of the Evangelicals who 'founded' the Australian colonies:

> In the 1820s, as Van Diemen's Land wrestled with its growing Aboriginal problem, the Evangelical movement was demanding the complete abolition of slavery in the British Empire, an objective it finally achieved in 1833 … In Van Diemen's Land itself, Evangelicalism remained an important religious and social force throughout the 1820s and 1830s. Lieutenant-Governor Arthur himself was, according to his biographer, 'a devout and convinced evangelical' who had already, in his previous administration, given a practical demonstration of his beliefs when he set free the Indian slaves of British Honduras.[20]

Windschuttle's is a self-innocenting narrative, casting our national forebears as caring, Christian civilisers motivated by concern for the hapless natives. He goes to considerable lengths to show that the 'orthodox school' exaggerated the numbers killed by the colonists and the extent of massacres. The legendary Risdon Cove massacre of 1804 was mere myth and Lyndall Ryan's account of a massacre of the Port Dalrymple people in 1827 'pure fiction'.[21] More whites were killed in frontier conflict than blacks.

Yet Windschuttle's own evidence suggests that the colonists – in fits of conscience – continually blamed themselves for the escalation of hostilities. To quote Lieutenant-Governor Arthur again: 'all aggression originated with the white inhabitants'.[22] It was the settlers' outrages – or, according to the gentry and officials, those of the lower orders, the convicts and bushrangers – that had led to understandable retaliation and a spirit of vengeance. As the Broughton Committee reported, Aborigines 'sustained the most unjustifiable treatment in defending themselves against outrages which it was not to be expected that any race of men should submit to without resistance, or endure without imbibing a spirit of hatred and revenge'.[23] In colonial memory, the story of the 1804 Risdon Cove massacre came to serve symbolically – like Eve's bite of the apple – as the originating transgression. In Arthur's words: 'the quarrel of the natives with the Europeans, occasioned by an unfortunate step of the officer in command of the Garrison on the first founding of the Settlement was daily aggravated by every kind of injury committed against the defenceless natives.'[24]

Patriarchs Doomed to Die

> The native in Australia … must disappear.
> – Mary Fullerton, *The Australian Bush*[25]

The logic of Windschuttle's self-innocenting account demands that he resurrect the old nationalist conceit that Aborigines were 'a dying race'. Windschuttle finds the chief cause and symptom of Aboriginal backwardness and 'vulnerability' to lie in the men's treatment of the women as 'drudges' and 'prostitutes'.[26] There was much evidence, writes Windschuttle, of their brutality towards their women and 'the violent nature of the relations between the sexes'.[27] The violence perpetrated by colonists is thus displaced onto Aboriginal men in a rhetorical move with a long tradition in imperial and nationalist writing.

One of the central fantasies of nationalist writing in Australia has been that the national character was born in the bush – Russel Ward was drawing on long-established precedent. The land thus acquired spiritual significance for non-Aboriginal as well as Aboriginal Australians. Mary Fullerton's *The Australian Bush* was a classic in the genre, published in London in the late 1920s and dedicated to 'the memory of the stout-hearted – The pioneer Men and Women of the Bush'. Her account of the development of the nation is haunted by the absent presence of the Aborigines, but she assures her readers that they 'must disappear'. As a 'menace to settlement' the Aborigine was 'practically dead', his extinction read as a foregone conclusion:

> He will linger on, a wretched remnant to be cared for by whites, for
> fifty years or so yet; when he must disappear, leaving hardly a mark of
> his poor vagrant existence on the face of the land.[28]

Her account prefigures Windschuttle's in the connection drawn between the patriarchal nature of Aboriginal society and their unfitness to survive.

As justification for the settlers' appropriation of Aboriginal country, Fullerton points to the alleged 'chattel' status of Aboriginal women:

> the female Aborigine, the lubra or 'black gin' as she is called … has no
> status, no right of any sort at any time. From start to finish she is a
> chattel to be claimed or disowned, beaten, burdened, or even killed at
> the discretion of her men-folk. The Australian lubra is veritably the
> most pitiful being in existence.[29]

Faithfully echoing this assessment, Windschuttle reports: 'The first European observers called the men "indolent" and "extremely selfish" and said they treated their women like "slaves" and "drudges".'[30]

Mary Fullerton revisited this theme in 1934 on the occasion of the centenary of the colony of Victoria, when she wrote a story she named, appropriately, 'A Fantasy'. As Jacqueline Rose argues, 'fantasy' plays a key role in the 'fierce blockading protectiveness' of nation-building. Fantasy 'plays a central, constitutive role in the modern world of states and nations'.[31] In Fullerton's account of the colonial encounter in Victoria, she imagines the response of the 'Yarra Yarra tribe' when they confront the first 'white men'. There were early warning signs, portents of change, most notably in an Aboriginal woman's defiance of her patriarchal master:

> That which had never been had happened now; a lubra had rebelled.
> They felt the dark approach of Change, were silent in the shade of
> things to be that had not been.[32]

When the 'lubra' returns to her tribe she has a fearful tale to tell of the arrival of the 'great white men'. While the younger tribal men are keen to defend their land ('The Bush that they would steal is ours; we shall preserve our own'), the king in his wisdom counsels resignation:

> The dark man's kingdom was to pass from his dominion. The great wide bush that their nomadic feet had trod since ocean made it land, would pass to these new lords. These pallid men ...[33]

Thus are the usurpers freed from the responsibilities of historical agency. Doomed by the laws of evolution and progress, the Aborigines must succumb to the logical succession of settlement.

In Windschuttle's account, Aborigines are also doomed, but he opts for anthropological/sociological discourse to explain their fate: their society is 'dysfunctional', 'maladaptive' and 'regressive'.[34] It is moreover morally unfit. The men brutalised the women and only 'men who held their women cheaply would allow such a thing to happen'.[35] The characterisation of Aboriginal women as the 'slaves', 'chattels' and 'drudges' of their men was central to the settlers' 'violent innocence'.

In recent decades – especially from the 1970s – a large body of scholarship has taken issue with this bleak account of gender relations in Aboriginal society, scholarship with which Windschuttle seems unfamiliar. This more recent anthropological and historical writing suggests that Aboriginal women's physical strength and capacity for labour was empowering rather than degrading; and that Aboriginal women's autonomy, independence and self-sufficiency may more accurately be read as a source of status and self-esteem rather than as subordination. The fact that sexual relations with white men led to women's infection with venereal and other diseases would seem to be reason for indictment of the white men who infected them, rather than the Aboriginal women who engaged in what Windschuttle calls 'self-prostitution'. Although he cautions elsewhere that the historian's duty is to try to see the world through the eyes of his subjects and enter their 'very different mentalities', in this instance Windschuttle simply recapitulates nineteenth-century moral judgments and sexist double standards.

Mary Fullerton's writing in the 1920s and 1930s was haunted by the fate of the Aborigines. With the advent of professional history in the 1950s and 1960s, however, Aborigines had disappeared from accounts of the Australian past, if not from Australia itself. But with new campaigns for Aboriginal citizenship rights launched by organisations such as the Aboriginal-Australian Fellowship and the Federal Council for the Advancement of Aborigines, indigenous leaders began to demand acknowledgment of past injustice and recognition of 'land rights'. Suddenly, Australian history had to come to terms with the fact that Aborigines had not disappeared, not even in Tasmania – as a demonstration against the premiere of the film *The Last Tasmanian* attested. Historians such as Henry Reynolds and Lyndall Ryan began to write a new national history, one that foregrounded frontier warfare and the political resistance of an emergent Aboriginal nation. Much of Windschuttle's passion is directed at discrediting the idea that Aborigines were patriots or nationalists fighting for their country. Rather, he says, they were opportunistic criminals, engaged in assault and murder, 'two customs they had come to relish'.[36]

As proof that Tasmanian Aborigines were not fighting in defence of their country, Windschuttle cites the example of the Port Davey Mob from the south-west, 'one of the most active bands in murdering and robbing white settlers' in the districts around Hobart. They had no patriotic or territorial motives, he argues, because no one 'had taken their land or disturbed their hunting grounds ... There was no white settlement in their area ... and still none, even today. It remains uninhabited wilderness.'[37]

Windschuttle's argument about the Port Davey Mob highlights one of the key weaknesses of his historical analysis: his failure to see that collective identities – nations and classes, 'Aborigines' and 'white men' – are themselves produced in historical process, in dynamic interaction between the colonised and the colonisers. As Martin Daunton and Rick Halpern point out in their introduction to the collection *Empire and Others*, 'the identities of both the British and indigenes were subject to constant re-negotiation.'[38]

Englishmen Becoming 'White Men'

> [Aborigines have] a strong thirst for revenge against all white men.
> – Lieutenant-Governor Sorell, quoted in the Broughton Report[39]

In her new book, *Civilising Subjects: Metropole and Colony in the English Imagination 1830–1867*, Catherine Hall offers an extended analysis of the racialisation of English identity which was central to 'the making of colonising subjects' in the early nineteenth century.[40] Much of her study is concerned with the same culture of Evangelical humanitarianism that Windschuttle calls up in his discussion of Lieutenant-Governor Arthur, but unlike Windschuttle, Hall shows the ways in which identities and selves were made and re-made in the often-violent relations of colonial rule. She understands history and the making of national identities as dynamic intertwined processes.

Windschuttle's historical subjects, by contrast, act out static and unchanging roles. Lieutenant-Governor Arthur is confined to his unchanging role as Evangelical humanitarian. The Port Davey mob must forever act as the Port Davey Mob, with no wider 'collective interests' or 'patriotic' motives. Aborigines in general had 'no sense of a collective interest of any kind'.[41] Yet it is clear that by the 1820s and 1830s a collective indigenous memory of brutality, murder and suffering was generating a new sense of collective identity. As Henry Reynolds has argued, the traumatic experience of colonisation united Aborigines. By the time of the 1846 Flinders Island petition, addressed to the Queen, it is evident that Aborigines from different regions and tribes had come to see themselves as one people, as fellow countrymen, as poor blackfellows.[42]

It is also clear that Aboriginal people were active in identifying all settlers – whether hut-keepers, clergymen, convicts or military officers – as one people, as 'white men', whom they held jointly responsible for taking their land. Older ethnic or national identities as English, Irish, Cornish or Jewish were subsumed in the racial classification of 'white'. As Robinson reported, Aboriginal people linked the injuries done to Aborigines with an emergent understanding of their 'white enemies':

They have a tradition among them that white men have usurped their territory, have driven them into the forests, have killed their game and thus robbed them of their chief subsistence, have ravished their wives and daughters, have murdered and butchered their fellow-country-men; and are wont whilst brooding over these complicated ills in the dense part of the forest, to goad each other on to acts of bloodshed and revenge for the injuries done to their ancestors and the persecutions offered to themselves through their white enemies.[43]

The colonial encounter was crucial, as historians of empire have recently argued, to new understandings of what it meant to be British, as well as what it meant to be Aboriginal:

It was not merely that imperial power, springing from many sources, classified, defined and sought to dominate indigenous peoples, but that equally the identities of Britons themselves took shape in relation to the colonised 'other'.[44]

Colonialism was a two-way encounter in which the British trans-formed the lives of indigenous peoples, but the colonial experience also re-defined British identities. The fact that Aboriginal retaliation and revenge were 'indiscriminate' (as Windschuttle argues) is explained by the Aboriginal perception that a group of people defined by their 'whiteness' had taken their country. The racialised identity of the colonists was itself one of the main outcomes of the colonial encounter. Aboriginal perception and response thus played a key role in producing the settlers' racial identity as 'white men' and by extension the racial identity of the emergent nation, in whose name the federal fathers would formulate the project of White Australia. 'In the catego-rization of other peoples and the marking of difference between the British and their others', as Hall writes, 'new selves were constructed, new identities demarcated for those who were ruling as well as those who were ruled.'[45] In identifying himself as a 'white man', the Australian colonist initially defined that emergent identity in terms of his difference from Aborigines, who were deemed deceitful, lazy, cunning, dependent, dishonourable and uncivilised.

As suggested at the beginning of this chapter, the project of

Australian history has conscripted the past into the service of the nation, constructing a story of national identity, development and achievement. Catherine Hall has suggested a different historical approach: 'A focus on national histories as constructed, rather than given, on the imagined community of the nation as created rather than as simply there, on national identities as brought into being through particular discursive work, requires trans-national thinking.'[46] Such trans-national thinking might begin by placing the colony and metropole in the one analytic frame so that we might better understand the 'mutual constitution' of coloniser and colonised. In the colonial encounter, Englishmen became 'white men'. By attending to the dynamic and violent nature of the colonial encounter, and the racialisation of colonial identities, we can also begin to understand the ways in which racial thinking became central to Australian identity and the national project, which themselves can only be understood in the larger imperial context.

NOTES

1. Mona Siegel, '"History is the Opposite of Forgetting": The Limits of Memory and the Lessons of History in Interwar France', *Journal of Modern History* 74, 4, December 2002.
2. Keith Windschuttle, *The Fabrication of Aboriginal History: Volume One, Van Diemen's Land 1803–1847*, Sydney, Macleay Press, p. 130.
3. Vance Palmer, *The Legend of the Nineties*, Melbourne University Press, Melbourne, 1966 edition, p. 9.
4. F. K. Crowley (ed.), *A New History of Australia*, Melbourne, Heinemann, 1974, pp. 1, 6.
5. *Ibid*, p. xi.
6. Geoff Eley and Ronald Grigor Suny (eds), *Becoming National*, Oxford, Oxford University Press, 1996, pp. 3–36.
7. Adam McKeown, *Chinese Migrant Networks and Cultural Change Peru, Chicago, Hawaii, 1900–1936*, Chicago, University of Chicago Press, 2001, p. 6.; see also Marilyn Lake, 'Nation gazing', *The Australian's Review of Books*, October 1999, pp. 10–12.
8. Jerry H. Bentley, 'Perspectives on Global History' in 19th International Congress of Historical Sciences *Reports, abstracts and round table introductions*, Oslo, 2000, p. 29.
9. Anna Clark, 'History in Black and White: a critical analysis of the Black Armband debate' *Country Special Issue of the Journal of Australian Studies*, UQP, 2002.
10. Sir William Deane, quoted in Windschuttle, *Fabrication*, p. 1.
11. Windschuttle, *Fabrication*, p. 377.
12. *Ibid*, p. 111.

13. *Ibid*, p. 100.
14. Lieutenant-Governor Arthur to Viscount Goderich 10 January 1828. Letter reprinted in *Bulletin of the Centre for Tasmanian Historical Studies* 1, 1, 1985, p. 21.
15. Windschuttle, *Fabrication*, p. 103.
16. *Ibid*, p. 128.
17. Jacqueline Rose, *States of Fantasy*, Oxford, Clarendon Press, 1996, p. 59.
18. Windschuttle, *Fabrication*, p. 130.
19. Rose, *States of Fantasy*, p. 61.
20. Windschuttle, *Fabrication*, pp. 298–99.
21. Windschuttle, *Fabrication*, p. 139.
22. Arthur to Goderich 10 January 1828, quoted in *Bulletin of the Centre for Tasmanian Historical Studies*, p. 23.
23. Windschuttle, *Fabrication*, p. 119.
24. *Bulletin of the Centre for Tasmanian Historical Studies*, p. 21.
25. Mary Fullerton, *The Australian Bush*, London, Dent and Sons, 1928, pp. 65–66.
26. Windschuttle, *Fabrication*, pp. 377–79.
27. *Ibid*, p. 380.
28. Fullerton, *Australian Bush*, p. 66.
29. *Ibid*, p. 68.
30. Windschuttle, *Fabrication*, p. 379.
31. Rose, *States of Fantasy*, p. 4.
32. Mary Fullerton 'A Fantasy' in Frances Fraser and Nettie Palmer, *Centenary Gift Book*, Melbourne, Robertson and Mullens, 1934, p. 44.
33. *Ibid*, p. 46.
34. Windschuttle, *Fabrication*, pp. 382–86.
35. *Ibid*, p. 386.
36. *Ibid*, p. 129.
37. *Ibid*, p. 112.
38. Martin Daunton and Rick Halpern (eds), *Empire and Others British Encounters with Indigenous Peoples, 1600–1850*, Philadelphia, University of Pennsylvania Press, 1999, p. 6.
39. *Ibid*, p. 119.
40. Catherine Hall, *Civilising Subjects: Metropole and Colony in the English Imagination 1830–1867*, Oxford, Polity, p. 13.
41. Windschuttle, *Fabrication*, p. 101.
42. Henry Reynolds, 'Aboriginal Identity and Nation' *Tasmanian Historical Studies*, 6, 1, 1998.
43. N. J. B. Plomley (ed.), *Friendly Mission: The Tasmanian Journals and Papers of George Augustus Robinson 1829–1834*, Hobart, Tasmanian Historical Research Association, 1966, p. 88.
44. Daunton and Halpern, *Empire and Others*, p. 6.
45. Catherine Hall, 'William Knibb and the constitution of the new Black subject' in Daunton and Halpern, *Empire and Others*, p. 303.
46. Hall, *Civilising Subjects*, p. 9.

Telling Us True

Greg Lehman

I

Australians don't need to be distracted and confused, or even bored with a history that reaffirms the Aussie imperialism. They need to know us, the indigenous people of this land. They need to understand that we are not the aliens. Aboriginal students want knowledge that provides a strengthening of Aboriginality and developmental themes for the future … Freedom is the aspiration, sovereignty is a name for freedom … Aboriginal education that does not contribute to the Struggle must ultimately contribute to the oppression.

– Jim Everett, Aboriginal Writer in Residence, University of Tasmania[1]

A time does not exist in human history without a story to mediate that time. Yet virtually all the history we are familiar with is written down. These stories are privileged by publication and, by the same means, they are made available for criticism. The extent of written history produced in the West can be awe-inspiring. From the painstaking and beautiful illuminations created in the abbeys of medieval Europe to the anarchic explosion of historical text on the World Wide Web, the wealth of record produced in the past few millennia surely offers us a diverse sense of what might be true among the happenings of the world. *The Fabrication of Aboriginal History* takes its place within this milieu.

Fabrication equates the idea of truth with the search for facts and proceeds to devote nearly 500 pages to the pursuit of these. Keith Windschuttle writes, 'The series has been written in the belief that the factual details are matters not to be waived aside but to be critically examined.'[2] It is at this point that I suspect he will lose a great many Aboriginal readers. You see, in Aboriginal English, the word 'true' has a very specific intent, but a rather elusive meaning. 'Aw – true!?' will be a familiar phrase to anyone who knows blackfellas. It is a question of authenticity and at the same time of an apprehension of reality. The phrase encompasses much of what it is to communicate within the cultural space inhabited by Aboriginal people. This is a space within which 'fact', 'reality' and 'certainty' are secondary considerations to the act of communication. 'Having a yarn' is more governed by the protocols of respect, trust and companionship than by the imperative to explore the veracity of a statement. Rather than listening with an expectation of photo-accurate observations of a subject, hearers of a 'yarn' listen for meaning, nuance and metaphor. And only by knowing the person speaking – or at least her family – are you likely to get more than a minimum of what is really being said.

For us, the 'truth' is made up of countless contradictory, ironic and provocative elements, woven together into an allegorical, sometimes fictive documentation of what it is to live our lives. As Marcia Langton describes it, 'When the cues, the repetitions, the language, the distinctively Aboriginal evocations of our experience are removed from recitals of our people, the truth is lost to us.'[3] Windschuttle's work clearly eschews this approach in favour of an empirical and objective historiography. In doing so, he disregards, or perhaps completely misses, the very elements of meaning and function that give life and reality to the conversation of Aboriginal experience. But, at the same time, he is just as embedded in the act of storytelling as those he decries as frauds and miscreants.

All of us, as communities, as peoples, travel from story to story. These stories are like the 'Melange' in Frank Herbert's science fiction trilogy *Dune* – a drug that is used to travel through time and space. We make these journeys in our imaginations. We continually remind each other of where we may be in these journeys, negotiating collective understandings; reinforcing these meanings with each re-telling of a well-known story. With each passing day – and the passing of our kin – these stories change, and their meanings along with them.

The historic event, which contains real acts; the archaeological site, containing real artefacts; the human life, containing real experience, are just snapshots in history. They are in themselves meaningless. Without an observer or an interpreter, they have no life, no implication for the present and no wisdom for the future. The space between these snapshots is a vacuum that necessarily fills – drawing interpretation from often competing and contradictory sources.

As Lacan reminds us, nothing is as it seems to be. This knowledge creates the space for a search for meaning and the opportunity for creation. Such a standpoint is in stark contrast with Windschuttle's project. *Fabrication* is a treatise against creation. It assumes that 'the truth *is* out there.' No one, therefore, has the right to interpret creatively the scraps of historical documentation that we have of early nineteenth-century Tasmania, because this may lead to an *authorship* of a history that should more properly be fixed in some objective frame. The problem with this project is that indigenous people all over the world, and growing hordes of postmodernists (who are rapidly approaching an indigenous epistemological paradigm), don't see things this way. There is diversity in understanding! This is nothing new – and certainly nothing that should warrant the outrage with which Windschuttle inflates his reputation. Unless of course, there is another purpose to his publication; a purpose which might attract the patronage of Australia's neo-conservatives. His is an attempt to drag us all back to a *status quo* which existed during the sheltered workshop of the early twentieth century, when naive Australian politicians sought to emulate the race-based policies common in that era. Their preferred ideological environment was one of absolute insistence on a specific doctrine intended to serve their cultural and economic interests – and to allay their paranoid fear of the growth of an off-white nation. This is not where Aborigines want to go. The price of this would be the loss of a freedom and understanding that has been hard won over the past four decades. Charlie Perkins spurred the nation to awareness of its arrogant racism and segregation with his Freedom Ride in 1965. Perkins recalled:

The scary part was not knowing how to confront people who were violently racist. None of us had ever done that before ... I think it changed the psychology of Aboriginal people. They realised, Hey, we don't have to cop this shit.[4]

If Charlie were alive today, he would see much that was familiar in the pages of *Fabrication*.

II

Observance of customs and laws can very easily be a cloak for a lie so subtle that our fellow human beings are unable to detect it. It may help us to escape all criticism, we may even be able to deceive ourselves in the belief of our obvious righteousness. But deep down, below the surface of the average man's conscience, he hears a voice whispering, 'There is something not right,' no matter how much his rightness is supported by public opinion or by the moral code.
– Carl Jung, from the introduction to Frances G. Wickes' *Analysis der Kinderseele*[5]

There are many types of historians. Our grandmothers, most important in Aboriginal culture, draw on their own experience and the collective memory of their family and their community. Nanna relied on her memories – memories that were not just biographical in nature but refashioned in the light of her experiences. Her memory was archival and a shaper of her own identity. Inevitably it also shaped ours. She knew that 'something was not right.' Her response was to try and protect her children from harm. Our generation has responded by shouting our views loudly, out of anger at the dishonour our ancestors experienced and the injustices that continue today. Historians such as Reynolds and Ryan have heard our cries and taken up the call. They are partisan and we celebrate that. Windschuttle, on the other hand, brands them as nothing short of traitors. But (to the horror of neo-conservatives) these scholars were just the vanguard. The partisan ranks are now swelling with narrative historians. Their interests are not restricted to the contents of archives, but involve them in the contents of people's lives – the meaning that human beings conjure from the past and the processes that take them into the future. For the narrative historian, perhaps the most fascinating terrain exists in the spaces between historical sources. The gaps between fact and fiction. This is the stuff of our dreams, our pain and our aspiration. It is where our identity resides.

Windschuttle is a different sort of fish. He is a technical historian. He is involved in the search for truth. Something factual and immutable. The sort of thing that may be useful in a court of law or a native title tribunal. Authoritative analysis to defend the past from irresponsible redefinition or undesirable claims for compensation. But, like most technicians, he can't resist the temptation to tinker, to adjust, so that things are *more* truthful. But truth, based on the interpretation of remote facts gathered with a minimum of context, can only ever be a result of social negotiation, agreement achieved by participants in particular conversations. These sources of 'social understanding' are usually referred to by sociologists as authority and tradition. But it is an error to consider these as fixed or providing a constant benchmark of truth as Windschuttle seems to do. And it is a judgement to privilege one tradition over another. The distinguished sociologist Earl Babbie describes tradition as a dynamic process:

> No individual is forced to start from scratch in his search for regularities and understanding. Knowledge is cumulative, and an inherited body of generalised understanding is the jumping off point for the development of more.[6]

Our whole society is based firmly around this idea. The notion that there is 'one true story' is firmly rejected as the motor for Western science and for progress. It is the stuff of revolution; the sort of revolution that saw Gandhi imagine the British out of India, and Mandela imagine an end to apartheid in South Africa. As a result we have an understanding that the earth rotates around the sun rather than vice versa (as in the pre-Copernican understanding), and that maggots hatch from the eggs of flies rather than mysteriously emerge from the substance of rotting meat (as the long-held theory of spontaneous generation maintained). Disbelief in a single, privileged truth is what frees us from the power of prejudice.

Early observations by European explorers are important in understanding how Europeans came to perceive Aborigines and subsequently place them in the colonial world. The location of Aborigines within the hegemonic framework of European-ness is maintained into the present by the persistence of these perceptions. Lyndall Ryan provides a comprehensive account of early European records of and attitudes to Tasmanian Aborigines in her book *The Aboriginal Tasmanians*.[7] The Dutch, who claimed Van Diemen's Land in 1642, did not meet an Aborigine. Instead, they concluded from the widely spaced notches cut into tree trunks that the island was inhabited by a race of giants. These impressions are likely to have seeped into official geographical accounts of this part of the world, generating an effective, if imaginary historical account of the island that served to prevent the imperial Dutch from ever returning! The French, led by Nicholas Marion du Fresne in 1772, were next to visit. Enamoured, according to Ryan, by his anticipation of a dialogue on the 'state of nature' with members of *la société naissante*, Marion sent naked sailors ashore at North Bay on Bruny Island to establish liaison with the 'noble savages'.[8] On the expedition's return to France, the philosopher Rousseau was horrified when told that his 'children of nature' had rejected the French landing with a violent assault and had had to be killed.

This early conflict, Ryan argues, tarnished the European image of the 'noble savage'. A later French expedition led by Bruny d'Entrecasteaux in 1792 contributed further difficulties. Among the expeditioners was the young Enlightenment scientist Jacques-Julien Houton de Labillardière. He had read Rousseau's *Discourse on the Origins of Inequality* and found the social organisation of the Aboriginal groups he met to be at odds with the patriarchy of Rousseau's archetypal model.[9] The native women, while appearing subordinate to the men, appeared to enjoy inordinate responsibility as providers. They seemed to have sole authority for gathering shellfish, hunting seals and providing many other essential resources. This must have challenged the patriarchal framework of gender roles that the French expected to find. Nevertheless, Labillardière perceived a place for the Tasmanian Aborigines in the

Republican ideology and imagined that these natives would be receptive to Western agriculture and would benefit from the 'proper' gender roles inherent in its practice.

All of these encounters by Europeans of the Tasmanian Aboriginal world are indications of how ready and willing the emissaries of the cutting edge of Western science and philosophy have been to impose their expectations on a people, without the benefit of even the slightest familiarity with the theoretical or epistemological framework of their subjects. The result? Fictive discourses rooted in the imaginary, rapidly taking on the mantle of historical fact. *Fabrication* treads the same well-worn paths. Windschuttle's comments about the 'decaying ... eroded ... and disintegrating'[10] state of the lands handed back to the Aboriginal community at Risdon Cove (meagerly evidenced by photographs of two broken signs) must be based on the same sort of blinkered prejudice exhibited by the Dutch and French. Either that or Windschuttle visited the area after nightfall! How else could he not have noted 20 hectares of native vegetation restoration, comprising thousands of seedlings protected by plastic enclosures? How did he miss the removal of willows that had been choking natural watercourses for a century, the brand-new bridge or the inspiring aesthetic of the Aboriginal school complex, designed by the award-winning architect Greg Burgess? No, all Windschuttle could see was the imagined basis of his outrage – all he could see was red (and black and yellow). The result? An ignorant and unjustified dismissal of thousands of hours of dedicated work by the local Aboriginal community and a misunderstanding of a culture. He would have learned so much more if only he had asked an Aboriginal person to show him around Risdon Cove. Instead he has insisted on keeping us at arm's length, maintaining Aborigines as a shadowy, threatening 'other'.

The attack on our treatment of country is a neat accompaniment to *Fabrication*'s assertion that Tasmanian Aborigines had no 'territorial instincts'[11] in the first place and, therefore, no attachment to territory – all of this appearing to suggest that land rights or native title are inherently wrong. Yet Plomley, whom Windschuttle refers to as 'the most scrupulous scholar',[12] provides a great variety of references to plant and animal use and clearly indicates the cultural associations that had developed around these. For example, Plomley records that, 'Those [tribes] of Oyster Bay ... the gum trees they claim as theirs and call them countrymen. The stringybark trees the Brune call theirs, as being their countrymen, the peppermint the Cape Portland call theirs, and the Swanport claim the honeysuckle.'[13]

Windschuttle's suggestion that proprietorial association with flora and fauna is unrelated to the land on which these species grow is naive and ignores the most basic anthropological understandings of how Aboriginal people conceive of country. Records and analysis of Tasmanian Aboriginal languages[14] also provide essential evidence for the complex inter-relation of people and their physical surroundings. Taylor asserts that 'all known words for hill, mountain and the like are clearly metaphorical in origin' and 'bear associations with words for spear, head, breasts and buttocks'.[15] The data presented by Taylor suggests that, as in other places throughout Australia, the Tasmanian Aboriginal cultural landscape was based on what Deborah Bird Rose terms a 'sacred geography',[16] where distinctions between the living and non-living, so convenient to Western ontologies, are less real. Windschuttle's expectation of evidence of Western proprietorial attitudes again places his perspective back in the company of the ethnocentric eighteenth-century French.

While trees are rooted in the land and different species have predictable associations with particular localities, the kangaroo is a highly mobile species that might not be expected to indicate Aboriginal association with land. But the kangaroo is a powerful metaphor for indigenous knowledge and identity in Tasmania. The animal was known to Aboriginal people as *Tarner*, a creation spirit and ancestor of *Parlevar*, the 'first man'.[17] Prior to British invasion, the sacred identity of *Tarner* was rekindled in each generation as traditional creation stories were passed down. *Tarner* was a central character of the sacred landscape in which Tasmanian Aborigines lived. Through customary kinship obligations, the kangaroo bound Aborigines intimately to the land and gave them a mythical identity as descendants of a creation spirit. In this way the values and beliefs of Tasmanian Aborigines were grounded in a mythological text that provided the theory and praxis of their life; an epistemology in which the kangaroo was central to the cluster of relations that characterises the complex of obligations and practices of indigenous customary law. The kangaroo featured in the totems of individuals, tribal songs and dances; it required elaborate ceremony for its hunting, killing and eating; and its ecological requirements motivated many traditional fire-based land-management practices.

The identity of the kangaroo as an ancestor is central to the association of Aborigines with their homeland. This is not an assertion of historical or evolutionary fact. It is an analogue of the Semitic tradition of creation recorded in *Genesis*. The Tasmanian Aboriginal genesis story even has a geographic location for the event of human creation – an Eden. Windschuttle's major limitation in his assertions about Tasmanian Aboriginal epistemology is his insistence on considering only European records made by people either decidedly disinterested in Aboriginal spirituality or heavily invested in its evangelical transformation. The process of critical analysis of Aboriginal historical narratives necessitates some degree of engagement with Aboriginal spirituality. This is not a difficult task in the context of an academic work, but without some effort in this direction, the resulting analysis is almost guaranteed to be superficial and ethnocentric. The mythical identity of the kangaroo provides a meta-narrative for the analysis of Aboriginal history – a system of mythical 'signs' which gives meaning to the physical evidence of Tasmanian Aboriginal reality.

III

Imagination is … a complex gift. The great difficulty in philosophy, which depends so much on thought experiments that are often preceded by invitation to imagine something or other, is to distinguish between an imagination that appears to make sense of nonsense by picturing it – and imagination that extends our sense of what is seriously possible to conceive.

– Raimond Gaita, *The Philosopher's Dog*[18]

So what sort of history do Aborigines want? Perhaps the sort of history that can be described as honest. Honest to the people that it seeks to serve. Honest to the reality that history is made out of representations and interpretations, either at its source or in its presentation. In his *Myths of Caribbean Identity*, Stuart Hall writes:

> What they felt was I have no voice, I have no history. I have come from a place to which I cannot go back and I have never seen. I used to speak a language which I can no longer speak, I had ancestors whom I cannot find, they worshipped gods whose names I do not know. Against this sense of profound rupture, the metaphors of a new kind of life can be reworked – can become a language in which a certain kind of history is retold, in which the aspirations of liberation and freedom can be for the first time expressed, in which what I would call the imagined country of Africa can be symbolically constructed.[19]

White Australians today, unfamiliar with the cultural worlds of their Celtic and Germanic ancestors, might be seen to occupy a similar space. Creating myths around historical figures such as Ned Kelly and the Anzacs, they give a recently constructed history depth and texture. Tasmanian Aborigines are not so different. We are heavily invested in the re-creation of our culture and history – a response to the destruction of so much of our heritage by the British. We aspire to inventing the possibility of a future for ourselves where conflict, racism and separatism might become just steps along the way to something much better. This future is not to be found in the pages of *The Fabrication of Aboriginal History*. All Windschuttle offers us is an ignoble death in the past. He is consumed by the absurd task of telling the dead how to die. Maybe he just wants to get noticed at our expense. As Lacan suggests, the desire for recognition produces a primordial confrontation leading to 'the desire for the disappearance of the other'.[20] When we encounter impasse from the affliction of others, we simply wish for them to vanish. The sort of historians I prefer are the ones who are busy constructing a new, negotiated place called Tasmania, where conflicts of the past can be talked about by all who are present and transformed – a place that we can imagine into existence.

NOTES

1. Jim Everett, *Aboriginal Studies Assessment*, unpublished report to Riawunna, Centre for Aboriginal Education, Hobart, University of Tasmania, 1993.

2. Keith Windschuttle, *The Fabrication of Aboriginal History: Volume One, Van Diemen's Land 1803–1847*, Sydney, Macleay Press, 2002, p. 9.
3. Marcia Langton, 'A Black View of History', *The Age*, 1/2/1981.
4. Stuart Rintoul, *The Wailing: A National Black Oral History*, Port Melbourne, William Heinemann Australia, 1993, p. 287.
5. Carl Jung, *Collected Works of C. G. Jung*, vol. 17, N. J., Princeton University Press, 1970.
6. Earl Babbie, *The Practice of Social Research*, Belmont, Wadsworth Publishing Co., 1975, p. 26.
7. Lyndall Ryan, *The Aboriginal Tasmanians*, second edition, St Leonards, Allen & Unwin, 1996.
8. *Ibid*, p. 49.
9. *Ibid*, p. 54.
10. Windschuttle, *Fabrication*, p. 418.
11. *Ibid*, p. 130.
12. *Ibid*, p. 433.
13. N. J. B. Plomley (ed.), *Friendly Mission: The Tasmanian Journals and Papers of George Augustus Robinson, 1829–1834*, Hobart, Tasmanian Historical Research Association, 1966, p. 369.
14. See N. J. B. Plomley, *A Word List of the Tasmanian Aboriginal Languages*, Hobart, Tasmanian Government, 1976; and J. Taylor, *Tasmanian Place Names – The Aboriginal Connection*, (published by the author), Launceston, (n.d.).
15. *Ibid*, p. 31.
16. Deborah Bird Rose, *Nourishing Landscapes*, Canberra, Australian Heritage Commission, 1996, p. 35.
17. Plomley, 1966, pp. 374–375.
18. Raimond Gaita, *The Philosopher's Dog*, Melbourne, Text Publishing, 2002.
19. Stuart Hall, 'Myths of Caribbean Identity', *The Walter Rodney Memorial Lecture Series*, Coventry, Centre for Caribbean Studies, University of Warwick, 1991, p. 10.
20. Jacques-Alain Miller (ed.), 'The See-Saw of Desire' in *The Seminar of Jacques Lacan, Book I: Freud's Papers on Technique, 1953–1954*, Cambridge, Cambridge University Press, 1988, p. 170.

IN PARTICULAR

Windschuttle's Debut

Neville Green

Keith Windschuttle's revision of Australian history began in late 2000 with the publication of three long pieces in *Quadrant* magazine.[1] The first of these was an analysis of the four famous massacres described in Phillip Knightley's book *Australia: A Biography of a Nation*. To assess the reliability of Windschuttle's scholarship, this essay will examine one of those massacres, the Battle of Pinjarra.

Between 1826 and 1852 at least 30 settlers and 121 Aborigines were killed in violent encounters in Western Australia.[2] The most tragic incident took place in 1834. While other multiple murders of Aborigines undoubtedly occurred as the western frontier advanced, the Battle of Pinjarra is the only irrefutable incident of this magnitude.

Concerning this battle, Windschuttle makes a series of claims. Pinjarra was not a 'massacre of innocents' but a 'real battle between warring parties with casualties on both sides'. It was not 'an ambush'; nor was it a 'punitive expedition'. Windschuttle claims that the leading authority on the battle is an historian, Frank Goldsmith. Following Goldsmith, he claims that between ten and twenty Aborigines were killed at Pinjarra. Most importantly, Windschuttle characterises the battle as a 'mission to capture the murderers of a British soldier', which was, as such, both 'lawful' and 'morally justifiable'. Let us examine what in fact happened at Pinjarra, on the basis of the available sources, as a way of assessing the quality of Windschuttle's debut as an historian of the Australian frontier.

The events leading up to the Battle of Pinjarra were these: in April 1834, members of the Murray River tribe raided a flour mill within sight of Perth. The ringleaders were arrested on their home territory (90 kilometres south of Perth) with the assistance of Thomas Peel, a local land-owner. They were brought to Perth and flogged; the senior man, Calyute, received 60 lashes and was imprisoned. On 16 July, soon after his release, Calyute and others killed Private Hugh Nesbitt and wounded another man, Edward Barron, at Peel's property. They also threatened to burn the barracks and farm buildings and destroy all the settlers of the district.

The governor of the colony, Sir James Stirling, was concerned that if the Murray people went unchecked, others might be encouraged to attack the settlers,[3] and in October 1834 he led an expedition south to apprehend the killers and punish the Murray tribe (and also, rather incongruously, to survey the site of a town). The party consisted of 25 citizens including the surveyors John S. Roe and George Smythe, troops and mounted police. On 28 October, the tribe, an estimated 70 to 80 men, women and children, were in or near their low bush huts at the Murray River. The battle began at 8.35 a.m.

Stirling gave the following report of it:[4]

Keeping the party out of sight, Captain Ellis, the superintendent of mounted police, was sent with Mr Norcott and three of his corps to re-cross the ford, and advance towards the natives, for the purpose of ascertaining whether they were the offending tribe. This he accomplished with great celerity, and on his approach towards them he recognized several of them to be those who were present at Nisbett's [sic] murder, and amounting in all to about 60 or 70. He accordingly made a preconcerted signal to me, and advanced towards them. The natives very resolutely stood their ground, as I am informed, and threw a volley of spears, by which Captain Ellis was wounded in the head, and one of his men in the right arm, and another was unhorsed. Stunned and dismounted by the blow, and having his horse speared, Captain Ellis's party was thus put into great peril; but at this critical moment the men with me got into position and commenced firing, and threw the natives into confusion. They fled to a ford about 100 yards below the other, but being headed by the corporal's party, they were forced back into the bed of the stream. The upper ford being also occupied by Mr Roe, as well as the two banks, they were thus completely surrounded and overpowered. The number killed, amounted probably to 15 men.

Three days later, on 31 October, Stirling met with George Fletcher Moore, the Advocate General. Moore summed up in his diary his impression of the incident: 'They came upon the offending tribe in a position which I dare say the natives thought was most favourable for their manoeuvres, but which was turned into a complete trap for them.'[5]

Lord Glenelg, the British Colonial Secretary, was not pleased, but he had to accept that Stirling's drastic action was justified. He chided the Governor:

> It is impossible however to regard such conflicts without regret and anxiety, when we recollect how fatal, in too many instances, our colonial settlements have proved to the natives of the places where they have been formed; and this too by a series of conflicts, in every one of which it has been asserted, and apparently with justice, that the immediate aggression has not been on our side.[6]

Glenelg is saying that he has heard this excuse too often in attempts to justify murder. He urged Stirling to seek out the real causes of hostilities and suggested that it began with acts of injustice, not by the Aborigines but by the settlers. If the leaders of the colony do not curb these injustices, it will lead to feelings of 'hatred and vengeance, which breaks out at length into deeds of atrocity; which, in their turn, make retaliation a necessary part of self-defence'. There are three elements to conflict: cause, clash and consequence. Glenelg was urging Stirling to look to the first and avoid the second.

A Real Battle?

In the conclusion to his *Quadrant* article, Keith Windschuttle states his agenda with regard to the incident. He seeks to convince readers that:

it was a real battle between warring parties, with casualties on both sides, rather than a massacre of innocents. It was not an ambush since the Aborigines were well aware of the troopers' presence beforehand. It was not a punitive expedition either.[7]

The contemporary reports clearly show that Windschuttle is wrong about the intention underlying the expedition. Stirling informed the Colonial Office that his objective was 'that a check should be put on the career of that particular tribe'. Lord Glenelg noted, 'It is with pain that I notice your holding out to the natives a threat of general destruction, extending even to women and children.' He referred to Stirling's chilling words to the women and children taken prisoner at Pinjarra:

> They were then informed that this punishment had been inflicted, because of the misconduct of the tribe; that the white men never forget to punish murder; that on this occasion the women and children had been spared, but if any other person should be killed by them, not one would be allowed to remain on this side of the mountains.[8]

Another witness account of the threat was reported in the *Perth Gazette* of 1 November 1834:

> … if they again offered to spear white men or their cattle, or to revenge in any way the punishment which had just been inflicted on them for their numerous murders and outrages, four times the present number of men would proceed against them and destroy every man, woman and child.

Glenelg warned Stirling that this was a dangerous course to take and while he may not carry through such a threat, '… the course threatened falls too much into the practice of native warfare, and was likely to create an impression among your uncivilized adversaries that the English, like themselves, regarded this as a legitimate mode of warfare.'

Was the encounter a 'real battle' or a 'massacre of innocents'? Was it an open meeting of forces or an ambush?

In addition to Stirling's account, we have three other witness accounts including a diary account of the affray by the surveyor John S. Roe entitled 'J.S. Roe with Sir Jas Stirling & party to Murray River &

back to Perth on which journey, the natives were punished at Pinjarra'.[9]

It was 8.35 a.m. and raining. The shouts by Peel and others failed to attract the attention of the camp. Roe continues:

Capt Ellis and Mr Norcott, with 3 of the mounted police were despatched across the ford to ascertain if the party belonged to the tribe of Kal-yute [aka Calyute] (which had recently committed some great outrages, and for which purpose jointly with that of protection for the present exploring party, the mounted force had accompanied us). In a few minutes the loud shouting and yelling of the natives told us the whites were discovered and firing immediately commenced on the left bank. Not having a gun, I was directed to take charge of the ford with the baggage and four soldiers, while the remainder of the force followed the Governor upwards. The firing continued upward and followed the retreating voices of the Natives for upwards of an hour. This is explained as follows. On the approach of the police towards the Natives, they started up from their fires about 70 or 80 in number and began retreating. However, as it was ascertained they were the obnoxious tribe, the firing commenced at a full charge, in which the chief, Captain Ellis was wounded in the temple and knocked off his horse by a spear thrown at 4 or 5 yards distance, and the natives wounded one of the police, P. Heffron in the right arm so as to completely disable him. The native was however instantly shot dead. After the first charge which killed 4 or 5, the natives retreated to the river intending apparently to cross over by another ford about half a mile lower down, in this they were completely frustrated by meeting the remainder of the armed force headed by the Governor as part of them were ascending the bank. In this dilemma they took to hiding themselves amongst the bushes and dead logs on the riverbanks and were picked off by the party on either shore. *This was not done without much resistance on the part of the natives, who although crouched in very small and scarcely discernible holes and places and in many instances had immersed themselves in the water, having only their nose and mouth above water, nevertheless threw numerous spears with amazing precision and force.*[10] In this way between 15 and 20 were shot dead, very few wounded being suffered to escape, until at length it being considered that the punishment of the tribe for the numerous outrages it had committed was sufficient and the firing ceased and the party secured 8 women and several children prisoners.

Keith Windschuttle accuses Henry Reynolds of giving 'a doctored version' of this battle by omitting the single line, 'and ready with a spear under water, to take advantage of anyone who approached within reach'. He then cites as proof that it was not a brutal one-sided affair just the one sentence given in italics above and omits the remainder of the report. When read in context, it contradicts Windschuttle's conclusion.[11]

As well as Roe's account, there is also the eyewitness account of an unnamed 'gentleman' published in the *Perth Gazette*, 1 November 1834. In this account the settlers' party crossed the Murray River and was less than half a kilometre on when Aboriginal voices were heard. The party returned towards the river, and 'His Excellency rode forward a couple of hundred yards with Messrs Peel and Norcott, who were acquainted both with the persons of the natives and with their language, and commenced calling out and talking to them for the purpose of bringing on an interview.' They could not be heard above the camp noises and Ellis, Norcott and three mounted police were sent across the river, 'to bring on the interview required'.

The 'gentleman's' description differs from those of Roe and Stirling. The main party with Stirling was some distance from the river and galloped forward upon hearing the shots:

... and arrived opposite Capt. Ellis's party just as some of the natives had crossed and others were in the river. It was just the critical moment for them. Five or six rushed up the right bank, but were utterly confounded at meeting a second party of assailants, who immediately drove back those who escaped the firing. Being thus exposed to a crossfire, and having no time to rally their forces, they adopted the alternative of taking to the river and secreting themselves amongst the roots and branches and holes on its banks, or by immersing themselves with the face only uncovered, and ready with a spear underwater to take advantage of anyone who approached within reach. Those who were sufficiently hardy or desperate to expose themselves on the offensive, or to attempt breaking through the assailants, were soon cleared off, and the remainder were gradually picked out of their concealment by the crossfire from both banks, until between 25 and 30 were left dead on the field and in the river.

This 'gentleman' admits that the death toll may be higher, adding, 'Notwithstanding the care which was taken not to injure the women during the skirmish, it cannot appear surprising that one woman and several children were killed.'

The encounter was not, as Windschuttle claimed, 'a genuine battle between two armed, warring parties with casualties on both sides'. It was the massacre of a group trapped between four armed parties. Stirling's deployment of his men and the ambush at the river with no call for surrender leaves no doubt that the purpose was to punish – and punish severely. As we have seen, the Governor's own report gave the impression of fierce resistance, but was this to justify the killing of so many Aborigines?

Windschuttle would expect us to believe that Aborigines, with only their mouths and noses out of the water, could fit long spears to the ends of their woomeras and leap out of the water to engage on equal terms with men with guns sitting a few yards away. What nonsense!

Those who submerged and tried to float downstream were vulnerable when they reached the ford where the river was 25 yards across and three foot deep. In Roe's words, 'between 15 and 20 were shot dead, very few wounded being suffered to escape'. When those trapped had been silenced, the men re-mounted and for another hour pursued Aborigines up and down the river.

Only Stirling referred to positioning men at the fords above and below the battle site. Only Roe referred to the men re-mounting and pursuing the fugitives for another hour. Only those killed at the camp and the river were counted, with at least 15 bodies being examined for identification. Neither Stirling nor Roe admitted to shooting women. This, however, was confirmed by Thomas Peel when he and Lieut. Armstrong interviewed survivors in March 1835 and obtained the names of the victims.[12]

Flawed Re-telling

Windschuttle's version of the events at Pinjarra seems to deviate from the known facts. He wrote in *Quadrant* that Stirling 'sent in an emissary, the local pastoralist Thomas Peel, who knew the tribe, to persuade them to come out and negotiate with Captain Stirling. This was unsuccessful and so the troops began to surround the camp.'[13]

Stirling's report made no mention of Peel being sent to negotiate with the Murray River tribe. Nor does any of the other reports. In fact, Peel (not a 'pastoralist' but a land-owner with little stock beyond a horse and a few goats) only went to the riverbank.

Windschuttle does not explain that it was raining and that the Aborigines were camped at least 200 metres away on the other side of the river. The Aborigines at the camp obviously did not sense the settlers' approach or they would have scattered. Neither was there an attempt by five men to 'surround' a camp of some 70 to 80 persons. The Aborigines were only aware of the three troopers and the two officers they could see approaching. If they knew another twenty armed men were at the river, they would hardly have retreated in that direction as they did.

The first public report of the affair in the *Perth Gazette* on 1 November challenges Windschuttle's account in another way. Windschuttle states that, 'The reports by expedition members are the only ones we have and, whatever one might think of their motives for saying so, they claimed the blacks threw their spears first and they fired in self-defence.'[14] Windschuttle did not read Stirling's report, but he did read the *Perth Gazette* report, or at least he appears to draw from it. However, the *Perth Gazette* report stated:

> The instant the police were observed approaching at about 200 yards distance, the natives, to the number of about 70, started on their feet, the men seized their numerous and recently made spears, and shewed a formidable front; but finding their visitors still approached, they seemed to feel unable to stand a charge and sullenly retreated, gradually quickening their pace until the word 'forward' from the leader of the gallant little party brought the horsemen in about half a minute dashing into the midst of them, the same moment having discovered

the well known features of some of the most atrocious offenders of the obnoxious tribe.[15]

So here we have a complete contradiction of Windschuttle. The Aborigines did not attack. They retreated.

Windschuttle also wrote in *Quadrant* that, 'Another Aborigine knocked Captain Ellis off his horse and speared him, fatally, in the head.' As Roe and Stirling both clearly indicate, Captain Ellis was not fatally speared while on the ground.

The *Perth Gazette* report of 1 November 1834 claims that the attack was justified by the identification of a wanted man, Noonar. On 22 November 1834, however, Norcott admitted that the man he shot was not Noonar but Munar.[16] An innocent man was shot and others were killed as a consequence of this false identification. Windschuttle allows this to persist as a justification – 'When Noonar saw he was recognised …'[17]

Windschuttle's dating of Nesbitt's murder to April instead of July is also a serious error because the murder was an act of vengeance following the arrest and punishment of Calyute. One is reminded of Glenelg's advice that murders are sometimes acts of revenge for a perceived injustice.

Windschuttle, in arguing that justice was being served and that self-defence was a justification, adopts the very stand that Glenelg abhorred when he told Stirling that in bringing an Aborigine to justice he must act as in the case of a settler. Had it been a settler accused of killing an Aborigine, one could not imagine Stirling leading an armed brigade into a country town and, after blocking the only exits, proceeding to shoot the residents. Yet Windschuttle seems to justify this behaviour for the capture of Aboriginal suspects.

The Death Toll

For a person who insists so publicly on accuracy of death tolls and up-front references, Windschuttle is remarkably casual in determining the total number of deaths at Pinjarra. In fact, his account has curious similarities to Battye's 1927 account, which was written without knowledge of both Stirling's and Roe's reports.[18]

Of the casualties, Battye wrote, 'One point in this report [*Perth Gazette*] was found on later investigation to have been greatly exaggerated. Instead of there being 25 to 30 men killed, as well as one woman and several children, the total death toll consisted of 10 men, 3 women, and one child.'

In 1951, F. Goldsmith, who had read Battye's article, wrote, 'Instead of there being 25 to 30 men killed, as well as one woman and several children, the total death toll consisted of ten men, three women and one child.'

Although Goldsmith cited only one original source, Windschuttle claimed that he gave 'the most credible modern estimate' and wrote in *Quadrant* that a third contemporary report 'said 25 to 30 were killed; but a fourth denied this last report and said the precise death toll was ten men, three women and one child.' The three authors share a common reluctance to provide either the name of this eyewitness or their source.

During November 1834, Captain Daniell and troopers of the 21st Regiment scoured the district searching for Calyute's band. They also examined the battlefield:

> On arriving at Pinjarra, they found that the bodies of the natives who were killed, were all decently interred, in one spot there being three graves of large dimensions, about twelve feet each in length, supposed to contain the members of separate families, and at a short distance from them were the graves of thirteen men.[19]

It was thought there were more graves in this area, but floods prevented Daniell from searching the area where the heaviest fighting had occurred. The alternative was that all or most of the dead had been carried to the 16 graves they observed. (Seymour Meares, who was with the 1834 expedition, settled at Pinjarra and years later stated that he had counted 18 graves.[20])

In 1838, G. F. Moore observed the burial customs of the Nyungar. Having selected the site and cleared the area, 'the grave was then dug in a direction due north and south, about 4 feet long, about 3 feet deep, and perhaps 18 inches wide.'[21] Given this information, one can surmise that each of the three large graves could have accommodated up to six bodies.

In 1835, Major F. C. Irwin, former Commandant of the 63rd Regiment at the Swan River, wrote:

> Though the loss of life in this affair is a very painful consideration, and deeply to be deplored. Yet it seems manifest that without some severe defeat to convince this tribe of their inferiority in power to the whites, a petty and harassing warfare may have been indefinitely prolonged, with ultimately much heavier losses on both sides.[22]

One may contrast with this a statement in Peel's 1 April 1835 report to Stirling by Ninda and Dollian, two Pinjarra survivors. Ninda and Dollian, wrote Peel, 'consider it very hard that the parties who were slain at Pinjarra by the soldiers and police should have been made to suffer for crimes in which they had had no participation'. This was followed by the names, including children, of ten males and four females killed at Pinjarra. Noonar and Munar were not listed. [23]

In 1973, I interviewed a Nyungar elder who as a young man was told by a local farmer, Mr Fawcett, that 750 people were buried in a field. The figure is not realistic, but it does demonstrate that handed-down stories may preserve the memory of the event but not the precise details. How would the 'battle' be regarded today if the only surviving contemporary statements were those by Ninda and Dollian? Perhaps, along with Mistake Creek, Bedford Downs and Forrest River, it would be a massacre myth attributed to 'stories my mum and dad told me'.[24]

NOTES

1. Keith Windschuttle, 'The myths of frontier massacres in Australian history, Part I: The invention of massacre stories', *Quadrant* 44 (10) 2000, pp. 8–21; 'The myths of frontier massacres in Australian history, Part II: The fabrication of the Aboriginal death toll', *Quadrant* 44 (11) 2000, pp. 17–24; 'The myths of frontier massacres in Australian history, Part III: Massacre stories and the policy of separatism', *Quadrant* 44 (12) 2000, pp. 6–20. The texts can be found at http://www.sydneyline.com.
2. Neville Green, *Broken Spears: Aborigines and Europeans in the Southwest of Australia*, Perth, Focus Education, 1984, Appendix 1.
3. Sir James Stirling to Rt Hon. E. G. Stanley, Secretary of State for Colonies, 1/11/1834, CO.18.14. (AJCP 299–300)
4. Stirling to Stanley, 1/11/1834, CO.18.14. (AJCP 299–300). Ellis died a little over a week later.

5. G. F. Moore, *Diary of ten years eventful life of an early settler in Western Australia*, Nedlands, UWA Press, 1978, p. 236.

6. Lord Glenelg to Sir James Stirling, 23/7/1835, CO. 18.14. (AJCP 299–300).

7. Windschuttle, 'The myths of frontier massacres in Australian history, Part I'. The text can be found at http://www.sydneyline.com.

8. Sir James Stirling to Rt Hon. E. G. Stanley, Secretary of State for Colonies, 1/11/1834, CO.18.14. (AJCP 299–300).

9. John S. Roe, Registered field book, no. 3, 1834–1838. Dept. of Land Management, Perth.

10. Windschuttle's words used in the italics differ slightly from other transcriptions.

11. Keith Windschuttle, ' Frontier Crimes: the debate', *The Australian's Review of Books*, April 2001, p. 5. Windschuttle adopts a similar tactic in his October 2000 *Quadrant* article on the Battle of Pinjarra.

12. Peel to Stirling, 1/4/1834, CSR 1834, vol. 38, SROWA.

13. Windschuttle, 'The Myths of Frontier Massacres, Part I'.

14. *Quadrant*, October 2000, p. 18.

15. *Perth Gazette*, 1/11/1834.

16. *Perth Gazette*, 22/11/1834.

17. 'Frontier Crimes: the debate', *The Australian's Review of Books*, April 2001, p. 5.

18. J. S. Battye, The official records of the encounter, *WAHS Journal* vol. 1 pt. 1, 1927, p. 37.

19. *Perth Gazette*, 22/11/1834.

20. Seymour G. Meares, *Perth Gazette and W.A. Times*, 3/7/1868.

21. G. F. Moore, *Diary*, p. 345.

22. F. C. Irwin, *The State and Position of Western Australia*, London, Simpkin Marshall, 1835, p. 27.

23. Peel to Stirling, 1/4/1834, CSR 1834, vol. 38, SROWA. See also W. C. Smart, *Mandurah and Pinjarra: History of Thomas Peel and the Peel Estate*, Perth, Paterson Brokensha, c. 1950. p. 32.

24. Rod Moran, 'Paradigm of the Postmodern Museum', *Quadrant*, Jan–Feb 2002, pp. 43–49.

Peggy Patrick
courtesy Jirrawun Aboriginal Art Corporation

John Glover (1767–1849)
Mount Wellington and Hobart Town from Kangaroo Point 1834
oil on canvas
76.2 x 152.4 cm

Tasmanian Museum and Art Gallery and National Gallery of Australia; purchased with funds from the Art Foundation of Tasmania Glover Appeal and the Nerissa Johnson Bequest.

Mistake Creek

Cathie Clement

The Fabrication of Aboriginal History 'examines how we can know about the past, the kinds of evidence we can regard as reliable, and how to detect false claims when they are made'. It is, according to its author, 'an excursion into the methodology of history'.[1]

The volume opens with Keith Windschuttle castigating Sir William Deane for Centenary of Federation speeches that 'focused on a great flaw that allegedly lay at the heart of the nation'. He condemns Sir William for expressing the view, both as Governor-General and as a High Court judge, that British colonisation dispossessed, degraded and devastated indigenous Australians.[2]

He attributes this 'politicisation' to historians' 'corruption' of the story of the nation's past. That 'corruption', Windschuttle says, left him 'no choice but to address the fabric of their scholarship in order to unpick their work and to establish what really happened'.[3]

Few people would consider tackling such a task. To 'establish what really happened' in one locality, if it were possible to do so, would require not only years of research but also unwavering objectivity and excellent analytical skills. To do the same for Australia would take a lifetime.

The author of this essay has been researching colonisation in Australia's north-west for two decades. Her extensive integration of written and oral sources has yielded considerable insight into that region's history but she would never claim to know what happened there.

Windschuttle's belief that one can 'establish what really happened' underpins his argument that Aboriginal history has been fabricated.[4] It is therefore ironic that, in his introduction to *The Fabrication of Aboriginal History*, his most prominent example of fabrication is a myth of his own making. The example relates to Sir William attending a remembering ceremony for Mistake Creek massacre victims in Australia's north-west. Windschuttle quotes Sir William's expression of personal sorrow that such events occurred but he also falsely claims:

— that the Governor-General made an 'apology for a massacre the local tribe suffered, and for all those perpetrated by whites on Aborigines';

— that he 'got the facts of this case completely wrong'; and

— that 'the tale he told about Mistake Creek is just one more of the many myths and legends now routinely recounted as historical fact but which, when properly examined, reveal a different story.'[5]

This essay shows that those false claims are part of a myth that was created by Windschuttle in 2001 and then recounted as fact. It also shows that, despite being told that he was making false claims and using sources selectively, Windschuttle stuck to his version of 'what really happened' at Mistake Creek.

Aboriginal Oral History

Sir William told no 'tale' at Mistake Creek. He did, however, allude to Aboriginal oral history relevant to a massacre.[6] That prompted Windschuttle to berate him for not being 'more familiar with the writings of his predecessor' and 'more sceptical of the oral history'. The predecessor was Paul Hasluck who, in 1942, identified 'two colossal fictions in popular accounts of the treatment of natives in Australia'.[7]

With no disrespect to Hasluck, Sir William would have benefited more from familiarity with papers from the East Kimberley Impact Assessment Project (EKIAP). Those papers include No. 28, *Impact Stories of the East Kimberley* (edited by Helen Ross, with Eileen Bray as translator), and No. 29, *Historical Notes Relevant to Impact Stories of the*

East Kimberley (written by the author of this essay to provide context for the stories). Both were published in 1989 and both contain material relevant to a 1915 massacre at Mistake Creek. The two papers came into being because people were thinking about two of the things that Windschuttle examines: 'how we can know about the past' and 'the kinds of evidence we can regard as reliable'.

The EKIAP acknowledged, first, that the perspective of people affected by impacts is of primary importance, and second, that the cumulative effects of development and other occurrences need to be understood within a social and historical context.[8] Discussions about an appropriate methodology led to Aboriginal elders deciding to use oral history to show how their communities fared after settlement activities began to affect their country. They took that approach because they wanted 'more than a "dry" report'. They wanted 'to make Kartiya [white people] understand'. They were also committed to 'redressing the lack of information available about what had actually happened to Aboriginal people in the region, and hence countering the non-Aboriginal "popular memory" which had been allowed to prevail'.[9]

Rod Moran would later applaud similar initiatives. The 'distortions of much early writing on Aboriginal/white contact', he wrote, make it important, especially in Western Australia, for 'victim-stories of Aboriginal experience' to be told.[10] He has since modified his attitude to Aboriginal oral history[11] but, when he wrote the book *Massacre Myth* in 1999, he mentioned his earlier comments and reiterated his view 'that the victim-stories have to be faced by contemporary Australia as a part of black and white reconciliation'.[12]

Moran's book, which denies the occurrence of other East Kimberley killings, was the catalyst for *The Fabrication of Aboriginal History*. Windschuttle read *Massacre Myth* and, because one aspect of Moran's research 'clicked' in his brain, he 'revisited Reynolds and his much quoted estimate that 20,000 blacks died in frontier violence'. He 'could see the whole thing unravelling immediately', and he thought, 'gee, this is a story.'[13] The story begins in Volume One of *The Fabrication of Aboriginal History*.

The Remembering Ceremony

It was while Windschuttle was writing his book that Sir William spoke at Mistake Creek. Journalists were there and, on 9 June 2001, the front page of *The Sydney Morning Herald* carried an article headed 'Straight from the heart: Sir William's final journey'. Written by Tony Stephens, it summarised the Governor-General's activities and quoted him saying, with regard to a Mistake Creek massacre, 'I'd like to say how profoundly sorry I am that such events defaced our beautiful land.' The article mentioned the 1915 massacre but made no reference to an apology or a perpetrator.[14]

On 11 June, the ABC's *7.30 Report* covered Sir William's journey and carried the words that Windschuttle described as an 'apology for a massacre the local tribe suffered, and for all those perpetrated by whites on Aborigines'. Sir William, after mentioning that a local elder had explained the Mistake Creek story as one of forgiveness, had said:

> The facts – nobody could claim the facts were crystal clear.
> What is clear is there was a considerable killing of Aboriginal women and children here.
> It seems it was over a mistaken belief that they were eating a stolen cow.
> In fact, the cow turned up afterwards …
> It's essential that we hear, listen to and acknowledge the facts of what happened in the past, the facts of the dispossession and the facts of terrible events such as what happened here at Mistake Creek in the 1930s, which is, in my lifetime. I'd like to say to the Kitja people how profoundly sorry I personally am that such events defaced our land, this beautiful land.[15]

It is obvious that the above quotation contains neither an apology nor a reference to perpetrators.

Windschuttle's 'Opinion'

The significance of *The 7.30 Report* is that it put a second date into circulation. Windschuttle responded by offering an 'Opinion' in which he drew on the EKIAP material to show that the Mistake Creek massacre had not occurred in the 1930s.[16] Most of his readers would have taken his point that 'Deane should have taken more care to get these particular facts right' before he 'sat in the red dirt with members of the Kija people in the East Kimberley and apologised for the brutality they had suffered'.

The same readers would not have known that Windschuttle, in borrowing five paragraphs of 'facts' from EKIAP Paper No. 29, had introduced five errors and turned three possibilities into certainties. Nor would they have known, unless they saw the transcripts of the speech and *The 7.30 Report*, that Sir William had neither apologised nor attempted to tell the story of the massacre. It was Windschuttle who went public with the oral history and its reference to a non-indigenous perpetrator named Mick Rhatigan.

The archival evidence summarised in the EKIAP paper showed that the massacre occurred on 30 March 1915. The eight people killed included Hopples, who was Mick Rhatigan's Aboriginal offsider. The survivors included Charlie, who was shot through the arm and reached a camp at Turkey Creek. Someone from that camp then informed the postmaster that 'Michael Rhatigan senior linesman and two boys Joe Wynn and Nipper had shot blacks at Mistake Creek'.[17] Nipper and Joe Wynn (also spelt Winn) were both Aboriginal and did occasional work for Rhatigan.

In Windschuttle's 'Opinion', Hopples, Joe Wynn and Nipper were 'Aboriginal station hands' from Mistake Creek Station, and Rhatigan was 'the white overseer of the station'. That corruption of the historical record is important because Windschuttle used it to dismiss the massacre as 'an internal feud between Aboriginal station hands'.[18]

No one will ever be able to prove what happened. Oral history related by Gija elders Bob Nyalcas and Winnie Budbaria placed Rhatigan at the scene and attributed his involvement to his belief that the people at Mistake Creek had killed and eaten his milking cow.[19] Archival records showed that, after a police party killed Joe Wynn, the police charged Rhatigan and Nipper with wilful murder and held them on remand for more than three weeks pending the outcome of an inquest.[20]

In one of two other accounts mentioned in EKIAP Paper No. 29, Matt Savage, a north Australian drover, attributed the massacre to 'a cold, heartless bloke' who had already killed 'plenty' of Aboriginal people.[21] Those killings might have been ones that occurred when Rhatigan worked as an East Kimberley police constable.[22] In the other account, Ion Idriess exonerated Rhatigan in a story that has one serious flaw but is otherwise, as the EKIAP paper noted, reasonably true to the police file on the massacre.[23]

Windschuttle seized on the Idriess account and concluded his 'Opinion' about the events at Mistake Creek with the following comments:

> This is not the kind of event for which the Governor-General of Australia should be apologising to Aboriginal people, or making theatrical gestures of reconciliation. Indeed, it reflects poorly on Deane's decision to stake his reputation on relations with the Aborigines when he displays such a cavalier attitude to their history and fails to do the most elementary research.
>
> Nor does the way this story was told on television reflect much credit on the ABC's Kerry O'Brien. It would have taken any competent researcher less than two hours to verify the information. O'Brien was prepared to spend the time to fly to the Kimberley with the Governor-General but not to instruct a researcher to check the facts.
>
> Had he done so, he might have had a few searching questions to ask Sir William about the symbolism of his performance at Mistake Creek.[24]

Correcting Windschuttle's Errors

Public debate followed with O'Brien refuting the allegation about the ABC's lack of research and stating that he had consulted four separate accounts of the massacre. He also criticised Windschuttle's selective use of sources and his omission of the EKIAP acknowledgment of Rhatigan's possible involvement.[25]

Windschuttle, ignoring the remark about selective use of sources, responded by writing:

> The oral history on which Deane based his speech was nothing more

than a statement the artist Charlene Carrington tagged to her 1999 painting of the site.

Carrington says her information came from 'my granny, Winnie, who was a little girl when this happened'.

The fact that Aborigines are now blaming whites for a massacre of Aborigines committed by Aborigines and that the Governor-General gives his imprimatur to the whole charade, is something that a journalist who did his job properly should have questioned, not accepted demurely.

O'Brien's research should have also made him question Peggy Patrick who appeared on his program claiming both her parents, two brothers and two sisters were massacred at the time. If her parents were killed in 1915, Patrick must now be at least 86 years old, yet on television she did not look a day over 50.[26]

Had Windschuttle examined the police file on the massacre, he would have known that the story of Rhatigan's involvement dated from the morning of the massacre. Had he been aware that Patrick, a Gija elder, does not speak standard English, he might have been less critical of her. She speaks Gija and Kimberley Kriol (the lingua franca for Aboriginal people in the region) and she had said 'My mum mother, father, and two brother, two sister got killed here too.' She had not, as Windschuttle asserted, claimed that those people were killed 'at the time' of the 1915 massacre. Nor had she claimed that her mother and father were killed. In using the words 'my mum mother, father' she had been referring to her mum's mother and father.[27]

O'Brien corrected two of Windschuttle's errors. He pointed out, first, that Patrick 'was referring to her grandparents (her mother's parents)', and second, that she gave her age as 71.[28] The debate about Mistake Creek continued but it needs no further discussion here. It is sufficient to note that O'Brien had drawn Windschuttle's attention to two of his errors and to his selective use of sources.

Myth Recounted as Fact

On 22 September 2001, *The Sydney Morning Herald* used a Mistake Creek photograph to introduce an article about Windschuttle's forthcoming book. In the article, Andrew Stevenson described Windschuttle as:

the historian the Prime Minister has been searching for all these years, someone with the scissors to snip through the black armband which Howard believes has cast a pall over Australia's past, present and future.

Then, discussing methodology, Stevenson wrote:

Windschuttle says it's about intellectual honesty – that he eschews politics and is willing and able to pursue the historical truth – unlike the Reynolds generation which, he claims, has sought to advance a political agenda by reworking the past.

That statement was at odds with Windschuttle's version of the events at Mistake Creek, and in another *Sydney Morning Herald* article on 30 October, Stevenson explored some of the inconsistencies. In doing so he also recounted as fact part of the myth created by Windschuttle. The former Governor-General had, according to Stevenson, 'apologised' for a massacre at Mistake Creek.

In another October development, a journalist writing about the Western Australian police contacted the author of this essay to obtain the accession number for the archival file on the Mistake Creek massacre. In his subsequent recycling of the Windschuttle myth, he made the peculiar claim that 'the silence of the irrepressible Mr Gribble', a Forrest River missionary, constitutes a 'negative piece of "evidence" that further undermines the *7.30 Report* version'.[29]

In November, *The West Australian* carried a feature article that asked, 'What really happened at Mistake Creek? And why is it so important to reconciliation between white and black Australia?' In that article, Moran embellished the Windschuttle myth, stating that Sir William had 'apologised for the massacre, presumably on behalf of the Australian people'. Moran also mentioned the earlier debate and elaborated on the EKIAP summary of archival evidence. In doing so, he argued that Rhatigan (correctly identified as the telegraph lineman) was innocent of any involvement. In closing, he mentioned that Sir William, despite having acknowledged that the massacre occurred in 1915 rather than the

1930s, was standing by his belief that the written record supported Aboriginal accounts of a white man's involvement.[30]

Moran knew that Rhatigan went free on an order of *nolle prosequi*, which is not the same as being found innocent. Yet, on grounds no more substantial than the archival evidence failing to mention a cow or a boab tree, he pronounced him innocent. The story in which Sir William had put his faith was, as far as Moran could see, one 'that could have been contaminated over generations by another Aboriginal story'. He did not reveal the source of the other story, which told of a bullock, a boab tree and killings at Horseshoe Creek.[31]

It would be very surprising if people to whom country is fundamentally important confused events at Mistake Creek with those at Horseshoe Creek. One of the events in that locality, which has historical links with Texas Downs Station, resulted in Aboriginal women showing a constable where a stockman named Tommy had killed Jimmy and Friday in 1901. Constable Thomson wrote:

> I seen burnt remains of a human being the fire was just about burnt out, also seen fresh shod horse tracks, could not find boot tracks, as all country is very stony and about 25 chains south of this body found another remains of a human body had been burnt about two weeks since.[32]

An inquest led to a charge of wilful murder, and a police report noted that:

> It is hard to get a Jury in Wyndham as there are so few people and they being in Business it is against their interest to give a verdict as the public of the East Kimberley are all siding with the Culprit Thomas McLaughlin.[33]

Another police report included the following comments:

> I consider there is a Very Poor case against McLaughlin as the natives give there [*sic*] evidence very bad. and it is a great trouble to get them to answer any question regarding the dead men.[34]

The wilful murder charge, like the later one against Rhatigan, was eventually withdrawn but the file provides the sort of evidence that both

Moran and Windschuttle believe must be present before Aboriginal oral history can be seen to be reliable. Such evidence is, however, often hard to find. Like the evidence of the Mistake Creek massacre and Rhatigan's killing of Aboriginal people at Argyle station, it was found only because the author of this essay did months of archival research to ascertain whether killings mentioned in the various stories in EKIAP Paper No. 28 were recorded elsewhere.

Reinforcement of the Myth

In December 2001, Windschuttle used the Mistake Creek massacre to argue that 'Aboriginal oral history, when uncorroborated by original documents, is completely unreliable, just like the oral history of white people'. He also argued that Deane 'made a fool of himself' when he 'used his last days in office to apologise to the Kija people for this incident and for all those that Aborigines had suffered at the hands of white settlers'. The myth had grown but few other changes were evident. Windschuttle mentioned that four Aboriginal accounts of the massacre had 'made their way into either print or television' but he gave no indication of having seen EKIAP Paper No. 28. He acknowledged Patrick's correct age but repeated his unfounded accusation that she had claimed that her parents were killed at Mistake Creek in 1915. He also persisted with his false claim that 'Aboriginal oral history later implicated the white overseer of the station' in the massacre.[35]

In May 2002, *Quadrant* published an expanded version of Moran's article, which laboured the point that Rhatigan could not have been involved in killings in the 1930s because he died in 1920.[36] That was hardly news when the obscurely titled police file used to date the massacre in EKIAP Paper No. 29 had been located by working backwards from the date of Rhatigan's death. Nor was it particularly relevant when Sir William had long since acknowledged his mistake regarding the date of the massacre. The approach did, however, lend unwarranted credence to Moran's assertion that nothing in the police file 'even remotely supports the version of events presented by Sir William Deane and Kerry O'Brien'.

Moran's arguments impressed Peter Walsh who wrote:

Rod Moran, a journalist from *The West Australian* newspaper has in recent years devoted considerable effort to exposing those who spice political propaganda with historical fraud.

Specifically he has exposed, by careful examination of extant contemporaneous records, the fiction of massacres at Forrest River and Mistake Creek.

The latter was heavily promoted when former Governor-General Sir William Deane, with eager assistance from the ABC and undisclosed cost to the Australian taxpayer, arranged a media stunt at Mistake Creek in the Kimberley region at which, on behalf of the Australian people, he apologised for the 'massacre' by whitey of several Aborigines in the 1930s.[37]

There was more in the same vein but it is enough to note that Walsh, while applauding the exposure of historical fraud, blithely recounted the myth of Sir William having 'apologised' for a massacre perpetrated 'by whitey'. Paul Sheehan adopted a similar approach. On 25 November 2002, he devoted the first seven paragraphs of an article to the myth. He took the line that 'Sir William Deane, then governor-general, apologised to the Kija people for an infamous massacre by whites'. Then, before promoting a pre-launch copy of *The Fabrication of Aboriginal History*, he suggested that 'Deane might one day reflect on his role in defaming the Australian people on the basis of shabby evidence'.[38]

Two days later, the *Herald* carried seven letters written in response to Sheehan's article.[39] It also carried an article by Sir William. He had responded, he said, 'only by reason of the hurt that Sheehan's article, if left unanswered, may cause to the Kija people of the region'. The remainder of the article read:

> As regards details of the killings, there is conflict between the Kija oral history and local police records about the nature and extent of the involvement of a non-indigenous former police constable named Rhatigan. Otherwise, there is a remarkable degree of common ground between the oral history and the police records. There was a killing by shooting of at least seven Kija people. Undoubtedly, two Aboriginal employees of Rhatigan were involved, riding Rhatigan's horses and

presumably using his firearms. There was pre-existing enmity between some of the Kija people and one of the Aboriginal employees, Wynn, who was from elsewhere in Australia. Wynn was apparently killed by an Aboriginal police tracker in the aftermath of the massacre. The other employee, 'Nipper', subsequently surrendered to the police.

According to Kija oral history, recounted in some published non-indigenous works and repeated with complete conviction by present-day Kija people, Rhatigan had led the attack because he mistakenly believed, presumably at the urging of Wynn, that the Aboriginal victims had taken and killed (and were eating) his milking cow. In fact, the cow had merely wandered and was found after the massacre.

According to police records, to which historian Cathie Clement drew attention in 1989, there was no basis for a conclusion of direct involvement of Rhatigan, notwithstanding his employees, his horses, his firearms and, apparently, his presence in the vicinity. On that version, Wynn and Nipper had carried out the killings on their own and on their own initiative.

At one stage I accepted that the killings occurred 'in the 1930s'. I now believe that Clement's work leads to the conclusion that they took place in 1915. In these circumstances, as Clement has stressed, one cannot simply ignore the indigenous oral history to the extent that it is not supported by police records.

It is clear that there was throughout Australia, including the Kimberley at these times, often reluctance on the part of police to file adverse reports or to bring proceedings against white settlers in respect of extreme physical retribution against Aborigines for the killing of live-stock on traditional lands. It needs little imagination to conceive that that reluctance could well be heightened in a case where a former police constable was involved.

At the same time, there would be few lawyers, at least of my genera-tion, with relevant experience who are unaware of how misleading and unreliable untested police reports of alleged verbal statements by illit-erate, particularly illiterate Aboriginal, accused or witnesses can be. If one were to restrict acceptance of oral indigenous history in relation to the killing of Aborigines to those cases where there was confirm-atory police evidence or action, the resulting sanitised version of the events of the dispossession would be contrary to plain fact and even commonsense.

In the case of Mistake Creek, the oral history is remarkably strong. As published and as recounted by Kija people, it lacks any dreamtime element of the kind that can occasionally lead to confusion between fact and allegory. The foundation of that oral history presumably lies in the eyewitness accounts of three Kija people who survived the massacre.

For another, the police initially arrested Rhatigan on suspicion of wilful murder. They did not proceed with the charge. Nipper, the Aborigine who had surrendered to the police, was charged with murder. The charge against him was also eventually dropped when the police failed to produce any acceptable evidence. He was subsequently taken to Perth where he was employed in the police stables.

No one was brought to justice for the killings and the police version of events, in so far as it differs from the strong Kija oral history, was never tested in a criminal trial.

It is also relevant to note, as regards the police evidence, that Clement, upon whose research Windschuttle expressly relied (*Australian Financial Review*, June 18, 2001), has dissociated herself from Windschuttle's use of her work in his efforts to discredit the Kija oral history.

The Sisters of St Joseph, who have selflessly served the indigenous peoples of the East Kimberley for many years, have erected a small monument at the foot of the old boab tree at Mistake Creek to mark the place where the killings occurred. There, on All Souls Day each year, representatives of the Kija gather in prayer and fellowship with non-indigenous fellow Australians, to mourn those who were killed. 'Theirs is', as I have pointed out, 'the path of true reconciliation.'[40]

The article prompted Windschuttle to assert:

— that 'Sir William Deane's version of what happened at Mistake Creek is as changeable as the oral history on which he relies';
— that Moran had 'forced' Deane to concede 'that it was a killing of Aborigines by Aborigines and it took place in 1915 not the 1930s';
— that Deane had defamed the Western Australian police by suggesting that they had invented witness statements; and

— that he had accused 'a white man of murder on the basis of nothing more than oral tales told 80 years after the event'.[41]

None of those assertions had substance but no journalist or editor is known to have challenged them. Instead, Windschuttle's myth gave rise to another 11 paragraphs (complete with the unfounded allegations about Peggy Patrick) on 1 December; an opening paragraph on the 6th; a headline on the 12th; and a paragraph on the 19th.[42] *Quadrant* mentioned it, too, with Peter Coleman writing, 'It is not enough to say with fine impartiality that the truth may lie somewhere between Deane and Windschuttle. The issue is one of truth or error and can be decided by evidence.'[43]

If only it were so simple. The evidence is there but, unless Windschuttle and those who accept his pronouncements start to do what he claims to be doing, truth will not prevail. He claims to be examining 'how we can know about the past, the kinds of evidence we can regard as reliable, and how to detect false claims when they are made'. That approach, as this essay shows, can be quite productive. It would be good to see it used, without bias, in the next two volumes of *The Fabrication of Aboriginal History*. It might not 'establish what really happened' but it would contribute to our understanding of the past. It might also prevent the denigration of Aboriginal people who have the courage to share their stories of past violence. That denigration has been mentioned above and, as Peggy Patrick shows in the statement that follows this essay, it has profound impact.

NOTES

1. Keith Windschuttle, *The Fabrication of Aboriginal History: Volume One, Van Diemen's Land 1803 –1847*, Sydney, Macleay Press, 2002, p. 10.
2 *Ibid*, pp. 1–3, 7–9.
3. *Ibid*, pp. 2–7, 9–10.
4. *Ibid*, pp. 3–7, 9–10.
5. *Ibid*, pp. 7–8.
6. Address by Sir William Deane, Governor-General of the Commonwealth of Australia, on the occasion of the Ceremony of Reconciliation with the Kiji [sic] people, Mistake Creek, 7/6/2001, copy viewed at
http://www.gg.gov.au/speeches/textonly/speeches/2001/010607.html;
and Transcript, *The 7.30 Report*, 11/6/2001, 'A look at Sir William Deane's term as Governor-General', copy viewed at http://www.abc.net.au/7.30/s311226.htm.

7. Windschuttle, *Fabrication*, p. 7.

8. Helen Ross, *Community Social Impact Assessment: A Cumulative Study in the Turkey Creek Area, Western Australia*, East Kimberley Working Paper No. 27, CRES, ANU, Canberra, 1989, pp. 1–6.

9. *Ibid*, pp. 10–17.

10. Rod Moran, 'Millennia-old oral culture puts down written roots', *The West Australian*, 2/4/1994, 'big weekend' section, p. 7.

11. See, for example, Rod Moran, 'Was there a massacre at Bedford Downs?', *Quadrant*, November 2002, pp. 48–51.

12. Rod Moran, *Massacre Myth: An Investigation into Allegations Concerning the Mass Murder of Aborigines at Forrest River, 1926*, Access Press, Bassendean (WA), 1999, pp. xxi–xxii.

13. *The Australian*, 6/12/2002, p. 12.

14. The information about the massacre came from an EKIAP Paper No. 29 extract circulated to journalists who covered the ceremony. The *Herald* mentioned the author's name but not the EKIAP paper.

15. Transcript, *The 7.30 Report*, 11/6/2001. It is noted that the language group to which the people belong is generally identified as either Gija or Kija.

16. Keith Windschuttle, 'Wrong on Mistake Creek', *The Australian Financial Review*, 18/6/2001, p. 54, 'Opinion', copy provided by Lindsay Peet.

17. State Records Office of Western Australia (SROWA), AN 5/2, Police Department, Acc 430, 1854/1915, Aboriginal Native Tracker 'Nipper'. From C. of P., pp. 21–4.

18. Windschuttle, 'Wrong on Mistake Creek'.

19. Helen Ross (ed.) and Eileen Bray (transl.), *Impact Stories of the East Kimberley*, East Kimberley Working Paper No. 28, CRES, ANU, Canberra, 1989, pp. 73–5.

20. SROWA, AN 5/2, Police Department, Acc 430, 1854/1915, Aboriginal Native Tracker 'Nipper'.

21. Cathie Clement, *Historical Notes Relevant to Impact Stories of the East Kimberley*, East Kimberley Working Paper No. 29, CRES, ANU, Canberra, 1989, pp. 17, 35, citing Keith Willey, *Boss Drover*, Rigby, Adelaide, 1971, pp. 15–16.

22. See, for example, SROWA, Acc 527, Colonial Secretary's Office, 823/1895, Correspondence regarding necessity for a police station at Negri River. That file records Rhatigan shooting four men who fled from the carcase of a dead cow on Argyle Station on 5 May 1895.

23. Clement, *Historical Notes*, p. 36, note 11, citing Ion Idriess, *Tracks of Destiny*, pp. 43–50.

24. Windschuttle, 'Wrong on Mistake Creek'.

25. Kerry O'Brien, 'Mistake Creek record used "selectively"', *The Australian Financial Review*, 20/6/2001, p. 51, 'Letters', copy provided by Lindsay Peet.

26. Keith Windschuttle, 'O'Brien accused of advocating implausible history', *The Australian Financial Review*, 21/6/2001, p. 58, 'Letters', copy provided by Lindsay Peet.

27. Linguist Frances Kofod, who assisted with EKIAP Paper No. 28 and continues to work with Gija speakers, advised (personal comment to Cathie Clement) that, because the English 's' sound does not occur in the Gija language, older Gija speakers cannot pronounce the combination 'ms' at the end of an English word. Further information about the pre-1908 massacre to which Patrick referred is available in *blood on the spinifex*, guest curator Tony Oliver, Ian Potter Museum of Art, University of Melbourne, Melbourne, 2002, pp. 36, 38. The account is presented

there as it was told by Patrick, in Gija interspersed with Kriol, with an English translation produced by Kofod.

28. Kerry O'Brien, 'Wider injustices remembered in massacre debate', *The Australian Financial Review*, 26/6/2001, p. 60, 'Letters', copy provided by Lindsay Peet.

29. Peter Conole, *Protect & Serve: A History of Policing in Western Australia*, Access Press, Bayswater, WA, 2002, p. 187.

30. Rod Moran, 'Mistaken Identity', *The West Australian*, 17/11/2001, 'big weekend' section, p. 3.

31. *Ibid*. See Ross and Bray, *Impact Stories*, pp. 3–5, 12–13, and Oliver (guest curator), *blood on the spinifex*, p. 44, for information about killings at Horseshoe Creek.

32. SROWA, AN 5/2, Police Department, Acc 430, 1382/1905, Alleged murder of two natives by Thomas McLoughlan, pp. [3–4]. See Cathie Clement, 'Monotony, Manhunts & Malice: Eastern Kimberley Law Enforcement, 1896–1908' in *Early Days* (Journal of the Royal WA Historical Society), vol. 10, pt. 1, 1989, pp. 93–4, for comment on the case.

33. SROWA, AN 5/2, Police Department, Acc 430, 1382/1905, portion of file marked C.O. 4560/01.

34. SROWA, AN 5/2, Police Department, Acc 430, 1382/1905, p. [25].

35. Keith Windschuttle, 'Doctored evidence and invented incidents in Aboriginal historiography' in *Frontier Conflict: The Australian Experience*, ed. by B. Attwood and S. G. Foster, Canberra, National Museum of Australia, 2003, pp. 106–7.

36. Rod Moran, 'Mistaken Identity: The massacre of Aborigines at Mistake Creek', *Quadrant*, May 2002, pp. 14–17.

37. Peter Walsh, '*Chutzpah* has no limits', *The Adelaide Review*, June 2002, p. 10, copy provided by Bernie O'Neil.

38. *The Sydney Morning Herald*, 25/11/2002, on-line edition, copy viewed at http://www.smh.com.au/articles/2002/11/24/1037697982065.html.

39. *The Sydney Morning Herald*, 27/11/2002, p. 14, copy viewed at http://www.smh.com.au/articles/2002/11/26/1038274301355.htm.

40. *Ibid*, 27/11/2002, p. 15, copy viewed at http://www.smh.com.au/articles/2002/11/26/1038274302698.html.

41. *Ibid*, 28/11/2002, p. 12, copy viewed at http://www.smh.com.au/text/articles/2002/11/27/1038386201394.htm.

42. Piers Akerman, 'Reconciliation begins with truth', *The Sunday Telegraph*, 1/12/2002, p. 111; Bernard Lane, 'Stripping the Armbands', *The Australian*, 6/12/2002, p. 12; 'The dispute over Mistake Creek', *The Economist*, 12/12/2002, Sydney edition on-line; and Miranda Devine, 'The book launch, bluster and backdowns', *The Sydney Morning Herald*, 19/12/2002, on-line edition.

43. Peter Coleman, '*The Fabrication of Aboriginal History: Volume One* by Keith Windschuttle' in *Quadrant*, December 2002, pp. 80–1, 'Books'.

Statement of Peggy Patrick

I bin born la bush. I never bin go school. We got own language, Gija, Miriwoong, Worla. We talk blackfella English not this gardiya [white people's] high English.

Early day gardiya bin really cruel la black fella. My mother bin little girl when her mum, her mum sister, her father bin get killed right in front of her. The read and write mob the one bin doing all the killing. They never write down what they did. We don't read and write but we hear about what bin happen before from our mother and father and we still got it in our mind. We never talk to gardiya about this cruel thing because people bin still frightened. If they say anything they might get killed themself.

Then lately we start talk about it. My big brother and his brother-in-law Paddy Bedford brought out the Joonba about what happen at Bedford Down. My friend Sir William Deane and ABC man Kerry O'Brien bin come la that boab tree la Mistake Creek where my mum mum bin get killed. They listened to me. I don't talk that high English but everybody who talk to me face to face understand properly what I bin tell 'em. My ganggay, my mum mum, bin get killed along with big mob more family.

Then people tell me that one gardiya call Windschuttle never listen to my word proper. He never come up here and talk to me face to face in my own country. He write bad way about me because he can't listen to my word proper way. He make fun of me. He reckon I bin say 'my mum' when I bin really talk 'ganggayi' or 'my mum mum' not 'my mum'.

First time when he say this bad thing about me Kerry O'Brien bin tell him good way la newspaper he bin make a mistake but he still never listen. He keep going pretending that I got a high English and try make me look stupid.

Bad enough this terrible thing bin happen before. That Windschuttle hurt my family feeling and it make us feel bad for all the relation bin get killed at Mistake Creek.

Even after Kerry O'Brien bin tell him he make a mistake and ABC mob put my word right way in gardiya high English on the ABC website he put out another story still saying the same bad thing about me.

I asked Peter Seidel the lawyer bin helping my Corporation and who work with that reconciliation man Mark Leibler to write to him ask him to apologise to me. He won't apologise and won't believe that I don't speak high English. He keep going saying that I really say my own mother bin get killed when I never say that. I bin talking for my ganggayi, my mum mum and her family.

He try say I change my word. I never change my word. I know what happen.

After that first lot of gardiya come here people were forced to go sit down la station and work for them. Policeman bin riding everywhere got a horse bringing people in. They work for tea, flour, sugar and tobacco, no money. We were treated like dog in we own country, just like a slave. Government mob never even think about we human being. We had no vote and no citizenship. We know people bin get killed all over the country. Now people like this Windschuttle try to say nobody bin get killed because gardiya never write 'em down what they bin do.

He make out I stupid because he can't understand my word. He reckon I gota put my word in high English myself.

He reckon he good one telling true story proper way. He say other people should make sure they got true story. He can't take notice when people tell him he make a mistake himself. Some of people say 'gardiya never believe blackfella.'

Sometime mum bin all day cry for it when he bin tell us story. Now gardiya talking bad way for my mum story. He rubbish my name and he rubbish all my relation that bin get kill. He make big shame for me all over. Make me and all my family real upset.

We bin bring out hard story what bin happen to blackfella. We talk about bad story so black and white can be friend when we look at true thing together. Look like nothing change. Gardiya killed blackfella with gun and poison now look like he killing our life making fun of my word. Not worth.

27 March 2003

Risdon Cove

Phillip Tardif

Keith Windschuttle calls the first chapter of *The Fabrication of Aboriginal History* 'The Killing Fields at Risdon Cove'. In it he seeks to reinterpret the massacre of Aborigines by settlers at Risdon Cove in Tasmania on 3 May 1804. For Windschuttle, the way this event has been recorded is a metaphor for his broader thesis. It shows, he says, 'how the conflict between Aborigines and settlers has long been exaggerated by people far removed from the scene and by rumours and myths that have perpetuated themselves'.[1]

Risdon Cove on the Derwent River was the site of the first European settlement in Tasmania. On 11 September 1803, a small party of soldiers, settlers and convicts led by 23-year-old navy lieutenant John Bowen arrived there from Sydney to pre-empt a rumoured French settlement. By 3 May 1804, the Risdon camp had been superseded by a new settlement at the present site of Hobart. A NSW Corps lieutenant, William Moore, was in command of the eighty or so people still living at Risdon Cove, Bowen being away at the time. Tension at Risdon was high, a near-mutiny by the soldiers having been put down less than a fortnight before. That day, a party of around 300 Aboriginal men, women and children came upon Europeans hunting and farming on the outskirts of the settlement. The settlers' reaction – the killing that occurred over the next three hours – became known as the Risdon massacre.

Windschuttle argues that historians of the Risdon massacre have been led astray by the testimony of those who were not there at the time. He says that if we stick to the 'facts' as told by the eyewitnesses, we see that the incident was merely an unfortunate misunderstanding in which just two or three Aborigines lost their lives.

Yet Windschuttle seems to find some 'facts' less convenient than others. While he accepts the word of two of the three eyewitnesses whose memories of that day were recorded, he goes to extraordinary lengths to wish away and discredit the testimony of the third. Is it a coincidence that this eyewitness, Edward White, claimed that 'there were a great many of the Natives slaughtered and wounded'?[2] White, an Irish ex-convict, left the most extensive account of the massacre under cross-examination before a committee of inquiry in 1830. The other eyewitnesses, Lieutenant Moore and Surgeon-Magistrate Jacob Mountgarret, were active participants in the attack.

How credible were these men? Moore, an officer of the infamous Rum Corps, was described as a 'mutinous rascal' by Risdon's commander, John Bowen. On one occasion Moore threatened to bring his troops out in arms against Bowen.[3] He later played a prominent role in the military coup that overthrew Governor Bligh. Mountgarret's credibility is equally flawed. He was sacked as Magistrate at Port Dalrymple in 1814 and later faced trial for assisting two bushrangers. Governor Macquarie wrote about the man's 'eternal disgrace and infamy'.[4]

Edward White, on the other hand, was one of the few convicts considered useful and reliable enough to retain at Hobart when the Risdon settlement was abandoned. When he testified before the Committee for the Affairs of the Aborigines in 1830, White had every reason to embellish the truth in favour of the soldiers. Anger in the colony was white-hot against the Aborigines following a series of killings. That he did not adds credibility to what he said. As the distinguished nineteenth-century historian J. B. Walker wrote, White's account 'looks probable, like the story of a man who had kept his head amidst the general panic'.[5]

Windschuttle's attempts to wish away the inconvenient evidence of the Risdon massacre began two years ago in a National Press Club debate with Henry Reynolds. Windschuttle implied that the reports of Moore and Mountgarret were the only first-hand accounts. White's evidence about the number killed was not mentioned at all![6] Similarly, in

The Fabrication of Aboriginal History, Moore's and Mountgarret's accounts are reproduced in full. White's is not.

White's testimony about the peaceable intentions of the Aborigines is ignored by Windschuttle. According to White, 'the natives did not threaten me; I was not afraid of them; … [they] did not attack the soldiers; they would not have molested them … they had no spears with them; only waddies.' On the contrary, the language in three accounts admits to aggression on the part of the Europeans. According to White, 'the soldiers came down from their own camp to the creek to *attack* the Natives.' Lieutenant-Governor Collins, after speaking to the officers involved, feared that the Aborigines would indiscriminately seek to exact revenge 'upon those who had no share in the *Attack*'. Even Lieutenant Moore wrote of 'the Circumstances that led to the *attack* on the Natives'.[7]

Elsewhere, Windschuttle uncritically accepts Moore's explanation of events. Moore's principal justification for the attack by the soldiers was that the Aborigines were beating the settler Birt at his hut. No other first-hand account refers to such an incident, although Windschuttle has falsely asserted that Surgeon Mountgarret made the same claim.[8] Even Moore admits he did not see it with his own eyes: 'I was *informed* that a party of them was beating Birt, the Settler, at his farm.'[9] White, who was working close to Birt's hut, swore that the Aborigines never came within 220 yards of it.

Having accepted at face value the stories told by Moore and Mountgarret, Windschuttle picks at the tiniest threads of White's evidence to try to show him as a mere peddler of gossip with a faulty memory. First, he claims White could have only seen a very small part of the action, because after he met the Aborigines he said he went back to his work hoeing new ground near Birt's hut. This, according to Windschuttle, was 'where he remained the whole time',[10] a claim backed by no evidence whatsoever. On the contrary, it is clear from White's statement that he was familiar with the entire incident at Risdon that day, not just the episode at Birt's hut. As he said, 'I could show [you] all the ground.'[11]

Windschuttle asserts that the soldiers would not have been physically able to kill as many Aborigines as White claims, because they only carried single-shot muskets. Yet this was a clash that lasted three hours – plenty of time for the soldiers to reload. The shooting commenced at about 11 a.m. and only ended at 2 p.m. when the military brought up and fired one of the settlement's two carronades. There were between 74 and 80 Europeans at Risdon that day. Easily two-dozen of them had access to a musket, a bayonet or a sword, enough to inflict a lot of harm on the several hundred unarmed men, women and children in the Aboriginal band over three hours.

As to the carronade, Windschuttle asserts that it must only have fired a blank because it was located at Risdon for ceremonial purposes. Whether the carronade was used on 3 May to frighten or to kill will never be known, but it cannot be asserted without any evidence that it fired a blank. The carronade, one of two taken from Matthew Flinders' *Investigator,* had been sent to Risdon 'with Shot and their other Materials'. Bowen had been warned to keep them under close guard lest the convicts rise up and use them against him.[12] Clearly their principal purpose at Risdon was to do what they were built for – to kill and to maim.

Windschuttle also questions the accuracy of White's memory in light of his claim that the hut of settler Birt was on the opposite side of the creek to that of settler Clark. Two plans made in 1803 do place Birt and Clark on half-acre allotments on the same side of the creek, but does that prove they were still there six months later?[13] By May 1804, both settlers were farming much larger allotments of five acres, an expansion that would have been hard to achieve without a change of location. There had been a considerable drought that year and it would have been logical to move nearer the creek. White's statement that Birt's farm was on the other side of the creek is backed by the report of the 1830 committee of inquiry, which stated Birt's hut was 'considerably advanced beyond the rest'.[14] Faced with two sets of 'facts' – an out-of-date map and an account from a person who was on the spot at the time – Windschuttle chooses the former to discredit the latter.

Finally, White's claim that Mountgarret sent the bones of some of the murdered Aborigines to Sydney in two casks is further proof of his unreliability, according to Windschuttle, because he was a convict and therefore wouldn't be directly aware of what members of the 'colonial elite' like Mountgarret were doing.[15] This argument is patently absurd. The Risdon 'colonial elite' in May 1804 comprised only Mountgarret, Moore, Bowen, storekeeper Thomas Wilson and a few settlers. Living as they did in small wooden huts, cheek-by-jowl with sixty to seventy soldiers and convicts, it is hard to imagine even the most minor piece of gossip passing at Risdon without every resident knowing about it, let alone the removal of bodies from the field, their dissection and their storage for shipping to Sydney three months later. We know from Mountgarret's own pen that he dissected at least one of the bodies. To have then removed the flesh and preserved the bones for further medical and scientific examination would have been entirely consistent with contemporary practice.

Keith Windschuttle has erred by weighting the facts to suit his thesis about what happened at Risdon Cove on 3 May 1804. The rest of his work warrants similar scrutiny. We will never know for sure how many were killed or wounded that day. Certainly it was more than two or three. Probably it was fewer than fifty. Somewhere in between lies the 'great many' spoken of by Edward White, whose poignant testimony remains for me the most credible description of this sorry episode.

Testimony of former convict Edward White before the Committee for the Affairs of the Aborigines, Hobart, March 16th 1830[16]

Was one of the first men who landed 27 years ago; built Lieutenant Bowen's house at Risdon; was then servant to a man named Clark; on the 3d May 1804, was hoeing new ground near a creek; saw 300 of the Natives come down in a circular form, and a flock of kangaroos hemmed in between them; there were men, women and children; 'they looked at me with all their eyes,' I went down to the creek, and reported them to some soldiers, and then went back to my work; the natives did not threaten me; I was not afraid of them; Clark's house was near where I was at work, and Burke's [Birt's] house near Clark's house; the Natives were never within half a quarter of a mile of Burke's house; the Natives did not attack the soldiers; they would not have molested them; the firing commenced about 11 o'clock; there were a great many of the Natives slaughtered and wounded; I don't know how many; some of their bones were sent in two casks to Port Jackson by Dr. Mountgarrett; they went in the Ocean; a boy was taken from them; this was three or four months after we landed; they never came so close again afterwards; they had no spears with them; only waddies; they were hunting and came down into a bottom; there were hundreds and hundreds of kangaroos about Risdon then, and all over where Hobart Town now stands; the Natives were driven from their houses afterwards, and their wives and children were taken from them by stock-keepers; lived three years as a shepherd in the Western Tier; was always afraid of them; afraid they would kill him; they often fell in with him; never pursued him; they carried spears in the bush; he never carried a gun; the soldiers came down from their own camp to the creek to attack the Natives; I could show all the ground; Mr. Clark was there; the Natives were close to his house; they were not on Burke's side of the creek; never heard that any of them went to Burke's house; is sure they did not know there was a white man in the country when they came down to Risdon.

The Natives leave their women and children behind them when they are going to war; believes the largest Natives were at Prosser's Plains; does not know any difference between the Natives of New South Wales and here; 'those at Port Jackson are savager'.

NOTES

1. Keith Windschuttle, *The Fabrication of Aboriginal History: Volume One, Van Diemen's Land 1803–1847*, Sydney, Macleay Press, 2002, p. 15.

2. Testimony of Edward White in 'Minutes of Evidence Taken Before the Committee for the Affairs of the Aborigines', *Commons Papers*, 1831, vol. 19, p. 53.

3. Minutes of Proceedings of Military Courts Martial and related papers, Lieutenant William Moore, 1804, Archives Office of NSW, 5/1155 17/9.

4. Macquarie to Davey, 24/5/1814, HRA Series III, vol. 2, p. 56.

5. J. B. Walker, 'The English at the Derwent, and the Risdon Settlement', 14/10/1889, in *Early Tasmania: Papers*, Government Printer, Tasmania, 3rd impression, 1950, p. 53.

6. National Press Club debate, 19/4/2001. Text can be found at www.sydneyline.com/ National%20Press%20Club%20debate.htm

7. Testimony of Edward White, p. 53; Collins to King, 15/5/1804, in HRA Series III, vol. 1, p. 238; Moore to Collins, 7/5/1804, in HRA Series III, vol. 1, p. 242. (Emphasis added.)

8. National Press Club, 19/4/2001.

9. Moore to Collins, 7/5/1804, in HRA Series III, vol. 1, p. 242, emphasis added.

10. Windschuttle, *Fabrication*, p. 22.

11. Testimony of Edward White, p. 53.

12. J. Bowen's sketch map of Risdon, 27/9/1803, in Walker; J. Meehan's survey of Risdon, 23/11/1803, in his fieldnotes (LSD 355/1), Archives Office of Tasmania.

13. King to Bowen, 18/10/1803, in HRA Series III vol. 1 p. 204.

14. Report of the Committee for the Affairs of the Aborigines, *Commons Papers*, 1831, vol. 19, p. 37.

15. Windschuttle, *Fabrication*, p. 24.

16. Testimony of Edward White, pp. 53–54.

John Glover's Mount Wellington

David Hansen

Keith Windschuttle's *The Fabrication of Aboriginal History* raises a number of important questions about the existence, form and context of historical evidence, and about its interpretation, presentation and acceptance by scholars and by the wider community. These are fundamental issues in historical method. They are particularly relevant in the uneven investigative terrain of the British imperial frontier, where the smooth archival field – the formal and generally credible bureaucratic reporting of the military and civil administration – is edged by a scruffy dystopia of letters, journals, newspaper reports and editorials, of gossip, hearsay and inherited traditions, and of scattered contemporary images and artefacts. In such an evidentiary environment, and at a time of much secondary text-based, cultural studies-inflected relativism, Windschuttle's call for close attention to primary sources is welcome and timely.

Unfortunately, Windschuttle's challenge to what he calls 'the orthodox interpretation of Tasmanian history'[1] is seriously compromised by his blatant ideological bias, by his journalistic selective emphasis and by his own failure to deal with empirical data. The caption to the illustration of *Mount Wellington and Hobart Town from Kangaroo Point*[2] is a case in point.

Windschuttle begins his text with the rhetorical headline, 'The last days of freedom of the Big River tribe?' and it soon becomes clear that the purpose of the reproduction and the caption is to discredit

Henry Reynolds, whose histories are a primary target of Windschuttle's revisionism. When *Mount Wellington and Hobart Town...* came on the market in late 2001, Professor Reynolds, in his capacity as a trustee of the Tasmanian Museum and Art Gallery, described the work as 'a painting of exquisite historical significance', stating that 'it captures the last days of freedom of the Big River tribe, who were brought to Hobart by George Augustus Robinson in January 1832 before being shipped to Flinders Island.'[3] Attacking this anodyne media sound-bite as if it were a formal historical argument, Windschuttle claims that Reynolds 'was mistaken'. He states that the Big River and Oyster Bay natives 'never visited Kangaroo Point', and that 'the painting depicts at least forty Aborigines, while there were only twenty-six members of the Big River tribe captured.' He also claims that 'none of [Glover's Aboriginal paintings] could have been drawn from life.'

In response to the first of these statements, it should be pointed out that the fact that there is no record of the natives having visited the eastern shore of the Derwent does not of itself prove that they did not. There is in fact no daily record of their activities during their brief (7–17 January) sojourn in Hobart Town, so their making a visit to the eastern shore must remain an open question.

With regard to the number of Aboriginal figures in the painting, Windschuttle points to the significant discrepancy between twenty-six and forty, but omits to mention the fact that Robinson's party included not only the Big River and Oyster Bay tribespeople, but also fourteen of his 'Friendly Natives'[4]

As for Glover's representation of Aborigines, the occasions of his encounters are quite well documented. John Richardson Glover records that on the arrival of the Glover family at the mouth of the Tamar River in 1831, 'our gun party went on shore and met with a party of Natives, one of whom was shot at and knocked over.'[5] Glover subsequently met and drew three Palawa in Campbell Town jail in August 1831,[6] a group in Launceston jail and Robinson's 'Friendly Natives' in September 1831,[7] the Big River and Oyster Bay Aborigines in Hobart Town in January 1832,[8] and Robinson's party again when they visited him at his 'Patterdale' farm in January 1834.[9] Isolated sketches of a bearded man in a kangaroo-skin cape[10] and another one (or two) with hands bound behind his back[11] look to have been drawn from life. The small figures of Aborigines (as individuals and in groups) that appear in numerous landscape sketches may be conventional 'staffage', or they may indicate other first-hand encounters. Glover also sketched John Batman's 'Sydney Blacks' in corroboree and on the ascent of Ben Lomond in January 1833.[12]

For Windschuttle, Glover's January 1832 drawings of Palawa posed around a tree, a sloping bank or rock and on tussocky native grasses 'must have been done ... at Robinson's place in Elizabeth Street'. This assumption appears without foundation. The only textual evidence of the location of the sitting is found in Glover's catalogue of his 1835 London exhibition, where he specifically notes, 'The natives danced and swam at the request of the artist. The Females are very expert in the Water, the Heels of one Woman are perceptible above the Water.'[13] There is no beach in Elizabeth Street, North Hobart.

While it is a simple matter thus to refute Windschuttle's arguments, the more significant point is that he deliberately ignores (or simply fails to understand) the nature of the painting as a work of art and as a historical document. *Mount Wellington and Hobart Town...* is not a snapshot, but an immensely complex and culturally determined artefact, its formal and allegorical codes reflecting Glover's forty years as a painter of British and Italian Picturesque landscape. In keeping with usual late eighteenth and early nineteenth-century practice, the work is based on at least three separate on-the-spot sketchbook drawings,[14] but in its finished form the landscape is an artificial, studio construction, a Picturesque confection. Thus, while in the layout and architectural features of the town Glover presents an accurate and informative descriptive record, elsewhere he can be seen to have taken substantial liberties with topography. He adjusts the form and scale of both Mount Wellington and Mount Nelson (on the left) in order to enhance the landscape's resemblance to the familiar British Lake District, as well as to emphasise the Sublime grandeur of the mountain backdrop.

Similarly, the placement of the Aboriginal group in the (eastern shore) foreground is in keeping with classical landscape conventions, where staffage is generally placed on the foreground plane. Moreover, it is likely that Glover's painting relates to 'The Course of Empire', the Romantic-era conceit in which all civilisations are seen to pass through a number of clearly identifiable stages, from initial barbarism to pastoral and agricultural domestication to urban-trading-imperial apogee and thence to decadence, decay and a collapse back into barbarism.[15] In painted representations of this idea, the conventionally shadowed foreground of classical landscape indicates the phase which is to be supplanted by the coming development visible on the sunlit centre stage. In view of common contemporary settler opinion and of Glover's own recorded comments,[16] *Mount Wellington and Hobart Town...* can properly be regarded as a conscious elegy to the Tasmanian Aboriginal people.

Windschuttle's errors of interpretation might charitably be excused as displaying nothing more than ignorance of art history and/or a failure of historical imagination. However, given the surgical footnote dissections and the mean arithmetic of ethnocide found elsewhere in his book, it is probably not unreasonable to conclude by noting that this one brief caption contains three egregious factual errors.

First, the picture's credit line is wrong. The painting does not belong to the Tasmanian Museum and Art Gallery but is in fact jointly owned by the TMAG and the National Gallery of Australia. Second, Professor Reynolds' comments did not 'help ... boost the price the Museum [*sic*] had to pay to $1.5 million'. That figure was the low estimate of the work prior to auction, and in fact the failure of the painting to realise a higher price prompted an (abortive) investigation by the Australian Competition and Consumer Commission. Finally, Windschuttle says bluntly that the picture 'was painted by John Glover in 1833'. The painting is not dated; Windschuttle's 1833 is nothing more than a guess, and an unlucky one at that. In fact, several of the Aboriginal figures are taken from the sketchbook drawings Glover made in January 1834, and the work was among those dispatched for exhibition in London in January 1835, permitting a sure dating to 1834.

As suggested at the beginning of this essay, there are good reasons to re-address the evidence pertaining to Aboriginal–settler relations in Van Diemen's Land in the early colonial period. Such a review, like all good history, will require a combination of accuracy, open-mindedness, imagination and humility. On the evidence of this single page alone, Keith Windschuttle shows himself to be unequal to the task.

NOTES

1. Keith Windschuttle, *The Fabrication of Aboriginal History: Volume One, Van Diemen's Land 1803–1847*, Sydney, Macleay Press, 2002. The field is defined on pp. 26–28.

2. *Ibid*, facing p. 218.

3. *The Mercury*, Hobart, 10/11/2001, p. 38.

4. *Hobart Town Courier*, 14/1/1832, quoted in N. J. B. Plomley (ed.), *Friendly Mission: The Tasmanian Journals and Papers of George Augustus Robinson 1829–1834*, Hobart, Tasmanian Historical Research Association, 1966, p. 573.

5. Letter, John Richardson Glover to his sister, Emma Lord, 15/9/1833, Mitchell Library, Sydney. A typical frontier assault, this encounter is not recorded in Windschuttle's table of documented Aboriginal killings (*Fabrication*, pp. 387–97). Though John Richardson Glover does state 'that they all finally escaped', there must remain the possibility of a subsequent death from wounds.

6. 'Timbruna, Sunamena, Muntena', sketchbook 43, f16r, Dixson Galleries, State Library of NSW.

7. 'Colammanea, Maccame, Wawwee' and 'Telliacbuya, Oredia, Umarah. Manalagura, Ludawiddia', sketchbook 43, f20v, Dixson Galleries, State Library of NSW.

8. 'The Natives that were sent from Hobart Town to Great Island' and 'Natives sent to Great Island', sketchbook 98, ff1r and 2r, Dixson Galleries, State Library of NSW.

9. Sketchbook 97, ff20r and 21v, Tasmanian Museum and Art Gallery.

10. Sketchbook 43, f21r, Dixson Galleries, State Library of NSW.

11. Sketchbook 43, f18r, Dixson Galleries, State Library of NSW.

12. Sketchbook 97, ff6r, 10v, 12r, 14v, 15r, and 16v, Tasmanian Museum and Art Gallery.

13. *A catalogue of Sixty-eight pictures descriptive of the scenery and customs of the inhabitants of Van Dieman's* [sic] *Land, together with views in England, Italy, &c. painted by John Glover, Esq. Now exhibiting, at 106, New Bond Street*, London, E. Morgan, 1835, cat. no. 46.

14. 'Wellington from Kangaroo Point' f3v; 'Kangaroo Point' f15r and (Hobart Town from Hunter Island) f13r, sketchbook 98, Dixson Galleries, State Library of NSW.

15. See Robert Dixon, *The Course of Empire: Neo-Classical Culture in New South Wales 1788–1860*, Melbourne, Oxford University Press, 1986.

16. In a letter to his daughter Emma Lord, 26/8/1831 (private collection, UK), he describes his first meeting with the Palawa, observing 'there are very few remaining now,' while the catalogue entry for The Cataract, Launceston describes the location as 'formerly a spot much frequented by the Natives ... but they are now nearly extirpated'. (*A catalogue of Sixty-eight pictures...* cat. no. 33.)

Who Is the Fabricator?

Lyndall Ryan

When Andrew Stevenson, a reporter on *The Sydney Morning Herald,* telephoned me one morning in November 2002 to ask for a response to allegations of 'fabrication' in my book *The Aboriginal Tasmanians,* I had no inkling that I was about to become the subject of a media witch-hunt.[1] The allegations had been made by Keith Windschuttle in his new book *The Fabrication of Aboriginal History: Volume One, Van Diemen's Land 1803–1847.* He accused me of fabricating footnotes to massacres that he claimed had never happened, and of providing false estimates of numbers of Aborigines killed on the Tasmanian colonial frontier. For his own part, he asserted that the Tasmanian Aborigines were among the most primitive people on earth, were too few in numbers at the onset of colonisation to survive this event, and lacked the political skills to engage in guerilla warfare. And he also claimed that they had killed twice the number of settlers for half the number lost on their own side.[2] These claims seemed so ridiculous that I could not believe they were being taken seriously.[3] The media, however, decided that I was the historian at fault and began a witch-hunt into my scholarship which continues to this day.[4]

I had researched the first edition of my book *The Aboriginal Tasmanians* over 30 years before and had long ago discarded the notes. In contrast to my predecessors in the field, who had depicted the Tasmanian Aborigines as at best passive victims of British colonial expansion, and as at worst the missing link between ape and man and destined to die out, I had represented the Tasmanian Aborigines as active agents in a living history. The focus of my story was not their extermination but their survival in the mid-twentieth century. It was this aspect of the book that gained it media attention when it was first published in 1981.[5]

When Allen & Unwin approached me in 1995 to prepare a second edition, the book had been out of print for ten years. They wanted to leave the original text largely intact while I updated the story of the Tasmanian Aborigines in the late twentieth century. This was a sensible decision because a new generation of scholars was re-positioning the story of the Tasmanian Aborigines on the more challenging terrain of postcolonialism and reconciliation. I saw the second edition of my book, published in 1996, as a starting point for this new work.[6]

So I was amazed that I should now be accused of fabricating my footnotes. While other historians had differed with my estimates of numbers killed on both sides of the frontier, and had drawn attention to minor errors that are bound to occur in a ground-breaking work of this kind, no one had ever accused me of falsifying my footnotes. I was even more puzzled by the fact that Windschuttle had no reputation as an expert in nineteenth-century colonial history, let alone Tasmanian history. This led me to formulate the following questions: Where had the term 'fabrication' come from? How had it entered Australian political discourse? How had Windschuttle read the primary sources to make accusations of fabrication about my work?

According to the *Shorter Oxford English Dictionary*, one of the meanings of the verb 'to fabricate' is '"to make up", to frame, or invent (a legend, lie etc)'. An example is provided from T. B. Macaulay's *History of England*: 'Numerous lies, fabricated by the priests were already in circulation.' The noun 'fabrication' means the action of 'making up' an invention, a forgery.[7] Thus a fabrication is a deliberate act, employed for propaganda purposes and designed to deceive an unwary public. This is a very serious allegation to make about any historian's work. While I am prepared to acknowledge, as any historian would, that my work may contain minor errors, I have certainly not engaged in any act of fabrication. Could it be that Windschuttle did not understand the difference between a minor error and a fabrication?

The term 'fabrication' entered Australian political discourse in 1995 when the Adelaide journalist Chris Kenny declared that some Ngarrindjeri women had 'fabricated' the claim that they were the custodians of important secret knowledge or 'women's business' that would be spiritually disrupted if a bridge were built across the Murray River from Goolwa to Hindmarsh Island. This led in turn to a royal commission which found the women guilty of 'fabrication'.[8] Although Judge Von Doussa in the Federal Court found, in August 2001, that there was no evidence of 'fabrication', by then the term had become so embedded in anti-Aboriginal discourse that it was regularly used by right-wing print-media columnists to vilify Aboriginal people.[9]

Given this, it is not surprising that Keith Windschuttle used the term in his attack on historians of the colonial frontier in a series of articles published in *Quadrant* in late 2000. There he alleged a conspiracy to promote the political cause of indigenous peoples by claiming that the British colonists had not always followed the principles of British law and order in colonial Australia. This conspiracy included the uncritical use of unreliable sources, in particular from Aboriginal people and from missionaries, in order to fabricate massacres on the colonial frontier.[10]

To prove that these historians were 'fabricators', Windschuttle applied a forensic model of analysis to investigate five well-known massacres of Aborigines. Only two passed his forensic test. The rest, he claimed, were fabrications.[11] However, when I examined how he had applied his model to investigate one of the massacres that had failed his test – the Waterloo Creek massacre of 1838 – I found that he had ignored several key sources and skimmed over the rest. I concluded that he had little understanding of the complexity of the sources and was more interested in pursuing his own political agenda of massacre denial than in the rigorous application of his own model.[12]

The same problem arises in *The Fabrication of Aboriginal History*. But this time Windschuttle has laced his forensic model with claims of 'fabricated footnotes' to seduce the unwary reader into believing that historians of the Tasmanian Aborigines like myself have invented footnotes to promote our case. His argument seems to be: if he can prove us wrong, then his version of the history of the Tasmanian Aborigines must be right. In his view, only 2000 Aborigines lived in Tasmania at the moment of British colonisation; their society was a dysfunctional one which was not based on attachment to land; and they lacked the political ability to conduct a guerilla war against the settlers. Instead, they were black marauders who raided settlers' huts in search of plunder, much like 'modern-day junkies, raiding service stations for money'.[13] In the end, the Aborigines themselves, rather than the policies of the colonial government and the actions of the settlers, were responsible for their own demise.[14]

How has Windschuttle reached this extraordinary conclusion? First, he is driven by the ethnocentric belief that the British colonists were so inculcated with the ideas of the Enlightenment that they were incapable of exterminating Aborigines. Rather the Aborigines were the problem. Second, he writes about the past as if it were one-dimensional – there can only be one true account and he has found it. The rest of us are wrong. Third, he structures his argument in an attempt to show that historians like myself are so driven by a pro-Aboriginal political agenda that we have fabricated massacres and grossly overestimated the numbers of Aborigines killed on the frontier. He can prove this by checking our footnotes. Last, he presents his case in the vitriolic language of a public prosecutor at a Moscow show trial. In this courtroom we, the historians, have been found guilty before the trial has even begun.

The central plank of Windschuttle's case against historians like myself is his critique of our footnotes. In this essay I will investigate a number of his allegations of fabricated footnotes in my book *The Aboriginal Tasmanians* as a way of demonstrating how Windschuttle constructs his case. I will show that he has little understanding of the process of footnoting and even less knowledge of the sources I have used. I will conclude by arguing that he is so driven by his own political agenda that he leaves himself open to the charge of fabrication.

'Footnotes', Windschuttle argues on page 133 of his book, 'function as a means of keeping historians honest.' Indeed they do, but if a footnote is incorrect, it does not automatically mean that it has been 'fudged' or 'fabricated'. It is more likely that it has been mistakenly rendered or, in the process of referencing for publication, has been omitted from the text. For example, my PhD thesis, which formed the basis of the first edition of *The Aboriginal Tasmanians,* contains 1351 separate references in just under 1000 footnotes.[15] These were reduced in the first edition of my book to 857 references in just over 500 endnotes. In the process of such substantial reduction, some were lost or scrambled. Every historian dreads this happening, but it is a fact of life. In this case, any historian who checks a colleague's footnotes usually refers to the surrounding footnotes or to the original thesis to see if they have indeed been scrambled and then resorts to the primary source to see if they have been lost. In his book, Keith Windschuttle rarely engages in any of these scholarly practices. Indeed, his lack of familiarity with the process of checking footnotes is revealed in two ways.

First, he complains that the style of footnoting adopted by Lloyd Robson and myself – of an endnote containing several references, located at the end of each paragraph – often made it difficult for him to check the reference.[16] Yet this is the form of referencing that academics in Australia have been using for the last 25 years. As a historian, Windschuttle should know this. Or is it that he has never conducted sustained research in primary sources before and is therefore unaware of footnote protocols?

Second, Windschuttle employs one standard of footnoting for himself and another for the rest of us. Like him, in my book I used endnotes in three ways: to identify quotes, statistics and incidents; to provide examples of how things happened; and to point the reader to other sources as a way of illuminating my argument. Windschuttle, however, cannot accept this. If the footnote is not exactly where and what he expects it to be, then it is fabricated.

A checker needs to have a detailed knowledge of the incidents discussed and of the archives in which the source is located. On several occasions Windschuttle misses the point of the reference. I suggest this tells us more about his lack of familiarity with research into primary sources than about the way I have used my footnotes.

Let's look at some examples of his footnote sleuthing.

The European/Aboriginal Death Toll, 1807–1808

On page 77 of my book, I wrote, 'The first European was killed by the Aborigines in 1807. By 1808, conflict between Aborigines and Europeans over kangaroos had so intensified that twenty Europeans and one hundred Aborigines had probably lost their lives.' This sentence is part of a two-paragraph discussion about the impact of kangaroo hunting on the Tasmanian Aborigines. At the end of the first paragraph, I provided three references to the diary of Robert Knopwood as examples of how kangaroo hunting was conducted. One noted the death of the first European in 1807. At the end of the next paragraph, I provided two further references: John Oxley's 'Account of the Settlement at the Derwent in 1810', published in *Historical Records of Australia*[17]; and his 'Remarks on the Country and Settlement formed in Van Diemen's Land, 1809', an unpublished report located in the NSW Archives.[18]

On pages 575–6 of his published report, Oxley noted that 20 to 30 kangaroo hunters from the Derwent and Port Dalrymple now lived permanently in the bush and were in conflict with the natives: 'Some of them have forced the Native Women after murdering their Protectors to live with them and have Families.' In his unpublished report, Oxley noted the deaths of 'a number of kangaroo hunters and bushrangers from conflict with the natives in the woods' and questioned the use of kangaroo meat as a source of food at the settlements on the grounds of cost and 'the considerable loss of life among the natives'. From the information in both these reports, I deduced that about 20 Europeans and 100 Aborigines had *probably* lost their lives. This is not an unreasonable estimate.

Windschuttle, however, asserts that only five Aborigines and two Europeans were killed during this period based on the evidence of the diary of Robert Knopwood and information from an article by Marie Fels.[19] This article appeared after the first edition of my book was published and only discussed incidents along the Derwent River. It is also deficient in information about the seasonal patterns of movement of the Aboriginal tribes in this area. Windschuttle conveniently ignores these facts. Instead, he makes out that I have deliberately based my estimate only on the information in the Knopwood diaries so that he can accuse me of fabrication. This is nonsense. Had he consulted my PhD thesis, as he professes to have done on many other occasions, he would have found the Oxley references in footnote 44 at the end of the original sentence on page 76. Windschuttle did not bother to do so. He is more interested in making an accusation of fabrication.

Northern Vigilantes and the Massacre of the Port Dalrymple Aborigines

On page 139 of his book, Windschuttle quotes a paragraph from page 92 of mine about bloody skirmishes along the Meander River in 1827. It's worth reproducing in full:

> West from Launceston, along the Meander River, some of the bloodiest skirmishes of the war were already taking place. In May 1827 the Port Dalrymple band of the North Midlands tribe visited Norfolk Plains (now Longford). First they killed a kangaroo hunter at Western Lagoon in reprisal for shooting Aboriginal men. Then in July they burnt down the house of a prominent settler because his stockmen had seized Aboriginal women. Finally in November they speared three more of this settler's stockmen and clubbed another three to death at Western Lagoon. In retaliation, stock-keepers at Norfolk Plains formed a vigilante group and in December massacred a number of Port Dalrymple Aborigines at the junction of Brumby Creek and the Lake River. At the same time the Big River and Oyster Bay Aborigines attacked stock-keepers with such skill and ferocity that some settlers feared that they had devised a uniform plan of attack. The deaths of thirty Europeans in 1827 appeared to support this view.

Windschuttle spends four pages of his book 'investigating' my seven references to these incidents and concludes on page 143 that they are 'a remarkable catalogue of misrepresentations for one paragraph – indeed, it must set some kind of record in Australian historiography – and can hardly be explained away as an accident or mistake'.

There are indeed seven references to this paragraph and, as we shall see, most of them are in fact correct. It is Windschuttle who is substantially incorrect. The first five relate to incidents between the Aborigines and the colonists that took place in the Norfolk Plains police district between June and December 1827. The last two references relate to the second-last sentence in the paragraph.

Let's look more closely at the references. The first four are in one cluster and concern incidents that took place in June 1827. The first three come from the same source in the Archives Office of Tasmania (AOT), the Colonial Secretary's Office (CSO) 1/316; the fourth is a newspaper reference.

The first reference, Smith to Col. Sec. May 1827, CSO 1/316, is partly incorrect. It should read Malcolm Laing-Smith (police magistrate at Norfolk Plains) to Colonial Secretary, 10 January 1831, CSO 1/316 (p. 803). This is a case of the wrong date but the right archival location. The reference is to a report summarising incidents recorded in the Norfolk Plains police district between 1827 and 1831. Laing-Smith (or Smith, as he was actually known to the Colonial Secretary) reported that the killing of the stockman/kangaroo hunter William Knight had taken place in May rather than June 1827– hence my mistake in dating the reference. In other words, Smith had provided inaccurate information which I reproduced. If Windschuttle is such a sleuth with footnotes, he should have readily found this mistake. I suggest that his lack of understanding of the incidents and the organisation of the archival sources precluded his checking this kind of reference properly.

The second and third references are correct. They refer to the report from Corporal John Shiners and others in his party who went in search of the Aborigines following the killing of William Knight on 23 June. Corporal Shiners made his report to his senior officer, Captain Dalrymple, who sent the report to his senior officer, Captain Montagu in Launceston, who then sent it to P. A. Mulgrave, the commanding officer in Hobart, on 1 July 1827. He in turn sent it on to the Colonial Secretary. Windschuttle claims that I have scrambled the dates and reports as well as the process. This is not so. Shiners' report ended up on the Colonial Secretary's desk and it can be readily found in the reference that I stated, CSO 1/316. The contents of Shiners' report are the key issue here. He went to great lengths to show that when his party of stockmen came upon the Aborigines, their dogs raised the alarm and in the ensuing melee one Aborigine, at most, was wounded. One of the stockmen, Hurling, in his deposition that accompanied Shiners' report, referred to the fact that Knight had been in an affray with the Aborigines about a month before. This was later corroborated by information provided to G. A. Robinson when he visited the area three years later and was told that Knight 'used to kill Aborigines for sport'.[20]

The fourth reference is incorrect. The reference to the *Hobart Town Courier*, 28 July 1827, should be to the *Colonial Times* of 6 July 1827. It was the only other newspaper published in Hobart at that time and contains a report of Shiners' sortie against the Aborigines. The report notes that Aborigines had killed six stock-keepers in the Quamby's Bluff area 'in the last month' and that the pursuit [Shiners'] party captured only dogs and weapons. It is interesting that Windschuttle could not find this newspaper.

The reference to the settler whose house was burnt down is also missing from my book. It was William Bryan's home at Glenore on the Meander (Western) River and took place in November when Aborigines killed one of his shepherds. The Aborigines had also killed one of his stock-keepers the previous June and burnt down his hut. I had mistaken the burnt hut in June for the burnt house in November. Both references can be found in CSO 1/316.

The fifth reference is correct. The *Journals of the Land Commissioners for Van Diemen's Land 1826–1828* for 3 and 5 January 1828 noted that the confluence of the Lake River and Brumby Creek was 'a resort for the natives' and that, 'Murders have been committed in this recess and have hitherto remained undetected.'[21] However, I neglected to include here two further references. The first is to the letter sent by Police Magistrate Smith to the Colonial Secretary on 12 November 1827 following the killing of three shepherds, all freemen. He wrote that he had 'dispatched military parties and Field Police guides to the different stations where the outrages were committed and gave directions that diligent pursuit be made after this audacious band'.[22] The second is to a report in *The Tasmanian* on 16 November 1827 about the killings of the three shepherds in the employ of the settlers Bryan, Laurence and Lyttleton. It continues:

We are just informed, that two parties of military were dispatched yesterday, in order to join the Field Police in putting a stop to these outrages; and we trust His Excellency will follow up this matter with such measures as will entirely prevent any future occurrence of a similar nature.

By matching these three pieces of evidence, and the fact that fewer Aborigines were in the area in the following year, I surmised that a massacre of the Aborigines had taken place in the location identified in the Land Commissioners' Journals and had been hushed up. The fact that so many stock-keepers and shepherds had been killed in this area led me to believe that their mates had joined the military and field police as a vigilante group in this action, as was customary. On re-reading the sources 30 years later, I am even more convinced of my conclusion, because no reports of the actual personnel of the parties sent out by Police Magistrate Smith have ever been found.

The sixth reference is correct. It refers to the second-last sentence in the paragraph, where I noted that 'some settlers feared that they [the Aborigines] had devised a uniform plan of attack'. This point was taken from a letter from Police Magistrate Thomas Anstey to Arthur on 4 December 1827 in CSO 1/320. In missing entirely the relationship of this reference to my text, Windschuttle reveals, yet again, his lack of knowledge of the relevant sources.

The final reference is once more correct. It refers to a Garrison Order in the *Military Operations* sending more soldiers to Norfolk Plains, the Western River and the Lake River.[23] This reference is evidence that this part of the frontier was in need of military back-up. Once again, Windschuttle missed the point of this reference.

So, in this now-famous footnote, there are actually five correct references out of seven provided, one misplaced reference, one incorrect newspaper reference which can easily be re-located and does actually report what is claimed; one missing newspaper reference; and three missing references that can be readily found in the Archives Office of Tasmania, CSO 1/316. These are the kinds of mistakes that any historian can make when working through a vast and complex array of primary sources for the first time. What is significant, however, is that these mistakes can be readily identified and corrected, and that there is no wilful 'fabrication'. Furthermore, the basic story they disclose is interpretively undisturbed. Windschuttle, however, has demonstrated that he does not know how to check these kinds of footnotes, or how to place them in the context of the issue under discussion. Instead, he takes a simplistic approach to the process – if the footnote is not as he expects it to be, then it must be fabricated. This is not the practice of a serious scholar.

Invented Atrocities

On pages 270–280 of *Fabrication*, Windschuttle dismisses my claim that atrocities took place at the Western Marshes/Western (Meander) River in the Norfolk Plains police district in northern Tasmania. Let me reproduce part of the paragraph in question:

> Between June 1827 and September 1830 the North people fell in number from two hundred to sixty. One stock-keeper shot nineteen people with a swivel gun charged with nails; another shot a group of Aborigines while offering them food; another ripped open the stomach of an Aboriginal while offering him a piece of bread at the end of a knife; others offered them poisoned flour. A party of soldiers from the 40th Regiment killed ten at the Western Marshes.[24]

The next three paragraphs outline further atrocities in this area. They provide powerful evidence of the extreme violence of the colonial frontier in this part of Tasmania. Except for the detail about the numbers of the 'North people', all this information comes from G. A. Robinson's journal between 8 August and 25 September 1830.

How does Windschuttle deal with these atrocities? First, he denies even the existence of the North people by claiming, 'This was a category invented in the nineteenth century by white observers in an attempt to make sense of the tribal divisions among the natives. There was never any good evidence from Aborigines themselves that they were members of such a tribe.'[25] In two sentences Windschuttle dismisses the painstaking research of scholars from the nineteenth and twentieth centuries on Tasmanian tribal structures, all of whom agree on the existence of an entity called the North tribe. Why does he do this? Is it because by denying the existence of a whole tribe, he does not have to account for its virtual disappearance?

How then does he account for the atrocities Robinson describes in his journal? Let's look at two examples. First, the swivel gun massacre. The informant, Henry Hellyer, told Robinson about this incident on 12 August 1830 while they were camped near St Valentine's Peak, which formed part of the Van Diemen's Land Company's Hampshire Hills property. Hellyer informed Robinson that a 'stockkeeper called Paddy Heagon at the Retreat … had shot nineteen of the western natives with a swivel charged with nails'.[26]

Windschuttle denies that the incident took place because it was not recorded in the Van Diemen's Land Company's records. He cannot find who Paddy Heagon was, even though he is prepared to acknowledge the existence of a place called 'the Retreat'. Then, for the next two pages, he tries to prove that it was most unlikely that anyone would have had access to a swivel gun in this part of northern Tasmania, but, with all his blustering, he inadvertently indicates that it was possible after all. This long and somewhat obsessive disquisition on the swivel gun serves to divert the reader's attention from the credibility of the informant, Henry Hellyer. Hellyer was a well-educated Englishman and chief surveyor of the most powerful private company in Tasmania. He was no friend to the colonial government or to Robinson, and had refused to provide the latter with a map of the company's lands.[27] Hellyer had no reason to 'fabricate' this horrible atrocity which reflected so poorly on the company's reputation. By any standard, Henry Hellyer was an outstanding informant. That is why I accepted his story. Windschuttle is unable to discredit it.

The second cluster of atrocities was told to Robinson on 24 September 1830 by Punch, the overseer of magistrate Captain Malcolm Laing-Smith. For a day and a night, Punch escorted Robinson eastwards along the Meander (Western) River to Westbury and told him about atrocities that had taken place in the area, including those perpetrated by soldiers from the 40th Regiment in 1827. Punch provided names, places and times for all these incidents with all the accuracy of a good informant.

Windschuttle dismisses this information on the grounds that Punch was an ex-convict who lived with a half-caste Aboriginal woman and was probably illiterate. For Windschuttle, honesty is clearly correlated with class. A few pages further on, he says, 'We might be able to understand Punch's motives, being a man living in an isolated outpost trying to both entertain and impress a visitor who was obviously eager for stories of this kind.'[28] Yet Punch was a trusted overseer in the employ of a respected police magistrate and a very credible informant. He knew intimately both sides of the frontier along the Western River. He had no reason to fabricate his information. It simply suits Windschuttle's case to disbelieve him.

Windschuttle then attacks me for not verifying Punch's information in the historical record. He claims there is no record of the names of the men whom Punch identifies, and he rejects the evidence that soldiers from the 40th Regiment committed this atrocity at the Western Marshes. But the *Colonial Times* for 6 July 1827, referred to earlier, contains two reports of encounters with the Aborigines by members of the 40th Regiment at the Western Marshes in June 1827, the first by Corporal Shiners referred to earlier, and a second as follows:

> The people over the second Western Tier have killed an immense quantity of blacks this last week, in consequence of their having murdered Mr Simpson's stockkeeper. They were surrounded whilst sitting around their fires when the soldiers and others fired at them about 30 yards distant. They report there must have been about 60 of them killed and wounded: they found muskets, cartridges, loose balls and gunpowder –etc. The man they murdered was formerly an associate of blacks at Sydney, altho' himself a white man.

Windschuttle has three responses to Punch's information about this incident. First, he claims that he must have confused it with a massacre perpetrated by the 40th Regiment in another part of Tasmania 18 months later.[29] But he provides no evidence to support this claim. Second, he claims the Aborigines could not have been shot in large numbers because the musket was an unreliable weapon and often misfired.[30] But, according to Robinson, Punch not only carried a musket, he wore a brace of large pistols and had a bayonet.[31] This is clear evi-

dence that the stockmen on this frontier knew how to look after themselves and had the capacity to kill numbers of Aboriginal people. Third,
he claims that if the stock-keepers did kill large numbers of Aborigines
along the Western River, then, 'instead of dutifully recording all clashes
between whites and blacks, Laing-Smith and others in authority must
have concealed the great majority of them.'[32] I am arguing that this is
indeed what occurred.

Windschuttle's evidence comes from the 'Reports of Murders and
Depredations committed by the Aborigines in the Police District of
Norfolk Plains between 1827 and 1831', prepared by Police Magistrate
Malcolm Laing-Smith on 10 January 1831 and found in CSO 1/316,
pp. 803–7. It lists four Europeans killed in 1827 and 17 casualties for
the entire period. This is the same source that I used, the one that
incorrectly dated the death of the stock-keeper William Knight to May
rather than June 1827. The report also neglected to record the deaths
of two stockmen in February 1827, two in May, another in June, and
three shepherds and two other stockmen in November of that year. In
other words, Laing-Smith's report is not reliable. Windschuttle should
have used the list of incidents in this area provided by N. J. B. Plomley
in *The Aboriginal/Settler Clash in Van Diemen's Land 1803–1831* and
checked them in CSO 1/316 and the colonial newspapers. According
to Plomley's table of incidents, 13 stock-keepers were killed by the
Aborigines in the Norfolk Plains police district in 1827 alone and 12
were wounded; eight more were speared in 1828; two more in 1829;
while a stockman was killed and two others speared in 1830; and two
settlers and one stockman were killed, two soldiers and nine stockmen
wounded in 1831 – a total of 52 recorded European casualties.[33] This
is more than three times the number recorded by Laing-Smith and
reproduced by Windschuttle. Plomley's evidence confirms the claim I
made on page 92 of my book that 'some of the bloodiest skirmishes of
the war' took place in this area.

Windschuttle also ignores other evidence about the intensity of the
conflict along the Western River: the use of horses to 'disperse' the
Aborigines. This evidence was provided by one of the land commissioners, Roderic O'Connor, in his appearance before the Aborigines
Committee in March 1830. It reads:

Captain Ritchie's men, to the westward of Norfolk Plains, used to hunt them on horseback, and shoot them from their horses; one of those men was known by them, and watched and followed till they killed him at Piper's Lagoon; he had told Mr O'Connor that he had thrown a woman upon the fire and burned her to death.[34]

These are the same incidents told to Robinson by Punch.[35]

How then can Windschuttle claim that the Western River was one of the 'least violent regions in Tasmania'?[36] He does so only by denying the actual existence of an Aboriginal tribe from this area, dismissing evidence of major atrocities from key white informants in favour of a report that was found seriously deficient by research published in 1992, and ignoring completely evidence about the use of horses to disperse Aborigines that was provided by one of the most respected civil officers in the colony to the official committee of inquiry into the origins of the Black War. This is not the work of an historian seeking to wrest truth from all the sources available.

The Pittwater Massacre and the Abyssinian Dispersal

On pages 134–139 of his book, Windschuttle discusses my account of what he calls the 'Pittwater Massacre and the Abyssinian Dispersal' in late 1828. I recorded both incidents in two sentences on page 92 of my book. It reads:

> The entry of the military and field police led to an immediate affray with forty Oyster Bay Aborigines at Pittwater in which fourteen Aborigines were killed and ten captured. Another group of Big River people were dispersed from the Abyssinia area and two were shot.

I provided three references to these incidents: Gordon to Col. Sec., 9 December 1826, CSO 1/331; the *Hobart Town Courier,* 15 November 1826; and the *Colonial Times,* 1 December 1826.

Windschuttle claims that he could not find the first reference in the CSO volume I cited nor in volumes CSO 1/316 or CSO 1/310. So convinced is he that I have simply fabricated this reference that he concludes, 'Indeed, there is no document anywhere in the Archives

Office of Tasmania written by Gordon either on this date or about this incident.'[37]

Yet the reference is where I cited it, in CSO 1/331, on pp. 194–5. It reads in part:

> I beg to report to Your Excellency that Information being received by the Police at Sorell yesterday evening of a Number of the black Natives being in the Neighbourhood of the Little Plains; the Constables accompanied by the Military proceeded to the Place where they succeeded in surprizing a Party of Nine – viz, 6 men and 3 women, one of whom has an infant, and amongst the men, Black Tom is of that number.

To be sure, the reference to the 14 Aborigines killed is missing from this particular source. It can be readily found, however, in the evidence of Gilbert Robertson to the Aborigines Committee on 3 March 1830, where he said:

> The Richmond police, three years ago, killed 14 of the Natives, who had got upon a hill, and threw stones down upon them; the police expended all their ammunition, and being afraid to run away, at length charged with the bayonet, and the Natives fled.[38]

The second reference, to the *Hobart Town Courier*, 15 November 1826, is certainly incorrect in both book and PhD thesis, but in the latter it is supported by a reference to a letter from the settler Thomas Wells, who reported the encounter at Abyssinia.[39] The incident is actually reported in the *Hobart Town Gazette* for 16 December 1826. In this case Windschuttle located the reference.

The third reference, to the *Colonial Times* for 1 December 1826 is also incorrect. It should read 15 December 1826. Again Windschuttle has located this reference.

Windschuttle denies that the capture of the nine Aborigines and an infant and the killing of 14 Aborigines at Pittwater are the same incident. This is a matter of interpretation, not fabrication.

With regard to the Abyssinia incident, Windschuttle chastises me for not realising that it involved two separate encounters over two days, and that four Aborigines were killed rather than two, and that the encounters occurred before rather than after Arthur's proclamation of

29 November 1826. Yet in pointing this out, Windschuttle fails to acknowledge that he has had the retrospective benefit of reading Plomley's chronology of these incidents, published in 1992.

Windschuttle also accuses me of misusing the term 'dispersal' in relation to the Abyssinia encounter. I certainly consider a hot pursuit of the Aborigines that ends in at least one death to be a 'dispersal'. The same term was used by a correspondent to the *Colonial Times* on 5 May 1827 to describe a very similar 'encounter' at the Macquarie River.

Overall, then, the reference that Windschuttle could not find can be found in the place where I cited it and is correct, another is missing but readily discovered, and two others are incorrect in source but not in substance and are easily corrected. The only substantive alteration is that Plomley's later work shows that two more Aborigines were killed than I first estimated. This does not constitute a fabrication.

The Shootings at Tooms Lake and Moulting Lagoon

Windschuttle claims on pages 160–161 of his book to have found a massacre of Aborigines at Tooms Lake that no other historian has mentioned. His discovery is based on two reports in the *Hobart Town Courier* for 9 and 13 December 1828. The first report states that a party of the 40th Regiment had returned to Oatlands with two captives, a black woman and her boy. The second report states that the military party was:

> led into the bush by John Danvers and Constable William Holmes …
> made an attack upon the Aborigines at the Great Lake at the source of
> the Macquarie River. Ten of the natives were killed on the spot and the
> rest fled.

Windschuttle cites no corroborating evidence of this encounter from any military officer, field police or magistrate. Nor was it recorded by Plomley in his *Aboriginal/Settler Clash in Van Diemen's Land*. In other words, this massacre has as much evidence to support it as the one that Windschuttle disputes was carried out by the 40th Regiment in the Western Marshes in 1827, which was reported in the *Colonial Times*, 6 July 1827, and later told to G. A. Robinson by Punch. Although

Windschuttle demands high standards of evidence from historians like me, he does not demand these of himself.

However, on page 102 of my book (which Windschuttle mistakenly cites as page 104), I wrote about the killing of Aborigines at Moulting Lagoon in January 1829:

> The settlers began to exploit their knowledge of the Aborigines' seasonal patterns of movement. When a band of the Oyster Bay tribe visited Moulting Lagoon in January 1829, they found the settlers waiting for them. Ten were shot dead and three taken prisoner.

As evidence of this incident, I cited the *Launceston Advertiser* of 9 February 1829. Let me quote the newspaper reference in full:

> A correspondent at Great Swan Port says – the grand topic of local interest here is the blacks and *the general combined movement against them* [my italics]. These savages in the district are particularly annoying. They rob every hut they can succeed in drawing the inmates away from, but there have been no more murders since Mr Hawkins' man. Parties are continually out in quest. We saw but one black during the whole of our journey, and he escaped among the scrub. There were doubtless others, but they would not show themselves. Two of Mr Meredith's huts and Mr Allen's have been robbed within the last fortnight. Mr David Ryner shot a black man near Mr Lyne's on Monday last. Nine were killed and 3 taken, near St Paul's River and about the same time ten were shot and two were taken, near the Eastern Marshes. A few weeks ago tribe attacked Mr Meredith's horses and barbarously put two to death. We are daily expecting them round at Schouten's, when all hands will be out in pursuit. We cannot think how cunning the black devils are. When the first of Mr Meredith's huts was robbed, they set fire to the fence, to entice the men out of the hut.

There are several incidents here. In my research, I followed up the statement about the 'attack on Lyne's hut on Monday last'. On this topic, Windschuttle says:

> The 'Mr Lyne' it mentions would have been William Lyne, a settler at

Little Swan Port on the east coast. In this case the report was credible. The correspondent gave the name of the man responsible, the farm where the shooting took place, and the date. It was unlikely that some-one would invent details as precise as this so close to the event.[40]

But where on the east coast was Lyne's hut? The map in the *Journals of the Land Commissioners of Van Diemen's Land 1826–28* locates it at the top of Moulting Lagoon, en route to Schouten Peninsula, where the Oyster Bay Aborigines were known to gather each January for egging and birding. The sentence from the *Launceston Advertiser*, 'We are daily expecting them around on Schouten's, when all hands will be put out to pursuit,' gave me further clues. Contrary to the story in the newspaper, I knew from the report of the roving party that no Aborigines had been shot or captured at St Paul's River. This led me to believe that the story of the incident in the Eastern Marshes (Tooms Lake) was also a false report. So I surmised that the massacre could have taken place at or near Moulting Lagoon. Under the circumstances, this was not an unreasonable assumption.

Windschuttle's reading of the evidence 30 years later has led him to conclude that the massacre took place two months earlier at Tooms Lake. In this case, he has had the benefit of using my research to make a new reading of the chain of events and to reach a different location and time of the massacre. In these circumstances, the historian, in adding new knowledge, would normally acknowledge the pioneering work of his predecessor. This point of etiquette has escaped Windschuttle entirely. Instead he accuses me of fabricating a massacre at Moulting Lagoon.

Use of Unreliable Sources: The Journals of G. A. Robinson

On page 270 of his book, Windschuttle accuses me of using uncritically the information provided by the journals of G. A. Robinson about atrocities in many parts of Tasmania and, in particular, about incidents such as those outlined above. Certainly the historian has to make judgements about the quality of the evidence provided by Robinson. Let me give two examples.

The Killings by the Port Davey people

On pages 113–114, Windschuttle accuses me of not accepting Robinson's claim that the killing of a settler at New Norfolk in December 1829 was perpetrated by 12 Aboriginal people from the Port Davey mob because it opposes my view that this group of Aborigines did not kill settlers. However, in comparing Robinson's claim with other accounts of attacks by Aborigines in the New Norfolk area described in the Colonial Secretary's Office correspondence, I came to the conclusion that this settler was killed by Aborigines from the Big River tribe. In this case Robinson was mistaken as to the identity of the perpetrators. He had not met the Big River people at this stage and was unaware of their seasonal patterns of movement. The New Norfolk area was well outside the territory of the South-West people and there is no evidence that they ever visited it. Windschuttle, however, accepts Robinson's account because it suits his case to do so.

The Death of Quamby, the Resistance Leader

On page 280 of his book, Windschuttle claims that I have uncritically accepted the information given to G. A. Robinson by the surveyor Henry Hellyer about Quamby, the Aboriginal resistance leader in northern Tasmania. Robinson writes 'that a native named Quamby had disputed the land occupied by the whites and that he had successfully driven them off, but he was afterwards killed with others'.[41] I wrote about this incident on page 141 of my book: 'In July the Pallittorre disputed territory occupied by stock-keepers and successfully drove them off. A short time later their leader, Quamby, was shot.'

Windschuttle has already rejected other information provided by Hellyer to Robinson, so he has to reject this as well. He seizes on the fact that the editor of Robinson's journal, N. J. B. Plomley, provides a footnote referring to James Bonwick's story of the name 'quamby' in relation to Quamby's Bluff, which he took from a report in the *Hobart Town Courier*, 14 March 1829. According to Windschuttle, 'quamby' was 'not the name of a man but an expression of the language', and this story 'pre-dates Robinson's diary entry by more than a year'.[42]

But neither Hellyer nor Robinson refer to the place Quamby's Bluff. Indeed, the latter had not seen it. I certainly surmised that the

Quamby described by Hellyer was the leader of the Pallittorre. Further, Plomley offers no view on which story may be the correct version. Rereading Robinson's journal 30 years later, I can find no other evidence to change my interpretation. Since Hellyer had lived in the area for five years and had witnessed many incidents between whites and Aborigines, I had no reason to doubt his information. Windschuttle is unable to discredit it.

The Roving Parties

On pages 151–153 of his book, Windschuttle disputes my claim on page 102 of mine that the roving parties killed 60 Aborigines. However, in reproducing my text, he runs the last sentence from one paragraph into the next and thus renders the endnote meaningless. Leaving aside this breach of academic practice, there are two other points at issues here – how do I apply the term 'roving parties'; and did they kill 60 Aborigines?

I applied the term 'roving parties' to include all the different kinds of military and paramilitary forces that were sent out on the orders of the police magistrates to track down Aborigines in the settled districts between 1 November 1828 and 31 January 1831. These parties ranged in size from four to 11 men and consisted of soldiers, district constables, field police, volunteer guides, settlers, stock-keepers and black-trackers, some of whom came from New South Wales. For example, the military party that Windschuttle claims killed the ten Aborigines at Tooms Lake in December 1828 consisted of nine soldiers from the 40th Regiment and two field police, one of whom was John Danvers. The latter was then ordered by the police magistrate at Campbelltown, James Simpson, to form his own roving party to track down Aborigines in the St Paul's River area. This roving party comprised two field police, an Aboriginal tracker, a volunteer guide and three others.[43]

Neither the magistrates nor the press made a clear distinction about the kinds of roving parties that operated in the settled districts at this time. For example, James Simpson wrote to the Colonial Secretary on 30 December 1828 that, 'I purpose sending him (a district constable called Loane) out immediately with *a roving party of military* [my italics] through the Eastern Tier.'[44] In another example, a correspondent in the *Colonial Times* on 17 January 1829 simply used the term 'parties' to describe all these different kinds of groups out in search of the Aborigines.

Windschuttle, however, uses the term 'roving parties' more narrowly to describe specifically those led by Gilbert Robertson and Jorgen Jorgenson. He claims that these parties killed no Aborigines at all.[45] However, the 'roving parties' as I defined them killed 60 Aborigines in the settled districts. Indeed, Windschuttle's own list of Aborigines killed in the settled districts between 1 November 1828 and 31 January 1831 records at least 40 Aborigines killed by parties according to my definition of the term, and another nine killed by stockmen in self-defence.[46] So, our estimates for the number of Aborigines killed in this period are remarkably similar. Our differences lie not in numbers killed but in our interpretation of who killed them. This is not a fabrication but a legitimate debate about the character of the frontier.

The Aboriginal Death Toll

On page 174 of my book, I wrote:

> In 1823, the estimated population of the Big River, Oyster Bay, North Midlands, North-East and North tribes was about a thousand. By 1832, 156 had been captured, 50 lived with sealers, and 27 lived with settlers. Of the remainder, 280 were recorded shot, which leaves some 480 unaccounted for. It seems that even on the Tasmanian frontier only about one third of the Aborigines killed were recorded and that a more realistic total would be about 700, or nearly four times as many as the 176 Europeans killed by the Aborigines.

The information in the first part of this paragraph is based on five years of close reading of the primary sources, from which I constructed an 'Appendix of Aborigines Accounted for in the Literature' in my PhD thesis.[47] Windschuttle dismisses it on the grounds of insufficient detail and provides his own list of Aborigines killed by colonists.[48] However, the two lists are not comparable. His is based on research in a very narrow range of sources to arrive at a claim of 118 Aborigines killed. Mine uses a far wider range of sources and accounts for 785 Aborigines killed, captured and living with sealers and settlers. I suggest that Windschuttle finds my estimates inconvenient for his own political agenda.

The estimated death ratio of 1:4 was (and remains) a cautious estimate. It was based on a close reading of the sources and a comparison of my findings with those of other historians who had researched race relations in other parts of Australia and who had provided estimates of closer to 1:10.[49] Windschuttle does not even discuss this.

In *Fate of a Free People*, Henry Reynolds provides a very useful discussion of this issue. While he thinks that my estimate might be too high because it is based on 1000 Aboriginal people being alive in the settled districts in 1823, he also points out that other historians, such as Robert Hughes and Noel Butlin, have claimed a much higher ratio applied. Reynolds then suggests that the European/Aboriginal death ratio in Tasmania could have been as low as 1:1, which he sees as further evidence of the intensity of the Black War.[50] Windschuttle, however, asserts that two Europeans were killed for every Aboriginal.[51] He reaches this statistic simply by applying his forensic model to deny most of the recorded killings of Aborigines by the colonists. Despite his confident assertions, his estimate is flawed on three main grounds:

1. Windschuttle reads the Tasmanian archival and newspaper records as if they are omniscient. However, as any seasoned researcher knows, they do not provide an account of every incident – even of every killing of a colonist. This is readily borne out in Plomley's book *The Aboriginal/Settler Clash in Van Dieman's Land*, where Plomley found no consistent correlation of recorded incidents between the Correspondence files in the Colonial Secretary's Office and the colonial newspapers, let alone between the CSO records and other sources such as settlers' diaries which Windschuttle barely used.[52]

2. Windschuttle naively assumes that the same level of care was taken in recording killings of Tasmanian Aboriginal people as those of colonists. This is nonsense. While Lieutenant-Governor Arthur did set up a system of reporting incidents on the frontier in 1829, from which the historian can make a reasonable assessment of the number of colonists who were killed, Arthur also knew that not all incidents were

reported, particularly not those incidents in which Aboriginal people were killed.[53] The colonists, of course, did the vast majority of the reporting: Aborigines had very little input into the record in order to present their interpretation, which undoubtedly would have told an even more repressive story.

3. Windschuttle provides no consistent account of what happened to the Tasmanian Aboriginal people in the settled districts between 1823 and 1830. I have found no new evidence to lead me to change my original claim that there were about 1000 Aboriginal people in the settled districts in 1823 and that only 60 were still alive at the time of the Black Line in October 1830. While I certainly acknowledge that not all were shot by the colonists, a great number probably were. The issue of how many is still wide open for debate.

But Windschuttle is not interested in debate. He tries to overcome the problem of numbers by contending that the pre-contact Aboriginal population of Tasmania was less than 2000. How does he reach this figure? On pages 366–372 of his book, he examines the work of N. J. B. Plomley (editor of G. A. Robinson's journals) and the archaeologist Rhys Jones, who estimated a pre-contact Aboriginal population of about 4000.[54] He concludes that they over-estimated the number of Aboriginal people on the west coast because G. A. Robinson had found only 108 during all of his travels in this region between 1830 and 1834. Yet Jones based his estimate for the West Coast tribes not only on the number of Aboriginal people that Robinson saw but also on his archaeological finds from excavations at West Point and Rocky Cape. And Plomley based his estimates on more careful readings of the Robinson journals than Windschuttle has been able to make. While neither Plomley nor Jones would claim that their estimates are set in stone – indeed, more recent work by the archaeologist Colin Pardoe suggests that the original number could sensibly be doubled – they would certainly demand a higher standard of evidence than Windschuttle can provide.[55]

For example, while he accepts evidence of post-contact numbers for Aboriginal people on the west coast, he simply ignores evidence of their post-contact numbers in eastern Tasmania. Two of the eyewitness accounts of the Risdon Cove massacre in May 1804 noted that at least

300 Aboriginal people were at the site, while a third estimated there 'was not less than 5 or 6 hundred'.[56] Taking the more conservative estimate of 300, this means that if there were 2000 Aboriginal people in the whole island, one-sixth of the entire population was present in the one place on the one day! Other accounts of large numbers of Aboriginal people gathered in the one place are found throughout the Correspondence files of the Colonial Secretary's Office, in settlers' diaries and in the colonial press. Windschuttle conveniently ignores them.

Instead, he chooses to accept the estimate of 2000 Aboriginal people provided by the nineteenth-century historian James Backhouse Walker in a lecture titled 'Some Notes on the Tribal Divisions of the Aborigines of Tasmania', delivered to the Royal Society of Tasmania between 1888 and 1898. Yet Walker acknowledged that he had arrived at this figure without the benefit of access to the journals of G. A. Robinson. Walker continues, '... so that the information available is not sufficient to enable us to determine with any accuracy either the total number of the aborigines or the limits of the respective tribes'.[57]

Robinson's journals were published in 1966 and have since become the basis for all estimates of the pre-contact Tasmanian Aboriginal population. Windschuttle clings to Walker's now superseded estimate because it fits his ideological position to do so. This is hardly sound scholarship.

Conclusion

What do Windschuttle's allegations against my work add up to? In the cases about footnotes I have outlined, I have placed one endnote before another; apparently used three inaccurate newspaper references for information quickly discoverable in other newspapers; used one source that has retrospectively been shown to be unreliable; and have left out five references for information that exists in the historical record. I may also have placed the site of a massacre that did take place in the wrong location. In each case, the mistakes can be identified and rectified. It is hard to see how any of these errors changes the fundamental story of what happened to the Tasmanian Aborigines. Rather they are minor infractions. They are certainly not 'fabrications'. Indeed, when one takes into account that this pioneering research was undertaken over 30 years ago, when the primary sources were in a much less accessible form than they are now, and that I was the first trained historian to use them in any consistent way, these kinds of errors are not only understandable, there are also remarkably few of them.

Windschuttle, however, has used outdated research to claim a pre-contact Aboriginal population that is too small to be sustained in a hunter-gatherer society; mis-read and relied on sources that any scholar with a knowledge of the Tasmanian archives would have readily found to be incomplete; denied the existence of an Aboriginal tribe; stubbornly refused to accept evidence of killings of Aborigines from credible white informants; and has been unable or unwilling to re-locate sources which are readily available in the empirical record. In assessing the contribution of historians like myself, he invariably adopts the most malicious of intellectual interpretations, in a manner almost unprecedented in Australian historical scholarship.

These are the transparent tactics of an opportunist seeking to claim credibility as a historian in a field in which he has conducted no previous historical or archival research, nor demonstrated an understanding of the relevant historical debates. Windschuttle's book is the work of a propagandist, determined to impose his own political agenda of denial about the past, rather than the work of a fair-minded historian re-assessing a critical period in Australian history. In the end, one must reasonably ask: Who, pray, is the real fabricator?

NOTES

1. Lyndall Ryan, *The Aboriginal Tasmanians*, second edition, St Leonards, Allen & Unwin, 1996. The page numbers in this edition are cited in this essay.
2. Keith Windschuttle, *The Fabrication of Aboriginal History: Volume One, Van Diemen's Land 1803–1847*, Sydney, Macleay Press, 2002, p. 3.
3. Lyndall Ryan, 'No historian enjoys a monopoly of truth', *The Australian*, 17/12/2002.
4. See for example Bernard Lane, 'Orthodox history under the gun', *The Australian*, 28–29/12/2002, p. 16; and 'Historians at War', *Sunday* program, Channel 9, 25 May 2003.
5. Lyndall Ryan, *The Aboriginal Tasmanians*, first edition, St Lucia, University of Queensland Press, 1981.

6. See for example, Ian Anderson, 'Re-Claiming TRU-GER-NAN-NER: Decolonising the Symbol', in Penny van Toorn and David English (eds), *Speaking Positions; aboriginality, gender and ethnicity in Australian cultural studies*, Melbourne, Department of Humanities, Victoria University of Technology, 1995, pp. 31–44; Rebe Taylor, *Unearthed; the Aboriginal Tasmanians of Kangaroo Island*, Kent Town, Wakefield Press, 2002.

7. *Shorter Oxford English Dictionary*, 2 vols, vol. 1, p. 716.

8. Chris Kenny, *It Would Be Nice if There Was Some Women's Business: The Story behind the Hindmarsh Island Affair*, Sydney, Duffy & Snellgrove, 1996.

9. Margaret Simons, *The Meeting of the Waters: The Hindmarsh Island Affair*, Sydney, Hodder, 2003, pp. 445–461.

10. Keith Windschuttle, 'The myths of frontier massacres in Australian history, Part I: The invention of massacre stories', *Quadrant* 44, 10, 2000, pp. 8–21; 'The myths of frontier massacres in Australian history, Part II: The fabrication of the Aboriginal death toll', *Quadrant* 44, 11, 2000, pp. 17–24; 'The myths of frontier massacres in Australian history, Part III: Massacre stories and the policy of separatism', *Quadrant* 44, 12, 2000, pp. 6–20. The texts can be found at http://www.sydneyline.com.

11. Windschuttle, 'The myths of frontier massacres in Australian history, Part I', pp. 9–13.

12. Lyndall Ryan, 'Waterloo Creek, northern New South Wales, 1838', in Bain Attwood & S. G. Foster (eds), *Frontier Conflict. The Australian Experience*, Canberra, National Museum of Australia, 2003, pp. 33–43.

13. Windschuttle used this expression at the Roundtable on Tasmanian History, Launceston, 16 May 2003.

14. See for example Windschuttle, *Fabrication*, p. 386.

15. Lyndall Ryan, 'The Aborigines in Tasmania, 1800–1974 and their Problems with the Europeans', PhD dissertation, Macquarie University, 1975.

16. Windschuttle, *Fabrication*, p. 133.

17. John Oxley, 'Account of the Settlement at the Derwent in 1810', published in *Historical Records of Australia*', Series III, I, p. 575.

18. John Oxley, 'Remarks on the Country and Settlement formed in Van Diemen's Land, 1809', NSW Archives, 2/8130.

19. Marie Fels, 'Culture Contact in the County of Buckinghamshire, Van Diemen's Land 1803–11', *Tasmanian Historical Research Association Papers and Proceedings*, vol. 29, no. 2, June 1982, pp. 1–15.

20. N. J. B. Plomley (ed.), *Friendly Mission: The Tasmanian Journals and Papers of George Augustus Robinson 1829–1834*, Hobart, Tasmanian Historical Research Association, 1966, journal entry for 25/9/1830, p. 219.

21. Anne McKay (ed.), *Journals of the Land Commissioners for Van Diemen's Land 1826–28*, Hobart, University of Tasmania in conjunction with the Tasmanian Historical Research Association, 1962, p. 74.

22. Laing-Smith to Col. Sec., 12/11/1827, AOT, CSO 1/316, p. 67.

23. *Van Diemen's Land. Copies of all Correspondence between Lieutenant-Governor Arthur and His Majesty's Secretary of State for the Colonies, on the subject of the Military Operations carried on against the Aboriginal Inhabitants of Van Diemen's Land*, with an historical introduction by A. G. L. Shaw, Hobart, Tasmanian Historical Research Association, 1971, p. 49.

24. Ryan, *Aboriginal Tasmanians*, p. 139.

25. Windschuttle, *Fabrication*, p. 271.

26. Plomley (ed.), *Friendly Mission*, 12/8/1830, pp. 197–8.

27. *Ibid*, 25/8/1830, p. 207.

28. Windschuttle, *Fabrication*, p. 280.

29. *Ibid*, pp. 279–80.

30. *Ibid*, pp. 260–1.

31. Plomley (ed.), *Friendly Mission*, 24/9/1830, p. 218.

32. Windschuttle, *Fabrication*, p. 278.

33. N. J. B. Plomley, *The Aboriginal/Settler Clash in Van Diemen's Land, 1803–1831*, Launceston, Queen Victoria Museum & Art Gallery, Tasmania, 1992, pp. 62–100.

34. Shaw (ed.), *Military Operations*, p. 54.

35. Plomley (ed.), *Friendly Mission*, 24/9/1830, pp. 218–9.

36. Windschuttle, *Fabrication*, p. 278.

37. *Ibid*, p. 135.

38. Shaw (ed.), *Military Operations*, pp. 21–2.

39. Ryan, 'The Aborigines in Tasmania', fn. 97, p.153.

40. Windschuttle, *Fabrication*, p. 159.

41. Plomley (ed.), *Friendly Mission*, 12/8/1830, p. 198.

42. Windschuttle, *Fabrication*, p. 281.

43. James Simpson to Col. Sec., 20/12/1828, AOT, CSO 1/316, p. 206.

44. *Ibid*, 30/12/1828, AOT, CSO 1/316, p. 213.

45. Windschuttle, *Fabrication*, pp. 152–4.

46. *Ibid*, pp. 390–395.

47. Ryan, 'The Aborigines in Tasmania', Appendix III, p. 373.

48. Windschuttle, *Fabrication*, pp. 387–397.

49. See for example John C. Taylor, 'Race Relations in South East Queensland, 1840–1860', BA thesis, University of Queensland, 1967; R. H. W. Reece, *Aborigines and Colonists*, Sydney, Sydney University Press, 1974, pp. 217, 219–20; Peter Corris, *Aborigines and Europeans in Western Victoria*, Canberra, Australian Institute of Aboriginal Studies, 1968, pp. 155–57.

50. Henry Reynolds, *Fate of a Free People*, Ringwood, Penguin, 1995, pp. 75–82.

51. Windschuttle, *Fabrication*, p. 399.

52. Plomley, *Aboriginal/Settler Clash*.

53. Minute by Arthur to J. Burnett, 13/7/1829, AOT, CSO 1/316, p. 284; Arthur to Murray, 10/1/1825, Shaw (ed.), *Military Operations*, pp. 3–4.

54. N. J. B. Plomley, *The Tasmanian Aborigines: A short account of them and some aspects of their life*, Launceston, published by the author in association with the Adult Education Division, Tasmania, 1977, p. 17; Rhys Jones, 'Tasmanian Tribes', Seminar paper, Department of Prehistory, Research School of Pacific Studies, Australian National University, March 1971.

55. Colin Pardoe, 'Isolation and evolution in Tasmania', *Current Anthropology*, vol. 32, no. 4, February 1991, pp. 1–11.

56. Shaw (ed.), *Military Operations*, p. 53; Mary Nicholls (ed.), *The Diary of Robert Knopwood 1803–1808*, Hobart, Tasmanian Historical Research Association, 1977, p. 51.

57. James Backhouse Walker, *Early Tasmania. Papers Read before the Royal Society of Tasmania during the Years 1888 to 1899*, fourth impression, Tasmania, T. J. Hughes, Government Printer, 1973, p. 267.

Robinson and Robertson

Cassandra Pybus

I have a photograph of myself standing in front of George Augustus Robinson's house in Bath, taken during a trip to England in 1989. I had been curious to see the house of the man who removed all the Aboriginal people of Tasmania to miserable exile on Flinders Island and who was also the good friend of my colonial ancestor. After scrutinising the photo it seems to me that the house speaks of modest prosperity. It is not the mansion Keith Windschuttle claims, any more than a ten-room house Robinson built in Hobart in 1835 should merit that description. Windschuttle employs inflated descriptions of Robinson's lifestyle to buttress his portrait of Robinson as a greedy and dishonourable man, 'the founder of a long tradition of those who made a lot of money out of the Aboriginal predicament while watching their charges die before their eyes'.[1]

His materialistic reading of Robinson reeks of old-fashioned disapproval of someone who has catapulted out of his class, but, more seriously, it shows that Windschuttle knows very little about the social, political and economic forces at work in early colonial Tasmania.

Windschuttle's failure to engage intellectually with the complex nature of Robinson, or with the everyday realities of the world in which he operated, is amply demonstrated by his almost total reliance on Vivienne Rae-Ellis's lurid caricature of the man. Aware of the depth of scholarly distaste for Rae-Ellis's *Black Robinson*, Windschuttle turns this to advantage by claiming the book as exemplary revisionist history.

He insists that the reason Rae-Ellis's contract with the Institute of Aboriginal Affairs was cancelled in 1984 was not because of suspect scholarship but because she 'had the temerity to break with the orthodox interpretation of her subject'.[2] What nonsense. The book was rejected because of a series of offensive and inaccurate assertions about Tasmanian Aborigines, most notably that they routinely engaged in cannibalism. It was after some years of the manuscript doing the rounds that Peter Ryan took it for Melbourne University Press, probably because he could see media hype would be generated by publishing Rae-Ellis's claims in the year of the bicentennial. Ryan released the book with provocative fanfare in January 1988 and championed the most outrageous assertions of the author as a matter of free speech.[3] Scholarly reviews of Rae-Ellis's book were uniformly critical. The acknowledged expert on Robinson, N. J. B. Plomley, was scathing, concluding that 'this is a very bad book because of its bias against Robinson – I use the word bias as meaning a point of view which holds evidence to be subservient to the end desired.' Others agreed, and also expressed concern about her 'absurd' treatment of ritual cannibalism and 'nonsensical' claims that Robinson used hypnotism on his Aboriginal guides.[4]

Windschuttle appears not to be acquainted with the publication history of *Black Robinson*, asserting that the book has been dismissed by scholars because Rae-Ellis 'affronts almost all the received views about her subject, especially that portrayed by Reynolds in his 1998 book *This Whispering in Our Hearts*'.[5] That is to say, a book published in 1988 can somehow challenge a reading of Robinson not articulated till a decade later. There was no orthodox interpretation of Robinson as a great humanitarian when Rae-Ellis's book managed to find a publisher, nor is there any such an orthodoxy now. Prior to 1988 the only extended work on Robinson was Plomley's exemplary edition of his journals, *Friendly Mission*. Far from being an admiring editor, Plomley was highly critical of Robinson's actions and motives. Lyndall Ryan's brief treatment of Robinson in *The Aboriginal Tasmanians* was even more censorious. As for earlier generations of writers, Windschuttle himself acknowledges that beginning with James Bonwick in 1870, criticism of Robinson has been consistent. My own study of Robinson in *Community of Thieves,* published three years after Rae-Ellis's, presented a deeply flawed man, driven by honourable motives, yet ultimately self-serving, manipulative and destructive of his Aboriginal charges. It was Henry Reynolds who flew in the face of received opinion when he articulated a very benign interpretation of Robinson's role in the fate of the Aboriginal Tasmanians that was not shared by others who had written on the subject.

It is important for Windschuttle to talk up Rae-Ellis's portrait of the Aboriginal conciliator as 'a liar, a cheat, a man of little honour'[6] because he needs to eliminate Robinson as a credible witness. It should come as no surprise, then, that the forensic scrutiny he applies to Lyndall Ryan's and Henry Reynold's scholarship is absent from his treatment of Rae-Ellis. He simply takes her word and repeats her claims with next to no contradiction. Content to rely entirely on Rae-Ellis's work for Robinson's early English experience, Windschuttle opens his own account of the Aboriginal conciliator with Robinson's appointment as storekeeper of a proposed Aboriginal establishment on Bruny Island in 1829. Almost immediately he introduces 'a particularly beautiful native girl, about seventeen years of age, named Trugannini'. Windschuttle tells us that even though she was tiny, this lovely native maiden 'made an immediate impression on him'.[7] His opening gambit is taken almost word for word from Rae-Ellis and points to her most notorious assertion, unquestioningly accepted by Windschuttle, that Robinson and Trugannini became lovers soon after he met her on Bruny Island, and this affair continued for at least seven years. He wants his readers to understand that the man was not only greedy and dishonest, he was also a sexual predator and hypocrite.

There is not a shred of credible evidence for Trugannini's sexual liaison with Robinson. In *Black Robinson,* Rae-Ellis produced only a few ambiguous references to support her claims and those fall apart under scrutiny. Although she cited Robinson's journals, they do not provide evidence of a sexual liaison between 'the conciliator and the beautiful black girl' in the wilds of Tasmania.[8] The journals indicate only that Trugannini was one of his close and trusted companions, demonstratively the most loyal. He also makes clear that she reeked from the animal fat used to smear her body and carried a potent form of venereal disease. For all the years that Trugannini and Robinson spent together in the wilderness, written up in expressive detail in Robinson's voluminous journals, there is nothing to indicate a sexual connection. Certainly, various eyewitnesses reported that Trugannini was very attached to Robinson, but I believe there are compelling reasons why Robinson would not have sex with her, even if other white men did. It wasn't just that he was repulsed by 'the loathsome disease' she carried; it was also the case that any sexual liaison would have completely undermined his powerful belief in himself as the sole protector and father figure of the Aborigines.[9]

The main evidence Rae-Ellis provided was a letter from Joseph Fossey, surveyor with the Van Diemen's Land Company based in the remote north-west of Tasmania. The letter was written after a visit from Robinson in late June 1830 where the Aboriginal guides sang and danced for him. Regarding Trugannini, Fossey wrote, 'I often think of her most singular expression respecting me, and could I meet with one as faithful as she is to *you* whether black or white, it might wreak a great change in me: an evening companion would be exceedingly agreeable in this secluded and remote quarter …' This missive, according to Rae-Ellis, is a clear reference to Robinson's sleeping with 'the beautiful black girl'. I do not think so. Fossey was a desperately lonely man and he was probably referring to nothing more than the pleasure of human company and affection. Rae-Ellis also cited Robinson's anger at a convict in the party, Alexander McKay, whom he believed had 'taken liberties' with Trugannini.[10] There was nothing in that matter either. Robinson abhorred men who sexually exploited Aboriginal women and his journals are full of his rants about it. Although still a convict, Alexander McKay was already a bushman of renown. Robinson's clash with McKay, and subsequent vilification of him in official reports, was typical of his dealings with everyone who could challenge his mastery in the Aboriginal conciliation stakes.

To seal her case, Rae-Ellis triumphantly produced evidence from Robinson's journal when he was the Commandant at Wybalenna on Flinders Island, noting a journal entry written 'with pleasure and some degree of secrecy' on 29 July 1837 that read, 'Had a pargener at Lydgugey's.' The Aboriginal word used here Rae-Ellis translated as 'kiss', based on information from Plomley.[11] However, Rae-Ellis failed to notice that Robinson had used Aboriginal words to mask his amorous activities several times before during 1835 and 1836. On every occasion he was referring to his none-too-secret affair with Mrs Dickerson, the white wife of the storekeeper.[12] Lydgugey was one of the several names that Robinson gave to Trugannini, but here too Rae-Ellis failed to notice Robinson did not say he had a kiss *with* Lydgugey, rather it is *at* Lydgugey's. In the full journal entry for 29 July 1837, Robinson recorded that Aboriginal women were away from Wybalenna on a hunting trip and that he had called to see the storekeeper. By my reading, this entry tells us that 'pargener at Lydgugey's' was yet another coded reference to his affair with Mrs Dickerson and that it describes an amorous exchange at the house usually occupied by Trugannini, from which she was probably absent.[13]

If the centrepiece of Rae-Ellis's construction of Robinson can be shown to be faulty, it follows from Windschuttle's own logic that the rest of her interpretation must be suspect. True, Robinson was vain, greedy and unscrupulous, but he had many other qualities as well. An ambitious tradesman of limited education from the east end of London, Robinson emigrated to the colony of Van Diemen's Land in 1824 hoping to secure a more comfortable social niche for himself and his large family. It was remarkable, therefore, that in 1829 he would be willing to throw over his potentially successful trade as a builder/bricklayer to become a custodian of blackfellows.

Rae-Ellis insisted that Robinson was in financial trouble in 1829, so took the job on Bruny Island for the money, but she provided no evidence for this. Robinson was an astute businessman, as his later financial dealings showed. In addition to his trade he owned several houses that he let out in 1829. There is every reason to believe he was motivated less by the meagre salary on offer than by the missionary impulses that had already involved him prominently in the Wesleyan Missionary Society, bible societies and a mission to seamen. His application for the job was couched in missionary language, stressing his desire to 'ameliorate the condition of the Aboriginal inhabitants ... as the degraded Hottentot has been raised in the scale of beings and the inhabitants of the Societies Island are made an industrious and intelligent race'.[14] For all that missionary zeal, he was canny enough to negotiate with the governor to double his salary once he had secured the post. Equally, he believed that in a mission to the Aboriginals he would gain a status that was denied him as a mere artisan in Hobart. His posturing as the governor's envoy on Bruny had no appreciable effect on the other white colonists, and his self-important diary entries would seem rather pathetic were it not for the unmistakable sense that Robinson saw the despised Aborigines as the key to the upward mobility he so craved. One of his most intriguing contradictions was that genuine humane impulses continually fuelled his baser drives for personal and economic gratification.

I have no doubt that Robinson was motivated by a strong desire to protect Aboriginal people from the terrible injustice he felt had been inflicted on them by white settlement. To him they were not mere objects of pity but fellow humans suffering grief and loss as profound as he might feel. Given that many colonists believed the population to be troublesome vermin, debased beyond any recognition on a scale of humanity, it was inevitable that Robinson's professed empathy would draw ridicule and abuse. On the streets of Hobart, just as on Bruny Island, he was subjected to open derision, highlighting the contrast between the airs he gave himself and his disreputable calling. To add further insult, his social background never failed to draw comment. The more he was ridiculed for his association with Aborigines, the more he sought to use them to transcend the social class that rendered him so vulnerable.

Ever since he had encountered a party from Port Davey on Bruny Island, Robinson knew that there were Aboriginal tracks he could follow to the west coast. He was determined to prove his mettle, not only as a conciliator of Aboriginals, but also as an adventurer and explorer. Yet another aspect of Robinson's complex character was a hankering to venture into the heart of darkness, to experience the challenges offered by the vast wilderness of the new world. He was a critical reader of the accounts of other European explorers, and it is clear that while he sought to move up the social scale of civilised society, he was also powerfully drawn to a place without civilisation, where the modifying impact of man was barely evident. Naturally, he reasoned to himself, his objective was to civilise such places, but his wholehearted embrace of life in the wild suggests a passion for elemental experience at odds with his evangelical posturing.

In February 1830, he set off to walk to the west coast with 12 surviving Aboriginals from the establishment at Bruny Island, his son Charles and a support team of six convicts. It was an astonishing feat. Had his reputation not become so completely linked to the awful fate of the tribal people of Tasmania, Robinson would probably be remembered kindly for having walked through the great south-west, which remains today much as he found it – one of the last tracts of wilderness in the world. His remarkable trek though the south-west and then up the west coast established a relationship of mutual dependence between Robinson and his Aboriginal companions that would continue, with only occasional interruptions, for another five years. This reciprocal relationship, only available to us through Robinson's self-deluding and self-serving journals, has all the elements of classic tragedy. Nearly two centuries later, I still find it heartbreaking that despite their long and intimate association, neither Robinson nor his Aboriginal companions ever managed to comprehend each other's motives and expectations.

One thing I am sure about is that the Aboriginal people who accompanied Robinson were intelligent human beings who acted on their own volition. They were not the traumatised victims portrayed in the nineteenth-century accounts, pitifully dependent on Robinson. Equally, they were not the dupes of Rae-Ellis's account who, she claimed, remained loyal to Robinson in his mission to conciliate the tribes of Van Diemen's Land only because he used his skills as a mesmerist to hypnotise them. Undoubtedly the Aborigines attached to Robinson's party had mixed motives for sticking with him – Robinson's journals reveal that they were far from diligent in support of his mission. However much they tried to subvert his mission, Robinson's Aboriginal guides understood he offered their best chance for independence and survival. They knew there were terrible risks in trying to go it alone in occupied territory, and once in the bush it seemed as if the conciliator was in the process of becoming one of them, in contrast to their previous experience on Bruny Island where he had sought to make them like himself. Robinson did not strip off his clothes and go hunting naked as they did, but he did share the food they caught, unlike the convict retainers, who spurned the blackfellow's food of crayfish, abalone and game and made do with spoiled rations of potatoes and salt meat. More pointedly, Robinson kept the convicts camped at a discreet distance at night, while he slept at the Aboriginal camp, often sharing his blanket with them (and their skin diseases). He was at pains to make himself part of the camp rituals. Evenings were spent singing and dancing. Every night Robinson would respond to the demand that he play his flute and chant a tune as part of this process. In his records of these interactions, Robinson showed a genuine interest in Aboriginal culture and an affectionate regard for the people. He sang with them, slept with them, hunted with them, learnt their language and marvelled at their mental and physical adaptation to the natural world. There is an awful irony in it, though. Despite his intense pleasure in elemental experience, which caused his impoverished puritan spirit to soar, Robinson wanted to ingratiate himself in order to secure the trust, and necessary support, of the Aboriginal people he met during his mission.

The greater his interaction with his Aboriginal companions, the more settled was his view that they were wretched, simple-minded dependants, without God and without hope – but for *him*. He could invest them with feelings of sadness and pleasure, even affection and loyalty, but to grant them complex reasoning would have destroyed the whole rationale of his activity. The idea that they could regard themselves as equal partners in the enterprise would not have entered his head. Consequently he was never troubled by his ultimate betrayal of his long-term companions when he despatched them to exile on Flinders Island.

In almost every instance, self-promotion and self-admiration overwhelmed Robinson's finer impulses. All that mattered, finally, was his mastery of Aboriginal conciliation. To effect that mastery, his humane persuasion gave way to force and duplicity, including his promise to the chief Mannalargenna 'that they could remain in their own country'.[15] He might have grieved for the damage he was inflicting on a proud people, but no ruse was too low in order to get them off the mainland

and onto the Bass Strait islands. His concern for Aboriginal well-being competed with his concern that they might elude his plans for them. Robinson's genius, as he saw it, was to combine the two concerns. A masterstroke was to issue European clothing to those Aborigines he conciliated. 'Trousers is excellent things and confines their legs so they cannot run,' he confided to his journal on 3 November 1830. The following day, when he had his captives embarked on a ship to be taken to one of the Bass Strait islands, he was pleased to grant himself heroic status: 'I said come and they came, go and they went.'[16]

By the time he had confined the entire remnant of Aboriginal Tasmanians on the Flinders Island settlement at Wybalenna, his humane impulse had been all but extinguished. He could still shed tears for the many deaths, but this was a small matter compared to his joy at being in control of a substantial domain of cottages, a chapel, hospital, tannery, bakehouse, store, cultivated gardens and military barracks, with the Commandant's quarters as the centrepiece. 'I was now addressed as the Commandant', he noted with immoderate pride.[17] So taken was he with his new status that for weeks his journal references were to 'the Commandant', as if he were in awe of himself; as if the authority vested in the role differentiated that self from the other who was participant and witness. 'The Commandant' moved about his new domain receiving guests, giving orders, making changes, acting 'as one having authority'.[18] All the while, Robinson provided his own admiring audience. On Flinders Island he had what he had always craved: authority, status, a good salary, official recognition, the promise of a pension; all of which were embodied in 'the Commandant'. But to be in charge at Wybalenna also meant being trapped amid the despair and disintegration of a people he had professed to save and for whom he alone had responsibility. The determined self-deception so obvious in his early journals, where he pointedly misinterprets what has happened, had permitted him to sidestep his responsibility. At the end of the line on Flinders Island he could no longer execute this manoeuvre. Instead he created a role for himself and then arranged events to reinforce it. He actually created fiction in his own diary, describing an elaborate fantasy of industrious Aborigines enjoying the fruits of civilisation, all the while simultaneously bombarding the government with utterly fraudulent reports. His journal accounts of activities at Wybalenna reveal that Robinson wrote his Aboriginal charges into the roles of dutiful Christian serfs he had made for them. Accounts of the sewing circle of Aboriginal women making dresses out of sackcloth or the fierce Big River people reaping corn as if they were born to the sickle (something that Windschuttle accepts without query) were constructed to fit the heroic narrative he had already mapped out. Before leaving Hobart for Flinders, he had drafted the outline of a book about his conciliation mission and commissioned John Glover to paint the frontispiece. In his mind's eye, his command at Wybalenna provided a culmination to his glorious achievement of peaceably clearing Tasmania of its troublesome blacks.

Robinson had made a fundamental connection between his own fortunes and those of the Aboriginal people, so it was not enough to fictionalise the process of civilisation for his black captives. For his own psychological health he needed it to be true. The inescapable reality was that, rather than a showpiece of amelioration and civilisation, Wybalenna was destined to be one great graveyard. His most pressing consideration became how to get away from there. He lobbied desperately for positions in the mainland colonies. Although he turned down the job of Protector of Aborigines in South Australia because the salary was too meagre, he did accept the job in Victoria with a handsome salary, land grants and a lifetime pension. In February 1839, he sailed away from Flinders Island with over a dozen of his closest Aboriginal associates. He left behind 60 Aboriginal survivors, most of them ill with influenza.

We do not need Rae-Ellis's crude portrait to see Robinson as a profoundly problematic character and to understand that his account of his dealings with the Aborigines is suspect. That much is apparent from Plomley's editions of his journals. It goes without saying that historians who use the journals need to take a critical attitude and scrutinise what he says in the light of all the other kinds of evidence, not the least of which are the flaws of character revealed within his journals. He is not always an unreliable witness, his veracity waxes and wanes according to his circumstances. This holds true just as much for his accounts of atrocities against Aborigines as it does for his account of their customs and practices. For example, we should be sceptical of his assertion that Aboriginal people could not make fire, a claim that Windschuttle gleefully accepts even in the face of the alternative explanations offered by H. Ling Roth in his authoritative book *The Aborigines of Tasmania*. The issue of Robinson's credibility is as challenging and perplexing as the man himself.

For historians to trust or doubt the evidence of the contemporary witness/participant in any particular instance, they need to know a good deal about the subject. They also need to understand the social, political and economic nuances of the historical circumstance in which that person was operating. Yet Windschuttle's decision to trust or to doubt the veracity of historical witnesses seems largely to be determined by personal whim. I will leave it to others to explore his judgments about the veracity and credibility of George Augustus Robinson, though, and consider instead another witness Windschuttle has discredited out of hand: Robinson's arch-rival, the District Chief Constable at Richmond, Gilbert Robertson.

Robertson was an even more mercurial fellow than his rival. At first glance he may seem to be a candidate for Windschuttle's approval as a trustworthy witness: a gentleman farmer with 1500 acres on the Coal River and the president of the local agricultural society. He had arrived in Van Diemen's Land in 1822, carrying a letter from the Secretary of State, Lord Bathurst, for a free land grant. Although Robertson had no money, his connections ensured him a grant of 400 acres that he increased by leasing the neighbouring farm of Thomas Birch. Within a year he made the first of the court appearances that were to become a fixture in his life in Van Diemen's Land, defending a series of dubious charges against him, all of which were heard, and proved, by the local magistrate, George Weston Gunning, a neighbouring landholder. In response to a complaint from Robertson, Gunning wrote an outraged letter to the Colonial Secretary objecting strongly to Robertson's assumption of intimacy between them, even though they were both prominent land-owners and neighbours. Gunning expostulated, 'You have seen this man,' going on to say, 'How dare he presume ... what impertinence and swaggering Gilbert Robertson conducts himself'.[19] This initial clash with Gunning set a pattern of conflict with men of

entrenched interest that persisted throughout Robertson's very che-
quered career in Van Diemen's Land. He was always in the courts,
suing or being sued, and he was unrelenting as the author of letters,
memorials and petitions. Scribbled in the margins are exasperated
notes from Governor Arthur or the Colonial Secretary about the man's
impertinence.

Having been raised by his grandfather who was a prominent cleric
in the dissenting Free Church of Scotland, Robertson also felt it his
duty to challenge the dominance of the established church in the
colony, which added the Anglican clergy to the chorus of his detractors.
By the time he gave his evidence to the Aborigines Committee, he had
thoroughly alienated almost every office holder and government crony
in the colony. He was not without important friends, though, and was
closely associated with the leading colonists opposed to the cronyism of
Arthur's government.

Robertson was appointed District Chief Constable at Richmond in
October 1828 and almost immediately landed himself in trouble by
arresting a drunken settler who, on the advice of Magistrate Gunning,
sued for assault. It was when he was caught up in several legal battles
and beset with debt that he set out on the first of his roving parties on
5 November 1828. He had early success, capturing five Aboriginal people, including the chief Eumarrah on 22 November 1828. Emboldened
by this success, Robertson petitioned Arthur to formalise the roving
parties, requesting a salary of £200 (in addition to his salary as District
Chief Constable of £75), a land grant of 2000 acres on his return and a
grant of 100 acres for each of his six children.[20]

Robertson was of the opinion that the Aboriginals he was tracking
were engaged in a guerilla war. 'They consider every injury they can
afflict upon white men as an act of duty and patriotic,' he explained in
his report on the capture of Eumarrah, 'having ideas of their natural rights which would astonish most other European statesmen'. He
insisted that the execution of Aborigines had led to murderous attacks
on settlers, arguing that Aboriginal people 'consider the sufferers under
those punishments as martyrs in the cause of their country'.[21] With
this line of reasoning, he persuaded Governor Arthur not to execute
Eumarrah but to treat him honourably as a prisoner of war.[22]

Robertson's awareness of Aboriginal concerns was probably influenced by his association with Kickerterpoller, known as Black Tom, a young man from Oyster Bay stolen when he was about nine and given to Robertson's neighbour Thomas Birch as a farmhand. When Robertson rented the Birch property, Kickerterpoller came with it. He and Kickerterpoller did appear to have a mutually supportive relationship, which Robertson held up to Governor Arthur as an example of what could be achieved by conciliation. I suspect it was Robertson who influenced James Gordon to recommend the release of Kickerterpoller and others from the Richmond gaol.[23] The lad then went to live with Robertson and became a guide for his roving party. Later, another boy who was captured with Eumarrah also went to live at Robertson's home, where he was known as Jack Woodburn. Eumarrah and several other adults held in Richmond gaol went almost daily to his house. His intimacy with Aborigines, and his view that they were patriots rather than murderous savages, did not endear him to his fellow settlers.

Lyndall Ryan is mistaken in attributing 19 deaths to Robertson's roving parties. Apart from the capture of Eumarrah's group, they neither captured nor killed anyone.[24] His various roving parties appeared to be so dilatory in Aboriginal hunting that they aroused suspicion they were just having a jolly fine time out in the bush, liberally provisioned at government expense. Robertson infuriated the Police Commissioner at Oatlands, Thomas Anstey, by his failure to supply proper reports.[25] By October 1829, Governor Arthur had tired of complaints from and about Robertson and decided that George Augustus Robinson would be cheaper and considerably less troublesome in the business of conciliation. In December, Arthur ordered that the Aboriginals living with Robertson be transferred to work for Robinson as guides. With relatively good grace, Robertson allowed Eumarrah and Kickerterpoller to be transferred to his rival. He held on to Jack Woodburn however, but the lad was taken away at Robinson's insistence. Robertson was outraged, protesting that the action was equivalent to someone walking into his house and taking away one or all of his children.[26]

This was background to the evidence Robertson gave to the Aborigines Committee in 1830. Windschuttle utterly dismisses this evidence, describing Robertson as 'a notoriously unreliable witness, prone to exaggerating violence done to the blacks'.[27] We are not told how Windschuttle arrived at the 'notoriously unreliable' label nor why he can state, 'this was how Robertson's peers regarded his evidence in 1830.'[28] We are only told that the final report of the Aborigines Committee did not mention Robertson's evidence. He does not say that the final report of the committee did not specifically mention any of the evidence given to them about contemporary events. So it is worthwhile considering what Robertson did tell the committee.

A great deal of what Robertson had to say concerns the *modus operandi* of Aborigines, based on what he had been told by his Aboriginal friends. His sympathies were evident when he argued that murders committed by them had been in retaliation for the judicial murder of Aborigines. This radical perspective was unlikely to inspire the committee to engage positively with his evidence. When reporting on the two incidents that so interest Windschuttle, Robertson presents *hearsay* evidence, so it is important to consider where he may have got this hearsay. He told the committee: 'The Richmond police, three years ago, killed 14 of the Natives, who had got upon a hill, and threw stones down upon them; the police expended all their ammunition, and being afraid to run away, at length charged with the bayonet, and the Natives fled.'[29]

Robertson did not say how he knew this to be true, although he was quite definitive. Before following Windschuttle in dismissing his claim, we should consider that Robertson had lived in the Coal River/Pittwater area for eight years and that he paid close attention to what went on in the district. As the chief constable at Richmond for nearly two years, he may well have had close contact with those same police constables, who could have supplied him with the details. Windschuttle insists this massacre could not have happened because the Richmond Police Magistrate, Thomas Lascalles, 'would have been obliged to report such an incident' and he had 'nothing to hide'.[30] Having searched Lascalles' papers in the Colonial Secretary's Office files, Windschuttle unearthed no such report. Anyone familiar with Van Diemen's Land society will smile at the suggestion that Lascalles would feel himself obliged to report anything, or that he would have nothing to hide, since he was one of the most corrupt officials in a notoriously corrupt society. He was removed from his position at Richmond for corruption in 1829. More importantly, Lascalles was not the police magistrate at Richmond at the time. He was appointed in March 1827 and appears to have taken up his duties some time later. The magistrate responsible was in fact Robertson's friend and political ally, James Gordon, who could have told him about what had happened. Gordon did report the capture of nine Aborigines at Pittwater in December 1828, and this may have been the same incident, as Lyndall Ryan has suggested.[31] If indeed such a massacre did take place, no police magistrate would feel 'obliged to report it', since the Colonial Office would certainly demand the police be tried for murder.

In the second incident Robertson gave evidence that:

> great ravages were committed by a party of constables and some of the 40th Regiment … that 70 of them were killed by that party; believes five or six men could destroy 70 of the Natives; the party killed them by firing all their ammunition upon them, and then dragging the women and children from the crevices in the rocks, and dashing out their brains; the Natives watch to recover the dead bodies of such as are killed on those occasions, and put them in hollow trees; believes, from Dugdale's account, who was one of the party, that the whole tribe was destroyed. Grant could give some clue to these murders; believes that there was provocation, that two whites had been previously murdered; Morley, as well as Dugdale, was with the party; never heard this great slaughter mentioned by any of the Natives.[32]

Robertson made no claim to any first-hand knowledge of this event. He made it clear that he got the information from members of the 40th Regiment who were with his roving party. He named them and invited the committee to interrogate the soldiers, yet they did not act on this suggestion. He was not alone in suggesting that many Aborigines were killed. In refuting the story, Dr Turnbull said it had been reported that '100, 70, 40, 50 then 17 of them had been killed,' although he could find no bodies. Another settler, William Robertson, who also refuted the story, was told by the soldiers they had 'killed seven' but when he went with them to look for the bodies, he was told by a corporal 'to tell you the truth we did not kill any of them.' Although Dugdale and

Morely were present with William Robertson, 'they said nothing.'[33] Windschuttle is happy to rely on the word of Dr Turnbull and William Robertson that no massacre took place, even though no attempt was made to interview the named participants, Morely, Dugdale and Grant.

Almost certainly, Robertson's hearsay of 70 Aborigines killed was inflated, but the absence of bodies reported by Turnbull and Robertson does not rule out the possibility of a massacre. In fact, there was a massacre of some kind in the area in 1828, as Windschuttle himself acknowledges, at a place now known as Tooms Lake. This incident was described (again as hearsay) in the *Hobart Town Courier*, on 13 November 1828, where ten were said to have been killed. Moreover, the diary of a settler named James George mentioned the same incident, reporting that a party of soldiers, constables and assigned men 'fired volley after volley in amongst the blackfellows, they reported killing some two score'.[34] The failure of the committee to seek evidence from first-hand witnesses and to ignore the evidence in their report does not show that they regarded Robertson as 'notoriously unreliable'. In my reading it shows that they did not want any hint of a massacre by members of the 40th Regiment to reach the Colonial Office. Settlers in Van Diemen's Land relied on the 40th Regiment for protection and knew that even hearsay evidence of a massacre by members of that regiment would certainly lead to a court martial of those involved.

The final report of the Aborigines Committee ignored any evidence about organised violence toward Aborigines during Arthur's government. The committee was happy to talk about what might have happened at Risdon in 1804, and the outrages of 'dissolute and abandoned characters' in an earlier period, but for the present they stressed only the threat to settlers from Aborigines possessed of 'a wanton and savage spirit impelling them to mischief and cruelty'. They did obliquely refer to Robertson's testimony when they emphatically rejected the theory that the Aborigines were 'retaliating for any wrongs which they conceive themselves collectively or individually to have endured'.[35]

One need only consider the make-up of the committee to see why they would reject what Robertson had to say. It was entirely composed of colonial officials and Anglican ministers who had come to regard Robertson as troublesome and impertinent. They were fed up with him and believed they had expended too much on his roving parties for too little return. That should not mean his word should not be trusted. Windschuttle entirely misjudges the man and his situation. It is clear to me, having ploughed through Robertson's astonishing output of letters, reports, memorials and legal defence, as well as his journalism as the editor of *The Colonist* and *The True Colonist*, that he had a compulsion for telling the truth as he saw it, no matter how detrimental to his personal interest, as it always was. Robertson's peers did not regard him as 'notoriously unreliable', as Windschuttle claims. They did not consider him to be their peer. This was first apparent in the outraged letter from Magistrate Gunning in 1823, in which he appealed to the class interests of the Colonial Secretary, saying, 'You have seen this man.' To understand what Gunning meant, we need to go behind the official correspondence, where Robertson was always described as a gentleman, to private letters and journals. In the journals of George Augustus Robinson, for example, there was a contemptuous reference to his rival as 'Black Robertson', implying that this appellation was in common use.[36]

Robertson was himself black. He was the bastard son of a Scottish plantation owner and his West Indian slave mistress, and was raised and educated in Scotland. Connected to one of the best families in Scotland, Robertson's colour was no hindrance in his early life. However, at the edge of empire in Van Diemen's Land, a place beset with racial anxiety, he was seen to be harbouring the savage other under his skin; a gentleman in name only, who could never be allowed full partnership in the colonialist enterprise. That Windschuttle does not take this into account in his assessment of Robertson is a significant failure of historical analysis.

NOTES

1. Keith Windschuttle, *The Fabrication of Aboriginal History: Volume One, Van Diemen's Land 1803 –1847*, Sydney, Macleay Press, 2002, p. 201.
2. Windschuttle, *Fabrication*, p. 199.
3. In a press interview, Rae-Ellis claimed her book had been censored by the Institute of Aboriginal Affairs – see *The Mercury*, 26/2/1988. Censorship and free speech were key issues in the review of the book by Christopher Koch in *The Australian*, 30/4/1988.

4. N. J. B. Plomley, 'Who Was the Real Robinson', *Overland*, vol. III, 1988, pp. 54–58; *Tasmanian Historical Research Association Papers and Proceedings*, vol. 35, no. 2, 1988, pp. 87–91; see also *Victorian Historical Journal*, vol. 59, no. 2, 1988, p. 55; see also *Australian Historical Studies*, vol. 23, no. 91, 1988, pp. 211–3.

5. Windschuttle, *Fabrication*, p. 200.

6. *Ibid*, p. 201.

7. *Ibid*, p. 203.

8. Vivienne Rae-Ellis, *Black Robinson: Protector of the Aborigines*, Melbourne, Melbourne University Press, 1988, p. 48.

9. Fossey to Robinson, 5/7/1830, quoted in N. J. B. Plomley (ed.), *Friendly Mission: The Tasmanian Journals and Papers of George Augustus Robinson 1829–1834*, Hobart, Tasmanian Historical Research Association, 1966, p. 234.

10. 1/10/1830, *Friendly Mission*, p. 224.

11. Rae-Ellis, *Black Robinson*, p. 49.

12. See entries for 27/11/1835, 7/1/1836, 11/1/1836 and 31/1/1836 in N. J. B. Plomley (ed.), *Weep in Silence*, Hobart, Blubberhead Press, 1987.

13. 29/7/1837, *Weep in Silence*, p. 466. In his review of Rae-Ellis's book in *Overland*, Plomley also pointed out that the reference was probably to Mrs Dickerson not Trugannini.

14. AOT 1/321/7578.

15. 27/8/1831, *Friendly Mission*, p. 413.

16. 4/11/1830, *Friendly Mission*, pp. 266–7.

17. 17/10/1835, *Weep in Silence*, p. 303.

18. 18/10/1835, *Weep in Silence*, p. 304.

19. Gunning to Burnett, 5/10/1823, CSO1/56/1185.

20. AOT CSO1/888/18829.

21. Robertson to Lascelles, 17/11/1828, CSO1/333/168.

22. The evidence for Robertson persuading Arthur comes from Henry Melville, *The History of Van Diemen's Land* [1835], Sydney, Horwitz-Grahame, 1965, p. 80, but Robertson makes the same point to the Aborigines Committee in 1830 – see A. G. L. Shaw (ed.), *Correspondence Between Lieutenant Governor Arthur and His Majesty's Secretary of State for the Colonies, on the Subject of the Military Operations Lately Carried on Against the Aboriginal Inhabitants of Van Diemen's Land*, Hobart, Tasmanian Historical Research Association, 1971, pp. 47–48.

23. Gordon to Burnett 5/1/1827, AOT CSO 8/109/60.

24. Both Lyndall Ryan and Keith Windschuttle are mistaken about Gilbert Robertson's activities. Both cite the somewhat ambiguous *Hobart Town Courier* on 7 March 1829 that reported one native being captured and five others shot. Ryan to attributes these five deaths to Robertson, while Windschuttle claims that the newspaper report was wrong and five were not shot. Close examination of the newspaper report and the two journals kept by Robertson's roving party clearly shows that the reference to five being shot did *not* refer to Robertson but to some other roving party or vigilante group. See CSO1/331/7578, pp. 79–92 and CSO1/331/7578, pp. 114–144.

25. AOT CSO1/888/188829.

26. See Robertson to Burnett 14/12/1829, AOT CSO1/888/18829. For the detail of the dispute between Robinson and Robertson over Jack Woodburn see *Weep in Silence*, pp. 448–9.

27. Windschuttle, *Fabrication*, 2002, p. 137.

28. *Ibid*, p. 137.
29. Shaw (ed.), *Military Operations*, p. 49.
30. Windschuttle, *Fabrication*, p. 137.
31. Gordon to Burnett, 9/12/1828, CSO1/ 331/194–5; see Lyndall Ryan, *The Aboriginal Tasmanians*, second edition, St Leonards, Allen & Unwin, 1996, p. 92.
32. Shaw (ed.), *Military Operation*, p. 47.
33. *Ibid*, p. 49.
34. Extracts from a diary belonging to James George, *Oatlands District Historical Society Chronicle*, no. 2, 2002, p. 13.
35. Shaw (ed.), *Military Operations*, pp. 35–46.
36. 14/2/1831, *Friendly Mission*, p. 317. This is another issue about which Rae-Ellis is mistaken. She claims that she chose her title, *Black Robinson*, because 'he was often referred to this way', yet the only evidence she has for this assertion is a letter in the *Cornwall Chronicle* of 13 June 1835 that refers to roving parties 'who acted under Black Robinson in catching the blacks here'. It is an obvious error, as the context makes it clear that the writer meant Gilbert Robertson. I have never seen George Augustus Robinson referred to in this way.

Cape Grim

Ian McFarlane

Chapter Eight of *The Fabrication of Aboriginal History* is largely devoted to Keith Windschuttle's case against a European massacre of Aborigines having taken place at Cape Grim in 1828 by members of the Van Diemen's Land Company.

At the time of the Cape Grim massacre, the Van Diemen's Land Company (VDL Co.) was administered by Edward Curr, who also held the position of magistrate, two roles that gave him inordinate power and autonomy. With no free settlers in the district, Curr presided over a virtual state-within-a-state, largely immune from the scrutiny of the colonial press and the policies of Arthur's administration in Hobart.

As Windschuttle points out, the Cape Grim massacre didn't appear in historical consciousness until 1966.[1] He proceeds to infer that because a long list of early historians made no mention of the event, it was considered an event of no great consequence; it is therefore a recent preoccupation, a modern construct. However, the reason for the late interest in the massacre lies simply in the fact that the main sources of reference are located in the VDL Co. records and in G. A. Robinson's journal. None of the historians listed by Windschuttle from Melville (1835) to Turnbull (1948) could access this essential material as VDL Co. records were not available for public scrutiny until they were deposited with the Tasmanian Archives Office. Originating from Circular Head and London, this material arrived gradually over a period from the late 1950s to the early 1970s. Robinson's journal only became readily accessible in 1966 with the publication of N. J. B. Plomley's *Friendly Mission*.

Windschuttle also sets the scene by proposing that the views of 'academic historians' are neatly opposed to those of the current managers of the VDL Co. and 'local historians' who take the company view that no massacre took place. There is no basis for this division: the 'academic historians' listed by Windschuttle have differing interpretations of many of the associated events, as do the listed 'locals'.[2] Kerry Pink, who is undoubtedly a local, does not deny the massacre but simply questions the magnitude of the casualties claimed: 'it is difficult to believe that four convict shepherds, untrained and unskilled in the use of cumbersome muzzle loading guns, could have ambushed and slaughtered 30 Aborigines renowned for their agility on land and as expert swimmers.'[3] Pink also challenges Robinson's claim to have found, nearly three years later, human bones and blood-stained rock at Suicide Bay, noting that whale skeletons usually disappear within months along the coastline.[4] Pauline Buckby, on the other hand, dismisses the whole incident as a myth: 'The legend arose, from this incident, whereby it was said that the last of the Aborigines were sent to their death at Slaughter Hill.'[5] In any case, as there is no oral tradition concerning the incident, the geographical location of the commentators would seem to have little bearing on the argument.

The massacre took place in the north-west of Tasmania on VDL Co. land grants, an area of land that roughly coincided with the lands occupied by the eight Aboriginal tribes that made up the North-West cultural/linguistic grouping. Cape Grim is a small, west-facing promontory, adjacent to and a little to the south of two small islands called the Doughboys. It is also part of a larger peninsula, the most northerly aspect of which is called Woolnorth Point.

When describing the geographical location of the massacre site, Windschuttle quite unfairly castigates Lloyd Robson for not even bothering 'to consult a map', accusing Robson of wrongly depicting the Doughboys as being to the south of Cape Grim.[6] Robson used the Doughboys as a reference point for the massacre site as it was one of the few local landmarks to have retained its identity over time. As Robson located the massacre site at a position immediately adjacent to the

Doughboys and considered Cape Grim to be north of the massacre site, he naturally described Cape Grim as being to the north of the Doughboys. The nomenclature of the area has changed a number of times since first sighted by Bass and Flinders. In Flinders' original 1798–99 map of *Terra Australis*, the whole peninsula was called Cape Grim. The 1824 government chart by Thomas Scott supports Robson by showing Cape Grim to be a little to the north of the Doughboys, while VDL Co. maps from the 1820s place Cape Grim directly opposite. In 1872, the present site of Cape Grim appears as Slaughter Hill.[7] These names remained constant until 1975, when Cape Grim is moved to where Slaughter Hill was, and the name Slaughter Hill disappears from all maps.[8] It was at this time that Suicide Bay first appeared on maps as the bay just to the south of the Doughboys and to the north of the newly named Cape Grim. Lloyd Robson's conception that the massacre site was to the south of Cape Grim would have been correct on a majority of charts until 1975.

Windschuttle, following previous historians, links the Cape Grim massacre to two earlier incidents:

> Early August, 1827 – Wounding of Thomas John in the thigh
> 31 December 1827 – Destruction of sheep by Aborigines
> February 1828 – Cape Grim massacre

As it happens, the wounding of Thomas John actually took place early in December 1827, making the destruction of sheep by Aborigines later in the same month more likely to have been a reprisal raid. Even more importantly, five events should actually be taken into consideration when examining evidence for a massacre:

> Early December, 1827 – Wounding of Thomas John in the thigh and killing of Aborigine(s)[9]
> 31 December 1827 – Destruction of sheep by Aborigines
> Early February, 1828 – Attack on Cape Grim Aborigines mounted from VDL Co. ship the *Fanny*, killing 12 Aborigines[10]
> 9 February 1828 – Company Superintendent Alexander Goldie visits men at Cape Grim on eve of incident[11]
> 10 February 1828 – Cape Grim massacre[12]

The addition of the *Fanny*'s raid to the list reveals that the company was involved in three encounters in which Aborigines were killed at Cape Grim in less than a three-month period.

Windschuttle observes that Curr was not personally present at any of the incidents and that although Goldie was later to refer to the massacre, he also 'was not present himself'.[13] The inference is that Curr's distance from events confers some innocence, while Goldie's absence discredits his value as a witness. To strengthen this position, Windschuttle avoids discussing the significance of either Curr's Superintendent visiting his Cape Grim servants on the eve of the massacre or the use of such a valuable asset as the supply vessel *Fanny* to mount an attack on Aborigines – a venture that almost certainly would have needed Curr's approval. Curr prepared a sanitised version of the event in a despatch to his directors:

> The Fanny went there a few days after this occurred for wethers for the Emu Bay Establishment, and being detained two days by an easterly wind, the Master [Richard Frederick], who is very well acquainted with that part of the country and with the habits of the Natives, took the opportunity of going in quest of them, with three other men. They came about nightfall on a tribe of about seventy men, but it was judged better to take day light for the intended attack, and the party drew off until morning. It rained heavily during the night and when they approached in the morning close to the Natives with the intent of attacking them, not a musket would go off and they were obliged to retreat without firing a shot.[14]

In this account, Curr concealed the Aboriginal deaths from his directors and portrayed the incident as an initiative of the Master of the *Fanny* who was simply an over-zealous servant protecting company property. The fact that the report contains no hint of condemnation or censure is revealing, as the Aboriginal targets of the raid were supposedly under Curr's protection as magistrate. There are also a number of problems with Curr's depiction of events. If the Master was as well acquainted with the 'habits of the Natives' as Curr maintained he was, he would know that the Aborigines were very reluctant to move during the night, being timid in the dark. It is highly improbable that men armed with that knowledge would sit in the cold and rain all night while their targets were silhouetted by campfires, awaiting the light of morning when they would lose their strategic advantage. Also, even men with only minimal experience of the bush would be well aware that after such prolonged exposure to the elements their muskets would be damp and too unreliable to risk against an armed enemy. The account given to Rosalie Hare directly by the men involved seems a more plausible version of the raid. Hare, the wife of the captain of the *Caroline*, was an independent and objective witness with no interest in either the VDL Co. or the affairs of the colony. She visited Circular Head on 19 January 1828 and noted in her diary:

> The Master of the Company's cutter *Fanny* assisted by four shepherds and his crew, surprised a party and killed twelve. The rest escaped but afterwards followed them. They reached the vessel just in time to save their lives.

Windschuttle critically reviews the differing accounts recorded by 'academic historians' regarding the circumstances of the Cape Grim massacre, as well as the casualties involved. Given the contradictions to be found in the primary sources, the disparities are not surprising. The reason for this confusion must be laid at Curr's door. It was Curr's duty as a magistrate to investigate the matter formally, since the Aborigines killed were under his jurisdiction. Yet there was no trial, no investigation nor even a rudimentary inquiry into the incident. Curr was not only remiss in his duties, he was also deceptive. He saw no need to provide his company with a detailed explanation of either the killings or the circumstances that had led to them. More seriously, Curr as magistrate failed to make a report of the matter to Lieutenant-Governor Arthur, who only learned of the incident 18 months later from Company Superintendent Goldie in November 1829.[15]

Windschuttle accepts the fact that an incident took place at Cape Grim, but he challenges the casualty figures, commonly accepted as 30 Aboriginal deaths, the claim that the VDL Co. servants were the aggressors, and most of the contemporary versions of the event. As I will discuss later in this essay, part of Windschuttle's argument is based upon Kerry Pink's doubts concerning the ability of inexperienced shepherds hampered by the limitations of Brown Bess muskets to inflict casualties of the order claimed. Windschuttle's position also relies heavily on his ability to discredit the witnesses used by Robinson to make a case for the massacre. These witnesses were Charles Chamberlain (the shepherd directly involved in the shooting), Superintendent Goldie and a local Aboriginal woman. Robinson's credibility as a reliable investigator is also challenged.

Windschuttle notes that Chamberlain, who informed Robinson that 30 Aborigines had been killed, was a convict with a serious criminal record, violent, brutalised and a persistent law-breaker, and argues that these are not the qualities one would look for in a reliable witness. Windschuttle seems to overlook that Chamberlain as depicted fits the profile of a potential slayer of Aborigines admirably.

Robinson was also able to interview another convict shepherd involved in the shooting, William Gunshannon. Gunshannon was less forthcoming about the casualty figures than Chamberlain, but when Robinson informed him that Chamberlain had already told him 30 had been killed, Gunshannon didn't deny this but, according to Robinson, 'seemed to glory in the act and said he would shoot them whenever he met them'.[16] Gunshannon not only accepted Robinson's charge but also revealed a great deal about the attitude of VDL Co. servants towards the Aborigines.

The Aboriginal woman who gave testimony to Robinson was visiting sealers near Robbins Island at the time of interview.[17] She was described by Robinson as 'from these parts'. Windschuttle makes the assumption that she was probably from the island itself and therefore would not be privy to information relating to the incident at Cape Grim. He uses the same argument to dismiss any possible testimony from Pevay, also present, who was a Paperloihener man and a native of Robbins Island. Here, Windschuttle appears to be unaware of local tribal seasonal movements. At the time of the massacre, February, most of the eight tribes that made up the North-West regional group would have been in the Robbins Island/Cape Grim area for traditional, economic and cultural purposes. Robinson's account of the Aborigines involved in the massacre – they were 'principally of women and children' who came to the islands to gather food – is consistent with known Aboriginal cultural patterns during that time of the year. As a number of tribes were in the area at the time, we have no way of knowing which tribe(s) was involved in any of the incidents.[18] However, given the interaction between the tribes during the spring/summer migrations, news of an incident as significant as the shooting of Aborigines would have rapidly spread throughout the region. Windschuttle challenges the Aboriginal testimony further by arguing that they could not count past four or seven. There is little doubt that the North-Eastern women at the meeting could speak English, having lived with and worked for sealers for years, work that presumably involved tallying the sealskins. This would account for their ability to count to 30, thereby resolving Windschuttle's difficulty in this regard.

Goldie's evidence is dismissed by Windschuttle as an attempt to discredit Curr in order to remove him from the position of magistrate. Goldie hoped to prevent Curr presiding over an investigation into the killing of an Aboriginal woman on 21 August 1829 by VDL Co. servants under Goldie's supervision. Windschuttle is under the impression that Curr was a diligent, fair-minded magistrate who would have dealt with any case of brutality or murder brought to his attention: 'there were settlers, including the chief agent of the Van Diemen's Land company, Edward Curr, who felt bound to bring such charges against their servants.'[19]

Curr, in fact, did everything he possibly could to avoid presiding over the case. It was Governor Arthur who compelled him to act. Curr informed his directors that, 'it is apparent that I cannot escape the painful duty of investigating that occurrence myself as I sincerely hoped I might have done.'[20] In any event, Curr delayed conducting the 'investigation' for four months and limited its activities to the taking of a statement from Thomas Watson, the storekeeper at Emu Bay. None of the men involved in the murder was interviewed. On no occasion did Curr ever voluntarily charge or investigate any of his servants for the murder or mistreatment of Aborigines. Windschuttle introduces the Goldie incident but then gives no detail of the circumstances surrounding the murder, which is unfortunate as they are most instructive. The field report that Goldie sent to Curr described the murder of one woman who had been wounded by a musket shot before being finished off with a blow to the neck with an axe while protecting her six-year-old child, as well as the taking into slavery of another woman. The report was cold, matter-of-fact and almost routine in tone.[21] In fact, Goldie was surprised by Curr's condemnation of the action. Curr's unexpected reaction may best be explained by the fact that, unlike previous incidents, this one had occurred close to the Emu Bay settlement and news was bound to leak to the authorities in Hobart. Curr's sensitivity to the scrutiny of Arthur's administration may be shown by his sending of servants to Hobart to reassure public opinion following the Cape Grim massacre. On 15 August 1828, the Hobart press reported that:

> Persons in the service of the V.D. Land Company, who have arrived in town from Circular head last week, inform us, that the black natives in that quarter are extremely quiet and do not possess the spirit of revenge so predominant in other parts of the Island; and much to the praise of Mr. Curr, orders had been given that they were not to be troubled in any way whatever, unless guilty of dishonest or improper conduct, (to the former they are much addicted) and on no account, to kill any of them.[22]

Likewise, Chamberlain, in his interview regarding the massacre, admitted, 'We was afraid and thought at the time the Governor would hear of it and we should get into trouble.'[23] Goldie, reasoning that he was to be made the scapegoat for the crime, wrote to Arthur not to make a case for another magistrate but to take the Nuremberg defence. He detailed previous attacks on Aborigines, some of which he had led, in order to implicate Curr as the authority that had given the orders which he had simply followed. Goldie went even further, embarking on a tour of the company huts to warn the men not to take part in any more attacks on Aborigines; they now ran the risk of being charged with murder as Curr would no longer support them.[24] Curr, in an attempt to re-assert control, personally led an abortive raid on some Aborigines and then offered his men rum for bringing in Aboriginal heads to place on huts.[25] By publicly detailing what he knew of previous outrages against Aborigines, Goldie would have anticipated corroboration and support from other company servants should that sort of evidence be required at any subsequent trial. The fact that this strategy entailed the risk of further personal incrimination – Goldie having played a central role in many of these activities – gives every reason to view his testimony to Arthur as having some credibility.

Another witness to some of the events at Cape Grim is overlooked by Windschuttle. Rosalie Hare stayed with the Curr family during her visit, keeping a diary of events during much of the period under question. Hare's diary serves to corroborate Superintendent Goldie's claim that:

> there have been a great many Natives shot by the Company's Servants, and several engagements between them while their stock was in that district. On one occasion a good many were shot (I never heard exactly the number) and although Mr Curr knew it, yet he never that I am aware, took any notice of it although in the Commission of the Peace and that time their [*sic*] was no proclamation against the Natives, nor were they (the Natives) at the time they were attacked at all disturbing the Company's flocks.[26]

Hare wrote in her diary:

> We have to lament that our own countrymen consider the massacre of these people an honour. While we remained at Circular Head there were several accounts of considerable numbers of natives having been shot by them [the company men], they wishing to extirpate them entirely, if possible.[27]

This brings us to the question, was a massacre of any scale possible given the expertise of the shepherds and the technology of the time, the Brown Bess musket? Much is made of the limitations of these weapons, their rate of fire, perhaps as poor as one round per minute, and their accuracy, probably 70 metres at best. However, the real solution to the problem can be found in the fact that the shepherds did not use their muskets in the military fashion by firing a single ball. The most common musket in use at that time was the Indian Pattern Smooth Bore musket.[28] These early muskets had smooth bores that, unlike rifles, were capable of using shot with no damage to the barrel. Far from being 'cumbersome', they had a calibre of .75 inches (19.05 mm), slightly larger than the current 12-gauge shotgun – a bore wide enough to handle a load of shot or pistol balls sufficient to cause devastating and widespread damage to human targets at close range. Lacking any means of treating shot wounds, wounded Aborigines faced a poor prognosis indeed. Armed with such weapons, the shepherds at Cape Grim were quite capable of killing the 30 Aborigines claimed by Robinson's witnesses.

The VDL Co.'s practice of using shot in their muskets is illustrated by an incident that took place at the Burleigh hut just seven months after the massacre. Following a serious and violent clash with Aborigines, a company surveyor, Joseph Fossey, sent a message to Circular Head complaining of having only '1¾ lbs Gunpowder and no shot'; he also asked to be supplied with 'Gunpowder Buckshot Muskets and Cutlasses' as a matter of urgency.[29] Windschuttle should have been aware of the practice of using shot against Aborigines, as he refers elsewhere in his book to such an occasion when describing how Batman's men used buckshot for ammunition in an incident near Ben Lomond in 1829.[30]

Another problem with the musket, according to Windschuttle, was that the Aborigines would time their assaults to take advantage of the time taken to reload once they became aware of the slow rate of fire. However, in the case of the North-West Aborigines, a lack of familiarity with European technology due to the absence of settlers and the brief period of VDL Co. occupation makes this argument unconvincing. Windschuttle goes on to make the rather sweeping assertion that his arguments relating to the limitations of the muskets at Cape Grim should be applied universally to 'any claim about the massacre of large numbers of Aborigines before the 1860s'.[31]

During the campaign to capture Pevay in the Victorian bush in 1841, Lieutenant Rawson and some police fired several shots in order to induce Pevay's band to surrender.[32] Rawson described the melee in his journal:

> We advanced down the hill, and were closing in upon them, I was about six feet from the fire, and could see them laying down, when a policeman who was on my left, catching a glimpse of a man's head,

without orders, fired and missed him … everybody fired at them as they got a sight of them. I fired both barrels, right and left, and I saw one drop. I had five pistol balls in each barrel.[33]

The practice of using shot or smaller ball in musket barrels was quite widespread. There was some resistance by troops to the adoption of rifled weapons for this very reason, as the smooth-bore muskets were used as shotguns for hunting game to supplement rations in the field.

While the regular use of muskets as a hunting weapon would account for the shepherds' expertise, the military record of one of the shepherds has also been overlooked. John Weavis was a former soldier who served in the 89th Foot as well as the York Chasseurs, a regiment raised from military deserters.[34] In the latter regiment, Weavis served in the West Indies from 1815 to 1817 and may well have taken part in the suppression of slave revolts during his tour of duty.[35] Weavis would have had ample time to pass on his military experience and train his companions in the competent use of the musket.

Windschuttle correctly points out that we will never 'know for certain exactly what happened'[36] on that day but, having said that, goes on to argue that we should accept the explanation of events provided by Curr. In this scenario, the incident took place not on the beach but adjacent the hill called Mount Victory. On seeing a large party of Aborigines on the hill, the four shepherds who were in their hut at the foot of the hill considered an attack imminent and marched out to engage the enemy. In the long battle that ensued, six Aborigines were killed. Windschuttle notes that, 'Under the circumstances, marching out under arms to meet them was a legitimate tactic.'[37] I would argue that abandoning the cover of a hut to engage a vastly greater force of Aborigines occupying the high ground would have been an act of gross stupidity – and not a manoeuvre one would expect from a soldier of Weavis's experience. As Windschuttle notes, the range of a Brown Bess musket loaded with ball was at maximum around 80 yards, an effectiveness that would be considerably reduced if loaded with shot and shooting uphill. Under these circumstances, in the open terrain and with the advantage of height, the Aboriginal spear was more than a match for the musket. James Calder noted that spears could be thrown with precision up to 70 yards (64 metres),[38] whilst Labillardière witnessed accuracy up to 100 yards (91 metres).[39] Jorgen Jorgenson described an official demonstration that took place before Governor Arthur:

> A large door was provided for the Blacks to make their spear exercise at. At the distance of about sixty or seventy yards they sent their spears through the door, and all the spears nearly in the same place. Oridia placed a crawfish on the top of a spear, then retreated sixty yards, and at that distance lodged two spears out of three in the crawfish.[40]

A large number of Aborigines armed with spears on the high ground would certainly have been victorious. That four shepherds could emerge from that shower of missiles unscathed is beyond the bounds of credibility.

Windschuttle's account still leaves us with the difficulty of two versions of events, that of Chamberlain, who states that the bodies were thrown down on the rocks and most of those bodies were men;[41] and that of Robinson, who states that the Aborigines attacked were a party made up of women, children and old people seated around cooking fires on the beach.[42] Robinson goes on to add a seemingly contradictory element to his story that gives some support to Chamberlain's account: 'I went to the foot of the cliffs where the bodies had been thrown down.'[43] These two versions of events are most likely two elements of the one story, an explanation consistent with traditional Aboriginal hunting patterns at that place. When out gathering food, according to custom the Aboriginal men would be upon the heights hunting for wallaby, while the women, children and the elderly would remain close to the sea harvesting any available seafood.[44] Under these circumstances, the wallaby hunters, probably less than half a dozen men, would have been the first Aborigines encountered by the shepherds and the first to be shot. It was their bodies that were later thrown upon the rocks after the shepherds had fired down upon those on the beach.[45]

The precise number of Aboriginal deaths sustained at Cape Grim will, of course, never be known, but it was physically possible for the shepherds to have killed 30, and from what we know of their attitude towards Aborigines, they certainly would have killed all they could. However, if like Windschuttle,[46] we accept Curr's initial report of a 'battle that resulted in Aboriginal casualties of six dead and several severely wounded'[47] as credible, we have to ask what happened to the several wounded. Even in modern warfare, the wounded considerably outnumber the dead; all that has changed are survival rates, not particularly good in those days. Already we are dealing with a double-digit figure, and when the wounded statistic is applied to the casualties sustained by the Aborigines in the Thomas John incident and in the raid by the *Fanny*, the potential death rate starts to climb.

Curr's subsequent reports refined the battle casualties downwards – his memory for detail improving two and a half years after the event – to six killed, one being a woman.[48] Later, when called upon to explain the situation to Arthur, he wrote, 'I have no doubt that some natives were killed on the occasion, my impression is that the real number was three.'[49] This revision downward of figures in order to mask the significance of the incident shows Curr to be an unreliable source of factual information. There is no compelling reason to accept his word against those of his servants, local Aborigines, a senior company supervisor and the observations of Rosalie Hare and G. A. Robinson.

Windschuttle seeks to undermine Robinson's credibility by questioning his claim to have found blood and bones at the foot of the cliffs some two and a half years after the event. It is worth noting that Robinson had Alexander McKay with him at the time of this discovery, a very experienced and respected bushman who had ample opportunity and motive to discredit Robinson's observations at a later date, when the two came into conflict. The presence of bones and a bloodstained cliff may be explained by the evidence of Goldie and Hare that a good many assaults on Aborigines occurred in the area. Robinson might well have found traces of a more recent murder, as evidence from the Cape Grim massacre would indeed long since have vanished.

Unfortunately for Windschuttle, his case relies heavily upon the reputation and credibility of Curr alone, not only for the numbers of casualties inflicted but also for determining who were the aggressors. The fact that the VDL Co. happened to be engaged in dispossessing the Aborigines of their lands, traditional culture and livelihood at the time doesn't enter into Windschuttle's conception of what constitutes aggression.

Prior to the establishment of the VDL Co. at Circular Head, Jorgenson's visit to the district confirmed the peaceful disposition of the Aborigines, who were blissfully unaware that their lands were now forfeit to the VDL Co.: 'The natives', he wrote 'seem an inoffensive and friendly race. Frank and generous treatment may render them of some service to white men who should visit this quarter.'[50] Shortly after arriving in the north-west in 1827, Curr reported to his directors with reference to the Black War that the Cape Grim Aborigines, while numerous, were 'in no way connected with the tribe which has caused so much bloodshed in the Island during the last few months'.[51] Later, Curr contradicted himself in an attempt to justify the ongoing bloodshed between his men and the Aborigines. He reported, 'But we found all the mischief done, discord has already gone to that length that there was no safety for a White man but in the destruction of his Black opponent.'[52] On an earlier occasion, Curr had expressed the view that, 'They [the Aborigines] have been the aggressors and strife, once begun with any of these tribes, has never yet been terminated, nor will, according to present appearances, but by their extermination.'[53] Later, in his submission to the Aborigines Committee, Curr made it abundantly clear that the whole responsibility for the Aboriginal 'problem' lay with the government: 'The Crown sells us lands, and is therefore bound to make good our titles and possession against *previous* occupants and claimants.'[54] Curr then argued that the government was faced with two stark choices: they must either 'submit to see the white inhabitants murdered one after another, or they must undertake a war of extermination'.[55] Here, Curr again advanced the opinion he had earlier put to his directors, that the extermination of the Aborigines was inevitable.[56] If this was Curr's long-held opinion, it is a reasonable assumption that his domestic policies were guided by the view. Curr closed his submission with the assurance, after making the suggestion of extermination, that he was 'far from advising such a proceeding' and he would not countenance bloodshed except in the case of 'aggression or self-defence'.[57] Windschuttle, in an attempt to defend Curr, criticises Reynolds for omitting to report the latter part of Curr's statement. Windschuttle argues that Curr was only 'canvassing' the possibility of the extermination of the Aborigines, not advocating it.[58] However, given Curr's habit of 'canvassing' the extirpation of Aborigines over a long period of time to anyone who would listen, this would seem a forlorn hope indeed. Curr also had rather a pro-active view of self-defence; he outlined some of his favoured measures in a letter to Police Magistrate John Lee Archer:

> I have tried the effect of spring guns in the huts, which they have once discharged, and must have escaped from almost by miracle.
> I am now trying a man-trap, also in one of the huts.
> I have for a week concealed an armed man inside one of the huts, with directions to fire upon intruders.[59]

Following the Thomas John incident, Curr had accepted John's charge that the Aborigines were the aggressors uncritically and, as usual, with no investigation. However, the same Aboriginal woman who provided information about the Cape Grim massacre informed Robinson that the company shepherds had 'got native women into their hut and wanted to take liberties with them'.[60] The Aboriginal woman's claim is consistent with Jorgen Jorgenson's earlier warning to Arthur that the VDL Co.'s men had 'designs of violating their women'.[61]

In relation to the Cape Grim massacre, Curr is ambiguous. He reported to the company directors that:

> the shepherds fell in with a strong party of Natives who, after a long fight, left six of their number dead on the field, including their chief, besides several severely wounded. I have no doubt that this will have the effect of intimidating them, and oblige them to keep aloof.[62]

The fact that Superintendent Goldie had visited his men the day before the attack raises the suspicion that whole incident may have been premeditated. In any case, Curr certainly seemed pleased with the outcome. The VDL Co. directors were not so convinced by Curr's report as Windschuttle apparently is. They responded:

> It is with no ordinary feelings of regret that the Court has read your

account of the encounter with the Natives near Cape Grim. It does not appear from the account who were the aggressors.[63]

Evidence indicating that the company's men were the aggressors, provided by Chamberlain, Gunshannon, Goldie and a local Aboriginal woman, is supported by what we know of Aboriginal seasonal cultural patterns – these suggest the group in question was made up of Aboriginal families involved in traditional food gathering. It is also worth noting that, after hearing Chamberlain's account of events at Cape Grim, Robinson concluded the interview by warning Chamberlain, 'You are not justified in using any arms except your life is in danger,'[64] indicating that any suggestion that the shepherds' lives were in any danger had not been raised.

The presence of women also makes the idea of an Aboriginal attack unlikely. Windschuttle uses the example of Walyer, an Aboriginal woman from the north-west region, to challenge Geoff Lennox's claim that the presence of women indicates that this was not a war party as women were not included in such ventures. Traditionally, Aborigines did not take women along with them on war parties, and in this incident we are dealing with traditional tribes. The VDL Co., the only European influence in the region, had arrived just 16 months prior to the massacre. Walyer was a member of the Tommeginner tribe from the Table Cape district. Along with two sisters and two brothers, she had been expelled for some tribal infringement. They soon took up with sealers, acquiring and learning how to use firearms in the process. After returning to the bush and recruiting Aboriginal survivors of different bands, they soon became a menace to any Aboriginal or European who crossed their path. Walyer was a creation of the sealers and European invasion; she was not representative of Aboriginal traditional society.

Windschuttle persists in treating the contact history in Tasmania as though it was a uniform experience for all involved. No importance is given to the various adaptive strategies employed by individual chieftains, and no reference made to the different forms, pace and nature of European settlement. The cultural traditions and movement patterns of North-West Aboriginal tribes are likewise ignored. The generalisation of Aboriginal culture and the experience of dispossession invites error.

The claim that Aborigines traded away their women, for example, does not hold up in the north-west. There is absolutely no evidence that this occurred and a strong case can be made to the contrary. As late as 1832, Robinson's records of the remnants of the North-West tribes show a relatively normal balance of males to females:[65]

Date	Place	Men	Women	Children*
15 July 1832	Hunter Island	6	5	7
3–4 Sept. 1832	Arthur River	10	14	12

*including adolescents

The names of the Aboriginal women present in these groups also reveal that, far from being exploited as objects of trade or instruments of diplomacy, there was a practice of offering protection to vulnerable women, including those from different tribes.

As well the Cape Grim massacre, Windschuttle challenges other reports of outrages committed against Aborigines in the VDL Co. lands, such as poisoning. Windschuttle is correct in stating that there is no hard evidence that Aborigines were poisoned with flour, and it would be wrong to say that this definitely occurred. However, there are indications that it was possible. On 8 August 1830, Robson, the superintendent of the Surrey Hills establishment, told Robinson he had offered the men some poison to kill the 'Hyaena' (Tasmanian Tiger). The men had responded that they didn't need it at that time, but they would have a use for it next summer. Robinson was of the opinion that hundreds of Aborigines had been destroyed that way.[66] All that can be gleaned from the exchange is that Robson was of the view that the men would poison Aborigines given half the chance. Eleven years later in 1841, the issue of poisoning was raised again when Curr wrote a rather anxious letter to his superintendent, Adolphus Schayer, on the subject:

> A report, resting on very good foundation I believe, that it was intended to get rid of the natives by leaving poisoned damper in the huts, having reached the Government, is the cause in my opinion, of this investigation being instituted … I beg you to communicate to me (and in a separate letter) any thing you may have heard connected with this topic.[67]

Again, this letter doesn't prove the deed was done, but it shows that Curr, like Robson, was of the view that some of the servants at least had the idea and the intention. The letter also indicates that, unlike Windschuttle, Curr was not so sure that poisoning had not taken place.

Windschuttle limits his research and confers great importance on Robinson by only using reports from his journal from 1829 to 1839 to create his list of Aboriginal casualties in the north-west. But Robinson was only in the north-west on three occasions: two months in 1830, six months in 1832 and a little under six months in 1834. His journals are therefore unlikely to provide a comprehensive account of casualties in clashes that took place between the VDL Co. and Aborigines in the 16 years between 1826 and 1842. While only three Europeans were killed by Aborigines on VDL Co. lands, we still have to account for the loss of most of the eight Aboriginal tribes in the eight years from 1826 to 1834. Only 91 Aborigines were ever taken into captivity and perhaps a dozen were still free after 1834, having evaded capture. If – ignoring many reports to the contrary about the north-west – we take Windschuttle's estimate of only 40 Aborigines to a band or tribe,[68] this gives a conservative total number of 320 Aborigines, leaving the disappearance of 217 unaccounted for. Windschuttle, trusting in the humanity of Curr and his servants towards the Aborigines, attributes the decline in numbers to introduced diseases such as colds and influenza. One of the problems in applying this theory to north-west Tasmania is the lack of contact between Aborigines and Europeans, there being no settlers in the region at the time in question. Contact was generally with VDL Co. men, and these encounters were usually lethal for reasons other than catching a cold. Curr actively dissuaded his men from establishing any social contact with the Aboriginal population:

> No one could feel more anxious than I have been, to avoid any kind of contention with these people, and I have always enjoined the men to have no communication with them whatever, either friendly or otherwise, knowing that their friendly visits are only paid for the purpose of ascertaining our means of defense and weak points, and are generally the forerunners of attacks.[69]

In fact, before Curr and his men even left Hobart for the north-west, prior to seeing or meeting an Aborigine from the region, Curr warned them:

> At the same time the well known character of the people must be kept in view and treachery must be guarded against. No person must suffer himself to be surprised by them at a disadvantage or without arms or to be seduced by any appearance of friendliness to trust himself in their power; the surest way to prevent bloodshed is to be always prepared to repel and punish aggression.[70]

It should also be noted that there is no account in the VDL Co. records of any of the company's shepherds or stockmen coming across sick or dead Aborigines, or commenting on any decline in population due to sickness.

Windschuttle's research brings no new arguments to the debate. Its only novel element is its faith in the testimony of a man like Curr, a magistrate who, while in the process of investigating Goldie for murder, personally led an attack on Aborigines. Curr reported the incident to his directors:

> My whole and sole object *was* to kill them, and this because my full conviction was and is that the laws of nature and of God and of this country all conspired to render this my duty ... And although I feel a perfect loathing to the idea of shedding human blood and know no difference in that respect between white and black, yet I regret upon principle that I was not successful against them. I think it would have done good, it would have alarmed the Natives more than anything else, prevented them from attempting our huts again, made them keep aloof, given them a lesson they would long have remembered and really been the means of saving more of their lives eventually than it would have cost them, as well as some of our own. As to my expression of a wish to have three of their heads to put on the ridge of the hut, I shall only say that I think it certainly would have the effect of deterring some of their comrades, of making the death of their companions live in their recollections, and so extend the advantage the example made of them.[71]

Windschuttle's confidence in Curr's character was certainly not shared by his contemporaries: this was a manager who physically assaulted his indentured servants for running away from his regime, which they did en masse.[72] A magistrate with his own personal flagellator, who regularly sentenced his assigned servants to be flogged at a rate twice that of other magistrates in the rest of Van Diemen's Land.[73] A man whom Arthur disliked intensely and whom Franklin refused to enter into correspondence with. Perhaps the last word on Curr should be reserved for the colonial press at the time of his sacking by the VDL Co.:

> The removal of the late superintendent, Mr Curr, from the charge of the Circular Head establishment, has occasioned unusual joy amongst the community at that place:– the result will be no less beneficial to the affairs of the company, we trust, than pleasing to its tenants and servants.[74]

NOTES

1. Keith Windschuttle, *The Fabrication of Aboriginal History: Volume One, Van Diemen's Land 1803–1847*, Sydney, Macleay Press, 2002, pp. 250–251.
2. Incidentally, Von Stieglitz is incorrectly included in Windschuttle's list of locals.
3. Kerry Pink, *And Wealth For Toil*, Burnie, Advocate Printers, 1990, p. 63.
4. *Ibid*, p. 63.
5. Pauline Buckby, *Around Circular Head*, Tasmania, Denbar Publishers, 1984, p. 21.
6. Windschuttle, *Fabrication*, p. 254.
7. VDL Map 343/5/1, 343/673; Jim Stockton, *Cultural Resources Information for Cape Grim*, Northwest Tasmania, Australian Heritage Commission, 1979, p. 31.
8. VDL Map 343/425; Stockton, *Cultural Resources*, p. 31.
9. Inward Despatch no. 1, Curr to Directors, 2/1/1828.
10. Rosalie Hare & Ida Lee, *The Voyage of the Caroline from England to Van Diemen's Land and Batavia*, Longmans, London, Green & Co., 1927, p. 41.
11. Inward Despatch no. 11, Curr to Directors, 28/2/1828.
12. Inward Despatch no. 150, Curr to Directors, 7/10/1830.
13. Windschuttle, *Fabrication*, p. 255.
14. Inward Despatch no. 2, Curr to Directors, 14/1/1828, AOT. VDL 5/1: BR LHC VDLC Microfilm Reel 33/1, p. 283.
15. G. Lennox, *The Van Diemen's Land Company and the Tasmanian Aborigines: A Reappraisal*, Sandy Bay, Tasmanian Historical Research Association Papers and Proceedings, vol. 37, 1990, p. 5.
16. N. J. B. Plomley, *Friendly Mission: The Tasmanian Journals and Papers of George Augustus Robinson 1829–1834*, Hobart, Tasmanian Historical Research Association, 1966, p. 196.

17. Windschuttle discounts any evidence from the other five Aboriginal women present at the meeting as they were from the east, even though after living and working with the sealers for a number of years they would have been able to communicate with at least one of the two local Aborigines in English and would have been made aware of significant events such as the massacre. Pevay, one of the local Aborigines present, became conversant with the English language while he was held captive for six months by the VDL Co., and had only recently been released (see Inward Despatch no. 86, Curr to Directors, 13/8/1829, AOT VDL 5/1). Although Robinson noted in his journal that the mission Aborigines were able to converse with the eastern women in their own language, he was quite specific that he received his information concerning Cape Grim from 'the aboriginal females'.

18. There is good reason to believe that the spearing of company sheep on 31 December 1827 was conducted by a band of Aborigines led by Pevay's brother Wymeruck – see N. J. B. Plomley, *Weep in Silence*, Hobart. Blubberhead Press, 1987, p. 836; see also fn. 24, p. 15.

19. Windschuttle, *Fabrication*, p. 192.

20. Lennox, *Reappraisal*, p. 16.

21. Letter from Goldie to Curr, 16/9/1829.

22. *The Tasmanian* (Hobart), vol. 11, no. 77, 15/8/1828.

23. Plomley, *Friendly Mission*, p. 175.

24. Letter from Goldie to Curr, 5/10/1829.

25. Inward Despatch no. 150, Curr to Directors, 7/10/1830.

26. Letter from Goldie to Arthur, 18/11/1830.

27. Hare, *Voyage*, p. 41.

28. Blair, Claude (ed.), *Pollard's History of Firearms*, Middlesex, Hamlyn, 1983, p. 137.

29. Letter from Hellyer to T. W. White, 25/9/1828.

30. Windschuttle, *Fabrication*, p. 156.

31. *Ibid*, p. 261.

32. *Port Phillip Herald*, Melbourne, 9/11/1841.

33. Jan Roberts, *Jack of Cape Grim*, Richmond, Greenhouse Publications, 1986, pp. 76–77.

34. Public Records Office, London, PRO WO12/12084.

35. *Ibid*, PRO WO17/292.

36. Windschuttle, *Fabrication*, p. 268.

37. *Ibid*, p. 268.

38. J. E. Calder, *The Native Tribes of Tasmania*, Hobart, Cox Kay, 1972, p. 33.

39. N. J. B. Plomley, *The Baudin Expedition and the Tasmanian Aborigines 1802*, Hobart, Blubber Head Press, 1983, pp. 186–187.

40. N. J. B. Plomley (ed.), *Jorgen Jorgenson and the Aborigines of Van Diemen's Land*, Hobart, Blubber Head Press, 1991, p. 114.

41. Plomley, *Friendly Mission*, p. 175.

42. *Ibid*, p. 183.

43. *Ibid*, p. 183.

44. The early date of 10 February would suggest seafood to be a more likely focus of the hunt than mutton-birds as it was too late in the season for the eggs, too early for decent-sized chicks and the adult birds would be away foraging for food at sea during the day. Robinson may have misunderstood what the Aboriginal women were trying to tell him: the common use of the term 'muttonfish' for abalone at that time could easily result in confusion. When Robinson depicted Aborigines with their

prepared supply of birds tied up with grass, he was clearly trying to reconstruct the scene of the massacre in his mind, as none of the witnesses had provided him with that sort of detail.

45. An alternative explanation for two parties of Aborigines could be that, given recent hostilities in the area, the Aborigines may have posted sentries on the high ground and these were the original casualties who were later to be thrown down upon the rocks.

46. Windschuttle, *Fabrication*, p. 266.

47. Inward Despatch no. 11, Curr to Directors, 28/2/1828.

48. Inward Despatch no. 150, Curr to Directors, 7/10/1830.

49. Letter from Curr to Colonial Secretary, 18/5/1831.

50. Plomley, *Jorgen Jorgenson*, p. 8.

51. Inward Despatch no. 42, Curr to Directors, 13/2/1827.

52. Inward Despatch no. 55, Curr to Directors, 17/1/1829.

53. Inward Despatch no. 11, Curr to Directors, 28/2/1828.

54. Curr's submission to the Aborigines Committee, AOT CSO 1/323/7578, vol. 8, p. 374.

55. *Ibid*, p. 376.

56. Inward Despatch No. 11, p. 304.

57. Curr's submission to the Aborigines Committee, p. 377.

58. Windschuttle, *Fabrication*, pp. 302–303.

59. Letter from Curr to Lee Archer, 10/8/1841, AOT VDL 23/10 BR LHC VDLC, p. 296.

60. Plomley, *Friendly Mission*, p. 181.

61. Arthur Papers A2209, memorial from Jorgenson of 5/1/1828 cited in Lennox, Reappraisal, Appendix 1.

62. Inward Despatch no. 11, p. 304.

63. Outward Despatch no. 83, Court to Curr, 28/10/1828.

64. Plomley, *Friendly Mission*, p. 175.

65. Plomley, *Friendly Mission*, pp. 702–703.

66. *Ibid*, p. 196.

67. Letter from Curr to Schayer, 6/12/1841; see J. Leslie Bruce, *A Gentleman from Silesia: Adolphus Schayer and the Van Diemen's Land Company 1830–1843*, Research Paper, Tasmanian State Institute of Technology, 1990. p. 72.

68. Windschuttle, *Fabrication*, p. 371.

69. Inward Despatch no. 11, p. 304.

70. Van Diemen's Land Company Orders no. 4, 22/3/1826.

71. Inward Despatch no. 150, Curr to Directors, 7 /10/1830.

72. Jennifer Duxbury, *Colonial Servitude: Indentured and Assigned Servants of the Van Diemen's Land Company 1825–41*, Clayton, Monash Publications in History, 4, 1989, pp. 49–51.

73. *Ibid*, p. 51. The average percentage of convicts sentenced to be flogged by other magistrates in the colony during 1834 was only 11%, one-fifth that ordered by Curr. Of those convicts assigned to the VDL Co. during Curr's period on the bench, one in two were flogged, while the average elsewhere in the colony between 1830 and 1835 was one in four.

74. *Cornwall Chronicle*, 19/3/1842.

Counting the Cost of the 'Nun's Picnic'

Mark Finnane

In a memorable phrase comparing Australia with other places settled by the European empires, Claudio Veliz described British colonisation of this country as 'like a nun's picnic'.[1] The occasion was his launching of Keith Windschuttle's book *The Fabrication of Aboriginal History*.

Rather than seeing evidence of the extensive violence of a colonisation process, Windschuttle argues that Aboriginal death during colonisation occurred because of the criminal behaviour of the Aborigines themselves. In a typical passage, which demands the scrutiny of criminologists as much of historians, Windschuttle argues that, 'Far from generating black resentment, the expansion of settlement instead gave the Aborigines more opportunity and more temptation to engage in robbery and murder, two customs they had come to relish.'[2] This is history and amateur criminology rolled into the most unapologetic advocacy of colonisation-as-civilisation that has been produced in this country for many years.

What kind of a 'nun's picnic' was this? Unpredictably, Windschuttle's book confirms that, at least in Tasmania, the experience of colonisation was a devastating one for the Aboriginal inhabitants. Even on Windschuttle's narrow definition of 'plausible' evidence, the rate of death from violence in the first 30 years of Tasmanian settlement was extraordinarily high. (And extrapolated to the Australian mainland, the rate of violent death in Tasmania delivers an unexpected challenge to Windschuttle's own revisionist account of events there.)

Yet Windschuttle does nothing to acknowledge the significance of this
rate because, when it comes down to it, he fails to fulfil one of the most
basic demands of social science – the need to take account of a population base and to compare the experience of different populations.

In a detailed accounting of 'plausible' documented deaths, Windschuttle argues that 118 Tasmanian Aborigines died in the three
decades after the first documented death in 1804.[3] To understand the
significance of that figure of 118 deaths, we have to remember the
population base concerned. The recent bombings in Bali help make
this point clearer. Most Australians have been touched in some way or
other by the Bali bombings – they know someone who was connected
with the many casualties and deaths. Yet the total number of
Australian deaths was 88 in a population of nearly 20 million. What
was the population of Tasmanian Aborigines that suffered this impact
of 118 'plausible' deaths? According to Windschuttle, historians bent
on emphasising the catastrophic impact of colonisation have grossly
exaggerated the pre-contact population. On reviewing the various
estimates, he concludes that the population of Tasmania in 1803
should be regarded as less than 2000.[4]

Since we have no census data or a proxy for it in computing pre-
contact populations, perhaps the best we can say about this as a starting point is that it relies on a high degree of speculation. Nevertheless,
it is important to work with some population base figure in order to
estimate with *any* degree of confidence the demographic impacts of
colonial violence. So let us start with that figure of 2000 and develop a
population count that takes into account the decline through disease
and lowered fertility, consistent with Windschuttle's estimates.[5] If we
use his population figures to calculate the rates of violent death at
the hands of settlers, the overall rate of violent death of Tasmanian
Aborigines in the 30 years of first contact (1804–34) was 365.9 per
100,000 population. On the hypothetical assumption of a stable, not
declining population (Windschuttle's 118 deaths in a population remaining stable at 2000 across the period), the death rate by violence *per
year* would be no less than 190 per 100,000.

What was the rate in the worst years of violence? In a passage dedicated to showing that colonists had no incentive to cover up deaths,

Windschuttle argues that after 1828, 'the documentary record does not show a sudden increase in the number of killings by whites.'[6] However, it is not clear which documentary record he is referring to, as the table later in the book documenting 118 plausible deaths shows quite the opposite.[7] Counting only Windschuttle's 'plausible' deaths, it appears that at least 40 of his total 118 deaths occurred in the two years after the declaration of martial law in November 1828. On the assumption, consistent with Windschuttle's arguments, that the population was not much more than 500 by 1828–30, the rate of Aboriginal violent death in the two years from the declaration of martial law would have been more than 3600 per 100,000.

Whichever way we look at it, these are very high chances of dying a violent death. In one of the world's most violent societies, the United States, the average homicide rate for the last quarter-century has been between 9 and 10 per 100,000. Historians of violence in early modern Europe are astonished at rates of violent death of between 10 and 60 per 100,000. In Tasmania in 1996, 35 people were shot dead at Port Arthur – that massacre sent the annual homicide rate in the state to 8.4 per 100,000, although it had a negligible impact on the total Australian homicide rate for that year.[8] During the two years from 1828, the year after which Windschuttle argues there was no 'sudden increase in the number of killings by whites', the violent death rate of Aborigines in Tasmania was more than three times the mortality risk of the Australian population during World War I, when over 60,000 soldiers died.

Are such comparisons appropriate in relation to the social process described in Windschuttle's book – the colonisation of a country occupied by hunter-gatherers? One exculpatory response to the argument put above has been that pre-contact Aborigines were accustomed to a more violent existence.[9] Indeed, that is explicit in Windschuttle's own indictment of their pre-contact society – these were people, he suggests, who enjoyed killing and among whom there was a high risk of dying a violent death at the hands of other indigenous people.[10]

A quarter of a century ago, Geoffrey Blainey's *Triumph of the Nomads* drew attention to evidence of the incidence of violent death in pre-contact Aboriginal societies. On the basis of only two accounts, his estimate was that the 'annual death rate in warfare' was between 1 in 270 and 1 in 300.[11] While Blainey's evidence base was thin and his statistical speculations no less than heroic, he usefully drew attention to the failure of previous scholars to generate mortality rates from the raw figures of deaths counted:

> As no prehistorian, to my knowledge, tried to convert the fighting deaths of hunter-gatherers into percentages, the illusion easily arose that in such societies fighting deaths, being numerically few, were not of great significance.[12]

This methodological criticism is one that we need to apply to Windschuttle's use of data.

Blainey's work was originally published in 1975. Subsequent research on warfare and disputes in hunter-gatherer and other pre-state societies largely confirms the serious levels of mortality that arose from internecine violent conflict, but also draws attention to the very significant range in these mortality rates. In a well-regarded recent overview of the subject, one only selectively cited by Windschuttle,[13] Lawrence Keeley used evidence from Australian anthropology of high rates of violence in tribes like the Murngin (or Yolngu) of Arnhem Land (studied by Lloyd Warner and also the basis of Blainey's 1 in 300 calculation) and very low levels of violence in tribes like the Mardudjara of central Australia who had no words for feud or warfare.[14]

Developing his general thesis of the commonality of warfare in all societies, Keeley embarked on the almost impossibly difficult exercise of computing annual warfare death rates. His comparison found that annual warfare death rates in pre-state societies regularly exceeded those of state societies – although his 'state society' calculations include decade ranges without significant wars (for example, he uses aggregated rates for Germany across the 90 years from 1900 to 1990, for only 11 years of which the country was engaged in major wars). Nevertheless, not one of the 31 examples of warfare death rates computed by Keeley[15] comes close to the fatal casualty rate of more than 2 per cent (or 2000 per 100,000) that I compute for Tasmanian Aboriginal death rates by violence during the years when Windschuttle argues that there was no war[16] (see Table 1, p. 305). And this violent death rate is more than three times that of the most violent warfare death rate attributed by Blainey to a pre-contact Aboriginal society in Australia.

Whatever the facts of pre-contact violence, after 1803 a new factor was introduced: the arrival of a non-indigenous settler population, which gradually made its presence felt throughout the island over the next three decades. The best possible analysis of the quantum of violence would be one that enabled us to compare this situation with similar historical examples. The dust-jacket of Windschuttle's book claims boldly that, 'The author finds the British colonization of the Australia [*sic*] was the least violent of all Europe's encounters with the New World.' The claim is developed on the inside cover leaf: 'The extensive and fully documented statistics produced in this book demonstrate that, in the entire history of Europe's colonization of the Americas and the Pacific, Van Diemen's Land was probably the site where the least indigenous blood of all was deliberately shed.' These claims are entirely unsupported by statistical information. If Windschuttle indeed looked for comparative statistics, he probably gave up in frustration. The fact is that the difficulties faced by Australian historians in estimating pre-contact populations are exactly those faced by historians of the European empires the world over. No reader of the well-documented history of the European empires in the Americas, in Africa, Asia and the Pacific can fail to notice the similarity between the Tasmanian situation in the early nineteenth century and that faced by hunter-gatherer, nomadic and semi-agricultural peoples in places like New England, north-western Canada, Brazil, south-western Africa and elsewhere from the sixteenth to the nineteenth century. Windschuttle has demonstrated nothing about these other situations beyond putting forward rhetorical claims about their being worse than Van Diemen's Land.

To confirm the emptiness of Windschuttle's claim about 'the entire history of Europe's colonization', we need only look across the Tasman to New Zealand. The early decades of Pakeha settlement of that colony were marked by sporadic negotiation and conflict, including a succession of wars at intervals from 1845 to about 1870. About 2000 Maori are reported to have died in the course of these wars, and more than 800 Pakeha, including some Maori allies.[17] A rough calculation of the violent mortality rates during these decades suggests a Pakeha death rate of just over 30 per 100,000, and a Maori one of over 140 per 100,000. These figures suggest a rate of violence considerably less than that prevailing in Van Diemen's Land in the decades studied by Windschuttle. They also force us to re-appraise the situation in Van Diemen's Land as something other than a massive crime wave.

Mortality rates, of course, are a statistical artefact. But any social science consideration of patterns, trends and experiences of violence has to take such calculations into account: they are our means of estimating the significance of social behaviours. I have shown that Windschuttle's failure to compute such rates perpetuates the illusion created by his putative demolition of what he calls the 'orthodox' account of Tasmanian history. A critic might respond that my calculations of mortality rates would look somewhat different if Windschuttle's contentious pre-contact population figure was revised to something more consistent with other anthropological and prehistorical evidence, say the upper end of Rhys Jones' 3500–5000 estimate.[18] However, the most this revision does is produce a violent mortality rate of still more than 200 per 100,000 across the whole 30-year period. And given the strong evidence of a very low Aboriginal population by the time of the worst violence (after 1826), it does nothing to alter the case against Windschuttle's gross underestimation of the seriousness of this colonial violence.

I have shown that Windschuttle fails to observe one of the most basic demands of social science: the need to take account of the population base of the at-risk population. Paradoxically, however, he is not even consistent in this failure. In fact, Windschuttle effectively disguises in his book the impact of Aboriginal fatalities while simultaneously emphasising the scale of white casualties. When he considers casualties among Aborigines, Windschuttle uses fatalities as the benchmark. In contrast, his estimation of settler victimisation adds evidence of wounding and even being 'harassed' to the calculus of violence. Consequently, his case inflates settler victimisation and diminishes the experience of the Aboriginal population.

The inflation of settler victimisation compared with that suffered by Aborigines is compounded by methodological mistakes. Discussing the evidence for settlers being killed *or wounded or being assaulted/harassed* for the years 1824–1831, Windschuttle concedes that Henry Reynolds is 'technically correct' in estimating the seriousness of settler/Aboriginal conflict during those years.[19] In contrast to his later discussion of the impact of violence on Aboriginal communities, Windschuttle here takes some account of the base population of the relevant community – in this case, the non-indigenous community. Yet his calculations are hopelessly wrong. Rather than 'roughly 2 percent' of the white population being serious victims of Aboriginal assaults, the estimated rate using his own victimisation and population figures would be 0.25 per cent – or 255 per 100,000.[20] This is a serious enough figure and indicates the scale of conflict in a period when Windschuttle argues Tasmania was not at war.[21]

	Aboriginal deaths[a]	Aboriginal population (based on 2000 in 1803)[b]	Aboriginal death rate	Aboriginal population (Plomley)[c]	Aboriginal death rate (Plomley base)	Settler deaths[d]	Settler population[e]	Settler death rate
1824	0	681	0.0	1500	0.0	10	12303	0.8
1825	0	647	0.0	1215	0.0	8	14351	0.6
1826	6	615	10.4	984	6.5	21	16399	1.3
1827	17	584	28.5	797	20.9	36	18447	2.0
1828	29	555	53.1	646	45.6	40	20496	2.0
1829	15	527	29.1	523	29.4	29	22544	1.3
1830	19	501	38.3	424	45.3	32	24592	1.3
1831	8	476	16.1	343	21.9	11	26640	0.4
	95		20.7		14.7	187		1.2

Table 1 – Estimates of violent mortality rates, Tasmania, 1824–1831, based on data in Keith Windschuttle, *The Fabrication of Aboriginal History* – death rates per 1000 population for Aboriginal and settler communities.[25]

a)   On the basis of information in Windschuttle[26] and his primary source material (Plomley's edition of the Robinson journals), 21 deaths with no date indicated have been pro-rata distributed to the years 1824–31.

b)   The population estimate is based on Windschuttle's claim of an original population at 1803 of less than 2000.[27] I have calculated a rate of decline of 5% p.a. to arrive at a population of no more than 500 by 1830 – a higher population in 1830 than Windschuttle is likely to accept.[28]

c) Using Plomley's population estimate[29] – 1500 in 1824 and 350 in 1831 – I have calculated a rate of decline of 19% p.a. for estimating years 1825–1830.

d,e) Settler population and death figures are derived from Windschuttle and his primary source material.[30]

The erroneous calculation, however, is not the main issue here. In this discussion of the relative victimisation of settler and Aboriginal communities, the tendentious quality of Windschuttle's account is exposed. *Nowhere* in his discussion of Aborigines as 'serious victims' of encounters does he add numbers of wounded to numbers of killed, let alone consider those who might have been 'assaulted/harassed'.[22] Even more seriously, nowhere in his discussion of Aboriginal casualties does he apply to them the same consideration that he applies in the course of estimating how victimised the settler community was.[23] To use a metaphor he is fond of, one can only conclude that in this respect Windschuttle has 'airbrushed' the evidence from his book, unless of course he never bothered to estimate what real casualty rates might have been. He certainly cannot claim that he hadn't thought about this dimension of his work – the detailed if tendentious account of research on pre-contact populations suggests quite the opposite.[24]

Perhaps some visual evidence can help make clearer the lessons of these calculations. The graph on page 307, based on the data in Table 1, represents an estimate of the death rates per 1000 population of the Aboriginal and settler communities between 1824 and 1831. It is based on Windschuttle's death counts. This table illustrates the real scale of the violence during these years and its extraordinarily unequal impact. Even taking Plomley's more generous population estimates, the lesson is clear. The figures illustrated in the graph, those based on an estimate of population closest to Windschuttle's figures, suggest a ratio of Aboriginal to settler mortality rates of at least 17:1 during the years 1824–1831. To put it even more starkly – if the settler population had suffered the same rate of violent death at the hands of Aborigines as the latter suffered at the hands of settlers, we would expect to find not 187 deaths during these seven years but more than 3200. If the Aborigines had suffered the same rate of violent death as the settlers during these years, there would only have been 6 deaths, not the 95 recorded by Windschuttle.

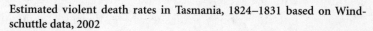

Estimated violent death rates in Tasmania, 1824–1831 based on Windschuttle data, 2002

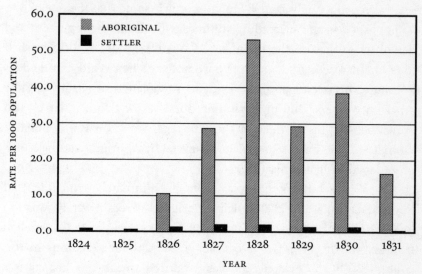

In his series of articles in *Quadrant* magazine and now in *The Fabrication of Aboriginal History*, Windschuttle has made it clear that the object of his substantial exercise in revisionism is to demolish what he sees as the 'orthodox' view of Australian history. He identifies Henry Reynolds as the high priest of this orthodoxy and contests the latter's estimate that 20,000 Aborigines suffered violent death during colonisation.[31] Now that we have finally seen the product of Windschuttle's own research, what are the implications of that work for Reynolds' estimate? It is my contention that Windschuttle's thesis collapses under the weight of his own evidence.

If we extrapolate to the Australian mainland the rates of violent death based on Windschuttle's evidence, then our estimates of the numbers of Aborigines killed by colonists in the first 30 years of settlement across all the different regions of Australia fall in the range 11,000 to 44,000. The high and low figures depend on whether we take a low (200,000) or high (750,000) estimate of the pre-contact indigenous population. The calculations also presume a rate of population decline in the various regions comparable to Tasmania's.

Is extrapolation from Van Diemen's Land to mainland Australia warranted? Well, Windschuttle concludes that 'in all of Europe's colonial encounters with the New Worlds of the Americas and the Pacific,' Van Diemen's Land 'was probably the site where the least indigenous blood of all was deliberately shed.'[32] One can only assume that the research to be published in the succeeding volumes will sustain the argument and demonstrate that on the mainland of Australia more blood was shed than in Van Diemen's Land. As I have noted earlier, Windschuttle does nothing in his book to examine evidence of violent death in any of these other encounters. But, in reminding ourselves of this fact, let us also remember that his death counts may be regarded as the lowest possible estimates of the impact of violence suffered by Aborigines at the hands of settlers during colonisations.

On Windschuttle's figures, we may legitimately conclude that Reynolds' estimate of 20,000 slain Aborigines across Australia was too low. Windschuttle has asked us to take a new view of the Australian frontier, and he promises a 'counter-history of race relations in this country'.[33] On the evidence he has produced so far, this history was closer to a catastrophic war than to Veliz's 'nun's picnic'. The chilling thing is that Windschuttle has achieved this new understanding through an exercise in sustained exclusion of uncertain evidence, as well as through a purported demolition of the orthodoxies of Australian frontier historiography. In spite of all the revisionism, Windschuttle's book ends up demonstrating the violence of colonial conquest in Australia. The question that remains is why he wants to evade the conclusions of his own version of Aboriginal–settler history.

ACKNOWLEDGEMENTS

This chapter is a slightly revised version of an article that was published in the journal *Current Issues in Criminal Justice*. I am grateful to the editor, Chris Cunneen, for permission to re-publish here. For their comments and discussion during preparation of successive drafts I would like to thank Bob Elson, Ross Homel, Janet Chaseling, Tim Rowse, Russell Smandych, Clive Emsley, Bruce Rigsby, Bain Attwood, Dirk Moses, Richard Hill, Barry Smith and Randolf Roth. Responsibility for the product remains mine.

NOTES

1. *The Australian*, 16/12/2002, p. 3.
2. Keith Windschuttle, *The Fabrication of Aboriginal History: Volume One, Van Diemen's Land 1803–47*, Sydney, Macleay Press, 2002, p. 129.
3. *Ibid*, pp. 387–397. The figure of 118 is used here because Windschuttle has put it into the debate. In fact, it appears that his own table accounts for 116 deaths, if one uses literally the key he provides, of 5 deaths for 'several' and 3 deaths for 'a few' or unspecified. In my own calculations in the later parts of this essay, I have assumed that the two cases listed by Windschuttle as 'wounded plausible, killed implausible' on 18 April 1830 are added to his count of 116.
4. *Ibid*, p. 371.
5. Population estimates based on various assumptions are given in Table 1 – in using Windschuttle's data, I have used an annual population decrease rate of 5%. Such calculations are of course speculative in the absence of definitive evidence of the size of the original or succeeding population, at least until the later 1820s.
6. Windschuttle, *Fabrication*, p. 361.
7. *Ibid*, pp. 387–397.
8. Australian Institute of Criminology (2003), 'Australia, states and territories, homicide victimisation rates 1989/90–1999/2000'. These rates can be found at http:/www.aic.gov.au/research/homicide/stats/hvr.html.
9. See letter of John Dawson in *The Australian*, 2/1/2003, p. 8.
10. Windschuttle, *Fabrication*, pp. 128–130.
11. Geoffrey Blainey, *Triumph of the Nomads*, South Melbourne, Sun Books, 1976, pp. 108–110. Blainey used only two sources for his own speculative comments on indigenous warfare: the memoirs of the nineteenth-century escapee convict William Buckley; and the commentary of anthropologist W. Lloyd Warner on 'warfare' in Arnhem Land. Buckley's account was taken down some years after his return to settler society; while Warner's calculation of tribal death rates from violence was computed by a speculative doubling of his recorded numbers of deaths over a 20-year period. This alone was the basis of Blainey's estimate of 1 in 300 deaths, though he did not comment on its methodological origins. The flimsy base of these statistical calculations seems not to bother Windschuttle in his eagerness to use Blainey as a source of evidence of the impact of internecine conflict. See Windschuttle, *Fabrication*, p. 382; and W. L. Warner, *A Black Civilization: A Social Study of an Australian Tribe* [1937], Gloucester, Mass., Peter Smith, 1969, pp. 146ff. For a critique of Blainey's sources, see Henry Reynolds, 'Blainey and Aboriginal History' in A. Markus and M. C. Ricklefs (eds) *Surrender Australia? Geoffrey Blainey and Asian Immigration*, Sydney, Allen & Unwin, 1985, pp. 85–87.
12. Blainey, *Triumph*, p. 265.
13. Windschuttle, *Fabrication*, p. 382.
14. L. H. Keeley, *War before Civilization*, New York, Oxford University Press, pp. 118–119, 30. Windschuttle's selectivity is hard at work in his use of Keeley. He fails to note the latter's citation of Tonkinson's work on the Mardu of the Western Desert. See *Fabrication*, p. 382, fn 105; and R. Tonkinson, *The Mardu Aborigines: Living the Dream in Australia's Desert*, Forth Worth, Holt, Rinehart and Winston Inc., 1991, p. 147.
15. *Ibid*, p. 195.
16. See Table 1.

17. W. H. Oliver and B. R. Williams, *The Oxford History of New Zealand*, Oxford, Clarendon Press, 1981, pp. 184, 492.

18. Rhys Jones in N. Tindale, *Aboriginal Tribes of Australia*, Canberra, ANU Press, 1974.

19. Windschuttle, *Fabrication*, pp. 84–5.

20. That is, 398 victims (killed or wounded) over the years 1824–1831. Even adding the 233 'assaulted/harassed' during this period brings the settler victimisation rate to just 0.41 per cent. Windschuttle's statistical error consists in his using figures for a number of years against a denominator of just one year's population – his averaging of statistics calculated on this basis only repeats the original error (see his letter to *The Australian*, 20 January 2003).

21. See in particular Windschuttle, *Fabrication*, chs 4 and 6.

22. Compare Windschuttle, *Fabrication*, Table 4.1, p. 85.

23. Windschuttle, *Fabrication*, pp. 84–86.

24. *Ibid*, pp. 364–371.

25. *Ibid*, pp. 84–85.

26. *Ibid*, pp. 387–397.

27. *Ibid*, p. 371.

28. See for example Windschuttle, *Fabrication*, p. 224.

29. N. J. B. Plomley, *The Aboriginal–Settler Clash in Van Diemen's Land*, Launceston, Queen Victoria Museum and Art Gallery, 1992, p. 11.

30. Windschuttle, *Fabrication*, pp. 84–5.

31. Keith Windschuttle, 'The myths of frontier massacres in Australian history, Part III: Massacre stories and the policy of separatism', *Quadrant* 44 (12) 2000, pp. 6–20. The text can be found at http://www.sydneyline.com.

32. Windschuttle, *Fabrication*, p. 398.

33. *Ibid*, p. 3.

Archaeology and History

Tim Murray & Christine Williamson

In *The Fabrication of Aboriginal History*, Keith Windschuttle makes several claims about the nature of pre-contact Tasmanian Aboriginal society that he maintains are supported by the available archaeological and ethno-historical evidence. Most memorably, when summarising the fate of the Tasmanians,

> They had survived for millennia, it is true, but it seems clear that this owed more to good fortune than to good management. The 'slow strangulation of the mind' was true not only of their technical abilities but also of their social relationships. Hence it was not surprising that when the British arrived, this small, precarious society quickly collapsed under the dual weight of the susceptibility of its members to disease and the abuse and neglect of its women.[1]

In this essay we consider what support Windschuttle's account of traditional Tasmanian society (particularly such aspects as population size, the treatment of women, the incidence of warfare and technology) receives from archaeological research. To this end we review current evidence for the size of pre-contact populations in Tasmania, the place of scaled fish in the late Holocene Tasmanian diet and the trajectories of change in traditional Tasmanian technologies.

We also consider the evidence for Windschuttle's three-fold characterisation of Tasmanian society prior to the arrival of the Europeans.

First, that it was internally maladapted,[2] quoting Robert Edgerton:

> There were no social or economic imperatives that drove Tasmanian men to treat their wives badly, to require them to carry out dangerous tasks, or to kill other men in pursuit of more wives, but there may well have been psychological imperatives that in the absence of social or cultural constraints led men to behave in these ways. Like many other small societies, Tasmanians failed to devise social and cultural mechanisms to control their destructive tendencies.[3]

Second, that it was precariously balanced:

> Into this setting, the British arrived. They soon put additional pressures onto Aboriginal women that probably tipped the balance of this already precarious population over the edge.[4]

Third, that it was dysfunctional:

> The real tragedy of the Aborigines was not British colonization *per se* but that their society was, on the one hand, so internally dysfunctional and, on the other, so incompatible with the looming presence of the rest of the world.[5]

Apart from showing that Windschuttle displays a far less forensic attitude to archaeological and ethno-historical evidence than he claims to bring to the analysis of written documentary evidence, we will establish that Tasmanian archaeological data tends not to support his claim that this was a society poised on the brink of extinction due to the consequences of long-term isolation. Indeed, we will observe that Windschuttle's account is based on a very partial and narrow understanding of the results of more than 30 years of archaeological research into the history of Tasmanian Aboriginal society. This is particularly apparent in Chapter 10 of his account, where his poor knowledge and understanding of that research culminate in a general statement about the forces that brought traditional Tasmanian society to an end. For these reasons we reject the implication that his 'counter-history' in some way or another mitigates the culpability of European dispossession as the primary cause of the destruction of traditional Tasmanian society.

Women and Warfare

The fate of women in traditional Tasmanian Aboriginal society looms very large in Chapter 10 of *Fabrication* and merits its own subheading: 'Cultural vulnerability and the position of women'. Windschuttle surveys some of the nineteenth-century literature, citing the opinions of Péron, Davies, Robinson, H. Ling Roth and others, in order to observe that, 'It was not only their technology that caused problems for the Tasmanians. The aspect of their society that left them most vulnerable in the face of the European arrival was the treatment of their women.'[6] In Windschuttle's account, Tasmanian Aboriginal women were brutalised, raped, kept as drudges and later prostituted or sold to European men. In short, they lived their lives in fear of violence or death at the hands of Tasmanian men, and were later wracked with venereal diseases resulting from their encounters with sealers and shepherds. Fighting between men over women was, for Windschuttle, 'one of the major causes of Aboriginal deaths. It was much higher than anything inflicted by British colonists'.[7] Thus the Tasmania Aborigines (following Edgerton) were a 'profoundly maladapted population'.

Archaeologists have long accepted that pathologies located on human skeletons can form the basis for reliable inferences about causes of death and/or injury, which can themselves support other inferences about diet and trauma – some of which can be further linked to age or gender profiles.[8] Nonetheless, it is also accepted that such inferences need to be made with caution. As it happens, in the Tasmanian case, evidence from human skeletons has played no part in reconstructing traditional Tasmanian Aboriginal society. Instead, arguments about the treatment of women or the incidence of violence have been based on fleeting glimpses gathered from the east coast by early French and English explorers, or on ethno-historical data collected during the disruption of Aboriginal society following the European settlement of the island.

These observations have been drawn from the most minute fraction of over 35,000 years of Tasmanian history.[9] Given the strong likelihood that Aboriginal society had probably undergone drastic changes by the time most European observations were recorded, it is extremely perilous to assume that all elements recorded are 'traditional'. Projecting these observations back into the prehistoric past also runs the risk of creating a timeless *ethnographic present* in which any sense of cultural flexibility and variability is replaced by a static, conservative and timeless image of pre-contact culture and society.

Population Size

Windschuttle notes that an accurate estimate of the size of the Aboriginal population of Tasmania prior to the arrival of Europeans is crucial because, 'the scale of the demise [of the Tasmanian Aborigines] and its possible causes depend upon the accuracy of these figures.'[10]

Pre-contact population size has been much debated, with early estimates ranging from a high of 22,000[11] to a low of 1500,[12] with George Augustus Robinson suggesting an original population of 6000–8000.[13] More recently, Rhys Jones advanced 3000–5000 as a reasonable figure,[14] while N. J. B. Plomley argued for about 6000.[15] Certainly there is a dearth of empirical evidence, and Windschuttle is probably correct to argue that there is nothing particularly compelling about either the Jones or the Plomley estimates (including arguments based on cross-cultural ethnographic analogy). However, the same applies to Windschuttle's suggestion of a small, pre-contact population of less than 2000 people, as he brings no new substantive evidence to the argument. The reality is that reconstructions of population size in Tasmania are merely more-or-less-educated speculation which cannot be validated by current archaeological or documentary data. To date, the only scientifically rigorous attempt is that of Pardoe, who used genetic evidence. While not offering an actual population figure, he suggested that Jones' figures require upwards revision, based upon the apparent lack of genetic drift between mainland and Tasmanian Aboriginal populations since the two populations were isolated from one another approximately 8000 years ago.[16]

One way forward is to develop a range of population models that would allow plausible predictions about crucial variables such as site locations, numbers, sizes and chronologies that could be explored through archaeological research. While significant problems arise with the development, testing and interpretation of such models, at least the opportunity arises to gain a clearer understanding of Tasmanian demography over a period of more than 35,000 years. But we are a very long way from being able to do this. As a result, we must conclude that the accuracy of estimation that Windschuttle rightly argues is central to his account of the consequences of European occupation of Tasmania is simply illusory.

Technology: the Tasmanian Toolkit

Windschuttle claims that, 'Instead of technological progress, the Tasmanians had experienced a technological regression.'[17] In asserting the 'reality' of technological and social regression he states that:

> From excavations of some long-used campsites and caves, the archaeologist and prehistorian Rhys Jones has concluded that several thousand years earlier their technology had actually been more complex. They once used bone tools, barbed spears and weaving needles made of fish bone. They also had wooden boomerangs, hafted stone tools, edge-ground stone axes and tools fashioned from volcanic glass. However, these had all long been abandoned by the time Europeans arrived.[18]

The first sentence of this quotation has a footnote referencing the work of Jones. However, the paragraph is structured in such a way as to suggest that the remainder is also based upon Jones' work (there are no further footnotes to indicate any additional sources). Other than bone tools and implements made of volcanic glass, though, there is no evidence that the technologies listed by Windschuttle were ever possessed by the Tasmanians, let alone abandoned. Furthermore, no archaeologist working on Tasmanian material (including Jones) has suggested anything of the kind. The Tasmanian archaeological record covering at least 35,000 years[19] (not 20,000 years as suggested by Windschuttle) holds no indicators of barbed spears, weaving needles made of fish bones (presumably Windschuttle's confused reference to the suggestion that bone implements were used for weaving fishing nets), wooden boomerangs, hafted stone implements or edge-ground axes. The Tasmanians never used any of these items.

The archaeological evidence indicates that the only items originally in the Tasmanian toolkit and later discarded were bone points (which we will discuss at greater length) and implements made of volcanic (Darwin) glass. The claim that the absence of Darwin glass from the cultural repertoire represents a technological regression can be rejected on two grounds. First, Darwin glass is found in sites in the south-western region during the Pleistocene period, close to the impact crater which is its source. It then disappears from the archaeological record around 10,000 years ago, because at this time the south-western region was abandoned and not re-occupied, except perhaps in a very limited way. Consequently, people no longer travelled to the source of this material and, hence, no longer used it to make implements.[20]

Second, if the absence of Darwin glass as a raw material is argued to be an indicator of regression, then logically the uptake of spongolite (a type of fine-grained stone) at about 2500 bp[21] must be interpreted as indicating progression.[22] But we fail to see how such simplistic readings of progress or regression enhance our understanding of what is clearly a dynamic cultural process.

Technology: Fish-Eating and Bone Points

Windschuttle argues that the absence of fish from the Tasmanian diet is evidence for both technological and social regression. This follows directly from Jones' argument that there is no coherent ecological explanation for Tasmanians not eating fish, and that this must therefore be interpreted as the outcome of cultural or religious choice.[23] The relative coincidence in the timing of the disappearance of fish remains and bone tools (not fish, fish-hooks and fish spears as suggested by Windschuttle[24]) from archaeological sequences led Jones to suggest that at this time the effects of the long isolation of the Tasmanian population from mainland Australia were being felt, as the social system might have been in the process of simplification or even winding down.[25] Consequently he viewed the loss of fish and bone implements as a maladaptation.[26]

The reasons for the disappearance of fish and bone implements from archaeological sequences after about 3500 bp, and the significance of that disappearance, have been (and continue to be) much debated. Jones has argued that fish and bone points were not related for three reasons. First, they do not have identical distributions throughout the Rocky Cape sequence; second, the wear on bone points is not consistent with their use as spear points; and third, bone points are found inland where no fishing could have occurred. He suggested that bone tools were used in the manufacture of skin cloaks.[27]

Sandra Bowdler has taken a different view, believing that fish and bone tools were related and that their apparently synchronous disappearance from the archaeological record is not a coincidence. Bowdler and Harry Lourandos suggest that the bone implements might have been used as netting needles and they argue that the consistent size and species of the Rocky Cape fish assemblage indicates that they must have been caught in nets.[28] They contend that bone tools were also found at inland sites because implements and nets were manufactured at these locations.[29]

Where Jones sees the loss of fish and bone tools as evidence of maladaptation, Bowdler argues that this change would initially have been based on sound economic reasoning and only later have gained the ritual connotations noted by Europeans.[30] Contrary to Jones, Bowdler has questioned whether fish were ever a particularly important part of the Tasmanian diet, given that only two sites, Rocky Cape and Sister's Creek (both excavated by Jones), had significant numbers of fish remains.[31] Bowdler has further argued that the loss of fish may have had to do with economic re-scheduling and probably would not have caused too much hardship. At this time (about 3000 years ago), Aboriginal people were in the process of moving into new areas due to environmental changes and the development of an effective firing regime which allowed for the creation of significant grasslands in the interior.[32]

Others have bought into this argument and also suggested that the loss of fish was not indicative of a maladaptive society but rather reflected the growing importance of other food resources and the unnecessarily high cost/benefit ratio of catching fish. On the basis of data from Louisa Bay, David Horton has argued for marked seasonal differences in diet.[33] Harry Allen also notes that even at Rocky Cape, fish were not the primary meat source and in fact ranked third behind seals and shellfish in terms of overall calorific contribution to the diet.[34] He further argued that the late Holocene evidence indicates that people shifted their economic strategies to more energy-efficient foods such as shellfish. Therefore the loss of fish from the diet can be seen as an adaptive act.[35]

The use of marine invertebrates is a feature of the Tasmanian economy as soon as the current coastline appeared at about 7000 bp (although the west coast appears not to have been used until after 4000 bp). Around that time there seems to have been a change in collecting practices in the north-west of the island when sub-littoral species began to be collected in quantity. Gary Dunnett found that in south-eastern sites sub-littoral resources such as abalone and crayfish only started to appear during the late Holocene (about 2500 years ago).[36] This marked a change from previous times when assemblages were pre-dominantly inter-tidal. Similar patterns of resource use were identified at Hunter Island[37] and Rocky Cape.[38] Dunnett also suggests that sub-littoral resources on the west coast might have been safer and more economical to obtain.[39] The coincidence between the timing of an effective strategy for obtaining sub-littoral resources in the north-west and the commencement of an archaeologically visible occupation of the west coast has been regarded as significant.[40]

Notwithstanding the wealth of information that has flowed from nearly 30 years of archaeological research, matters remain unresolved and probably irresolvable, given that it is highly unlikely that a single explanation applies to all cases and to both fish and bone tools. Furthermore, the observation of food taboos among the Tasmanians by European explorers and settlers does not, in itself, provide a secure explanation for changing strategies of resource exploitation that might have occurred thousands of years ago. Finally, the archaeological record around the world is littered with similar unexplained economic and technological shifts that do not necessarily require explanations of maladaptation and/or regression. Other archaeological evidence from late Holocene and Pleistocene Tasmania lends strong support to this view.[41]

Strangulation or Variation? Late Holocene Tasmania in Context

Windschuttle quotes the suggestion that Rhys Jones made in his 1971 PhD dissertation that late Holocene Tasmanian Aboriginal society, isolated from the mainland, might have undergone a 'slow strangulation of the mind'.[42] However, Windschuttle's subsequent discussion of the issue fails to acknowledge the complexities of late Holocene cultural variation in Tasmania, complexities that were well understood by Jones and his opponents. Indeed, Jones himself argued that the period after 2500 bp was one in which the Tasmanians expanded their social and cultural universe. As they widened their coastal economy to focus increasingly on the hinterland, they incorporated exotic raw materials into their stone toolkit, commenced rock art at Mount Cameron West (and possibly other known, but as yet undated petroglyph sites), opened up inland areas by firing the landscape, and moved onto the offshore islands. Other researchers have gone further, seeing the late Holocene as an expansive period characterised by intensification and increasing social complexity.[43]

While neither of us concurs with the intensification agenda of Lourandos and others (because it is not necessary to adopt processes of linear progress to account for change), the bulk of archaeological data clearly indicates that the ways in which the Tasmanians were using landscapes and resources changed (and continued to change) at this time. But it was ever thus – even when Tasmania was connected to the continent of Sahul (the island joining New Guinea, the Australian mainland and Tasmania). A close examination of more than 35,000 years of Tasmanian history reveals similar patterns of change and variation in technology and human behaviour as people coped with changing climates and ecologies and, by inference, changing social and cultural strategies. During this time there is considerable evidence for variability and change through time and across space, which argues against simplistic assumptions that changes apparent in the late Holocene are proof of maladaptation and cultural regression. The evidence also provides a sound basis for rejecting Windschuttle's extraordinary assertion that survival over such a long period 'owed more to good fortune than to good management'.[44]

One of the best examples of the reality of change in Tasmania can be found in the south-west. At Kutikina Cave, Jones found evidence for a marked change in stone tool technology and raw material usage at about 17,000–18,000 bp.[45] Thumbnail scrapers are generally only found after about 18,000 bp.[46] It has been suggested that these changes reflect a general re-organisation of society after the Last Glacial Maximum[47] towards greater mobility and with a consequent emphasis upon curated technologies.[48] It is widely accepted that the cultural and social systems that underwrote human occupation of the south-west came to an abrupt end at approximately 13,000 bp.[49] Whether this meant that human occupation contracted back to the coasts and major river systems, or that the abandonment of long-occupied rock shelters in the hinterland can be explained by changing strategies of occupation and land use,[50] the primary cause of this major change has been linked to the warming of the environment and a change in vegetation patterns.[51]

Post-Contact Archaeological Evidence

Of course, archaeological data are often equivocal and require the use of inferential reasoning to be developed to the point where they may count critically as historical or anthropological evidence. However, this does not mean that they must be either inherently insecure or mute. Fortunately, our stock of both archaeological and historical evidence, drawn from the first 45 years of European occupation of Tasmania, further strengthens the argument against regression. There is clear evidence that during this period Aboriginal people rapidly adopted new animals (dogs) and material culture (guns and blankets), sometimes modifying them to traditional uses (glass for tools and rust as a substitute for ochre). Clearly, the descendants of those who had coped with an Ice Age and the separation of Tasmania from Sahul had not lost their desire (or indeed their capacity) to cope with change. The picture that is slowly emerging from recent archaeological research is one of cultural dynamism and adaptation, although it is certainly the case that much work remains to be done to find more sites and to date more securely those that have been located.

Christine Williamson has demonstrated that the majority of archaeological sites that display clear post-contact archaeological evidence in

Tasmania are undated, and the majority of such sites are found in the eastern half of the island.[52] This is not surprising, as the location of the main settlements in the east meant that incidental finds of 'curios' were more likely to occur here than in any other part of the island. However, the observed distribution may also be a reflection of the longer and more intensive period of Aboriginal–European interaction in the east and the greater access of Aboriginal people in this region to European goods.

The high number of relevant sites around the mouth of the Tamar River and stretching into the Midlands and south to the Derwent is often attributed to the activities of the more active North Midlands, Oyster Bay and Big River tribes.[53] These groups raided European huts across this region and would have had greater access to European items than any other Aboriginal group. This post-contact patterning of sites in the Midlands is in stark contrast to the late Holocene pattern, where no dated sites have been recorded in the region around the Tamar River. In the south-west, where Aboriginal people had limited and late contact with Europeans, and consequently little access to European items, there are no sites containing post-contact materials and only three sites that may have modern dates (at two standard deviations). Most recorded, undated, post-contact Aboriginal items are flaked glass scrapers collected by non-archaeologists as curios. Other individual items include an abraded musket ball that may have been used as a pounder,[54] one of the bronze medals given to the south-eastern Aboriginal people by Captain Cook in 1777,[55] and flaked pieces of ceramic.[56] The original contexts of these items and any associated finds, such as stone artefacts and food remains, were not recorded. Therefore these artefacts are able to provide little insight into post-contact Tasmanian Aboriginal behaviour, other than to demonstrate the use of European materials in the manufacture of 'traditional' implements.

However, the available data from Aboriginal post-contact archaeological sites that has been recorded in more detail does suggest that these sites may differ from prehistoric sites. At Sandy Cape in the north-west, a deflated midden (or Aboriginal garbage dump) containing a piece of white glazed ceramic plate that had been fashioned into a concave scraper was noted to be one of only two such sites in the region with a visible bone assemblage.[57] Similarly, Steve Brown recorded a midden in the Derwent estuary that contained sheep bones.[58] Although the presence of faunal remains is rare in Derwent River middens, Jones has argued that the incorporation of dogs into the hunting process may have led to a higher level of animal foods in the diet during the post-contact period, and these sites may reflect this.[59]

Possible changes in resource exploitation strategies have also been noted at other sites. Along the South Esk River in the north-east, Sue Kee recorded the presence of freshwater mussel shell in a midden which also contained an artefact manufactured on porcelain. This is one of only three archaeologically identified instances of the possible exploitation of freshwater shellfish in Tasmania.[60] It may be that Aboriginal people turned to alternative food sources when access to foods they had exploited in pre-contact times became difficult or dangerous.

Several recorded sites containing post-contact materials are also extremely large and diverse compared to prehistoric sites in the same region. For example, Brown describes a very large artefact scatter approximately 10 km from the junction of the Derwent and Jordan rivers in the south-east containing 594 stone and 497 glass artefacts.[61] It is not known if all these items are contemporary and date to the post-contact period, or if the presence of both stone and glass artefacts indicates the continued use of locations favoured in pre-contact times. A stratified midden in the north-east at Campbells Point with incorporated glass and ceramic items was also noted to contain a large number of artefacts for sites in the region.[62] It is possible that in some instances, as movement became more restricted due to the presence of Europeans, Aboriginal groups became less mobile and tended to concentrate their activities at particular locales where they felt safe and where resources were still available, thus leading to the formation of larger sites.

As most sites containing post-contact items are undated, open sites or isolated finds, it is difficult to demonstrate these possibilities. An exception to this is the important ochre quarry of Toolumbunner in the Gog Range that, on the basis of radiocarbon dates, was exploited for at least 500 years.[63] The flaked glass assemblage recovered from the surface of the site, as well as accounts in Robinson's journals, indicate that the site was still in use after the arrival of Europeans. Antonio Sagona argues that it was during this post-contact period that the most intensive mining activities were carried out,[64] possibly because it was one of the few quarries that the European presence had not rendered inaccessible.

The archaeological record therefore suggests that sites in the post-contact period sometimes contain new or unexpected materials, often in larger quantities than in previous times. It is possible to interpret this evidence as representing post-contact changes in economic strategies and mobility. Alongside these indicators of change, there is also evidence for continuity – such as the continued construction along the north-west coast of huts built into hollowed-out depressions in dunes,[65] the continued use of locations favoured in the pre-contact period, and the presence of artefacts forms, sometimes made on new materials, that are also found in pre-contact contexts.

Burghley

A lack of research into the nature of the archaeological record of post-contact Aboriginal Tasmania has made it difficult to view this evidence as more than just a series of intriguing clues yet to be worked into more general statements about the nature of post-contact society. Burghley, a partially excavated stratified site in the north-west, demonstrates the potential of archaeology to contribute to our understanding of the Aboriginal experience of contact, while at the same time emphasising the resilience and adaptability of traditional Tasmanian society and culture.

Located between the Medway and Leven Rivers and established in 1825 as one of the sheep stations established in north-west Tasmania by the Van Diemen's Land Company, Burghley was excavated in the early 1990s. During the excavation, an assemblage of Aboriginal artefacts was recovered – among which were items such as flaked glass tools clearly dating to the post-contact period.

It was common practice in the Australian colonies at this time for sheep to be extensively grazed under the care of shepherds, who lived for long periods at 'stations' such as Burghley. During the ten or so

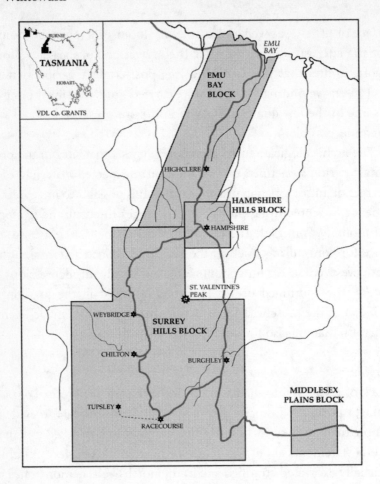

Figure 1. The location of the VDL Co. landholdings in the Surrey and Hampshire Hills region. The main stations, including Burghley, are indicated, as is the VDL Co. road through the area (adapted from an illustration drawn by Wei Ming).

years that Burghley was occupied, it is widely acknowledged that relations between the men stationed there and the Aboriginal population of the region were anything but friendly.[66] Violence began almost as soon as the company arrived in the region, as it rapidly placed settlements and sheep runs on Aboriginal hunting grounds, made use of native paths and roads (in particular that running from Emu Bay into the Surrey and Hampshire Hills) and generally disrupted the movements of Aboriginal people throughout the area.

By 1835, G. A. Robinson was claiming that all Aboriginal people had been removed from Tasmania.[67] However, the VDL Co. continued to report attacks on their stations, and in November 1836, Robinson sent out one of his sons to round up the stragglers for whom a £50 reward had been offered.[68] The party encountered a family of six near Cradle Mountain but could not convince them to make the trip back to Launceston.[69] Until recently, it was thought that these people were the only free Tasmanians left on the island after 1835, and that they were most likely to have been responsible for continuing attacks on VDL Co. servants.[70] The family consisted of a middle-aged man, Lanna (John Lanna), a woman, Nabunya/Nabrunga, two young men aged 18–20 (Banna/Manney [Barnaby Rudge] and Pleti) and three children under ten (Albert [Charley], William and Francis [Frank]).[71] They were captured in 1842 and sent to Flinders Island.

When the site of Burghley was re-located, the only surface evidence that remained was a pile of collapsed rocks indicating the position of a chimney. Two seasons of excavation uncovered a total of 145 square metres. Initial excavation focused on the collapsed chimney butt and attempted to delineate the boundaries of the associated hut structure. The excavation process revealed the outlines of a hut measuring 10 x 4 metres, a stone chimney and hearth with flagstones, a cobbled outside area where it was thought that a doorway had been located, another cobbled area further from the house that led into a drain structure, and a dump zone. It is not known if these are the remains of the officer's lodgings or one of the other eight cottages recorded in historic description of the site, as the existence and placement of other structures was not determined before excavation was terminated.

During the excavation, it became apparent that the hut had burnt down – probably when the chimney caught fire. While the flaked glass implements identified at the site are clearly the result of a post-contact Aboriginal presence, it also became apparent that much of the Aboriginal flaked stone assemblage overlay this destruction layer and therefore also dated to the post-contact period. Aboriginal artefacts were located in the upper few spits of deposit and were also found lying on the cobbled surface near the doorway. A quartz flake was found inside the hut lodged between the burnt floorboards and the fallen

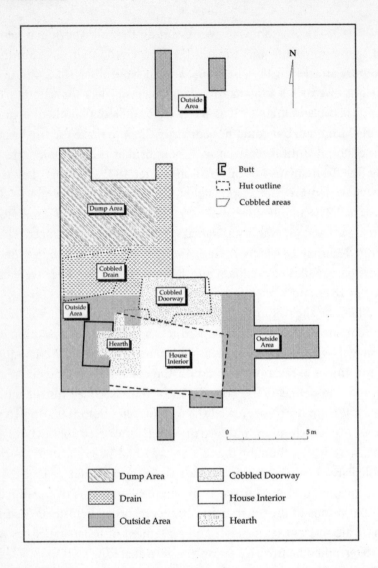

Figure 2. **Analytical areas used in the analysis of the materials excavated from Burghley** (adapted from an original drawing by Wei Ming).

chimney stones, indicating that its deposition had occurred prior to the destruction of the hut.[72]

It is clear from the historical records that Aboriginal and European people did not co-exist at Burghley. At no time during the station's European occupation would it have been left unattended, so there would not have been opportunities for Aboriginal people to make sporadic use of the site in the absence of company servants. Any post-contact Aboriginal occupation of the site must have occurred after the company abandoned it in the late 1830s – probably around 1836 or 1837. The family group captured in 1842 is the most likely candidate.

Burghley offers a unique opportunity to investigate the Aboriginal experience of contact through the archaeological record. It also provides the basis of a secure and detailed archaeological refutation of Wind-schuttle's claims concerning the adaptability of traditional Tasmanian society. However, the analysis of the recovered assemblage by William-son has also highlighted the problems encountered when attempting to disentangle the materials, remains and discard patterns of two dif-ferent cultures when they overlap at the one site.[73] Generally, items of European and Aboriginal manufacture can be relatively easily distin-guished, but the re-occupation of Burghley by Aboriginal people has meant that some of the observed discard patterns of European items may reflect Aboriginal rather than, or as well as, European behaviours. However, unless the European artefacts have been clearly modified in form by Aboriginal people, any Aboriginal use and/or movement of these items cannot be unequivocally demonstrated.

The obviously Aboriginal assemblage is limited to artefacts of flaked stone and re-touched items of glass. The distribution of Aboriginal flaked stone indicates that the cobbled doorway area was a primary focus of stone flaking and many hearth-based activities. What is not so clear is what part Aboriginal people played in the rest of the discard patterns discernible at the site. However, the drawing together of several threads of evidence leads us to conclude that some of the observed dis-tribution patterns might have been produced or modified by later Aboriginal re-use.

The presence of bottle and container glass in front of the hearth and in proximity to the cobbled doorway suggests that some of this glass might have been moved to these areas from locations away from the hut where it had been dumped by Europeans. Similarly, an anomalous distribution of ceramics in the same area may reflect Aboriginal re-use of this material. Although no ceramics modified by Aboriginal people were positively identified, it is possible that broken pieces of ceramic might have been used opportunistically. It is also possible that the dense cluster of clay pipe fragments in the region to the west of the cobbled doorway may mark a location where Aboriginal people were smoking while working stone and sitting around their fireplaces.

It is not possible to determine the origin of the bone assemblage, but the presence of a great deal of material in the region of the hearth suggests that this area was used after the hut had been abandoned by Europeans and the interior of the hut had ceased to be cleaned and maintained. There is also a suggestion that some of the European flint present at the site might have been worked through Aboriginal flaking, although the possibility that the presence of this material also reflects European activities cannot be discounted.

The analysis of the Burghley stone and glass assemblages by Williamson, which has been only very superficially reported here, has opened a window into the Tasmanian experience of contact with Europeans. At the very least it provides a significant body of site-specific evidence to weigh against the accounts of settlers, explorers or conciliators such as Robinson.

Concluding Remarks

The available archaeological evidence does not support Windschuttle's account of Tasmanian society before or after the arrival of the Europeans. In addition, we have argued that the available data is simply too equivocal to carry the burden Windschuttle has assigned it in two critical cases, those concerning the status and treatment of women and the size of the pre-contact Tasmanian population.

Windschuttle has made much of the virtues of empiricism and the potential dangers of theory – in the main, more properly *a priori* assumptions rather than true relational statements. In our view, Windschuttle's negative assessment of the nature of traditional Tasmanian society owes at least as much to such assumptions as it does to a lack of knowledge about, or understanding of, more than 35,000 years of Tasmanian history. But, as archaeologists frequently observe, somewhat ruefully, he is hardly alone in this. Historians of Aboriginal Australia, whatever their 'theoretical' or ideological stances, tend not to pay very much attention to what archaeologists have been up to since the 1970s. Perhaps the much-needed focus on the historical archaeology of Aboriginal Australia, as distinct from a concentration on remote antiquity, might make communication more natural and effective.[74] Either way, it is long overdue.

It is also clear that conflict between the data created by archaeologists and those ethno-historic and written documentary sources traditionally used by historians may not be resolved in every case. For example, much has been written about whether the Tasmanians knew how to make fire, and if they did not, whether this provides clear evidence of cultural regression after separation from Sahul at the end of the Pleistocene. Gott has thoughtfully reviewed the issue, concluding that it is most probable that the Tasmanians knew how to make fire, but that we simply cannot be certain.[75] It is also true, as many have observed, that absence of evidence has made it relatively easy for historians, anthropologists, even archaeologists, to construe Aboriginal Tasmania to suit their needs.[76] Nonetheless, we believe that through research, criticism and debate, progress can be made and – following the example of Julia Clark – we can reach a clearer understanding of the richness and strength of Tasmanian society and the impact of dispossession upon it.[77]

Windschuttle's critique of the history of Aboriginal/settler contact in Tasmania reminds us of the importance of clarity and openness in the way we seek to communicate such histories. It is indeed important to separate evidence from opinion, but it is equally important to identify and explore the deeper matters that underlie and shape our 'facts' and the ways we interpret them.

ACKNOWLEDGEMENTS

Richard Cosgrove for advice and Wei Ming for assistance with the illustrations.

NOTES

1. Keith Windschuttle, *The Fabrication of Aboriginal History: Volume One, Van Diemen's Land 1803–1847*, Sydney, Macleay Press, 2002, p. 386.
2. *Ibid*, p. 382.

3. Robert Edgerton, *Sick Societies: Challenging the Myth of Primitive Harmony*, New York, Free Press, 1992, p. 52

4. Windschuttle, *Fabrication*, p. 383.

5. *Ibid*, p. 386.

6. *Ibid*, p. 379.

7. *Ibid*, p. 382.

8. See for example S. G. Webb, *Palaeopathology of Aboriginal Australians: health and disease across a hunter-gatherer continent*, Melbourne, Cambridge University Press, 1995.

9. See R. Cosgrove, 'Late Pleistocene behavioural variation and time trends: the case from Tasmania', *Archaeology in Oceania*, 30, 1995. pp. 83–104; and R. Jones, 'Tasmanian archaeology: establishing the sequences', *Annual Review of Anthropology*, 24, 1995, pp. 423–446.

10. Windschuttle, *Fabrication*, p. 364.

11. J. Bonwick, *Daily Life and Origin of the Tasmanians*, London, Sampson, Low, Son and Marston, 1870, p. 83.

12. J. Milligan, 'On the dialects and language of the Aboriginal tribes of Tasmania, and on their manners and customs', *Papers and Proceedings of the Royal Society of Tasmania*, 1858, p. 275.

13. J. Backhouse Walker, 'Some notes on the tribal divisions of the Aborigines of Tasmania', *Papers and Proceedings of the Royal Society of Tasmania*, 1897, p. 176.

14. Rhys Jones, 'Tasmanian Tribes' appendix to Norman Tindale, Aboriginal Tribes of Australia, Canberra, ANU Press, 1974, p. 321.

15. N. J. B. Plomley, *Jorgen Jorgenson and the Aborigines of Van Diemen's Land*, Hobart, Blubber Head Press, 1991, p. 15.

16. Colin Pardoe, 'Isolation and evolution in Tasmania (including comments and reply)', *Current Anthropology*, 32, 1991, pp. 1–21.

17. Windschuttle, *Fabrication*, p. 378.

18. *Ibid*, p. 378.

19. R. Cosgrove, 'Thirty thousand years of human colonisation in Tasmania: new Pleistocene dates', *Science*, 243, 1989, pp. 1703–1705; R. Cosgrove, 'Late Pleistocene behavioural variation and time trends: the case from Tasmania', *Archaeology in Oceania*, 30, 1995, p. 83.

20. See R. Cosgrove, *The Illusion of Riches: Scale, resolution and explanation in Tasmanian Pleistocene human behaviour*, Oxford, BAR International Series No. 608, 1995.

21. R. Jones, 'Tasmanian archaeology: establishing the sequences', *Annual Review of Anthropology*, 24, 1995, p. 426.

22. It is a scientific convention in the reporting of radiocarbon dates that these be given in years 'before the present' or bp. The 'present' is conventionally pegged to 1950 AD. Thus 2500 bp is approximately 2500 years ago.

23. R. Jones, 'The Tasmanian paradox', in R. V. S. Wright (ed.), *Stone Tools as Cultural Markers*, Canberra, Australian Institute of Aboriginal Studies Press, 1977, p. 196; R. Jones, 'Hunters and history: a case study from western Tasmania', in C. Schrire (ed.), *Past and Present Hunter Gatherer Studies*, pp. 2–65, Orlando, Academic Press, 1984, p. 47.

24. Windschuttle, *Fabrication*, p. 378.

25. R. Jones, 'The Tasmanian paradox', pp. 202, 196; R. Jones, 'Hunters and history', p. 47.

26. See also S. Bowdler, 'Fish and culture: a Tasmanian polemic', *Mankind*, 12, 1980, p. 337.
27. Jones, 'The Tasmanian paradox', p. 196.
28. S. Bowdler and H. Lourandos, 'Both sides of Bass Strait', In S. Bowdler (ed.), *Coastal archaeology in eastern Australia*, Canberra, Department of Prehistory, Research School of Pacific Studies, Australian National University, 1982 p. 124.
29. S. Bowdler, 'Prehistoric archaeology in Tasmania', *Advances in World Archaeology*, 1, 1982, p. 42; Bowdler and Lourandos, 'Both sides of Bass Strait', p. 123.
30. Bowdler 'Fish and culture', p. 339.
31. S. Bowdler, 'Tasmanian Aborigines in the Hunter Islands in the Holocene: island resource use and seasonality', in G. Bailey (ed.), *The Archaeology of Prehistoric Coastlines*, Cambridge, Cambridge University Press, 1988, p. 49; see also H. Allen, 'Left out in the cold: why the Tasmanians stopped eating fish', *The Artefact*, 4, 1979.
32. Bowdler, 'Fish and culture', p. 339; see also H. Lourandos, '10,000 years in the Tasmanian highlands', *Australian Archaeology*, 16, 1983, pp. 39–47.
33. D. Horton, 'Tasmanian adaptation', *Mankind*, 12, 1979, p. 30.
34. Allen, 'Left out in the cold', pp. 1–10.
35. *Ibid*, pp. 4, 7.
36. G. Dunnett, 'Diving for dinner: some implications from Holocene middens for the role of coasts in the late Pleistocene of Tasmania', in M. Smith, M. Spriggs and B. Frankhauser (eds), *Sahul in Review*, Canberra, Occasional Papers on Prehistory No. 24, Research School of Pacific Studies, Australian National University, 1993, p. 252.
37. S. Bowdler, *Hunter Hill, Hunter Island: Archaeological investigations of a prehistoric Tasmanian site*, Canberra, Terra Australis Series No. 8, Department of Prehistory, Research School of Pacific Studies, Australian National University, 1984.
38. Dunnett, 'Diving for dinner'.
39. *Ibid*, p. 251.
40. *Ibid*, p. 252.
41. Pleistocene (1.6 million years ago to approximately 10,000 years ago). Holocene (approximately 10,000 years ago to the present).
42. R. Jones, 'Rocky Cape and the problem of the Tasmanians', unpublished PhD dissertation, University of Sydney, 1971.
43. See Lourandos, '10,000 years', p. 43.
44. Windschuttle, *Fabrication*, p. 386.
45. R. Jones, 'Tasmanian archaeology: establishing the sequences', p. 430.
46. *Ibid*, p. 435.
47. The Last Glacial Maxiumum is the scientific term for the height of the last Ice Age, which in Tasmania is conventionally dated to approximately 18,000 bp.
48. Ian McNiven, 'Mid-to-late Holocene shell deposits at Hibbs Bay, southwestern Tasmania: implications for Aboriginal occupation and marine resource exploitation', in J. Allen (ed.), *Report of the southern forests archaeological project. Volume one. Site descriptions, stratigraphies and chronologies*, Bundoora, La Trobe University, 1994, pp. 219–247.
49. Cosgrove, *The Illusion of Riches*; Jones, 'Tasmanian archaeology: establishing the sequences', p. 438.
50. See for example I. Thomas, 'Late Pleistocene environments and Aboriginal settlement patterns in Tasmania', *Australian Archaeology*, 36, 1992, pp. 1–11.
51. See also R. Cosgrove, J. Allen and B. Marshall, 'Paleo-ecology and Pleistocene

human occupation in south central Tasmania', *Antiquity*, 64, 1990, pp. 59–78; J. Freslov, 'The role of open sites in the investigation of Pleistocene phenomena on the inland southwest of Tasmania', in M. Smith, M. Spriggs and B. Frankhauser (eds), *Sahul in Review*, Canberra, Occasional Papers in Prehistory No. 24, Department of Prehistory, Research School of Pacific Studies, Australian National University, 1993.

52. C. Williamson, 'A history of Aboriginal Tasmania: 3500 BP to AD 1842', unpublished PhD dissertation, La Trobe University, 2002, pp. 274–278.

53. *Ibid*, pp. 275–278.

54. A. Sagona, *Bruising the Red Earth*, Melbourne, Melbourne University Press, 1994, p. 132.

55. D. J. Mulvaney, *Encounters in Place: Outsiders and Aboriginal Australians 1606–1985*, Brisbane, University of Queensland Press, 1989, p. 35.

56. Sagona, *Bruising the Red Earth*, p. 132.

57. Ingereth McFarlane, *A regional archaeological site survey of north-west Tasmania*, Occasional paper No. 3, Hobart, Department of Parks, Wildlife and Heritage, 1993, p. 100.

58. S. Brown, *Aboriginal archaeological resources in south east Tasmania*, Occasional Paper No. 12, Tasmania, National Parks and Wildlife Services, 1986, p. 70.

59. R. Jones, 'Tasmanian Aborigines and dogs', *Mankind*, 7, 1970, p. 267.

60. S. Kee, *Aboriginal archaeological sites in Northeast Tasmania*, Hobart, Department of Parks, Wildlife and Heritage, 1991, p. 37; McNiven, 'Mid-to-late Holocene shell deposits', p 224.

61. Brown, *Aboriginal archaeological resources*, p. 92.

62. Kee, *Aboriginal archaeological sites*, p 30.

63. Sagona, *Bruising the Red Earth*, p 66.

64. *Ibid*, p. 124.

65. T. Richards and P. Sutherland Richards, 'Chapter three: archaeology', in D. Harris (ed.), *Forgotten wilderness: North west Tasmania*, Hobart, Tasmanian Conservation Trust Inc., 1992, p. 28.

66. See for example G. Lennox, 'The Van Diemen's Land Company and the Tasmanian Aborigines: a reappraisal', *Papers and Proceedings of the Tasmanian Historical Research Association*, 37, 1990, pp. 165–208; Ian McFarlane, 'Aboriginal Society in North West Tasmania: Dispossession and Genocide', unpublished PhD dissertation, University of Tasmania, 2002; T. Murray, 'The childhood of William Lanne: contact archaeology and Aboriginality in Tasmania', *Antiquity*, 67, 1993, pp. 504–519; N. J. B. Plomley, *Friendly Mission*, Hobart, Tasmanian Historical Research Association, p. 196.

67. Plomley, *Friendly Mission*, p. 926.

68. D. Davies, *The Last of the Tasmanians*, London, Frederick Muller Ltd, 1973, p. 153.

69. Plomley, *Friendly Mission*, p. 926.

70. McFarlane, 'Aboriginal Society in North West Tasmania: Dispossession and Genocide'.

71. Murray, 'The childhood of William Lanne'.

72. *Ibid*, p. 509.

73. Williamson, 'A history of Aboriginal Tasmania', esp. chs 9, 10 and 11.

74. See for example T. Murray, 'Epilogue: An Archaeology of Indigenous/Non-Indigenous Australia from 1788', in R. Harrison and C. Williamson (eds), *After Captain Cook*, Sydney, Sydney University Archaeological Methods Series 8, 2002, pp. 213–223.

75. B. Gott, 'Fire-Making in Tasmania: Absence of Evidence is Not Evidence of Absence', *Current Anthropology*, 43, 4, 2002, pp. 650–656.

76. See for example T. Murray, 'Tasmania and the constitution of "the dawn of humanity"', *Antiquity*, 66, 1992, p. 730.

77. J. Clark, 'Devils and Horses: Religious and Creative Life in Tasmania Aboriginal Society', in M. Rowe (ed.), *The Flow of Culture: Tasmanian Studies*, Canberra, Australian Academy of the Humanities, 1987, pp. 50–72.

IN CONCLUSION

Revisionism and Denial

A. Dirk Moses

During the 1980s and 1990s, North American politicians, educators and intellectuals engaged in bitter debate over the status of 'Western civilisation' in their school and university curricula. Was it the source of a venerable canon of classical literature with which to assimilate minorities into the American 'melting pot', or rather a pernicious tradition of 'dead white males' that prevented the development of an authentic multiculturalism? The American 'culture wars' were watched with great interest from abroad, but they were far from unique.[1] All modernising societies comprise factions within their intelligentsia that struggle with one another to impose an authoritative interpretation of political and cultural reality on their respective public spheres. In this rivalry for cultural capital – prestige and influence – they deploy an arsenal of rhetorical devices to discredit the opposition and enhance their own position in the public-intellectual field. Two of the most common are 'political correctness' and 'revisionism'.

'Political correctness' was invented in the 1980s by American neo-conservatives who re-named the term that the left had used to discipline itself – 'ideological soundness' – to attack the perceived dominance of postmodern/multicultural ideas in the academy. By playing on the liberal unease about taboos and commitment to freedom of expression, the charge of 'political correctness' has proven a remarkably effective weapon. Much has been written on the subject, but the term has seen less service since the mid-1990s after its users began setting the political and cultural tone in a conservative direction.[2]

The origins of revisionism are much older. The term was used first in the 1890s in a fractious debate among socialist intellectuals in Germany and during the Dreyfus affair in France. Since the 1970s, it has appeared in a number of countries in debates about national myths. The simultaneous rise of Holocaust denial has made it all the more controversial because Holocaust deniers want to claim they too are revisionists, seeking merely to set the record straight. Revisionism could appear – or be made to appear – morally dubious. While the content of revisionism varies from case to case, its meaning as a speech act is constant: revisionists assail orthodoxies.

Accordingly, revisionism is not a coherent movement but a rhetorical weapon wielded in the symbolic struggles that constitute any free academic and public sphere.[3] As such, it can obscure as much as it reveals. Revisionism posits an orthodoxy that often exists solely in the mind of its proponents, just as political correctness implies moral and intellectual censorship that may or may not exist. Yet there is a difference between the terms. Political correctness always carries a negative connotation, while revisionism can be seen as heroic by those wishing to storm the parapets of official interpretation. At the same time, it can appear heretical if the orthodoxy is regarded widely as legitimate. Predictably, the 'orthodox' opponents of 'revisionists' will attempt to tar them as 'deniers'. One of the aims of belligerents in culture wars, then, is to define the parameters of legitimacy and public 'common sense'.

It is no accident that the vocabulary of religious discipline suffuses these debates. They concern moral and ethical issues in which intellectuals believe passionately. Their personal identity is also at stake. Collective ego ideals, like 'the nation', constitute a core component of the selves of the protagonists. For the nationalist, attacks on his cherished ideal are experienced as a diminution of his personhood (usually male), sometimes to the extent of inducing castration anxiety.[4] Whether they love or hate their nation, or entertain rival conceptions of it, the pride or shame that intellectuals feel is the source of the moral fervour underlying the many debates about revisionism.

What gives them a religious dimension is that they involve questions of good and evil. More often than not, the bone of contention is whether a loved/hated collective or cause is implicated in mass crimes. Because communists, to take another example, ascribed to their ideal a salvific role in world history, they scrambled to save its reputation against the accusation that it was intrinsically totalitarian (often by wilful blindness to Stalinist crimes), just as surely as anti-communists sought converts to liberal democracy which they saw as the redeeming force in global affairs.[5]

The Australian culture wars are no exception. Most recently, the eschatological urge of conservatives to claw back the left-liberal gains of the 1980s and 1990s has culminated in the self-publication by media analyst Keith Windschuttle of *The Fabrication of Aboriginal History*. Its target is what he calls the 'orthodox interpretation' which supposedly views Australian history as genocidal or even holocaustal.[6] Not only does he dispute the facts presented by the 'orthodoxy', he also proposes a 'counter-history' of British colonialism in Van Diemen's Land that identifies closely with the settlers. His accusation that historians concocted the evidence of massacres has proved seductive to many, who have folded his 'discovery' into their closely nurtured prejudices against 'intellectuals' and the 'new class'.[7] As might be expected, his critics have labelled him both a revisionist and denier.[8]

Windschuttle's book and articles have provoked considerable public controversy not only about the facts of the past, but also regarding the production of historical knowledge, the status of intellectuals and the public role of history. My aim here is to further understanding of these issues by situating his 'revisionism'/'denial' in historical and international context. Does the Australian situation bear any resemblance to culture wars in other countries? Is Windschuttle a revisionist, a denier, or both?

Revisionisms and Denial

Revisionism had two meanings when it appeared a little over a century ago. The first one varied according to the identity of the dominant interpretation or official position. In the famous 'revisionism controversy' in

German social democracy, for example, orthodox Marxist intellectuals hurled it as a term of abuse against fellow socialist Eduard Bernstein, who advocated gradualist reformism. The revolutionary goal could not be abandoned, they insisted. Marxism was a scientific, not ethical, socialism.[9] Revisionism was officially condemned by the Social Democratic Party of Germany, and Bernstein was lucky to escape expulsion. In Marxist circles and countries, revisionism became synonymous with heresy, and excommunication was its dire consequence.

More important still was the contemporaneous Dreyfus Affair, the controversy surrounding the notorious imprisonment in 1894 of the French-Jewish army officer Alfred Dreyfus for allegedly selling secrets to the Germans.[10] The revisionists were the left-liberal intellectuals – the so-called Dreyfusards – led by the novelist Emile Zola, who in 1898 launched a crusade to revise the judgement and prove the innocence of the man languishing on Devil's Island. Here the meaning of revisionism was determined in the same way as with the German socialists: as a challenge to an orthodoxy or official position.

Yet the eventual success of the Dreyfusards led to a fateful inversion of its content. After Dreyfus's pardon in 1906, Catholic-monarchist intellectuals – the anti-Dreyfusards – began calling themselves revisionists and insisted truculently on his guilt no matter how much evidence was presented to prove his innocence. Any testimony in his favour was disqualified on one spurious ground or another.[11] Theirs was the posture of denial, the second meaning of revisionism. This comes as no surprise. Many of the anti-Dreyfusards lived in a never-never world of paranoia and conspiracy, believing that Jews, Protestants, and freemasons were out to destroy the country by blackening the reputation of the army.

How could they believe in such fantasies? Why do people deny the Holocaust? We are dealing here with the operation of a psychic defence mechanism with which denialists protect themselves from the traumatic consequences of having to incorporate uncomfortable facts into a closed and rigid ideological framework. Freud called this mechanism 'repression'. It has two key symptoms. One is 'splitting', that is, protecting both the love object and self from their own corrupting features by separating and projecting these features onto an external source. The second is 'repetition', whereby someone acts out his or her pathological attachment by repeating the type of destructive behaviour that led to the controversy in the first place. The denier is unaware of his or her own repression, yet the uncomfortable facts will not go away.[12]

Holocaust revisionism is revisionist in both the senses I have described: heretical and denialist. And because of revisionism's dual meaning, 'orthodox' intellectuals often attempt to discredit their 'revisionist' critics by suggesting they embody both aspects. Whether they do needs to be examined on a case-by-case basis.

Revisionism and Denial in Other Countries

Most twentieth-century revisionism has been of the first mode: its meaning was dependent on the position of contending parties in a dispute. The inter-war Zionist Revisionists, for example, agitated against what they perceived to be a supine Zionist leadership, seeking instead 'maximalist' aims in Palestine: a Jewish majority in a Jewish state on both sides of the Jordan backed by military power. Their targets were both their own communal leaders and the 'minimalist' (i.e., non-Jewish state) reading of the British Balfour declaration.[13]

This meaning was also evident in the revisionism controversies of the immediate post-war decades, three of which concerned Marxism. The first instance mimicked the polemics of the original German dispute, this time concerning the orthodoxy of internal party reformers in eastern European states.[14] In the second, American new left historians in the 1960s challenged the conventional wisdom that Soviet aggression was to blame for the Cold War.[15] Then there was Anglo-French historiography of the French Revolution in which revisionist anti-communist English historians and their ex-communist French counterparts dismantled the dominant Marxist interpretation of the Revolution as a 'bourgeois' and 'world-historical' event.[16]

Revisionism sometimes tended towards denialism. In the 1920s, the American historians Sidney B. Fay and Harry E. Barnes rejected the war guilt clause of the Treaty of Versailles and the historical consensus that held Germany and her allies responsible for World War I. But Barnes went further than correcting the one-sided blame of the axis powers.

He exculpated Germany altogether and pronounced the 'unique guilt of France and Russia'. Nothing, it seems, could dissuade him from such an extreme position, leading commentators to place him in an incipient denialist camp.[17]

What about the present? The first meaning of the term has endured since the 1970s in Ireland, Israel, the USA and West Germany, but bloody-minded denialism is evident in relation to Japanese and Holocaust history (although it was not German historians who engaged in such denial). All these cases concern the status of powerful national foundation myths. Here is a global phenomenon that has accompanied the rise of humanistic counter-elites within the intelligentsia, which has been dominated by conformist nationalists and technocrats.[18] The appearance of critical intellectuals, especially since the 1960s, and their incremental seepage into influential institutions is the origin of the 'culture wars'. Would nation states remain in thrall to their foundation myths, or would they open themselves to cosmopolitan influences and universal values by recognising the dark side of their histories? Both wings of the intelligentsia could be revisionist depending on the state of the debate, that is, depending on which wing held the commanding heights of cultural transmission. Revisionism of the denialist variety occurs when conservatives convince themselves that their cherished ideals and beliefs remain viable and credible despite being unmasked as morally and factually compromised legends. The question to ask is whether Australian revisionists belong in the first or second group? Let us examine each in turn.

Most revisionisms in the first group concern cases of left-liberals storming conservative citadels. In Ireland, historical consciousness has been firmly indentured to the myth of national redemption. The great drama was the struggle of the Irish people to achieve national consciousness and political independence in the face of British imperial oppression. The purpose of historical scholarship was to remind the population of these facts. Although it had roots in 1920s positivist historiography, revisionism gained momentum in the 1970s among historians who thought that intellectual and public life should not be politicised in this way. The republican teleology made for bad history, and it justified violence, even terrorism.[19] The dispute peaked in the

1990s with the seventy-fifth anniversary of the 1916 Easter Rising. In the official version, the rising was the culmination of the national liberation project, but by the time of the anniversary revisionist historians had begun chipping away at iconic republican legends, like the 'genocide' of the Irish by the English in the potato famine of the mid-nineteenth century.[20]

As might be expected, nationalists struck back. Most influential was the historian Brendan Bradshaw, who expressed the traditional position with endearing candour. Revisionists, he charged, had alienated the historical discipline from 'the people':

> Invited to adopt a perspective on Irish history which would depopulate it of heroic figures, struggling in the cause of national liberation; a perspective which would depopulate it of an immemorial native race, the cumulative record of whose achievements and sufferings constitutes such a rich treasury of culture and human experience; a perspective, indeed, from which the modern Irish community would seem as aliens in their own land; in the face of such an invitation the Irish have clung tenaciously to their nationalist heritage. Who could blame them?[21]

Bradshaw entreated historians to empathise with the trauma of the Irish, and to abjure clinical detachment in writing about their suffering, lest a 'credibility gap' open between them and the reading public. Worse still, they might be too soft on the British.

Undeniably, revisionism 'has been crucial in forming a more liberal, internationalist and secular political culture' in Ireland, as one observer has noted.[22] It has found favour in parts of the political establishment – politicians, media commentators, academics – oriented to Europe and modernity, while simultaneously provoking the ire of traditionalists who can still make their presence felt. Typical of a threatened orthodoxy, Bradshaw and his supporters regard revisionism as the new orthodoxy, but in fact a healthy pluralism pervades Irish historiography and public culture.[23]

Revisionism is also post-national in Israel. Since the 1980s, so-called 'new historians' began shaking the Zionist foundation myth by showing that, contrary to official opinion, the Palestinians did not voluntarily leave their land for Jewish settlement in 1948. Israel, the prominent 'new historian' Benny Morris has argued, cannot deny co-responsibility for the Palestinian refugee problem because its military violently expelled many of them. A generational struggle was clearly taking place as younger historians and social scientists challenged the sacred truths of older Israelis that they were peace-loving victims of Arab aggression. Interestingly, Morris rejects the label 'revisionist' not because of its denialist connotations, but because it implies the existence of a legitimate historical orthodoxy. What Israel had, he avers polemically, was not scholarship but publicly sponsored nationalist propaganda that cannot be dignified with a revision. Serious historical research had to start from scratch.[24]

The evidence that the 'new historians' were able to muster for their conclusions soon had practical effects. School textbooks were altered to include the new explanation for the Palestinian flight, and the Israeli intelligentsia's push for peace negotiations was strengthened.[25] Predictably, their critics have labelled them 'post-Zionists' to suggest disloyalty, although Morris, for one, insists he is a committed Zionist. Much like Bradshaw in relation to Ireland, Zionists were dismayed that Jews could engage in an 'Israeli suicide drive', as one novelist put it despairingly.[26] One of them, Ephraim Karsh, published a book interestingly titled *Fabricating Israeli History: The 'New Historians'*, in which he scrutinised the new historians' footnotes, including those of Morris's landmark work, *The Birth of the Palestinian Refugee Problem, 1947–1949*.[27] Like Windschuttle, Karsh holds Edward Said's anti-imperialism (for Karsh this means anti-Zionism) responsible for politicising scholarship, as if problems in Israeli society were not stimulus enough for critical reflection.[28] Finding some archival errors, Karsh triumphantly claimed the new historian's scalp, but Morris's response showed that he had picked up only minor problems and missed the main points, systematically ignoring or glossing over facts that told against his argument. Ironically, Morris concludes by associating his critic with the dubious form of revisionism: 'Karsh resembles nothing so much as those Holocaust-denying historians who ignore all evidence and common sense in order to press an ideological point.'[29]

If left-liberals were the revisionists in Ireland and Israel, in Germany and Japan they were conservative nationalists. The Federal Republic of

Germany is the classic example, and it has even been called the 'storm centre of "revisionism".[30] This is not surprising. Where else have the crimes committed by the nationals of a country been so heinous yet so freely debated for such a long time thereafter? The 'Historians' Dispute' (*Historikerstreit*), played out in newspapers and public affairs journals in the mid-1980s, has become well known around the world, thanks to the translation of its key texts and the extensive secondary literature it has generated. It began when the maverick historian Ernst Nolte published a newspaper article entitled 'Between Historical Legend and Revisionism' that expressed concern about the mythically evil status of the Nazi period in public consciousness. What really bothered Nolte was not that Nazism was unpopular but that the new left-liberal politics and historiography of the 1970s attributed the Nazi regime and the Holocaust to pathological national traditions. As a nationalist, the purpose of his self-conscious 'revision' was to rehabilitate these traditions by showing that historical guilt, or at least the cause of the Holocaust, was *located outside German national history*. In a system of cause and effect, Germany was simply a link in the chain of exterminatory politics that had infected Europe since the French Revolution. The Holocaust was a response to the threatened class-murder of the Bolsheviks. 'Auschwitz ... was the fear-borne reaction to the acts of annihilation that took place during the Russian Revolution', he averred famously.[31]

Nolte's plea for a revision was answered immediately by West Germany's most prominent anti-fascist philosopher, Jürgen Habermas. Discerning a neo-conservative backlash against the tentative consensus about the uniqueness of the Holocaust since the Christian Democratic (CDU) Kohl government took office in 1982, Habermas lashed out at 'apologetic tendencies' in politics and historical writing.[32] As might be expected, he was roundly condemned by conservative historians and newspaper editors for enforcing 'moral taboos' and 'politicising scholarship', while left-liberal intellectuals rallied to Habermas's defence, mobilising clichés of their own. Conservatives, they said, were 'relativising' the Holocaust (by linking it to Bolshevik crimes), and rendering it 'harmless' (*Verharmlosung*).[33]

By the late 1980s, it was clear that the left-liberals had won the day, in part because liberal intellectuals, who had become alienated from the left during the 'red decade' between 1967 and 1977 (when terrorism and left-wing violence had plagued the country and university campuses), supported Habermas. Appalled by the nationalist drift of parts of German society, which reminded them of the bad days of hysterical anti-communism and illiberal clericalism of the 1950s, they affirmed the uniqueness of the Holocaust. The other reason for the defeat of retention of 'Holocaust consciousness' was the gradual realisation in the CDU, especially after the Bitburg debacle in 1985 when President Reagan and Kohl caused an international scandal by visiting a West German military cemetery containing graves of *Waffen SS* soldiers, that the country's international credibility depended on playing down its nationalist rhetoric.[34] Indeed, West Germany's rehabilitation depended on being seen to face the past honestly. Consequently, Kohl became a proponent of the Holocaust memorial in Berlin, an unthinkable proposition a decade earlier. Despite periodic challenge from the right, the Holocaust has become the centre of German state consciousness, which casts the country as an anti-genocidal polity.[35]

Certainly, the same cannot be said of the crimes committed by Japan's military during the 1930s and 1940s, and for this reason Germany's reckoning with the past is often compared favourably with the Japanese one.[36] Indeed, the continuing international disquiet over Japan's handling of the war's legacy indicates that involvement of public authority in the country's memory politics is highly controversial.

Yet there are no easy answers. It is not true that, considered as a whole, the Japanese have made no effort to 'come to terms with their past', as is sometimes alleged.[37] Like the other countries considered here, Japan's politics of history needs to be understood in the context of competing factions in the intelligentsia. The complexity of the Japanese case stems from the difficulty of identifying an orthodoxy, a problem reflected in terminology. Denialist writers are called the 'official school' by left-liberal historians, yet are also known as revisionists, and they like to call themselves 'liberals'. The fog begins to lift when we consider the early post-war years of Japanese democracy. The United States imposed a pacifist constitution on the vanquished country, and educational reforms gave greater autonomy to teachers and their union, who tended to the left and supported the new system. Similarly, many Marxists were now to be found among university historians who proffered an anti-military understanding of Japanese history. This new faction of the intelligentsia supported the Tokyo war crimes trials and viewed the Nanking Massacre as the culmination of Japanese military traditions of imperialism and racism.[38] The left was ensconced in the key institutions of cultural transmission at the outset of post-war Japan, while in West Germany it only made such advances after the 1960s.

For the conservative elites, whom the Americans permitted to regain power and retain the emperor system because of their worries about communist China and the Japanese left, the trials and the accompanying interpretation of Japanese history were anathema.[39] Since the 1950s, nationalist groups within the ruling Liberal Democratic Party (LDP) and general population have sought to strengthen the ability of the Ministry of Education to 'screen' (i.e. censor) school textbooks in order to erase the critical elements of the pacifist perspective. Left-wing historians, especially the university historian Saburo Ienaga, have challenged such censorship in the courts, leading to celebrated legal battles. The censorship shows that facts are not value-free and that the language in which they are presented determines their meaning. Thus, where one of Ienaga's textbook drafts read, 'The Japanese army everywhere murdered inhabitants, burned out villages and violated women, inflicting immense harm to the lives, property and chastity of the Chinese', the Ministry ordered him to:

> Delete references to 'violating women' and 'chastity'. The phenomenon
> of assault on women by troops is something that occurs commonly
> throughout the world, so to refer to this in relation to the Japanese
> army alone is unsuitable in terms of selectivity and sequence, as well
> as overemphasizing particular incidents.[40]

This battle of perspectives indicates what sections of Japan's business, bureaucratic and political elites continue to believe, namely that Japan was a victim of the war it waged to liberate Asia from Western imperialism. For this reason, these sectional groups have had great difficulty dealing with the 'comfort women', the Nanking Massacre, the notorious Unit 731 that conducted biological warfare and experiments, and the forced labour programs, all of which attest to systematic criminality by the revered military. Only in the 1990s have some women dared to come forward and demand reparation for their abuse.[41]

Yet the 1990s also saw a resurgence of nationalist activity. Many politicians and publicists, as well as a small number of historians, have consistently played down the 'Rape of Nanking'. It is either referred to as an 'incident' typical in wartime, or denied as a 'fabrication', as in Tanaka Masaaki's *The Fabrication of the 'Nanking Massacre'*.[42] In another publication, *What Really Happened in Nanking: The Refutation of a Common Myth*, Masaaki attacked the Chinese-American author Iris Chang for 'engineering hatred of Japan and the Japanese in the hearts of Americans' in her 1997 book *The Rape of Nanking: The Forgotten Holocaust of World War II*. He proceeded to offer a forensic treatment of the documentation which dismissed photographs of Japanese soldiers beheading and torturing Chinese civilians as inventions and instead showed religious ceremonies and happy locals welcoming their liberators. 'These photographs', writes the author, 'prove that Japanese military personnel adhered to the *bushido* code by praying for the repose of the souls of the enemy dead. They should also negate the evil demagoguery that led the world to believe that Japanese soldiers murdered Chinese indiscriminately or orchestrated a Holocaust.'[43]

How do we account for such crude polemics? An important factor is a change of government and public culture. In 1993, a change of government brought a new prime minister who conceded that Japan had waged an aggressive colonial war, and the Diet adopted a formal motion of regret. The state finally admitted that women had been compelled to work in 'comfort houses'.[44] This significant, albeit modest gesture toward the wartime victims of Japan provoked a vehement response from nationalists, who now regarded themselves as an embattled minority responsible for saving the country from self-destruction. Some members of the Diet formed associations in the name of a 'Bright Japan' and the 'Passing on of a Correct History', while new nationalist organisations sprang up among the conservative intelligentsia. Their articles receive extensive coverage in the popular press, including a national daily newspaper.[45] These revisionists are called 'official' because they articulate the historical resentments of 'official Japan', which regards itself as constricted by a victor's justice and its 'anti-Japanese' view of history.

One group closely aligned with the establishment calls itself the 'Liberal School of History'. Trying to sound reasonable and main-stream, it polemicises against 'taboos' in the name of 'free discussion' and 'rational arguments', yet it has taboos of its own. When 'comfort women' appeared in junior high school textbooks in 1997, the Liberal School complained about 'the spiritual disintegration of the Japanese State'.[46] Furthermore the Liberal School's arguments display denialist traits. It insists that no government source exists to prove that Asian women were compelled to work as sex slaves, and that their testimony is unreliable because it is uncorroborated. As one commentator of Japanese revisionism noted:

> this position is no different from that of the neo-Nazis who claim that the Holocaust did not occur on the grounds that there are no docu-ments signed by Hitler ordering the extermination of the Jews. The danger of exclusive reliance on documentary sources with regard to these problems should be plain to anyone, since it is well known that the great majority of potentially damaging documents were destroyed in anticipation of the Allied occupation.[47]

Likewise, the revisionists consider the Nanking Massacre to be a myth. Under no circumstances can the Japanese war campaign be compared to the Nazi one, they declare, despite the strong parallels in imperial aims, numbers of victims, racial ideology and resort to forced labour.[48]

Although they have a high profile, these revisionists have not been able to impose themselves, at least not yet. While prime ministers may court the nationalist vote by visiting the Yakusuni military shrine where war criminals are buried, Ienaga was able to win his case against the Ministry of Education in 1997. And the new textbook written by the Liberal School, though approved by the Ministry of Education, has not been adopted by many school districts. Japanese scholars are under-taking serious research into the war and the crimes of the Japanese military, and the government is not oblivious to its image abroad.[49] The struggle between revisionism and orthodoxy seems finely balanced.

Revisionism or Denial in Australia?

Where does Australia stand in this schema? Its experience resembles aspects of both the West German and Japanese experiences. As in West Germany, the left-liberal perspective only came to the fore in the 1970s. As in Japan, it is under serious threat from conservative imperialists who deny the national past contains much to be regretted. For them, it is an uplifting, even glorious story of progress shielded from the public by left-liberal historians who opportunistically purvey shameful untruths at taxpayers' expense.[50] Whether the Australian left-liberal intelligentsia can see off this national-conservative challenge remains to be seen.

Revisionism in Australia has arisen over controversies about national history since the 1970s. The post-war orthodoxy, the historian Bob Reece noted in 1976, was that Aborigines were peripheral to the dominant narrative of British expansion of the continent: 'The idea that has most influenced white Australians' attitudes to Aborigines is that they were dying out in accordance with some natural and inevitable process stemming from failure to adapt to European civilization.'[51] The national past was seen from the Europeans' point of view. Reece himself belonged to a younger generation of historians who challenged this view and proposed an alternative, namely, taking seriously the indigenous perspective. 'These revisionist historians', as Bain Attwood and Stephen Foster noted recently, 'represented colonisation as a matter of invasion, depicted the frontier as a line between conflicting parties, regarded the conflict as war, treated the Aborigines' response as resistance, and explained the violence of the frontiersmen in terms of racism as well as other factors.'[52]

These historians re-cast the moral drama of Australian history. No longer were Australians forging a 'New Britannia', rather they were making good the British abuse of Aborigines, non-Anglo immigrants and the environment.[53] Their labours have been effective. In the early 1990s, the Labor Prime Minister, Paul Keating, advocated reconciliation with indigenous peoples on the basis of a left-liberal perspective of the national past, one strongly influenced by his speechwriter, the historian Don Watson. The High Court took much the same view in two key decisions on native title, Mabo (1992) and Wik (1996), based as they were on a generation of revisionist scholarship on frontier violence.[54]

For conservatives, the institutional endorsement of an Australian history that for the first time gestured to the indigenous perspective represented a grave threat to a nation whose material success and moral probity they had invested with world-historical significance.[55] Throughout the 1980s and 1990s, these conservatives complained bitterly about the 'political correctness' of the Labor Party's shibboleths of multiculturalism and Aboriginal land rights, which appeared to criminalise the national past. These policies, they accused, were propounded illegitimately by 'elites' that brainwashed the public through left-liberal domination of the key institutions of cultural transmission: universities, schools, museums and the Australian Broadcasting Corporation (ABC).[56]

For this reason, members of the conservative intelligentsia regard themselves as beleaguered outsiders, having to rely on privately funded think-tanks and non-academic journals like *Quadrant* for research and publication support.[57] Since the Howard government came to power in 1996, the conservative intelligentsia has benefited from indirect state patronage and the increased sympathy of the print media.[58] Despite such support, however, 'black armband' history, as the left-liberal perspective is derisively called, did not disappear. On the contrary, the *Bringing them home* report on stolen Aboriginal children hit the headlines in 1997, prompting calls – backed by massive public demonstrations across Australia in 2000 – for an official apology to the victims. The formal 'reconciliation' process, initiated in 1991 after the recommendations of the Royal Commission into Aboriginal Deaths in Custody, culminated in a controversial 'Australian Reconciliation Convention' in 1997 at which the distance between the conservative government and left-liberals and indigenous leaders was readily apparent.[59]

These developments, and subsequent talk of a treaty between indigenous and non-indigenous Australians, were met with paroxysms of sneering by conservatives, who fell upon any doubt about the veracity of indigenous victim narratives with malicious alacrity. All this noise about Aboriginal issues, they snorted, was merely the expression of a self-loathing left-liberal elite parasitically ensconced in the nation's cultural institutions. Suddenly there was very little separating such conservatives and far right figures like Pauline Hanson and her One Nation party.[60]

The conservatives' charge sheet having been written, they are abuzz with projects. One of them is to stack the ABC with members of the conservative intelligentsia, such as Ron Brunton, a former 'senior research fellow' at the Institute for Public Affairs (a right-wing think-tank), a columnist with the Murdoch-owned *Courier-Mail* and the most prominent opponent of the *Bringing them home* report.[61] Another project is to transform the National Museum of Australia in Canberra, which, according to its most trenchant critic, Keith Windschuttle, is in thrall to a trendy postmodernism and postcolonialism that exaggerates frontier conflict and gives unwarranted space to the experience of minorities. Scandalously, it does not display the redeeming story of nation building.[62] A forum rather than a temple, he appears to be saying, the museum is not performing its traditional sacred role of constructing the collective subject – the national 'us' – that visitors can behold and narcissistically identify as their origin.[63] It is no coincidence that Christopher Pearson, columnist for *The Australian*, editor of the conservative *Adelaide Review*, former speechwriter for John Howard and member of editorial board of the magazine, *Quadrant*, that published Windschuttle's screed, is the government appointee on the museum council that was instrumental in contriving a review of the museum's exhibits by a select group of conservatives that includes no historians.[64]

Windschuttle clearly has clout. Each month, the Prime Minister and his cabinet rush out and buy *Quadrant* to see what new historical scandal he claims to have exposed.[65] Not for nothing did one journalist quip that, 'If Keith Windschuttle hadn't existed, John Howard would have been sorely tempted to invent him. He's the historian the Prime Minister has been searching for all these years, someone with the scissors to snip though the black armband which Howard believes has cast a pall over Australia's past, present and future.'[66] He has been given a platform by the country's only daily broadsheet, *The Australian*, forcing historians to reply immediately in public lest his claims of fraudulent research go unanswered. The doyen of conservative historians, Geoffrey Blainey, has blessed him, gushing of his book that it 'will ultimately be recognised as one of the most important and devastating written on Australian history in recent decades'.[67] Even school teachers have been convinced by Windschuttle's arguments.[68] But are they playing with fire? Is he like the Japanese deniers, or indeed the Holocaust deniers, in the sense of sharing their method? Certainly, he rejects the parallel.[69] Only by comparing his work with the approach of these groups can we answer this controversial question.

The Denialist Syndrome

Holocaust denial has emerged from the shadows of the cyberworld into the glare of public scrutiny because of the celebrated libel trial in London involving one of its most famous proponents, David Irving. In the late 1990s, he sued the American academic Deborah Lipstadt for calling him a Holocaust denier in her book *Denying the Holocaust*.[70] She and her publisher mounted a successful defence by assembling a formidable team of expert witnesses, mostly professional historians, who could show that Irving was an anti-Semite and not an 'objective historian'. The case generated enormous press, and at least five books on the trial and related issues have been published since it ended in 2000.[71] Yet Holocaust negationism, as denial is sometimes called, is an unusual instance of revisionism because most of its proponents are not defending their own nation or tradition. In France, for example, most of the deniers come from the anti-Zionist left.[72] If we consider the Japanese and Turkish repression of their respective pasts, a pernicious denialist syndrome becomes apparent. It comprises the following elements.

Denialists are documentary positivists in a fundamentalist sense. They claim that a factual statement can be authenticated as true only if backed up by a circumscribed category of documents. Direct evidence like official correspondence and eyewitness accounts are good sources of evidence, but indirect ones like hearsay are not. This sounds reasonable enough until the conclusions to which this limitation leads become apparent. Holocaust deniers cast doubt on the existence of gas chambers at Auschwitz because no direct evidence exists to attest to their construction and use for this purpose. Survivor testimony is rejected because it is hearsay; after all, the victims perished, and survivors cannot claim they ever saw them operating. Indeed, survivors who have appeared as trial witnesses have been forced to concede that they only heard about the gas chambers from kapos and camp rumour.[73] Similarly, the oral testimony of 'comfort women' is rejected by Japanese denialists because it is difficult to corroborate with documents, just as the anti-Dreyfusards spurned such testimony that exculpated Dreyfus. Irving denies that six million Jews were killed because documents cannot be adduced to attest to each death. The figure is a guesstimate, he says, based on a comparison between pre-war and post-war Jewish populations and is therefore not a documented historical fact.[74] Robert Faurisson, a prominent French Holocaust denier, typifies their narrow, forensic approach when he insists that if the holes in the roof of the now-ruined chambers through which the poison was poured cannot be identified, the case for gassing collapses: 'no holes, no Holocaust'. Revisionism, he insists, simply demands documentary proof. It is a 'matter of method and not an ideology'.[75] If so, as a commentator on the Irving trial remarked, its method is a 'crazed positivism'.[76]

Needless to say, professional historians reject this standard of proof. Instead, they rely on the 'convergence of evidence', that is, inferences made on the basis of indirect sources. If a sufficient number of them point in the same direction, namely the existence of gas chambers, historians conclude that we may reasonably infer their existence. In this case, such evidence includes testimonies, confessions and memoirs, as well as architectural plans.[77] Certainly, the trial judge thought that Irving was not operating according to this orthodox method because he had 'misstated historical evidence; adopted positions which run counter to the weight of the evidence; given credence to unreliable evidence and disregarded or dismissed credible evidence'.[78]

The fetishisation of direct evidence to underwrite every historical conclusion is the basis of denialists' peculiar self-understanding as authentic historians; indeed, as the only serious ones. As in Turkey and

Japan, they conduct research and observe the conventions of scholarship (footnotes and so on). Holocaust deniers have established their own pseudo-professional organ, the *Journal of Historical Review*.[79] They spurn professional historians as creatures of a smug club whose members habitually cite one another's books without doing sufficient legwork in the archives. Only his research is reliable, insists Irving, because he does not rely on that of his competitors who produce politically driven moralism. Hitler's bad reputation is the product of 'inter-historian incest', he charges, as each historian copied the judgements of his or her predecessors, not bothering to consult the original documents: 'Real History is what we find in the archives.' Because he is merely a conduit for 'the facts', allowing them to speak for themselves, Irving, with apparent sincerity, claimed in 1993 not to

> have any kind of political agenda, and really, it's rather defamatory for people to suggest that I do have an agenda. The agenda I have, I suppose, is, all right, I admit it, I like seeing the other historians with egg on their face. And they're getting a lot of egg on their face now, because I'm challenging them to produce the evidence for what they've been saying for fifty years.[80]

As deniers think they have uncovered the truth concealed by corrupt elites, they mount crusades to ensure its proclamation to the people. And this truth, of which they are the sole custodians, will save the nation or cause that they believe plays a redemptive role in world history. As might be expected, there is a whiff of paranoia and a proclivity to believe in conspiracy theories in the denialist mentality.

Denialists customarily uncover minor flaws in the claims of genocide and then claim that the entire case fails.[81] As one of the expert witnesses for Lipstadt's defence, Richard J. Evans, noted, 'Irving's technique was to present ... minor mistakes and propaganda legends at Nuremberg while ignoring the overwhelming mass of evidence on major matters of fact, using the former to discredit the latter.'[82] Or as Hugh Trevor-Roper similarly observed:

> He seizes on a small but dubious particle of 'evidence'; builds up on it,
> by private interpretation, a large general conclusion; and then over-

looks or re-interprets the more substantial evidence and probability against it. Since this defective method is invariably used to excuse Hitler or the Nazis and to damage their opponents, we may reasonably speak of a consistent bias, unconsciously distorting the evidence.[83]

Denialists offer preposterous counter-explanations or redefine words and contexts to render harmless the charge of genocide. Holocaust deniers, for example, claim the gas chambers at Auschwitz were in fact air-raid shelters for the SS, and that most Jews died of disease.[84] Japanese denialists, by contrast, discount the Nanking Massacre by defining massacre narrowly as 'the unlawful, premeditated, methodological killing of large numbers of innocent people'. Since the casualties in Nanking were overwhelmingly combatants or combat-related, it could not have been a massacre.[85] The Turkish establishment places blame for Armenian deaths on ideological fanatics, bandits or ignorant peasants. True, the Christian minority was being re-settled during the crisis of the First World War, it admits, but the casualties were a regrettable side-effect, and were by no means calculated. There was no genocidal plan, and therefore no genocide.[86]

Because of their fanatical commitment to their 'truth', denialists cannot accept sources that compromise it. Consequently, they define counter-evidence in such a way as to render their propositions unfalsifiable. For example, in response to a massive new book on Auschwitz and its gas chambers that relies on much oral testimony, Samuel Crowell, in the *Journal of Historical Review*, retorted that:

> the revisionist position that testimony may be doubted, not only because of the social and judicial pressures surrounding such testimony, but also because the gassing claims themselves originated in an atmosphere of anonymous rumour which makes all testimony potentially derivative, is irrefutable.[87]

Deniers are not necessarily disreputable cranks. In Turkey, the state itself is denialist, as are many members of the Japanese establishment. For a long time, Irving was taken seriously as a historian, publishing with commercial presses and receiving praise for his tireless archival efforts.

Finally, deniers pick on events in isolation and ignore the broader context. What was the Japanese army doing in China in the first place? Why were Armenians being deported in 1915 at all? Why were Jews in the camps to begin with? By focussing on iconic episodes, like the gas chambers, and ignoring the enabling conditions, deniers implicitly endorse the general policies of the perpetrators. They are not mounting scholarly investigations but prowling around for a 'scoop' with which to undermine the accusation of genocide.

Is Windschuttle a Denier?

How does Keith Windschuttle's work appear in light of this syndrome? Is he a denier or the upholder of those scholarly standards that university historians have neglected in pursuing their supposedly dubious ideological goals? This is a grave question. Reputations are at stake. It will not do to smear Windschuttle as he has smeared historians with his insinuations that they are cheats who invent sources. Facile parallels should be avoided. It is not decisive, for example, that the titles of the publications of denialists and of Windschuttle are so similar ('The Fabrication of X', 'The Myth of Y'). Likewise, his proclivity to sue critics, as Irving does, is not a reliable indicator. That he vigorously opposes the left-liberal intelligentsia is not a salient consideration either. As we have seen, conservatives can attack this group without resorting to denial. Nor is Windschuttle an anti-Semite. There is no evidence to suggest he doubts the veracity of the Holocaust, Armenian genocide or Japanese war crimes. But the question is whether he denies frontier violence in Australia in the same way as these other events are denied. Accordingly, we must ask whether the formal structure of his argumentation fits the denialist syndrome sketched out above. An examination reveals sufficient troubling parallels that Windschuttle should clarify where he stands in relation to each of its points.

Typical of denialism is Windschuttle's accusation that the history profession conspires to conceal a great truth, central to the welfare of humanity, of which he is the anointed prophet. World history is simple: it consists of the Manichaean struggle between good and evil. The truth in this case is not German culture, the Turkish state or Japanese destiny, but Western, above all, British civilisation: as the inheritor of 'Roman law, government, culture, and religion' that guarantees intellectual and political freedom, Windshuttle thinks its spread throughout the world drives historical progress. And the discipline of history is one of its central features, guaranteeing an open society and development of civilisation by challenging myths and legends.[88]

This progress, he is convinced, is threatened by an alternative Western tradition that, born of alienation, yearns for the romantic, idealises the primitive and results in the revolutionary utopianism of totalitarian dictatorships.[89] Leftist intellectuals now articulate this counter-tradition by pouring scorn on imperialism and attributing all contemporary ills to Western civilisation. They 'adopt a politically correct stance against their own society', yet are merely instrumentalising indigenous deaths to gain the moral high ground in the culture wars, 'a transparently insincere political gesture'.[90] Most recently, he warns that this evil irrationalism has manifested itself in postmodernism and policies of self-determination for Aborigines.[91] For these self-loathing elites, 'Western superiority, though patently obvious to everyone, has become a truth that must not be spoken.'[92]

Like deniers everywhere, Windschuttle proposes to rescue the truth by uncovering 'the facts'. Accordingly, he professes no ideological intent. 'My political agenda', he told a journalist in terms strikingly similar to Irving, 'is that I think history has been ruined by political agendas … I'm trying to find out the truth of the matter … My self is really irrelevant in this.'[93] At the same time, he is well aware of the political stakes in the culture wars, declaring, 'It's about the foundation of Australia – whether it was a legitimate foundation or whether it was just an imperialist invasion in which they rode roughshod over the Aborigines.'[94] Plainly he thinks the foundation was legitimate because the British colonisation 'brought the cultural inheritance of Rome and its successors to this continent'.[95] There is an obvious contradiction here between claims of neutrality and ardent partisanship. He can only avoid it by using the same evidentiary criteria and practices – crazed positivism – as deniers. Let us see how.

To begin with, he entertains the same view of sources as deniers, favouring the fundamentalist use of documents and abjuring evidential convergence. Consequently, where no government-authorised documents of eyewitnesses can be adduced, we cannot infer that a massacre or violent confrontation took place. And where such evidence does exist, we must take the death toll noted in such documents rather than in indirect sources of evidence, despite the obvious problem of using the testimony of perpetrators. A still more serious problem in Windschuttle's method of argument, however, is his willingness to claim that European diseases accounted for most indigenous deaths, although little documentary evidence exists of the sort he demands in relation to violence. This inconsistency is telling.

Like deniers, he also rejects *a priori* any material that tells against his case, in this instance the indirect testimony of missionaries in particular. Their voices are discredited on the grounds that they habitually exaggerated frontier violence so they could mount a case for government assistance to operate missions on which to 'protect' the Aborigines. In this way, Windschuttle continues, the missionaries, rather than British racism, are responsible for the adjustment difficulties of indigenous people today: their segregationist policies prevented natural integration into Australian civilisation. The tension between advocating such integration last century and ascribing indigenous fatalities to European disease is obvious.[96]

This attribution of blame to the rival, evil counter-tradition of the West is typical of another denialist problem, namely 'splitting'. It pervades Windschuttle's writing and mires him in contradictions. The blame for post-colonial ethnic messes, for example, is pushed on to the critics of imperialism (do-gooders like the missionaries) who forced European states to pull out before they had sorted out the natives. 'Indeed, the uncivilized conditions in which many people in the old imperial realm now live is evidence that the world would be a better place today if some parts of it were still ruled by the British Empire'![97] Yet, in another article, he pointed to these Western critics of imperialism to show that European civilisation was complex and should not be rejected out of hand. Suddenly, the anti-imperialists were the moral beacons of Western civilisation. But because he has to concede that they could not prevent the European powers from carving up Africa in the late nineteenth century, he must contrive an escape route from the corner into which he has painted himself. Ingeniously, he concludes that the British imperialists were driven by imported Hegelian philosophy – a manifestation of the evil counter-tradition – thereby rescuing British traditions from complicity in unjustifiable chauvinism![98]

What is more, Windschuttle hopes to show how the frontier was an essentially peaceful place of British law and order by engaging in four sleights of hand. To begin with, by taking the same episodic and forensic approach as deniers, he diverts attention from the larger colonial context. Violence, on those few occasions it occurred, he claims, was incidental rather than intrinsic to the European settlement of the continent. Its causes were local not systemic.[99] But Windschuttle can only advance this fanciful idea by ignoring the proposition that violence was an inherent aspect of the colonial encounter, and that its escalation was a potential rooted in the nature of its structure: because the settlers did not recognise native title and took the land without negotiation or compensation, Aborigines were bound to resist, and in turn sometimes provoke exterminatory reprisals by the settlers, who lobbied the authorities to eliminate the threat.[100]

Second, he hopes to pour cold water on the proposition that massacres were widespread, but ends up adopting the style of the Japanese deniers by redefining the concept of massacres into meaninglessness. He believes that documented killings of Aborigines by state troopers could not have been massacres because Aborigines were criminals and the British were conducting authorised arrests, which they resisted.[101]

Third, Windschuttle mis-states the views of historians regarding 'racial' conflict. He has them claim that many large-scale massacres typified frontier relations, when in fact they have written of pervasive but small-scale violence. His agenda is clear. On the one hand, he wants to highlight that colonial authorities were not complicit in massacres on the rare occasions when they occurred. On the other, he wants to ignore the pervasive settler racism but is prepared to concede the killing of Aborigines in 'ones and twos'.[102] To ask after the reasons for these phenomena could force him to concede the exterminatory violence inherent in the colonial encounter.

No example of the various straw men he sets up is more flagrant than his recent declaration that, 'For some reason, the academic historians who dominate this field want to portray their own country as the moral equivalent of Hitler's Germany or Stalin's Russia.'[103] In fact, no historian has advanced such an absurd thesis. To be sure, some journalists and popular writers have indulged in hyperbole, but they have been criticised by historians for doing so.[104] Windschuttle is saying nothing new yet claims to have uncovered a sinister plot like a tabloid reporter on the hunt for sensation. Similarly, he insists that an 'orthodoxy' holds the British committed a genocide upon the Tasmanian Aborigines, conveniently ignoring the fact that Henry Reynolds and this author – representatives of this orthodoxy, in his view – argued against this notion several years ago.[105] What is more, the 'black armband' view of history is not an orthodoxy at all. Considerable pluralism characterises the history profession, as Bain Attwood has shown. Even Gerard Henderson agrees.[106]

Fourth, as the denialists do in the German, Turkish and Japanese contexts, Windschuttle answers the question of the legitimacy of indigenous resistance to such police actions by presuming the justice of the British presence in Australia and identifying openly with them. The settlers in Tasmania, whom Windschuttle has to admit murdered blacks, were merely defending themselves from the Aborigines, whom he criminalises:

> In every case, even the hardest of attitudes was generated solely by the desire to stop the blacks from assaulting and murdering whites. They would have been a peculiar people had they not felt the urge to retaliate. Despite the restraints of their culture and religion, and the admonishment of their government, the settlers of Van Diemen's Land were only human.[107]

This is precisely the cycle of escalation built into the structure of colonial relations to which historians have pointed and Windschuttle has chosen to ignore because it compromises the decency he thinks characterises the colonisation project. Were he to recognise this point, of course, he would have to acknowledge that Aborigines were 'only human' too, and that their resistance could not be put down to the primitive instincts of a people who had to make way for a superior culture.

If Windschuttle wants to move beyond the dramatisation of history in terms of victims and perpetrators, he has done a very poor job. This could be a classic case of what psychoanalysts call 'transference', that is, adopting the perspective of the historical figure or cause to which one has formed a libidinal attachment. Good historians work through such inevitable and highly charged emotional investments by critical self-reflection, and the sure sign of success is the development of an *independent viewpoint*, that is, a viewpoint not that of any of the historical agents. Where historians allow themselves to become mouthpieces of a favoured protagonist, they often 'act out' their own emotional lives.[108] It makes for bad history, or worse.

The problem of perspective plagues Windschuttle's work more generally. Now he thinks that the great moral drama of Australian history, which has indeed become widespread since the 1970s, should be rejected because Aborigines, and indeed all minorities, were not nation-builders like great white men.[109] He himself accepted this drama as the central story of Australian history as late as the mid-1990s but has since reverted to the colonial orthodoxy that, in his own words, 'confined Aborigines to the first few pages of their general surveys ... and allowed them to disappear'.[110] Likewise, he has rejected any methodological sophistication he may have once embraced. Relentlessly positivist as his book *The Killing of History* is, it at least recognised that the historian's 'artistry' as a writer allows 'us to see things from a new, unexpected and illuminating perspective'. Facts do not speak for themselves after all. The most outstanding example of artistry for him was C. D. Rowley's *The Destruction of Aboriginal Society*, which showed that 'what most people had assumed to have been small, isolated outbreaks of violence against blacks, coupled with some sporadic, pathetic gestures at welfare, actually formed a great unbroken arch of systematic brutality, dispossession and incarceration stretching from the late eighteenth to the twentieth century'.[111]

Although Windschuttle considered Rowley's achievement to be the fruit of the traditional narrative mode of historical writing, it was also one that took seriously the indigenous perspective. But now, in the face of all arguments to the contrary, he thinks he can divest himself of *any* perspective and write from a culturally neutral standpoint and thereby show, rather than advocate, the superiority of Western civilisation. And yet all he has done is make a loaded choice to redeem the settler perspective and demonise that of the indigenous people because he presumes the justice of the former's cause. This methodological confusion, as naive as it is morally questionable, is the basis of his much-vaunted 'counter-history' of Australian settlement.

So far, Windschuttle has not proposed ridiculous counter-arguments to explain the catastrophic decline of the indigenous population. Disease is the main culprit, he insists, as indeed many historians have before him. But there are worrying signs when he proposes, before having conducted the research, that we should not expect large Aboriginal death tolls on mainland Australia because the British colonies 'were civilised societies governed by both morality and laws that forbade the killing of the innocent'.[112] It appears as if he knows the answer before visiting the archives.

Given these parallels between the denialist syndrome and Windschuttle's approach, it is not surprising that many historians suspect he is not playing by scholarly rules. Of course, he thinks he is faithful to the facts while his opponents are in thrall to a 'paradigm' of frontier violence in light of which any evidence is perverted to fit the desired conclusion. *They* are like David Irving, he would retort, not me. Where Windschuttle has uncovered unwarranted inferences or idle speculation, he has rendered a service, as indeed Irving did with the documents he dug up in obscure places. But his blanket rejection of virtually all sources that point to frontier violence indicates that he shares the deniers' dismissal of the convergence-of-evidence method shared by historians around the world.

So is Windschuttle a denier? The signs are not good. Once a fanatical communist, he has radicalised to the right in the past decade, stunning former friends with the asperity of his censure and his touching faith in the white civilising mission. Will he keep going? It all depends on how he responds to this book. One of the hallmarks of deniers is their refusal to enter into serious dialogue with historians, picking out as they do easily dismissed criticisms and ignoring the telling ones. Windschuttle can prove his seriousness of purpose by addressing *each* of the responses to his work. Henry Reynolds and Lyndall Ryan have amended their accounts in light of his valid criticisms. Is he prepared to address the specific criticisms of his?

Some may note that my challenge is futile, because if Windshuttle suffers from the denialist syndrome then he will not be able to reply rationally. For such people cast themselves as actors in a cosmic drama between good and evil, and thus automatically spurn what the agents of error – those postmodern relativists and postcolonial anti-imperialists – the university historians, can teach them. But while the paranoid are impervious to reason, we must hope that Windschuttle is true to his word about rational inquiry. Historical scholarship and Aboriginal history are too valuable to be reduced to the culture wars that he and his ilk want to wage. The answer to the question of whether he is a denier is in his hands.

ACKNOWLEDGEMENTS

My thanks go to Elise Tipton and Rikki Kersten for references on Japanese revisionism, and to Alexa Moses and Neil Levi for numerous editorial suggestions. I also thank the students of my 'revisionism' honours seminars in 2002 and 2003 for intellectual stimulation and unfailing enthusiasm.

NOTES

1. Mary E. Williams (ed.), *Culture Wars: Opposing Viewpoints*, San Diego, Greenhaven Press, 1999. A thoughtful criticism of the debate that shows the limitations of viewing the issue in these starkly polarised terms is Martin Jay, 'European Intellectual History and the Specter of Multiculturalism' in Martin Jay, *Cultural Semantics: Keywords of our Time*, Amherst, University of Massachusetts Press, 1998, pp. 31–36.

2. Marilyn Friedman and Jan Narveson, *Political Correctness: For and Against*, Lanham, Maryland, 1995. For an ironic inversion of its use, see Julia Gillard, 'Political Correctness, John Howard-Style', *The Age*, 13/3/2003.

3. Michael Schermer and Alex Grobman, however, think there is a revisionist movement: *Denying History: Who Says the Holocaust Never Happened and Why Do They Say It?*, Berkeley, University of California Press, 2000.

4. In this context, castration anxiety refers to the anxiety felt by men when their powerful collective ego ideals that make them feel good about themselves are threatened by perceived authority figures, who in Freudian theory represent the paternal figure that interdicts the boy's illicit desire for his mother. It is, thus, a fantasised (as opposed to an actual) danger to their genitals symbolised by the national ideal.

5. Tony Judt, *Past Imperfect: French Intellectuals, 1944–1956*, Berkeley, University of California Press, 1992.

6. On this general issue, A. Dirk Moses, 'Genocide and Holocaust Consciousness in Australia', *History Compass*, 1, 2003, AU 28, pp. 1–11 at www.history-compass.com.

7. Michael Duffy, 'Massacre of the Truth', *The Courier-Mail*, 14/12/2002; P. P. McGuinness, 'Tackling Fakery in the Halls of Academe', *The Sydney Morning Herald*, 24/12/2002; Roger Sandall, 'Mr Windshuttle versus the Professors', *The Australian*, 23/12/2002; Peter Ryan, 'All Hail the Unlikely Saviour', *The Australian*, 10/1/2003.

8. Ben Kiernan, 'Cover-Up and Denial: Australia, the USA, East Timor, and the Aborigines', *Critical Asian Studies*, 34:2, 2001, pp. 163–192; Colin Tatz, 'Confronting Holocaust Denial', *Aboriginal History*, 25, 2001, pp. 16–36; Henry Reynolds, 'From Armband to Blindfold', *The Australian's Review of Books*, March 2001, p. 9; Richard Hall, 'Windschuttle's Myths', in Peter Craven (ed.), *The Best Australian Essays 2001*, Melbourne, Black Inc., 2002, pp. 117–30; John Pilger, *The New Rulers of the World*, London, Verso, 2002, pp. 193–95; Phillip Tardif, 'So Who's Fabricating the History of Aborigines?', *The Sunday Age*, 6/4/2003.

9. Peter Gay, *The Dilemma of Democratic Socialism*, New York, Columbia University Press, 1952; Leszek Kolakowski, *Main Currents of Marxism*, vol. 2, Oxford and New York, Oxford University Press, 1978, pp. 98–114.

10. Jean-Denis Bredin, *The Affair: The Case of Alfred Dreyfus*, New York, George Braziller Inc., 1986.

11. Pierre Vidal-Naquet, *Assassins of Memory: Essays on the Denial of the Holocaust*, New York, Columbia University Press, 1992, pp. 54, 79.

12. Stanley Cohen, *States of Denial: Knowing about Atrocities and Suffering*, London, Polity, 2001, pp. 118f.; Michael A. Milburn and Sheree D. Conrad, *The Politics of Denial*, Cambridge, Mass., MIT Press, 1996, pp. 13–17.

13. Yaacov Shavit, *Jabotinsky and the Revisionist Movement, 1925–1948*, London, Frank Cass & Co., 1988; Walter Laqueur, *A History of Zionism*, New York, Holt Rinehart Winston, 1972, pp. 338–383.

14. Leszek Labedz (ed.), *Revisionism: Essays in the History of Marxist Ideas*, London, George Allen and Unwin Ltd., 1962. Of course, here there was little possibility of learning processes.

15. Joseph M. Siracusa, *New Left Diplomatic Histories and Historians: the American Revisionists*, Port Washington, NY, Kennikat Press, 1973.

16. François Furet, *Interpreting the French Revolution*, trans. E. Forster, New York, Cambridge University Press, 1981; Eric Hobsbawm, *Echoes of the Marseillaise*, London, Verso, 1990; George Kates (ed.), *The French Revolution: Recent Debates and New Controversies*, London and New York, Routledge, 1998.

17. Sidney B. Fay, 'New Light on the Origin of the World War', *American Historical Review*, 25, 1920, pp. 616–39; Harry E. Barnes, *The Genesis of the World War*, New York, Knopf, 1926, pp. 434, xii; Vidal-Naquet, *Assassins of Memory*, New York, Columbia University Press, 1992, pp. 80f.

18. Alvin Gouldner, *The Future of Intellectuals and the Rise of the New Class*, New York, Oxford University Press, 1979; Daniel Bell, 'The New Class: A Muddled Concept?' in his *The Winding Passage*, New York, Basic Books, 1980, pp. 144–64.

19. Ronan Fanning, 'The Meaning of Revisionism', *The Irish Review*, 4, Spring 1988.

20. Mary Daly, 'Revisionism and Irish History: the Great Famine', in D. George Boyce and Alan O'Day (eds), *The Making of Modern Irish History: Revisionism and the Revisionist Controversy*, London, Routledge, 1996, pp. 71–89.

21. Brendan Bradshaw, 'Nationalism and Historical Scholarship in Modern Ireland', in

Ciaran Brady (ed.), *Interpreting Irish History: The Debate on Historical Revisionism*, Dublin, Blackrock, 1994, p. 214.

22. Stephen Howe, 'The Politics of Historical "Revisionism": Comparing Ireland and Israel/Palestine', *Past and Present*, August 2000, p. 252.

23. Nancy J. Curtin, '"Varieties of Irishness": Historical Revisionism, Irish Style', *Journal of British Studies*, 35, 1996, pp. 195–219.

24. Benny Morris, 'The New Historiography: Israel Confronts its Past', *Tikkun*, November-December 1988, pp. 19–23, pp. 99–102; Jonathan Mahler, 'Uprooting the Past. Israel's New Historians take a Look at their Nation's Origins', *Lingua Franca*, August 1997, pp. 25–32.

25. Philip Mendes, 'The Israeli Historian Benny Morris and the Changing Politics of the Palestinian Refugee Debate', *Australian Quarterly*, November-December 2002, pp. 23–27.

26. Neil Caplan, 'The "New Historians"', *Journal of Palestine Studies*, 24:3, Summer 1995, p. 96.

27. Ephraim Karsh, *Fabricating Israeli History: The 'New Historians'*, New York, Frank Cass Publishers, 1998; Benny Morris, *The Birth of the Palestinian Refugee Problem, 1947–1949*, New York, Cambridge University Press, 1987.

28. See the excellent discussion of Paul Kelemen, 'Zionist Historiography and its Critics: A Case of Myth-Taken Identity?', *Economy and Society*, 27:4, November 1998, pp. 353–379.

29. Benny Morris, 'Fabricating Israeli History: The "New Historians"', *Journal of Palestine Studies*, 27:2, Winter 1998, p. 96.

30. D. George Boyce and Alan O'Day, 'Introduction; "Revisionism" and the "Revisionist" Controversy', in Boyce and O'Day (eds), *The Making of Modern Irish History*, p. 2.

31. Ernst Nolte, 'Between Historical Legend and Revision', *Forever in the Shadow of Hitler*, Atlantic Highlands, NJ, Humanities Press, 1996, pp. 1–15. See Daniel Levy, 'The Future of the Past: Historiographical Disputes and Competing Memories in Germany and Israel', *History and Theory*, 38, 1999, pp. 51–66.

32. Jürgen Habermas, 'A Kind of Settlement of Damages: The Apologetic Tendencies in German History Writing', *Forever in the Shadow of Hitler*, pp. 34–44.

33. Geoff Eley, 'Nazism, Politics and the Image of the Past: Thoughts on the West German *Historikerstreit* 1986–1987', *Past and Present*, 121, 1988, pp. 171–208; Charles S. Maier, *The Unmasterable Past*, Cambridge, Harvard University Press, 1988; Richard J. Evans, *In Hitler's Shadow: West German Historians and the Attempt to Escape from the Nazi Past*, New York, Knopf, 1989; Peter Baldwin (ed.), *Reworking the Past: Hitler, the Holocaust, and the Historians' Debate*, Boston, Beacon Press, 1990.

34. Geoffrey Hartman (ed.), *Bitburg in Moral and Political Perspective*, Bloomington, Ind., Indiana University Press, 1986.

35. Bill Niven, *Facing the Nazi Past: United Germany and the Legacy of the Third Reich*, London and New York, Routledge, 2002.

36. Ian Buruma, *The Wages of Guilt: Memories of War in Germany and Japan*, London, Jonathan Cape, 1994. Carol Gluck, 'The Past in the Present', in Andrew Gordon (ed.), *Postwar Japan as History*, Berkeley, University of California Press, 1993, pp. 64–95.

37. Iris Chang, *The Rape of Nanking: The Forgotten Holocaust of World War II*, New York, Penguin, 1997.

38. Takashi Yoshida, 'A Battle over History', in Joshua A. Fogel (ed.), *The Nanjing Massacre in History and Historiography*, Berkeley, University of California Press, 2000, pp. 72–79; Daniel A. Metraux, 'Japan's Historical Myopia', *East Asia*, 18:3, Fall 2000, pp. 95–109.

39. Rikki Kersten, 'Revisionism, Reaction, and the "Symbol Emperor" in Post-War Japan', *Japan Forum*, 15:1, 2003, pp. 15–31; Curtis Anderson Gayle, 'Progressive Representations of the Nation: Early Post-War Japan and Beyond', *Social Science Japan Journal*, 4:1, 2001, pp. 1–19.

40. George Hicks, *Japan's War Memories: Amnesia or Concealment?*, Aldershot, Ashgate, 1997, pp. 117f.

41. Ueno Chizuko, 'The Politics of Memory: Nation, Individual and Self', *History and Memory*, 11:2, 1999, pp. 129–152. Elazar Barkan, *The Guilt of Nations: Restitution and Negotiating Historical Injustice*, New York and London, W. W. Norton, 2000, pp. 46–64.

42. Buruma, *The Wages of Guilt*, pp. 121f.

43. Tanaka Masaaki, *What Really Happened in Nanking: The Refutation of a Common Myth*, Tokyo, Sekai Shuppan, 2000, pp. 1, 126; Chang, *The Rape of Nanking*.

44. Gavan McCormack, 'The Japanese Movement to "Correct" History', in Laura Hein and Mark Selden (eds), *Censoring History: Citizenship and Memory in Japan, Germany, and the United States*, Armonk, N. Y. and London, M. E. Sharpe, 2000, p. 54.

45. *Ibid*, pp. 56f.

46. Rikki Kersten, 'Neo-Nationalism and the "Liberal School of History"', *Japan Forum*, 11:2, 1999, p. 198.

47. Chizuko, 'The Politics of Memory', p. 131.

48. McCormack, 'The Japanese Movement to "Correct" History', pp. 61–64.

49. Daqing Yang, 'Convergence or Divergence? Recent Historical Writings on the Rape of Nanjing', *American Historical Review*, 104: 3, 1999, pp. 842–865.

50. Here I disagree with Colin Tatz who thinks Australia resembles Turkey in its government-sponsored denial of the Armenian genocide: Tatz, 'Why Denialists Deny', in Colin Tatz et al, *Genocide Perspectives II*, Sydney, 2003, pp. 267–84.

51. R. H. W. Reece, 'The Aborigines in Australian Historiography', in John A. Moses (ed.), *Historical Disciplines and Culture in Australasia*, St. Lucia: University of Queensland Press, 1979, pp. 253–55.

52. B. Attwood and S. G. Foster, 'Introduction', in Attwood and Foster (ed.), *Frontier Conflict: The Australian Experience*, Canberra, National Museum of Australia, 2003, pp. 1–30. It should be noted that Reece expressed reservations about this revisionism from the beginning. A good survey of the literature regarding revisionism and its critics is B. Attwood, 'Aboriginal History', *Australian Journal of Politics and History*, 41, 1995, pp. 33–47.

53. Manning Clark, 'The Beginning of Wisdom', *Time Australia*, 25/1/1988, pp. 12–15.

54. Bain Attwood (ed.), *In the Age of Mabo: History, Aborigines and Australia*, Sydney, Allen and Unwin, 1996.

55. Geoffrey Blainey and John Howard, for example, insist that Australia's democracy is virtually unique in its longevity and beneficence: Blainey, 'Drawing Up a Balance-Sheet of our History', *Quadrant*, July-August 1993, pp. 10–15; Howard, 'Confront our Past, yes, but let's not be consumed by it', *The Australian*, 19/11/1996). See also Claudio Veliz, 'History as Alibi', *Quadrant*, April 2003, pp. 21–24.

56. See, for example, the editorials of P. P. McGuinness in *Quadrant* since the late 1996.

An excellent analysis of this nationalist worrying is Ghassan Hage, *White Nation: Fantasies of White Supremacy in a Multicultural Society*, Sydney, Pluto Press, 1998.

57. For a sober reading of these years, see Robert Manne, *The Way We Live Now: The Controversies of the Nineties*, Melbourne, Text Publishing, 1998; idem, *The Barren Years: John Howard and Australian Political Culture*, Melbourne, Text Publishing, 2001.

58. The membership of the quaintly named Bennelong Society includes former conservative government ministers of Aboriginal Affairs, Peter Howson (1971–72) and John Herron (1996–2001): see www.bennelong.com.au. It is no coincidence that prominent newspaper conservative columnists Christopher Pearson (*The Australian*), Miranda Devine (*The Sydney Morning Herald*) and Imre Salusinszky (*The Australian*) are on the editorial board of *Quadrant*.

59. For the Council of Aboriginal Reconciliation and related Reconciliation Australia, see www.reconciliation.org.au and www.reconcilationaustralia.org.au.

60. Typical, once again, were the *Quadrant* editorials and newspaper columns of McGuinness. See the dissection of the arguments by Robert Manne, 'In Denial: the Stolen Generations and the Right', *Quarterly Essay* 1, Melbourne, Black Inc., 2001.

61. Cosimar Marriner, 'Anthropologist on ABC Board', *The Sydney Morning Herald*, 3–4/5/2003), p. 4. Brunton's criticisms of the report, predictably enough, were published in *Quadrant* and on the IPA website: 'Shame about the Aborigines', *Quadrant*, May 1997, pp. 36–9; idem, 'Genocide, the "Stolen Generations", and the "Unconceived Generations"', *Quadrant*, May 1998; idem, 'Justice O'Loughlin and Bringing them Home: A Challenge to the Faith', *Quadrant*, December 2000, pp. 37–42; idem, 'Correcting the False Scholarship Syndrome', *Institute for Public Affairs*: www.ipa.org.au/Reply/falsescholar.html.

62. Keith Windschuttle, 'How Not to Run a Museum: People's History at the Postmodern Museum', *Quadrant*, September 2001, pp. 11–19 . Also at www.sydneyline.com/National%20Museum.htm.

63. For the function of myths of national origins, see Mircea Eliade, *Myth and Reality*, New York, Harper & Row, 1963, pp. 21–53.

64. Gerard Henderson, 'Over the Top in the Culture Wars', *The Sydney Morning Herald*, 14/1/2003.

65. In fact, in 2003 the Prime Minister awarded him a 'Centenary of Federation' medal for his services to history: Jane Cadzow, 'Who's right now, then?', *Good Weekend*, 17/5/2003, p. 18.

66. Andrew Stevenson, 'A Voice from the Frontier', *The Sydney Morning Herald*, 'Spectrum' Supplement, 22/9/2001.

67. Geoffrey Blainey, 'Undermining a Bloody Myth', *The Australian*, 14/4/2003, p. 9.

68. Bernard Lane, 'Teaching Mr. Windschuttle', *The Weekend Australian*, 10–11/5/2003, p. 24.

69. Keith Windschuttle, 'The Fabrication of Aboriginal history', *The New Criterion*, 20:1, September 2001.

70. Deborah Lipstadt, *Denying the Holocaust*, New York, Free Press, 1993.

71. Eva Menasse, *Der Holocaust vor Gericht*, Berlin, Siedler Verlag, 2000; D. D. Guttenplan, *The Holocaust on Trial*, New York and London, W. W. Norton, 2001; Richard J. Evans, *Telling Lies about Hitler: History, the Holocaust and the David Irving Trial*, London, Verso, 2002; Robert Jan van Pelt, *The Case for Auschwitz: Evidence from the Irving Trial*, Bloomington: Indiana University Press, 2002; Peter Longerich, *The Unwritten Order: Hitler's Role in the Final Solution*, London: Tempus, 2003.

72. Alain Finkielkraut, *The Future of a Negation: Reflections on the Question of Genocide*, Lincoln, University of Nebraska, 1998.

73. Lawrence Douglas, *The Memory of Judgement: Making Law and History in the Trials of the Holocaust*, New Haven and London, Yale University Press, 2000, ch. 9; Guttenplan, *The Holocaust on Trial*, pp. 158, 176.

74. Evans, *Telling Lies about Hitler*, p. 126.

75. Robert Faurisson, 'Impact and Future of Holocaust Revisionism', *Journal of Historical Review*, 19:1 at www.ihr.org/jhr/v19/v19n1p-2_Faurisson.html.

76. Guttenplan, *The Holocaust on Trial*, p. 191.

77. Van Pelt, *The Case for Auschwitz*, pp. 88, 102; Schermer and Grobman, *Denying History*, pp. 31–35, 117–19, 249–5; Evans, *Telling Lies about Hitler*, p. 130; Guttenplan, *The Holocaust on Trial*, p. 306.

78. *The Irving Judgement: Mr. David Irving v Penguin Books and Professor Deborah Lipstadt*, London, 2000, p. 339. See Wendie Ellen Schneider, 'Objective Historian Standard Applied to Libel in Irving v. Penguin Books', *Yale Law Journal*, 110:8, June 2001, p. 1531.

79. It is the journal of the 'Institute for Historical Review': www.ihr.org/jhr.

80. Irving cited in Evans, *Telling Lies about Hitler*, pp. 22, 27.

81. Roger Eatwell, 'The Holocaust Denial: A Study in Propaganda Technique', in Luciano Cheles et al (eds), *Neo-Fascism in Europe*, New York and London: Longman, 1991, pp. 137f.

82. Evans, *Telling Lies about Hitler*, p. 133.

83. Trevor Roper cited in van Pelt, *The Case for Auschwitz*, p. 20.

84. Evans, *Telling Lies about Hitler*, pp. 115f.

85. Masaaki, *What Really Happened in Nanking*, pp. 7–9.

86. Vahahn N. Dadrian, *The Key Elements in the Turkish Denial of the Armenian Genocide*, Toronto, Zoryan Institute, 1999.

87. Samuel Cowell, 'A Holocaust Expert moves from Moral Certainty toward Open Debate', *Journal of Historical Review*, 21:1 at www.ihr.org/jhr/v21/v21n1p39_vanpelt.html.

88. Keith Windschuttle, *The Killing of History*, Sydney, Macleay Press, 1994, pp. 221–23.

89. Keith Windschuttle, 'The Break-Up of Australia', *Quadrant* September 2000, p. 16.

90. Windschuttle, *The Killing of History*, p. 67.

91. Windschuttle, *The Killing of History*; idem, 'The Fabrication of Aboriginal History', *The New Criterion*, 20:1, September 2001.

92. Keith Windschuttle, 'September 11 and the End of Ideology', *Quadrant*, December 2001, at www.sydneyline.com/September%2011.htm.

93. Stevenson, 'A Voice from the Frontier'.

94. Jane Cadzow, 'Who's right now, then?', p. 22.

95. Windschuttle, 'The Break-Up of Australia', p. 16.

96. Keith Windschuttle, 'The myths of frontier massacres in Australian history, Part II: The fabrication of the Aboriginal death toll', *Quadrant*, November 2000, pp. 17–25.

97. Keith Windschuttle, 'Rewriting the History of the British Empire', *The New Criterion*, May 2000, at: www.newcriterion.com/archive/18/may00/keith.htm.

98. Keith Windschuttle, 'Liberalism and Imperialism', *The New Criterion*, Dec. 1998; repr. in Hilton Kramer and Roger Kimball (eds), *The Betrayal of Liberalism*, Chicago, 1999, at http://www.sydneyline.com/Liberalism%20and%20Imperialism.htm.

99. Keith Windschuttle, 'Exposing academic deception of past wrongs', *The Sydney Morning Herald*, 19/9/2000.

100. A. Dirk Moses, 'An Antipodean Genocide? The Origins of the Genocidal Moment in the Colonization of Australia', *Journal of Genocide Studies*, 2:1, March 2000, pp. 89–105.

101. Keith Windschuttle, 'The myths of frontier massacres in Australian history, Part I: The invention of massacre stories', *Quadrant*, October 2000, pp. 8–21.

102. Windschuttle, *Fabrication*, ch. 9; idem, 'The Myths of Frontier Massacres. Part II', p. 23.

103. 'White Settlement in Australia: Violent Conquest or Benign Colonisation? Keith Windschuttle in debate with Pat Grimshaw', Melbourne Trades Hall, 5/3/2003. http://www.sydneyline.com/RMIT%20debate%20with%20Grimshaw.htm.

104. Philip Knightley, *Australia: Biography of a Nation*, London, Jonathan Cape, 2000, p. 107; Michael Cannon, *Who Killed the Koories?* [*sic*], Melbourne, Heinemann, 1990, ch. 22; Jan Roberts, *Massacres to Mining: The Colonisation of Australia*, Melbourne, Dove Communications, 1981; Norman C. Habel, *Reconciliation: Searching for Australia's Soul*, Sydney, Harper Collins, 1999, pp. 48–50, pp. 171–73. Criticisms include Reece, 'The Aborigines in Australian Historiography'; and Moses, 'Coming to Terms with Genocidal Pasts in Comparative Perspective', p. 102: 'There was no Holocaust in Australia'.

105. Henry Reynolds, *An Indelible Stain? The Question of Genocide in Australia's History*, Ringwood, Viking, 2001; and Moses, 'An Antipodean Genocide?'

106. Bain Attwood, 'Frontier Warfare', *Australian Financial Review*, 28/2/2003); Gerard Henderson, 'The Howard View of History', *The Sydney Morning Herald*, 4/4/2000.

107. Windschuttle, *Fabrication*, pp. 348f.

108. Dominick LaCapra, *Representing the Holocaust: History, Theory, Trauma*, Ithaca, Cornell University Press, 1994.

109. Windschuttle, 'How not to run a Museum'. For a counter-argument, see Ann Curthoys, 'Cultural History and the Nation', in Hsu-Ming Teo and Richard White (ed.), *Cultural History in Australia*, Sydney, UNSW Press, 2003, pp. 22–37.

110. Windschuttle, *The Killing of History*, p. 117.

111. *Ibid*, p. 117.

112. Windschuttle, 'The Myths of Frontier Massacres, Part II', p. 23.

Acknowledgements from the Editor

Deepest thanks are due to Morry Schwartz for his willingness to support both this book and our new enterprise, Black Inc. Agenda, and also to the splendid editor at Black Inc., Chris Feik, without whom this book could not have been produced. My gratitude goes also to Henry Reynolds for his advice. As always I am most deeply indebted to my wife, Anne, for her wisdom and her love. This book is dedicated to my daughters, Kate and Lucy, who I hope will be able to feel pride in a country which has shown the capacity to face honestly the shameful chapters in its past.

Notes on Contributors

James Boyce is a PhD candidate at the Centre of Environmental Studies, University of Tasmania, researching Van Diemen's Land history. He is the author of *God's Own Country? The Anglican Church and Tasmanian Aborigines* and 'Journeying Home: The British invasion of Van Diemen's Land 1803–1823'.

Dr Shayne Breen has taught Tasmanian Aboriginal History at the University of Tasmania since 1990. He is the author of *Contested Places: Tasmania's Northern Districts from Ancient Times to 1900,* published in 2001 by the Centre for Tasmanian Historical Studies in Hobart.

Dr Cathie Clement, MPHA is a Perth-based historian and heritage consultant. She specialises in researching and writing about people, places and events in Australia's north-west.

Mark Finnane is Professor of History at Griffith University and specialises in criminal justice history. His books include *Police and Government* (1994), *Punishment in Australian Society* (1997) and most recently *When Police Unionise: The Politics of Law and Order in Australia* (2002).

Dr Neville Green, MPHA is a Western Australian historian specialising in Aboriginal education, Native Title research and the study of contact and change in indigenous societies. He is the author of *The Forrest River Massacres* (1995).

David Hansen is Senior Curator of Art at the Tasmanian Museum & Art Gallery and curator of the exhibition 'John Glover and the Colonial Picturesque' (TMAG, 2003–04).

Robert van Krieken is Associate Professor of Sociology at the University of Sydney and is writing a book on *Social Theory and the Field of Law.*

Martin Krygier is Professor of Law at the University of NSW. In 1997 he delivered the Boyer Lectures, published as *Between Fear and Hope: Hybrid Thoughts on Our Public Values.*

Marilyn Lake holds a Personal Chair in History at La Trobe University. She formerly held the Chair in Australian Studies at Harvard University. Her most recent book is *Faith: Faith Bandler, Gentle Activist,* winner of the HREOC Arts Award for non-fiction in 2002.

Greg Lehman is Indigenous Research Associate at Riawunna, Centre for Aboriginal Education, University of Tasmania. He is a widely published writer whose research concerns indigenous identity, history and land management. He is a descendent of the Trawulwuy people of north-east Tasmania.

Robert Manne is Professor of Politics at La Trobe University and a regular commentator for *The Sydney Morning Herald* and *The Age*. His books include *The Culture of Forgetting: Helen Demidenko and the Holocaust* (1996) and *In Denial: The Stolen Generations and the Right* (2001).

Ian McFarlane graduated with honours in history and politics from Monash University before gaining a PhD in history from the University of Tasmania.

Dirk Moses teaches modern European history and genocide studies at the University of Sydney. He is the editor of *Genocide and Settler Society* (New York, forthcoming).

Tim Murray has been Professor of the Archaeology Program at La Trobe University since 1995. He is the author and editor of 15 books and has published numerous papers and book chapters in his major fields of research.

Peggy Patrick is a Miriwoong/Gija woman of the eastern Kimberley region of Western Australia.

Cassandra Pybus is ARC Professorial Fellow in the School of History and Classics at the University of Tasmania. She is the author of many books including *Community of Thieves* and *The Devil and James McAuley*, winner of the 2000 Adelaide Festival Award for non-fiction.

Henry Reynolds is currently an ARC Senior Research Fellow at the University of Tasmania at Launceston. He was for many years at James Cook University in Townsville. He is the author of many well-known books including *The Other Side of the Frontier, Law of the Land, Fate of a Free People* and *Why Weren't We Told?*

Lyndall Ryan is Professor of Australian Studies at the University of Newcastle and the author of *The Aboriginal Tasmanians*.

Phillip Tardif was born in Tasmania and studied at the ANU. His second historical work, *John Bowen's Hobart*, will be published later this year by the Tasmanian Historical Research Association to mark the bicentennial of European settlement in Tasmania.

Christine Williamson is with the Archaeology Program at La Trobe University.

Index

References to Aborigines are to Aborigines of Van Diemen's Land unless otherwise indicated.

Page numbers with the suffix 'n' relate to references in a notes section.